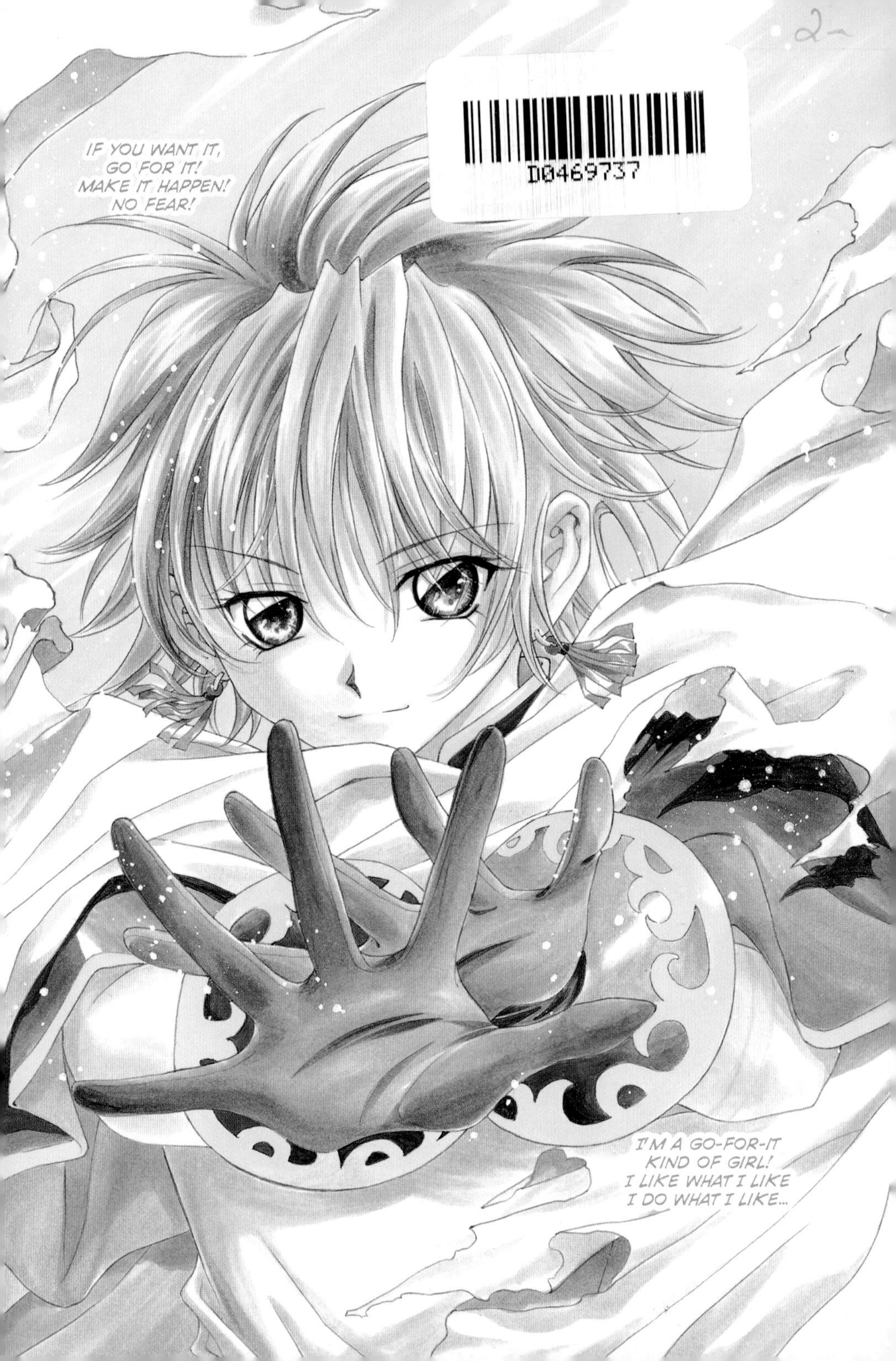
IF YOU WANT IT, GO FOR IT! MAKE IT HAPPEN! NO FEAR!
I'M A GO-FOR-IT KIND OF GIRL! I LIKE WHAT I LIKE I DO WHAT I LIKE...

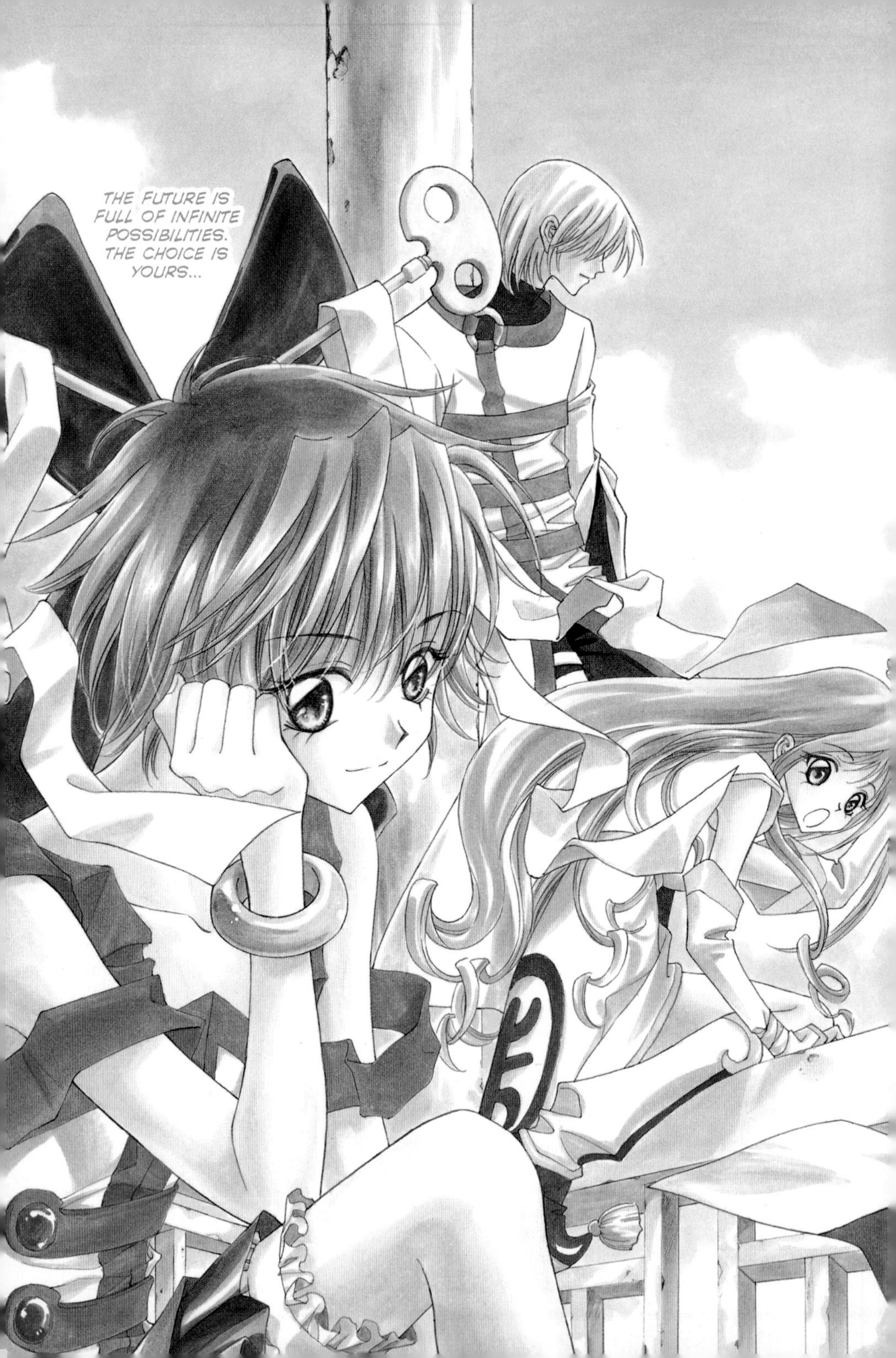
THE FUTURE IS FULL OF INFINITE POSSIBILITIES. THE CHOICE IS YOURS...

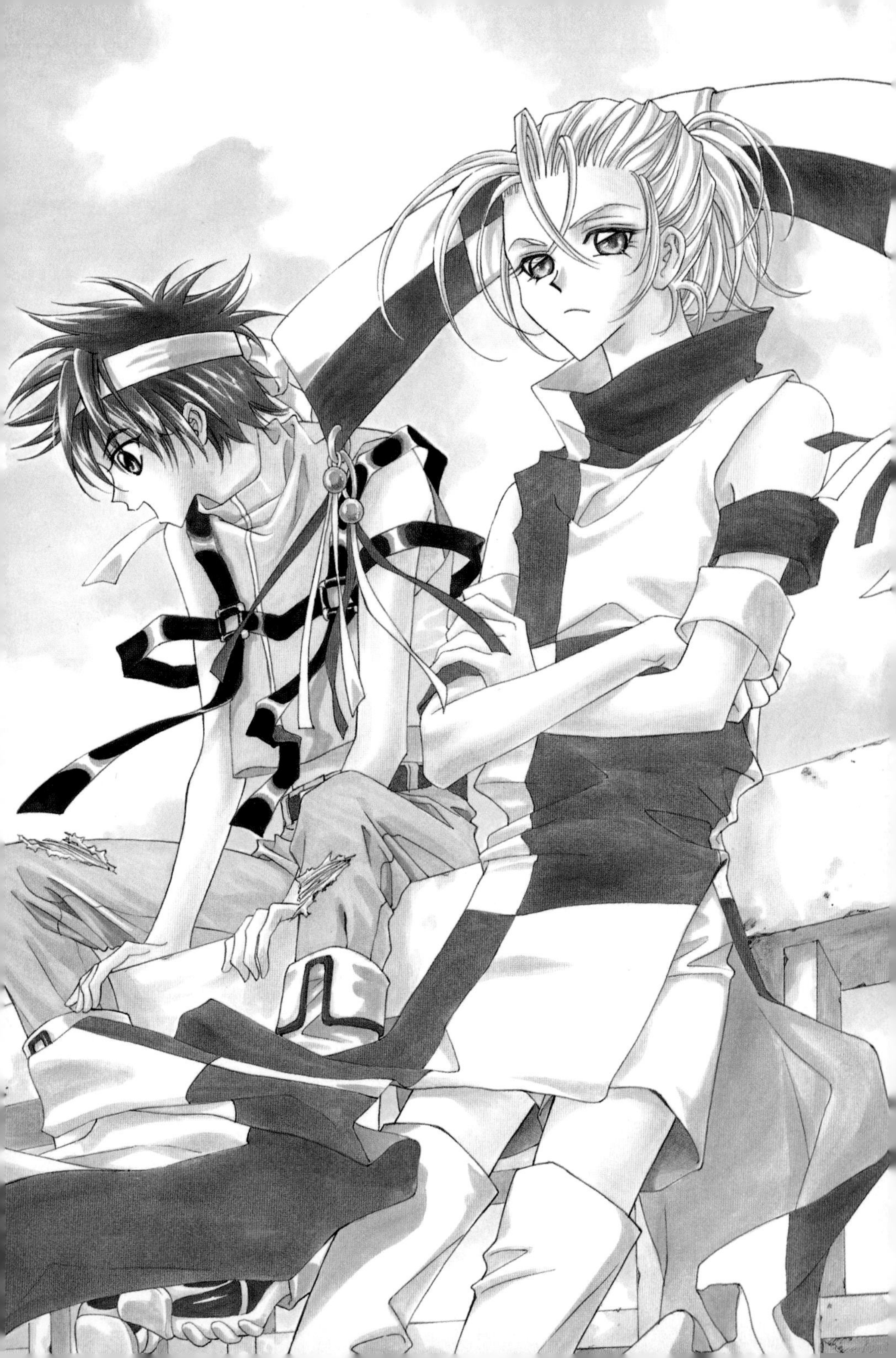

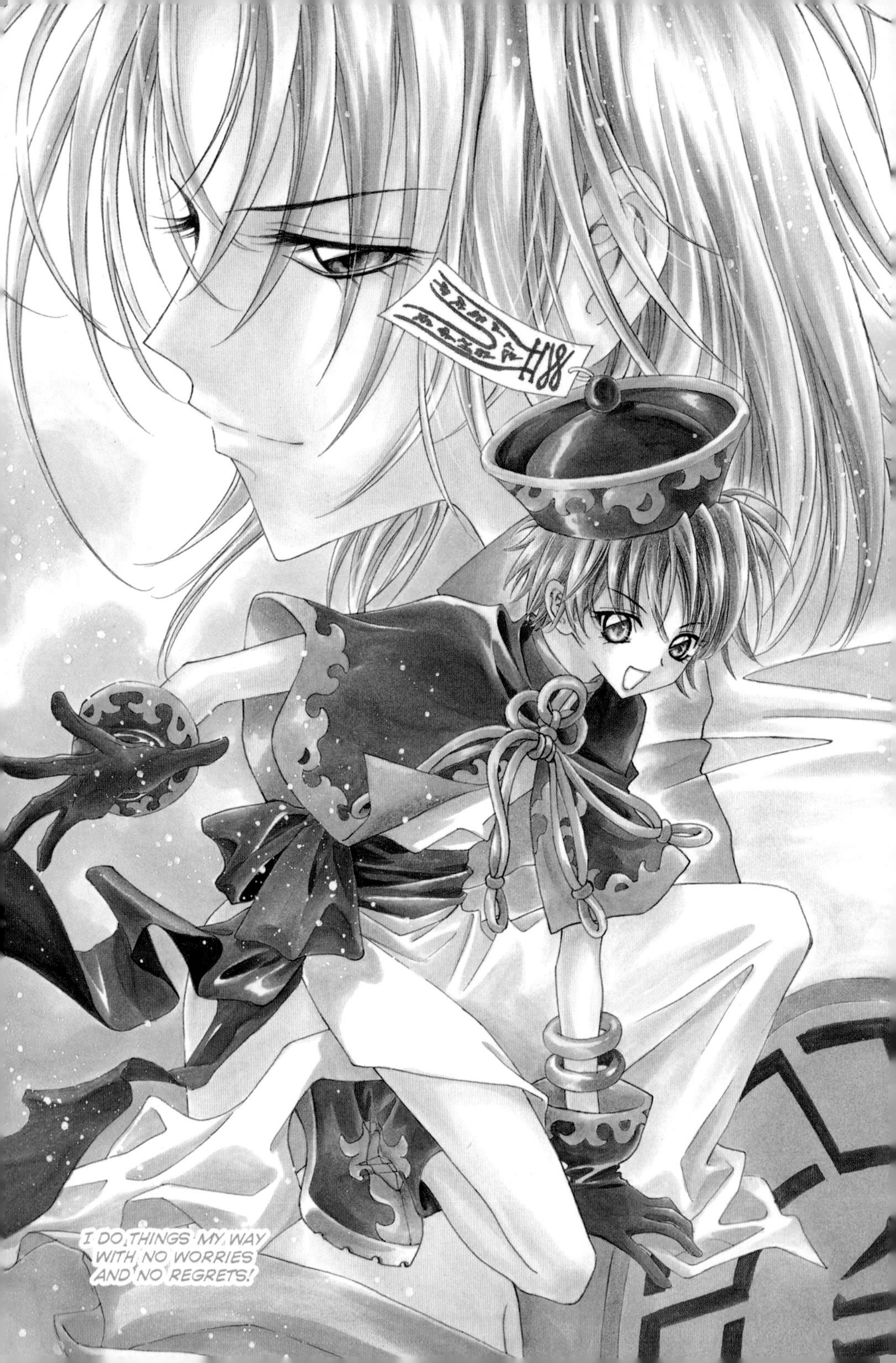
I DO THINGS MY WAY WITH NO WORRIES AND NO REGRETS!

Angel Diary

vol.1

Kara · Lee YunHee

ice
Kunion

WORDS FROM THE CREATORS

SINCE ITS INCEPTION, ***<ANGEL DIARY>*** HAS BEEN A CHALLENGING PROJECT FOR US. WE DIDN'T GET AS MUCH TIME AS WE WOULD HAVE LIKED TO DEVELOP DIFFERENT ELEMENTS OF THE SERIES. WE HAD A LARGE CAST OF CHARACTERS TO FLESH OUT, LOTS OF COSTUMES TO DESIGN, NOT TO MENTION ALL THOSE PAGES TO DRAW! BUT YOU CAN'T ALWAYS GET WHAT YOU WANT, RIGHT? WITH OUR FIRST ISSUE SCHEDULED RIGHT AFTER WE FINISHED OUR PREVIOUS PROJECT ***<DEVIL DIARY>,*** WE WERE REALLY PRESSED FOR TIME. WE EVEN HAD TO HOLD OFF RESPONDING TO OUR FAN MAIL. IT WAS ALL ABOUT FOCUSING ON ***<ANGEL DIARY>*** AND DOING OUR BEST ON THIS SERIES. OH, ALL THOSE SLEEP-LESS NIGHTS...

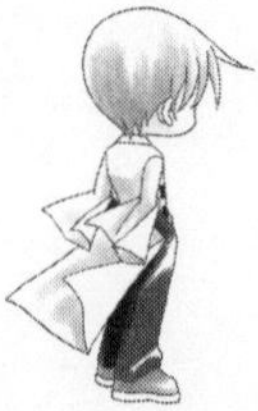

SPEAKING OF FANS, A QUICK WORD ABOUT THE ART IN THIS SERIES: ANGEL DIARY LOOKS DIFFERENT FROM ***<DEVIL DIARY>***. SOME PEOPLE MAY LIKE THE ART STYLE IN ***<DEVIL DIARY>*** BETTER, BUT AFTER READING THE FIRST SCRIPT FOR ***<ANGEL DIARY>,*** WE THOUGHT IT CALLED FOR A LIGHTER, UPDATED LOOK. WE HOPE BOTH OLD FANS AND NEW WILL ENJOY OUR NEW STYLE!

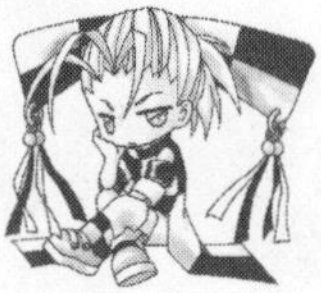

---KARA
(EVOLVING ARTISTS)

I'VE ALWAYS WANTED TO WRITE A STORY FEATURING CUTE AND QUIRKY GIRLS AND BOYS. IN ***<ANGEL DIARY>***, YOU GET TO SEE THAT STORY AND THE CHARACTERS I CAME UP WITH IN THAT VEIN.

DURING THE WRITING PROCESS, ONE OF THOSE CHARACTERS, *DONG-YOUNG*, TOOK OVER ANOTHER CHARACTER, *AH-HIN*, AS THE STAR OF THE SHOW. I STILL HAVE A LOT OF AFFECTION FOR *AH-HIN*, THOUGH. I LOVE BEAUTIFUL CHARACTERS. DON'T YOU?

WELL, EVEN THOUGH I'VE SURROUNDED OUR HEROINE WITH FRIENDS WHO ARE WEIRDOES AND PERVERTS (DOES THAT MAKE ME IRRESPONSIBLE?), I BELIEVE *DONG-YOUNG* MAKES A COOL CENTRAL CHARACTER!

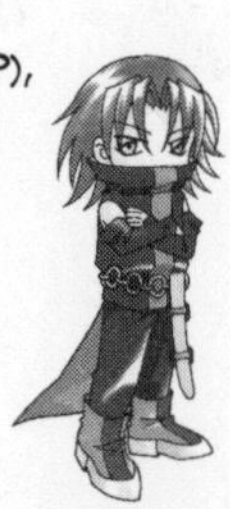

AND OUR ANGEL'S ADVENTURES ON EARTH BEGIN HERE...

--YUN-HEE LEE
(WRITER)

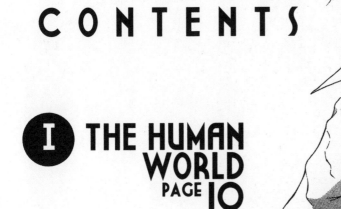

CONTENTS

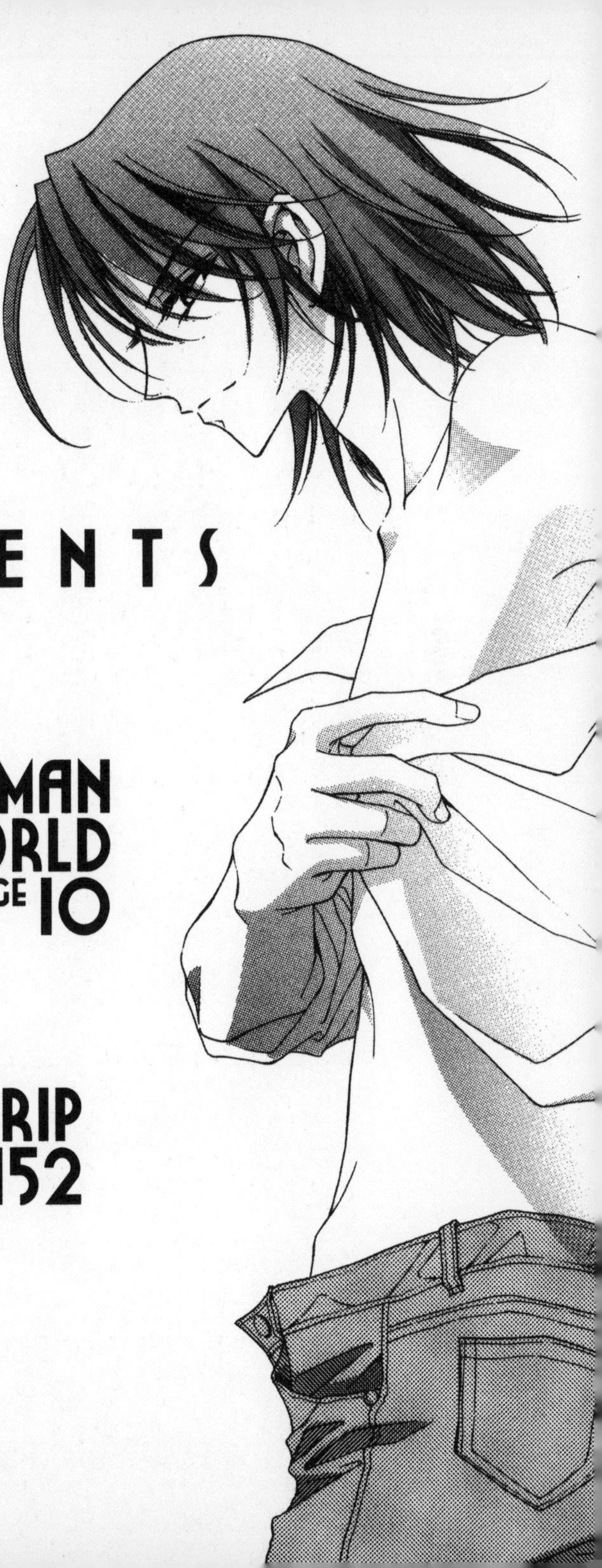

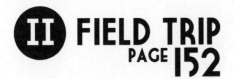

I THE HUMAN WORLD

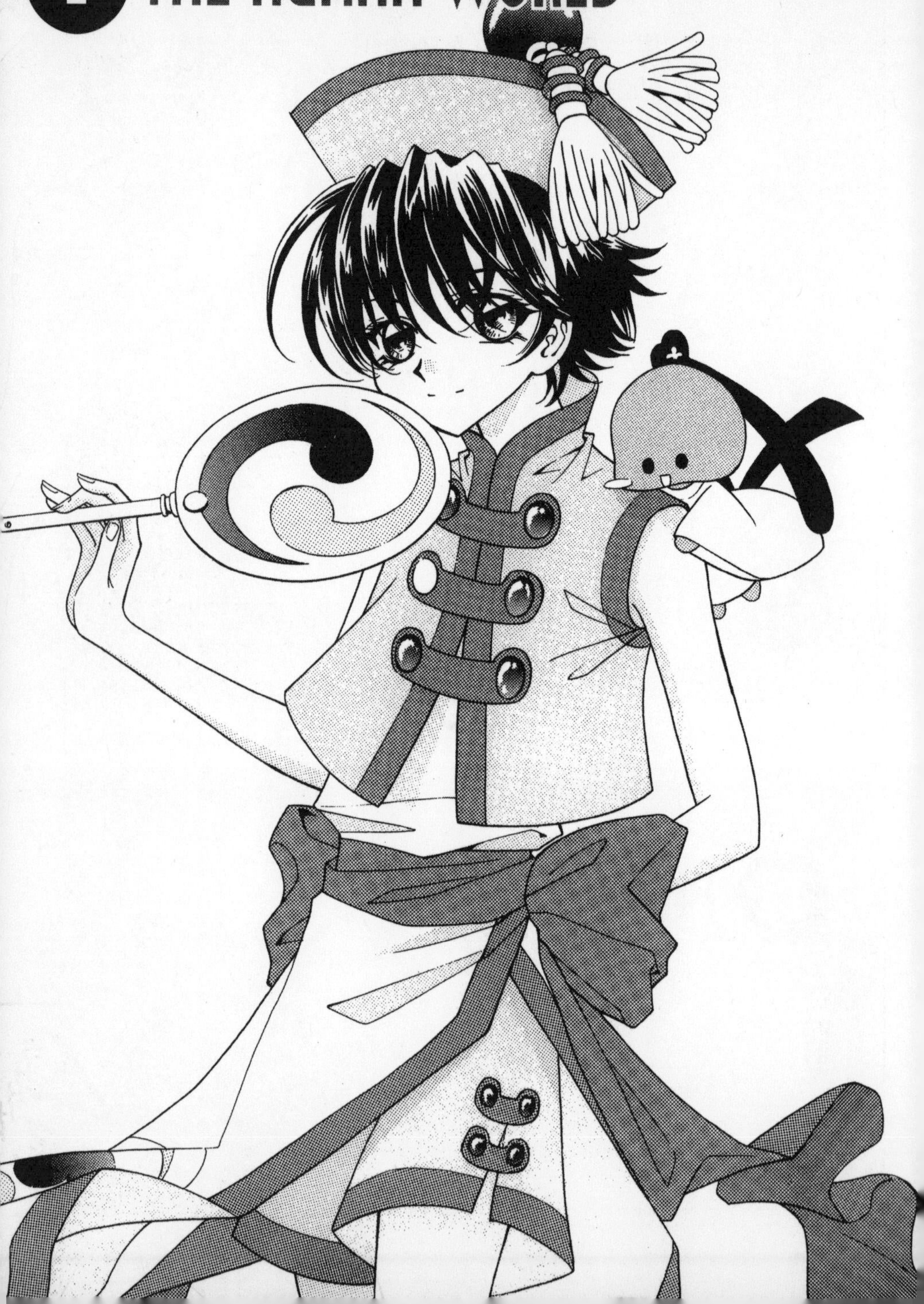

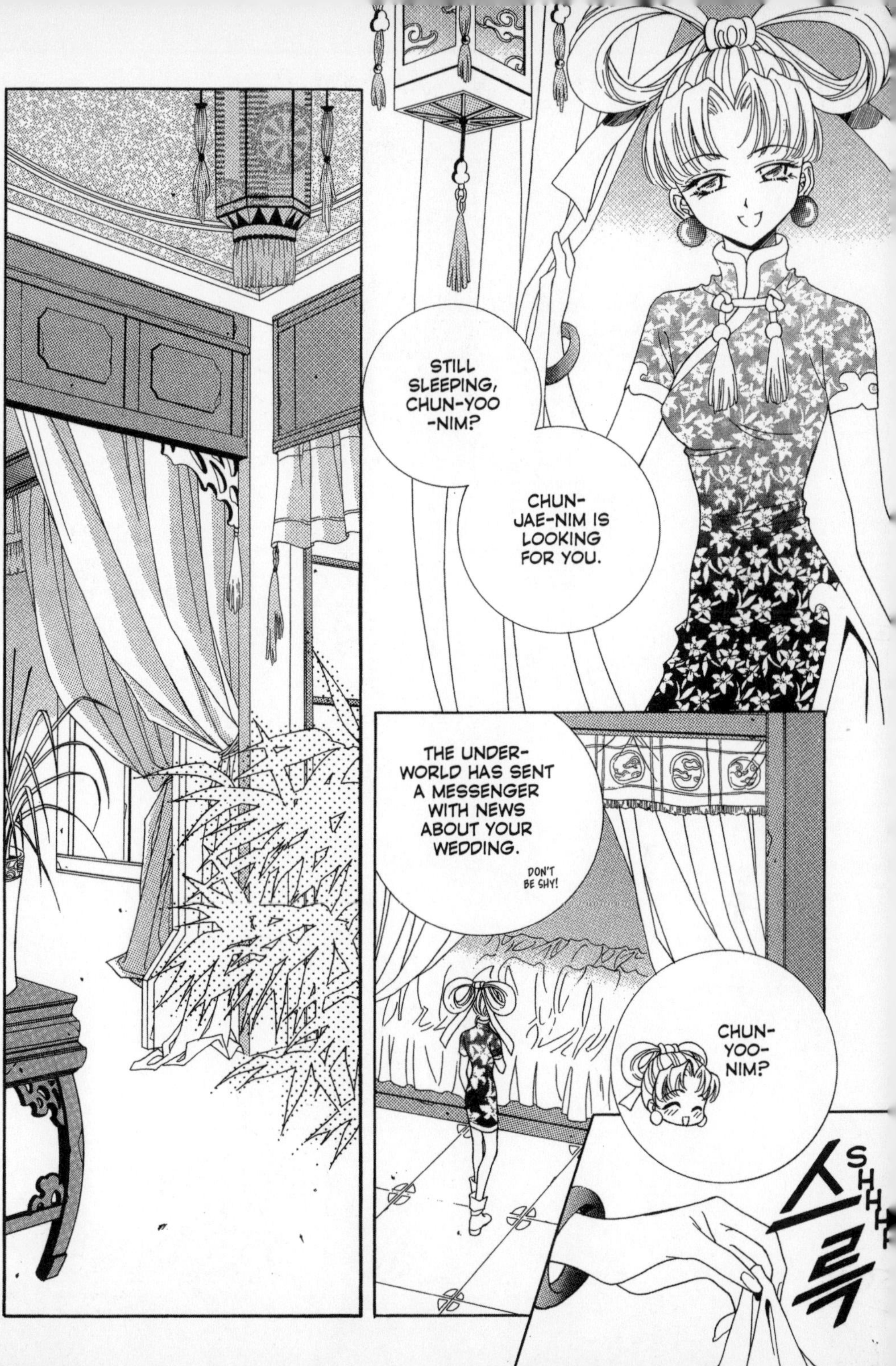
STILL SLEEPING, CHUN-YOO -NIM?
CHUN-JAE-NIM IS LOOKING FOR YOU.
THE UNDER-WORLD HAS SENT A MESSENGER WITH NEWS ABOUT YOUR WEDDING.
DON'T BE SHY!
CHUN-YOO-NIM?
스르륵
SHHH

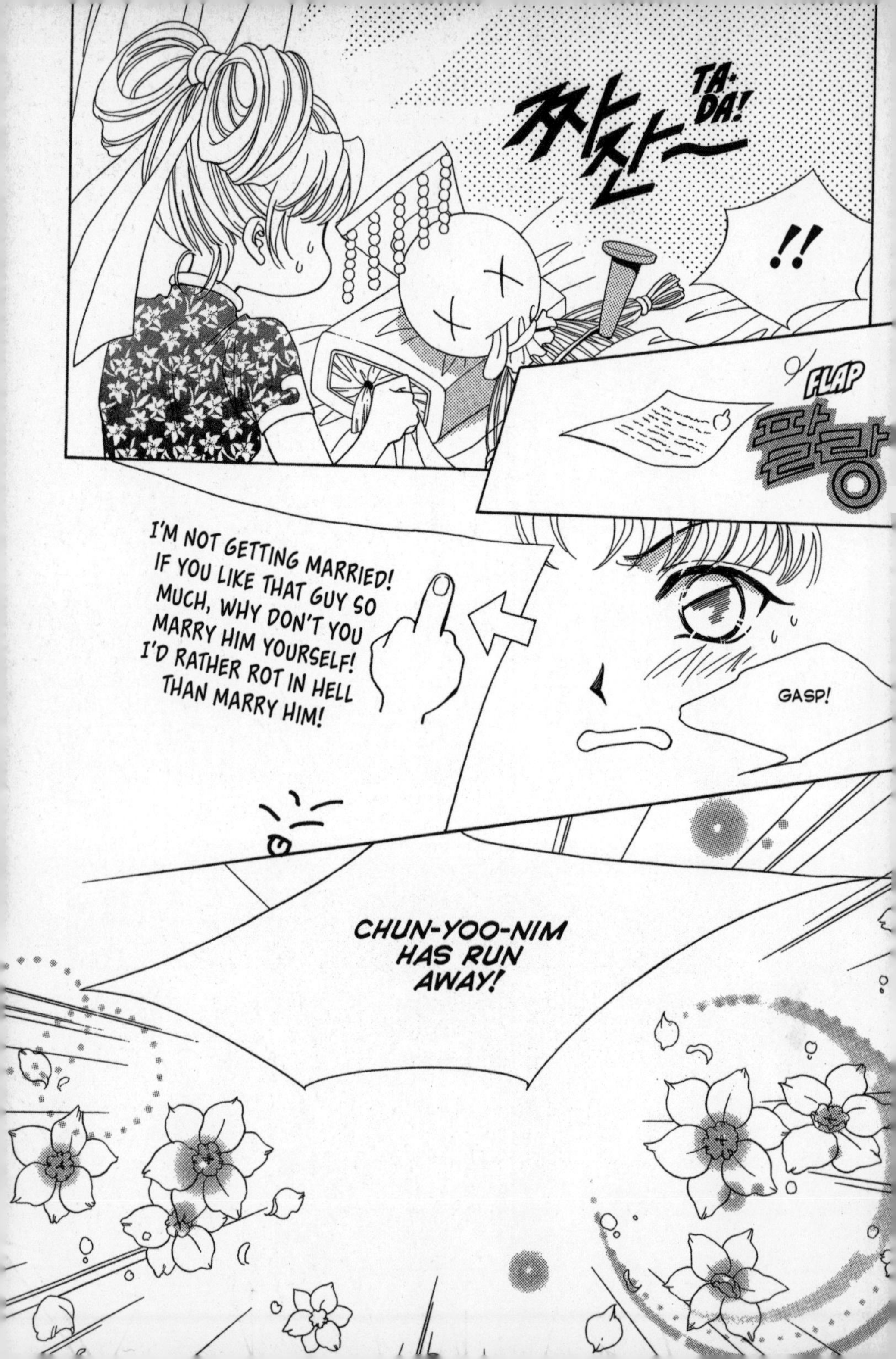

짜잔~
TA-DA!
!!
FLAP
펄럭
I'M NOT GETTING MARRIED! IF YOU LIKE THAT GUY SO MUCH, WHY DON'T YOU MARRY HIM YOURSELF! I'D RATHER ROT IN HELL THAN MARRY HIM!
GASP!
CHUN-YOO-NIM HAS RUN AWAY!

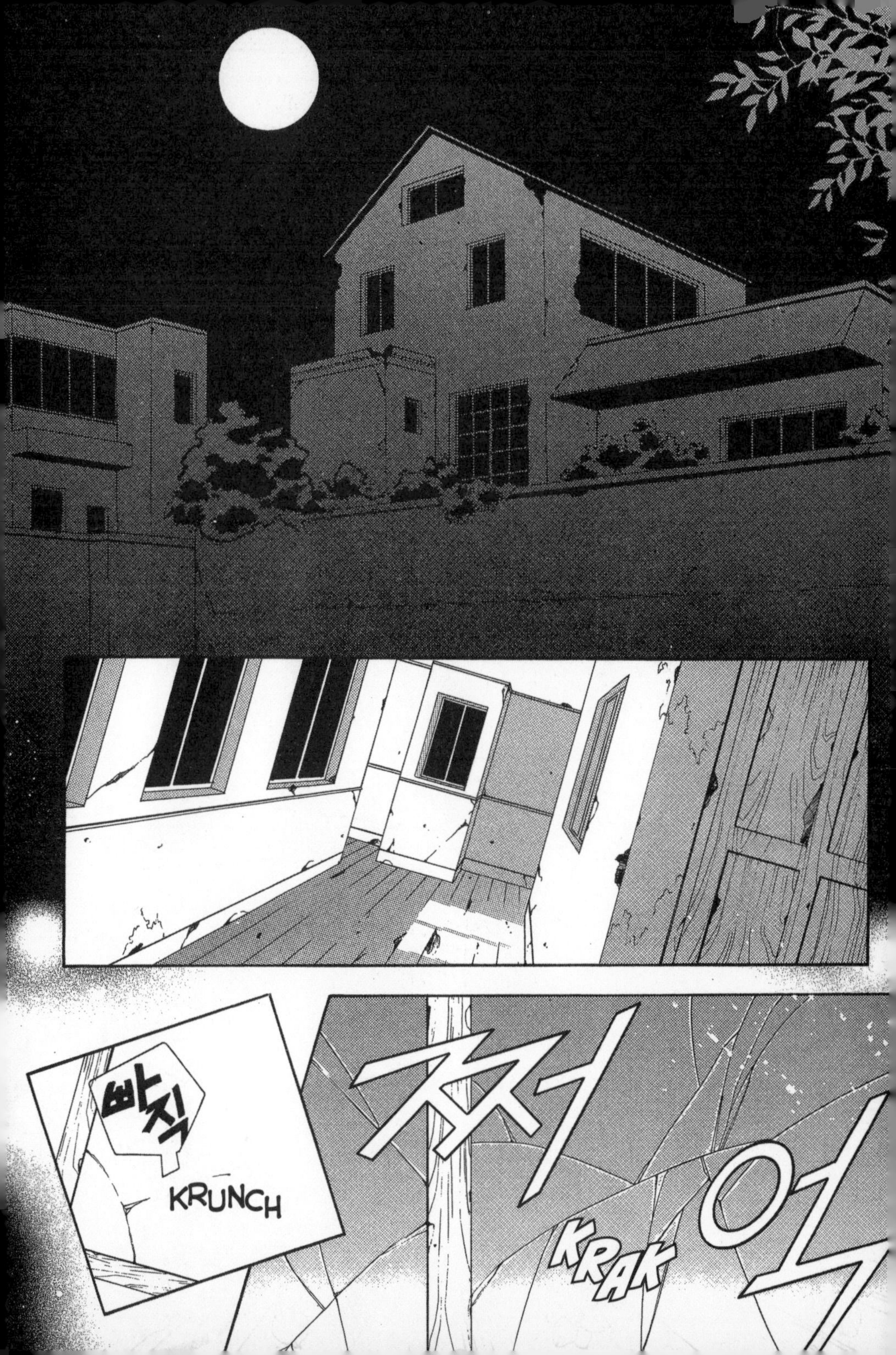
빠직
KRUNCH
쩌억
KRAK

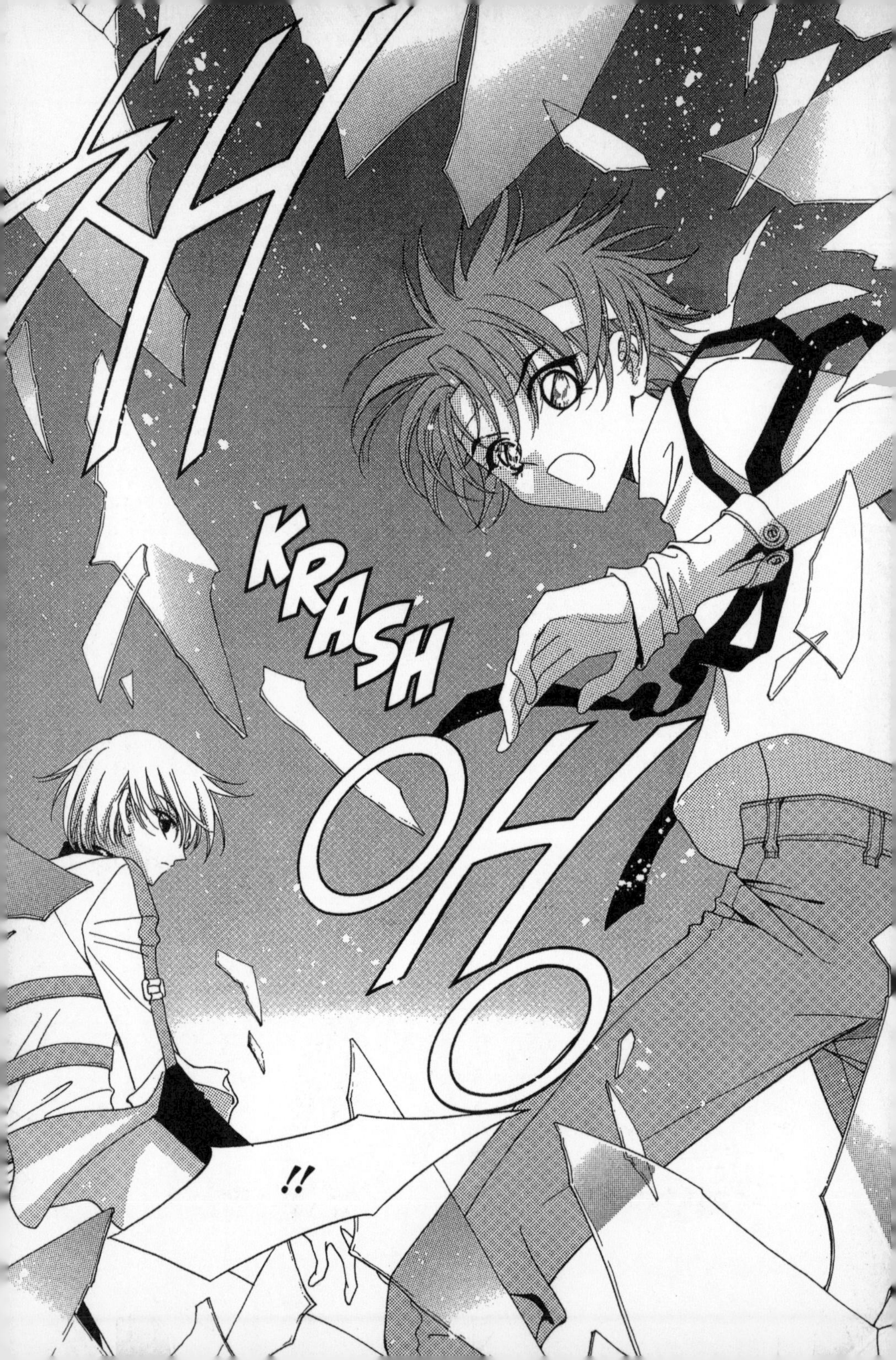
KRASH
!!

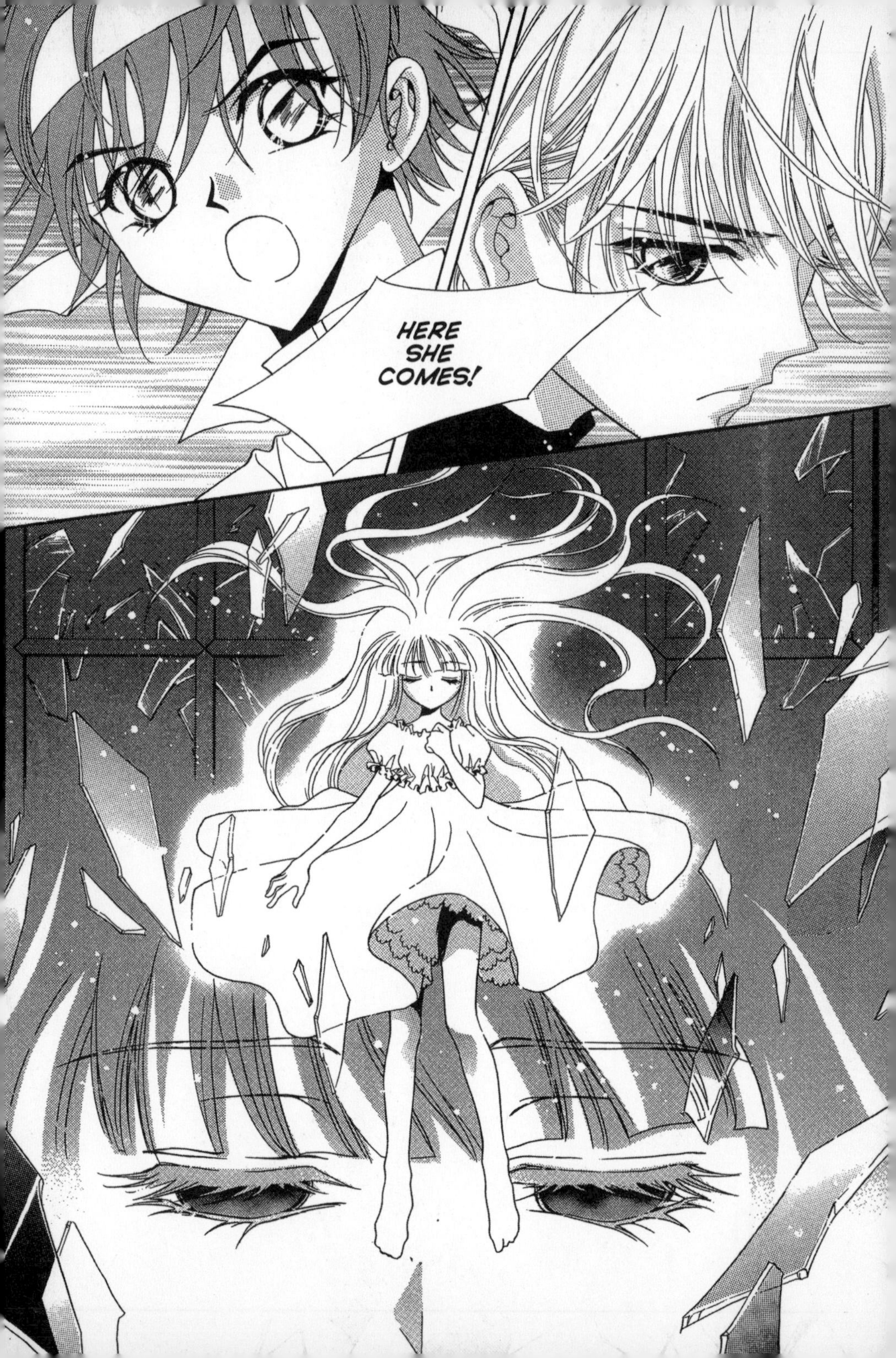
HERE SHE COMES!

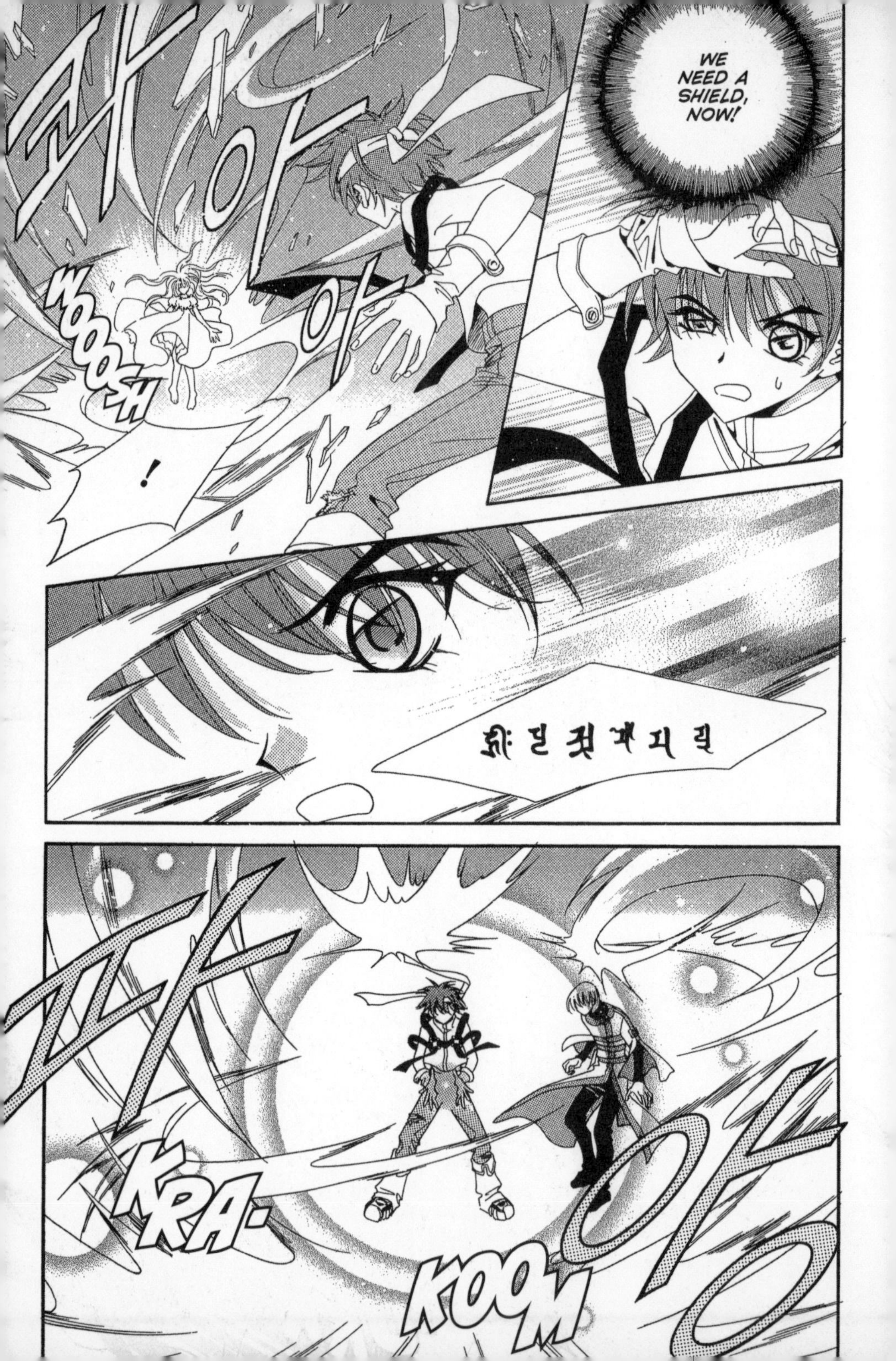
WOOOOSH
!
WE NEED A SHIELD, NOW!
KRA-
KOOM

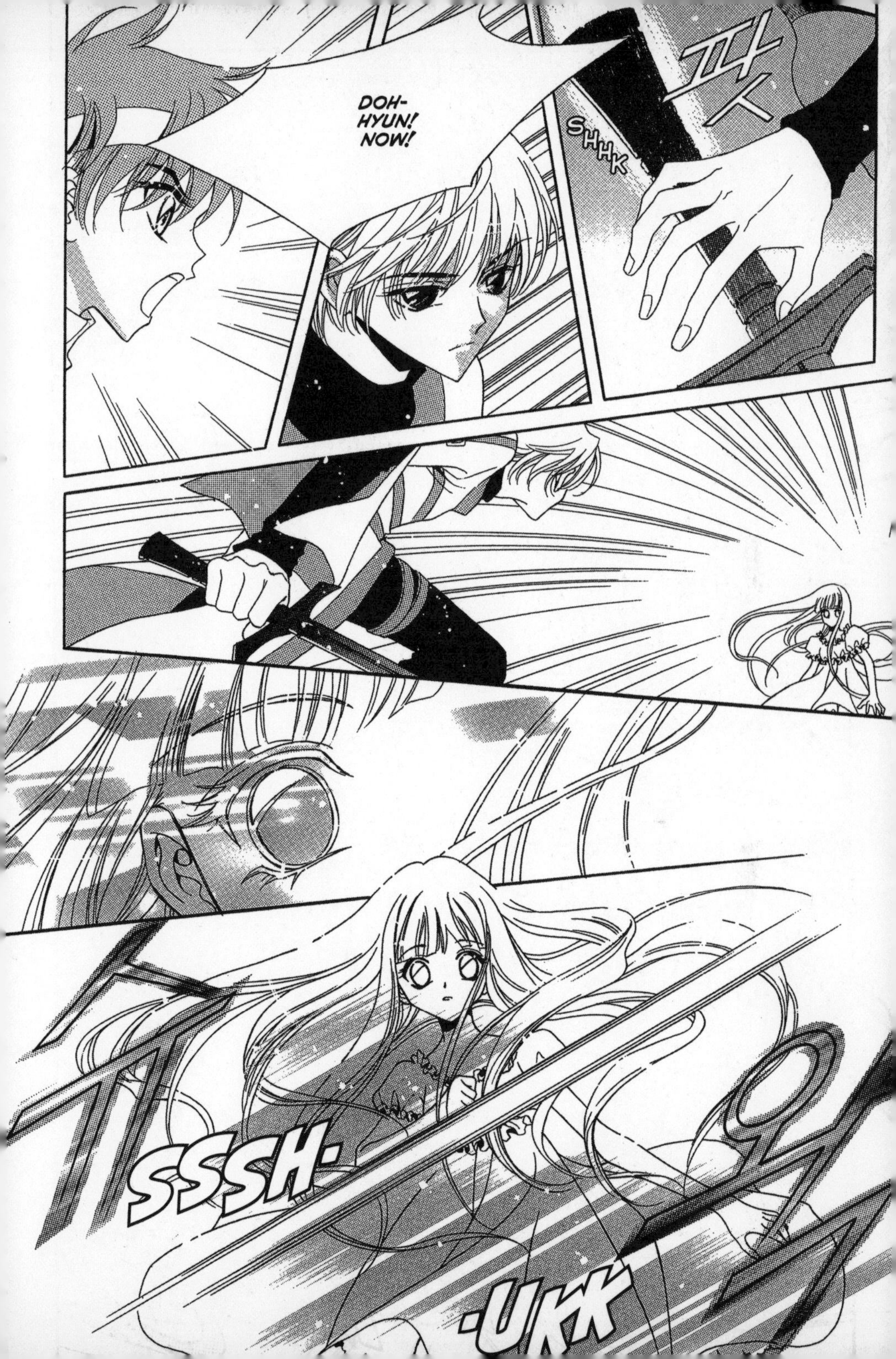
DOH-HYUN! NOW!
SHHK
SSSH-
-UKK

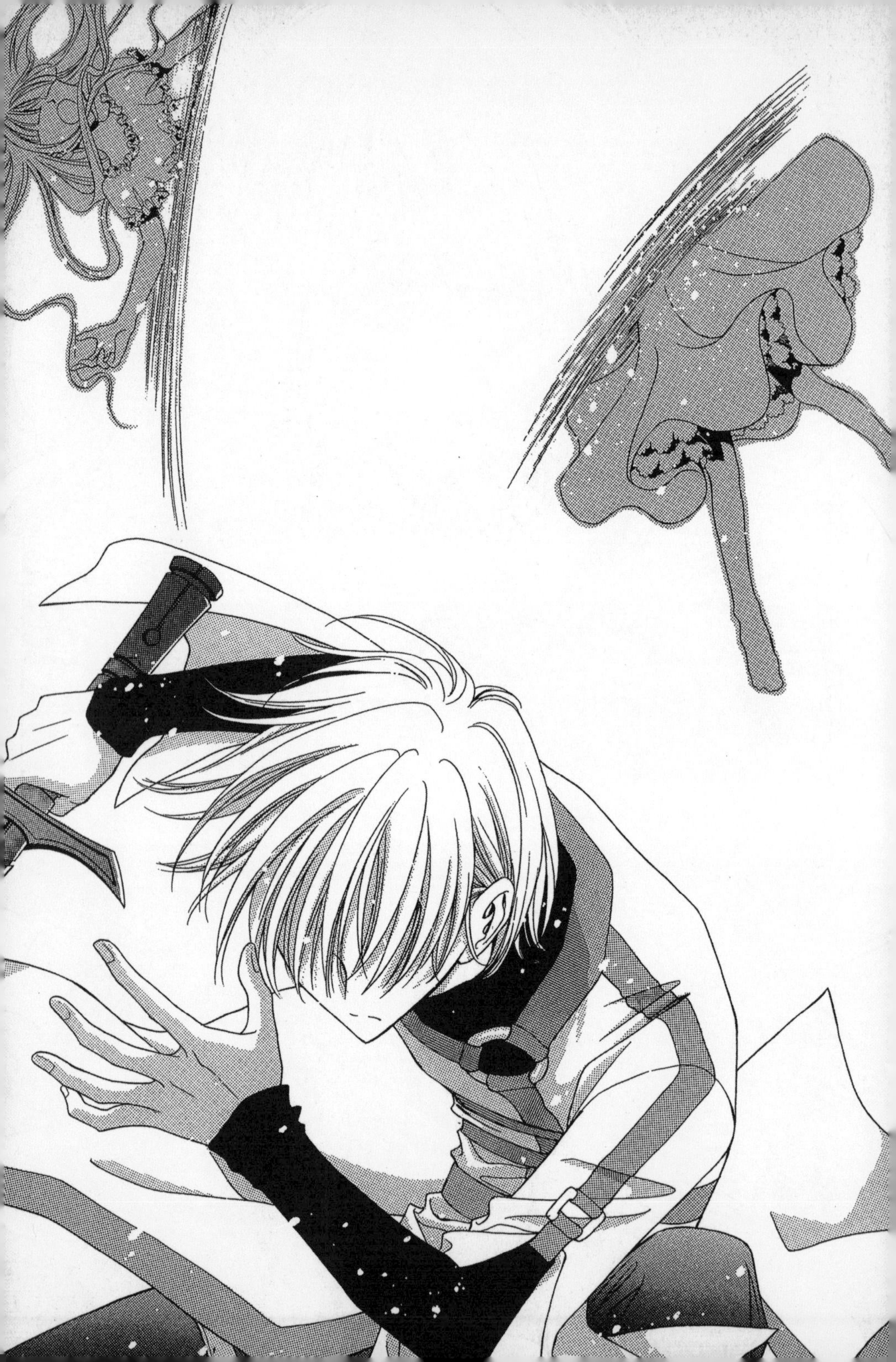

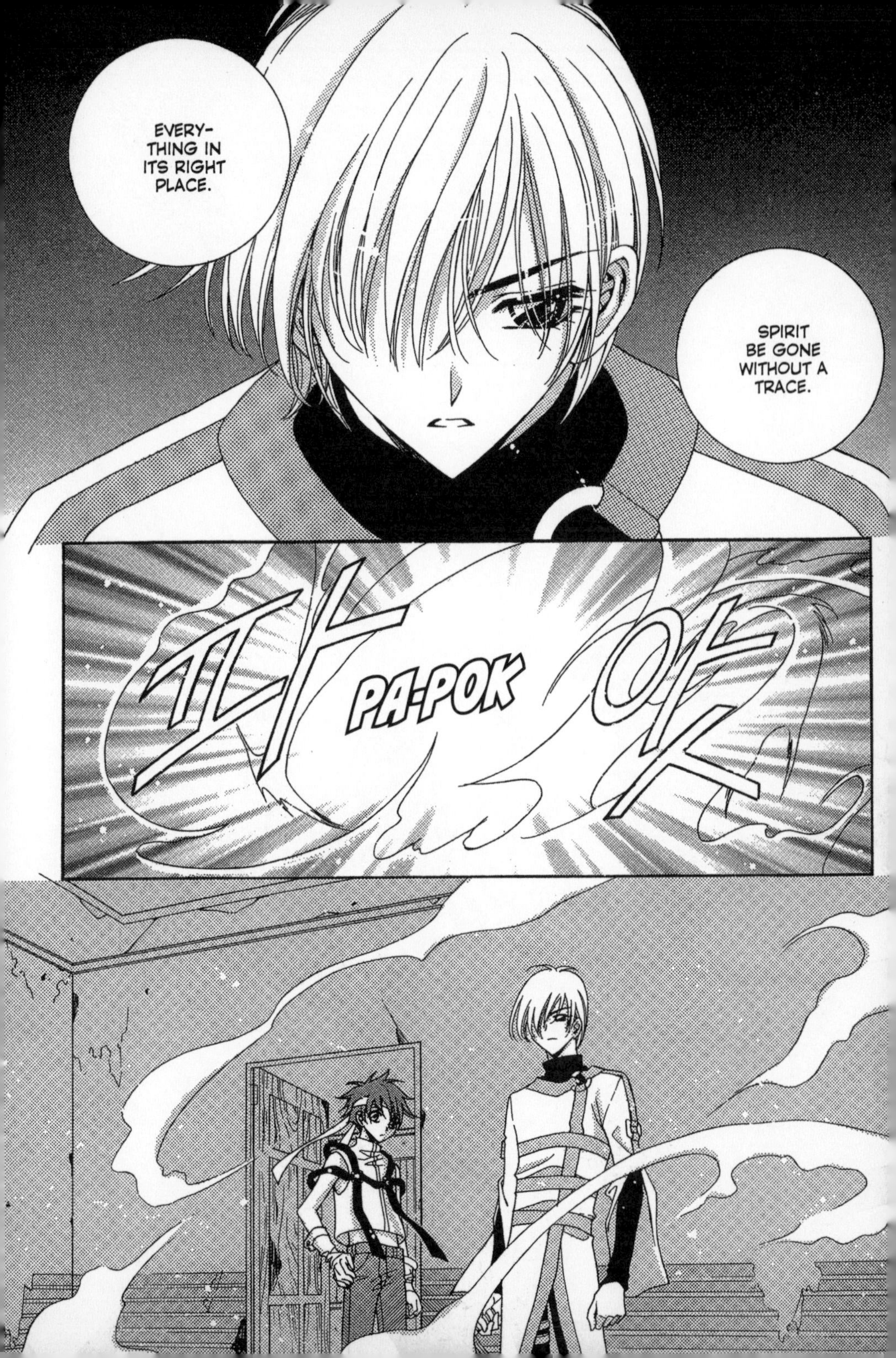
EVERY-THING IN ITS RIGHT PLACE.
SPIRIT BE GONE WITHOUT A TRACE.
PA-POK

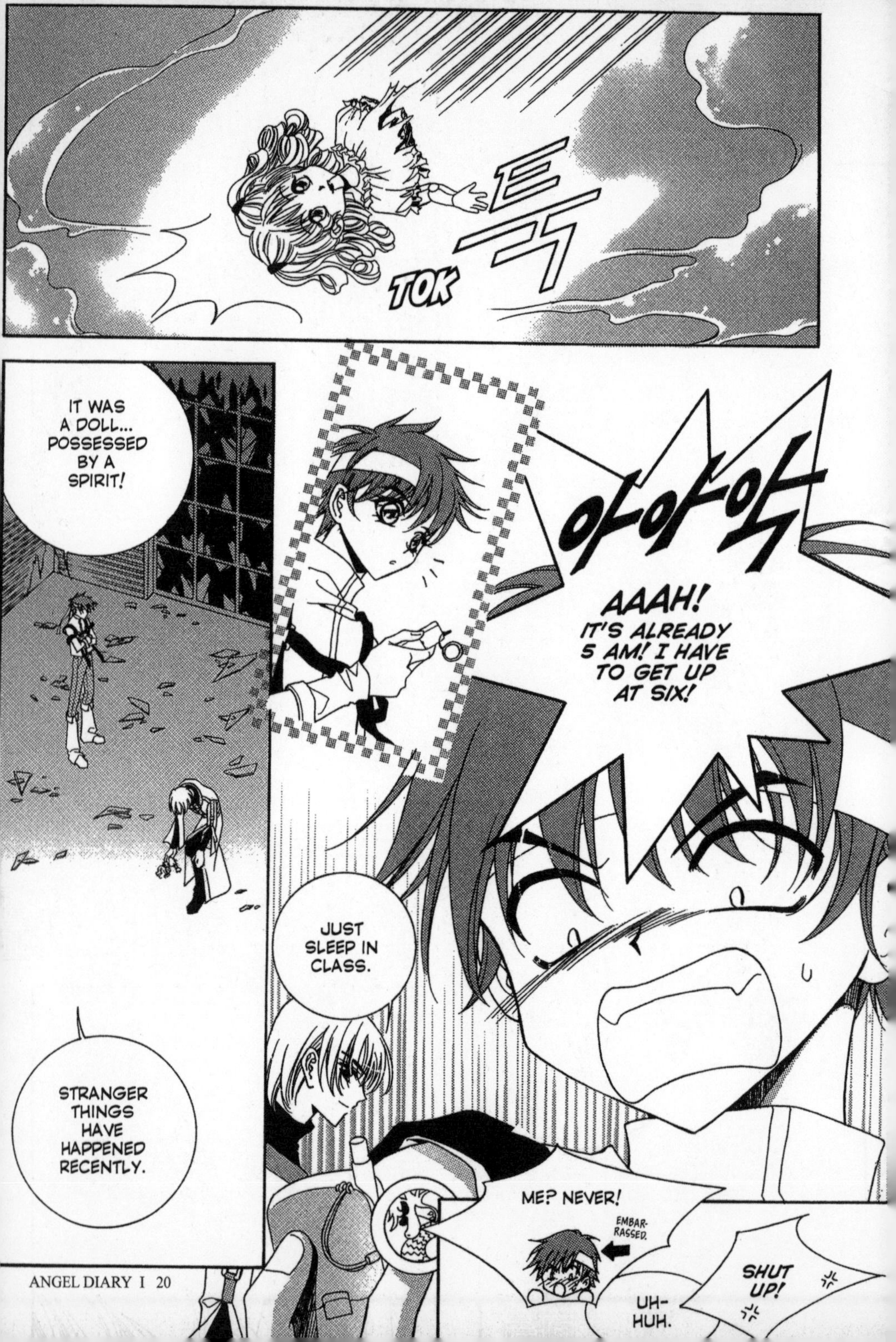
TOK
IT WAS A DOLL... POSSESSED BY A SPIRIT!
STRANGER THINGS HAVE HAPPENED RECENTLY.
AAAH! IT'S ALREADY 5 AM! I HAVE TO GET UP AT SIX!
JUST SLEEP IN CLASS.
ME? NEVER!
EMBARRASSED.
UH-HUH.
SHUT UP!

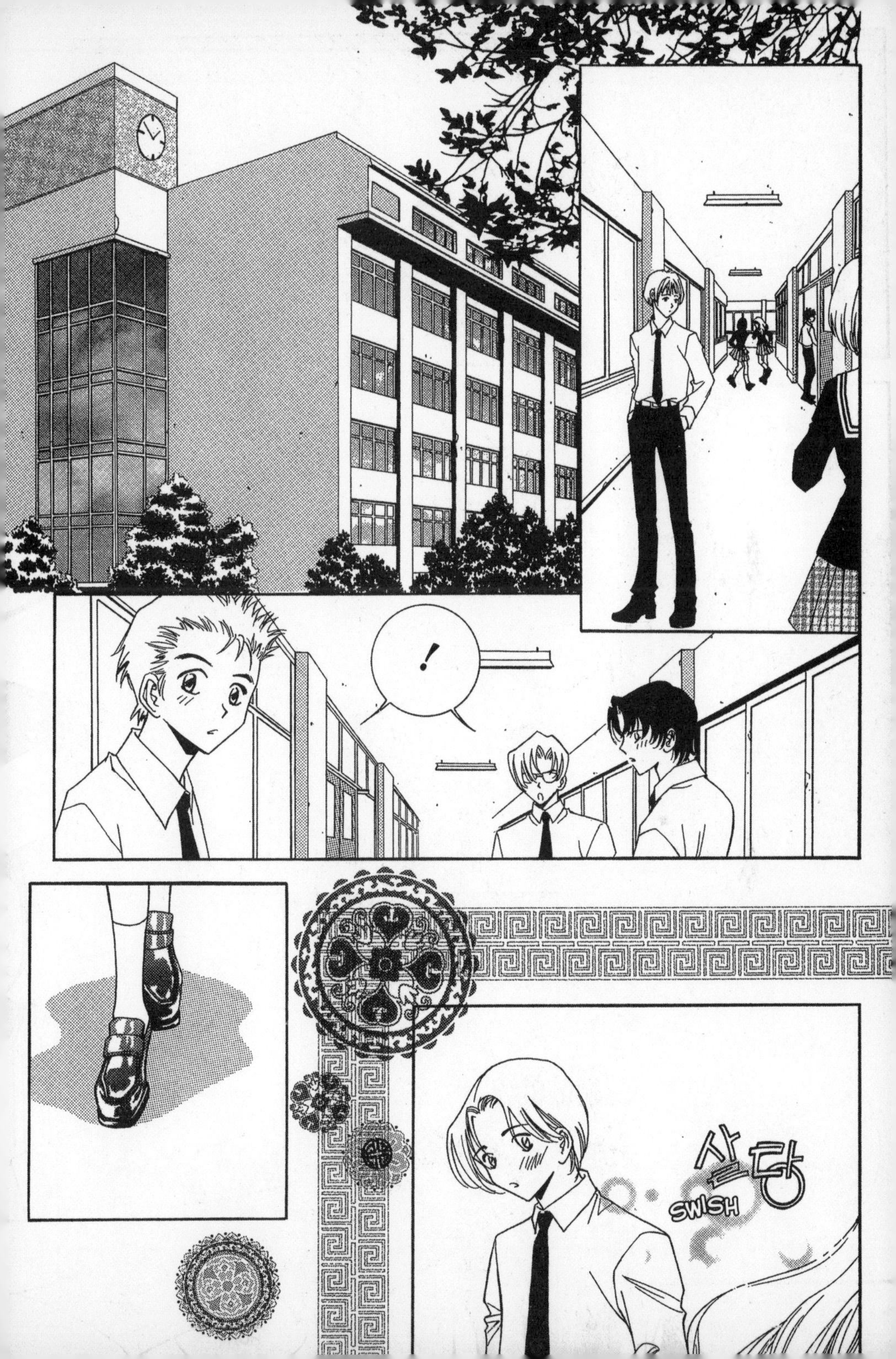
!
살랑
SWISH

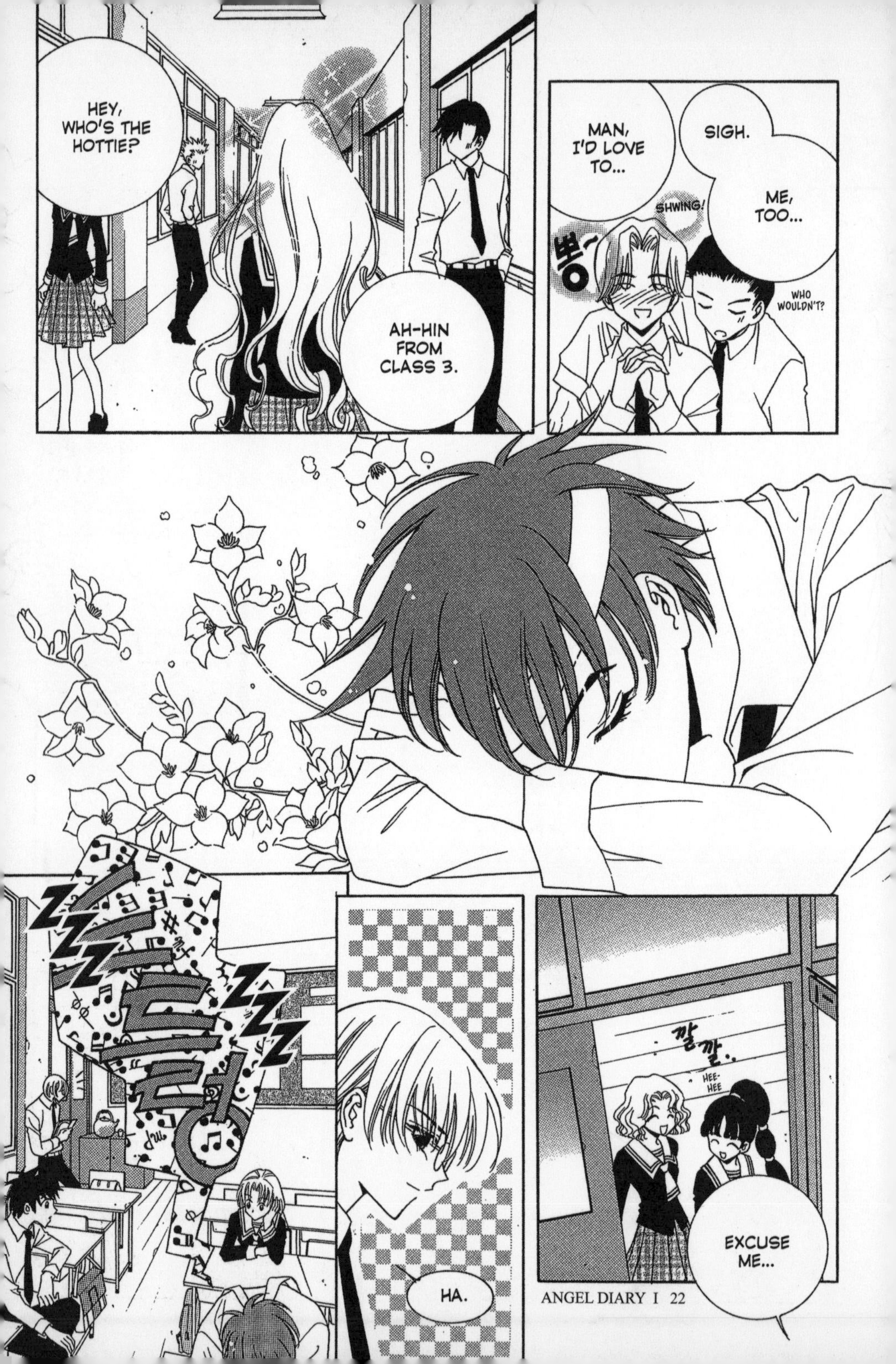
HEY, WHO'S THE HOTTIE?
AH-HIN FROM CLASS 3.
MAN, I'D LOVE TO...
SIGH.
SHWING!
뿅~
ME, TOO...
WHO WOULDN'T?
HA.
깔깔..
HEE-HEE
EXCUSE ME...

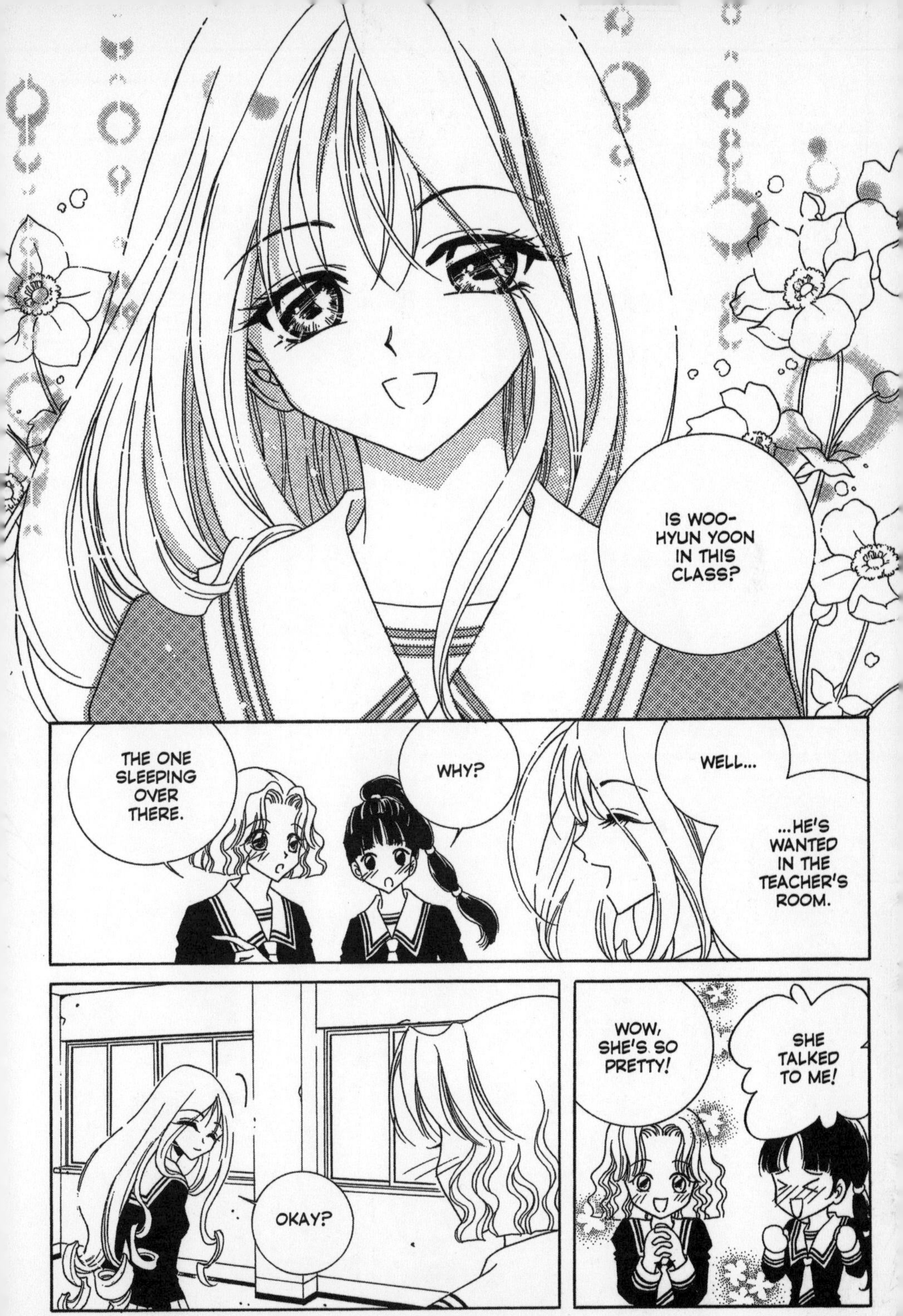
IS WOO-HYUN YOON IN THIS CLASS?
THE ONE SLEEPING OVER THERE.
WHY?
WELL...
...HE'S WANTED IN THE TEACHER'S ROOM.
OKAY?
WOW, SHE'S SO PRETTY!
SHE TALKED TO ME!

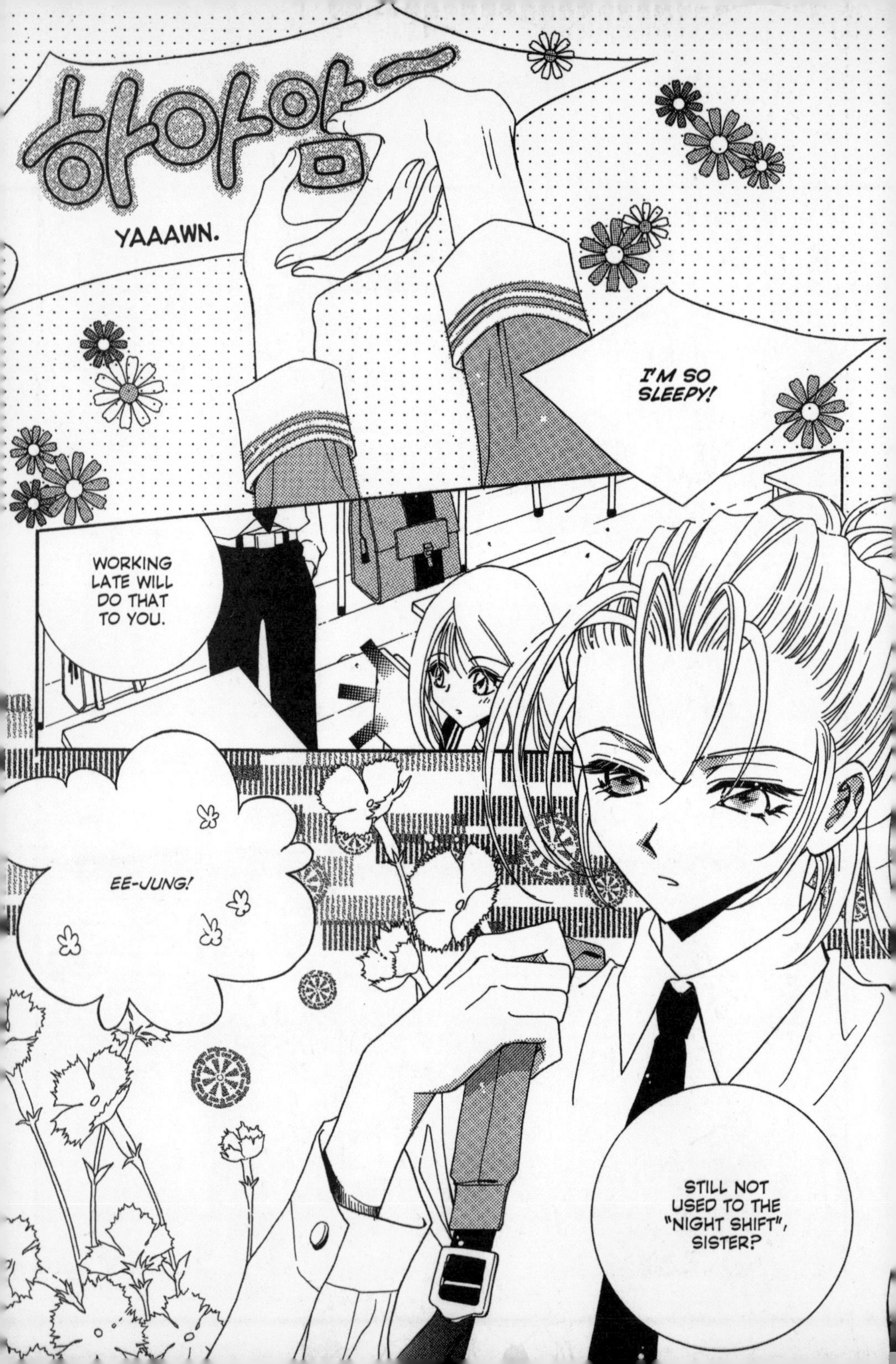
하아암~
YAAAWN.
I'M SO SLEEPY!
WORKING LATE WILL DO THAT TO YOU.
EE-JUNG!
STILL NOT USED TO THE "NIGHT SHIFT", SISTER?

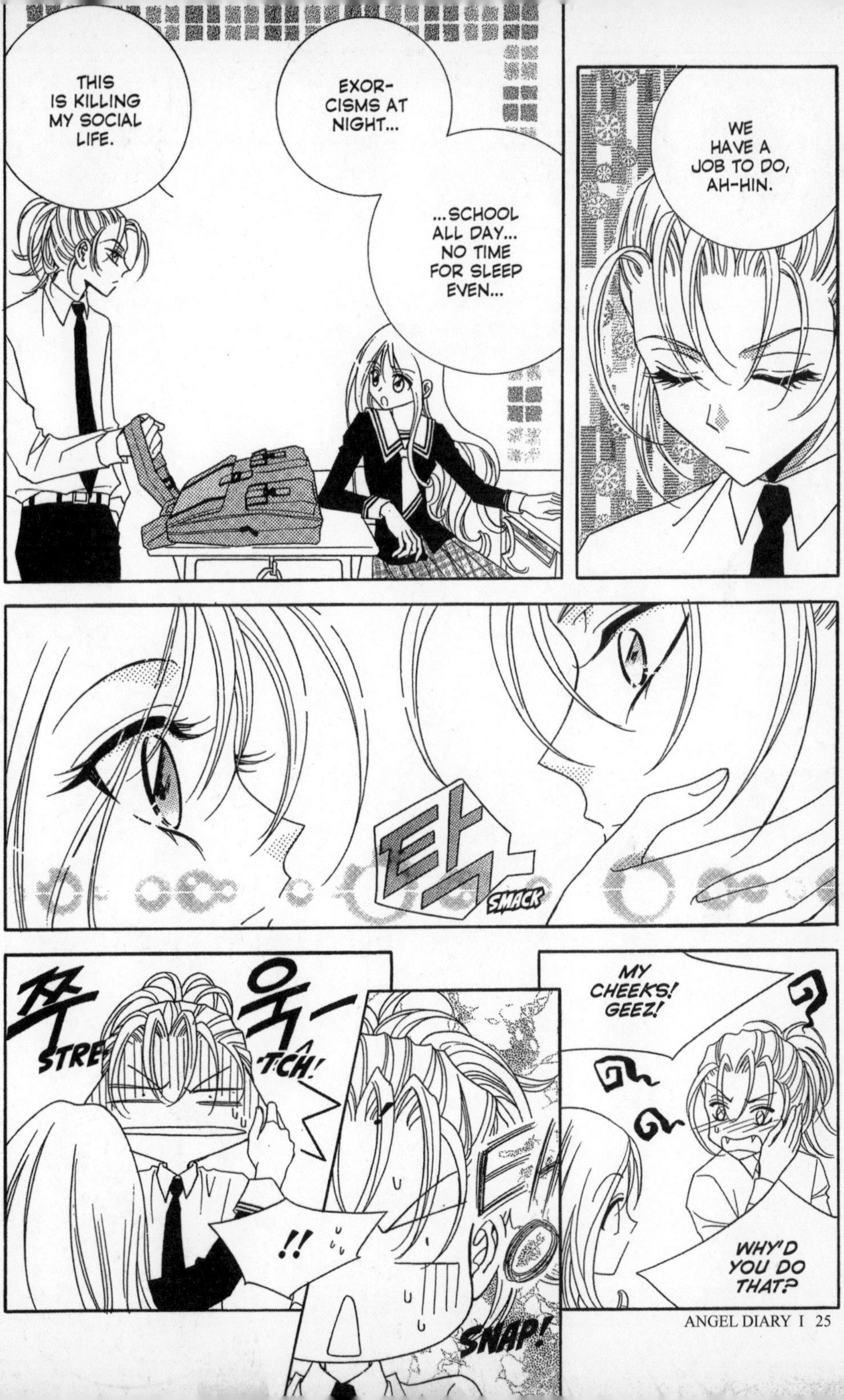
THIS IS KILLING MY SOCIAL LIFE.
EXOR-CISMS AT NIGHT...
...SCHOOL ALL DAY... NO TIME FOR SLEEP EVEN...
WE HAVE A JOB TO DO, AH-HIN.
탁
SMACK
쭈
욱—
STRE-
-TCH!
EH
!!
SNAP!
MY CHEEKS! GEEZ!
WHY'D YOU DO THAT?

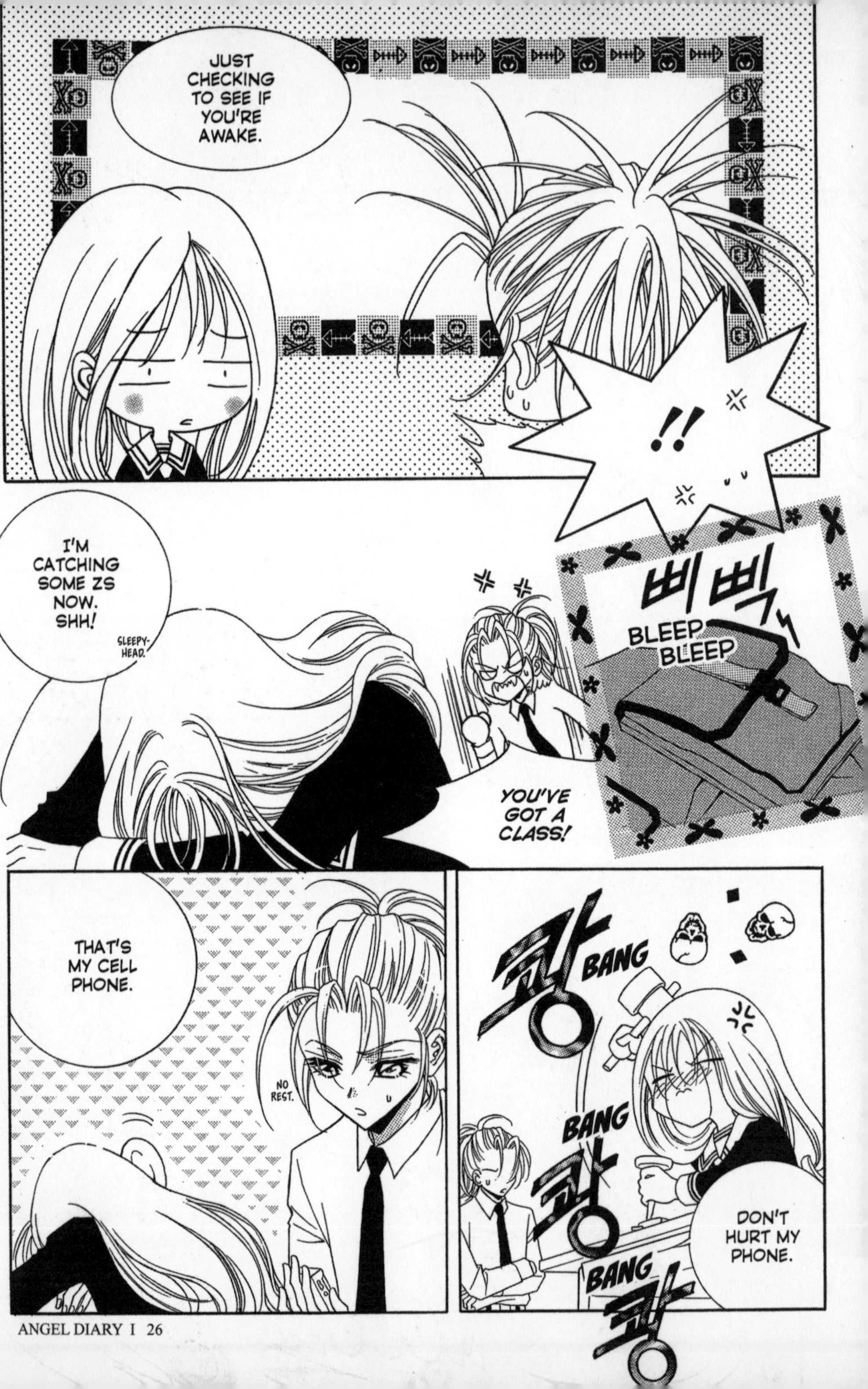
JUST CHECKING TO SEE IF YOU'RE AWAKE.
!!
I'M CATCHING SOME ZS NOW. SHH!
SLEEPY-HEAD.
YOU'VE GOT A CLASS!
삐삑
BLEEP BLEEP
THAT'S MY CELL PHONE.
NO REST.
쾅
BANG
BANG
쾅
BANG
쾅
DON'T HURT MY PHONE.

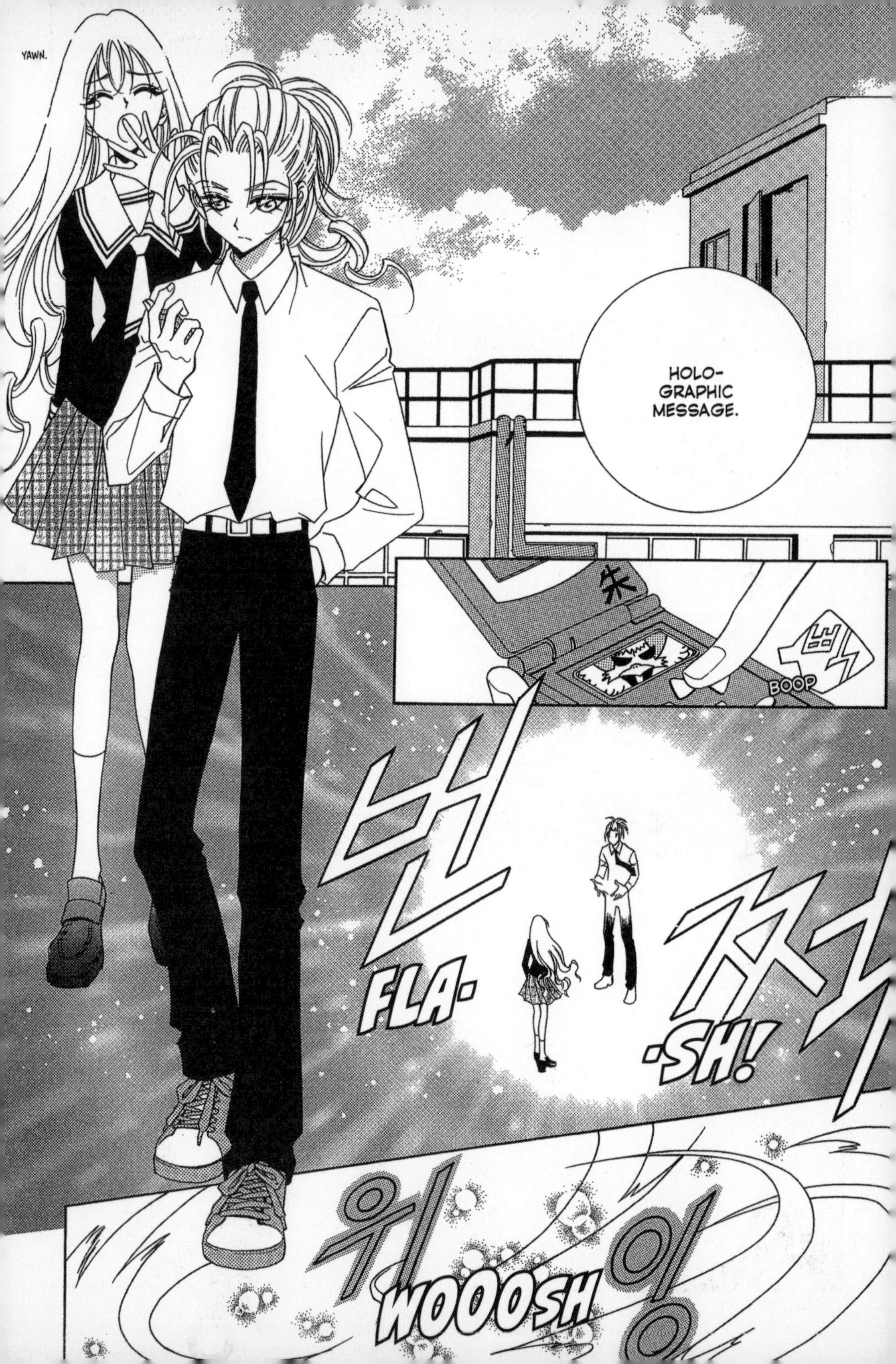
YAWN.
HOLO-
GRAPHIC
MESSAGE.
BOOP
FLA-
-SH!
WOOOSH

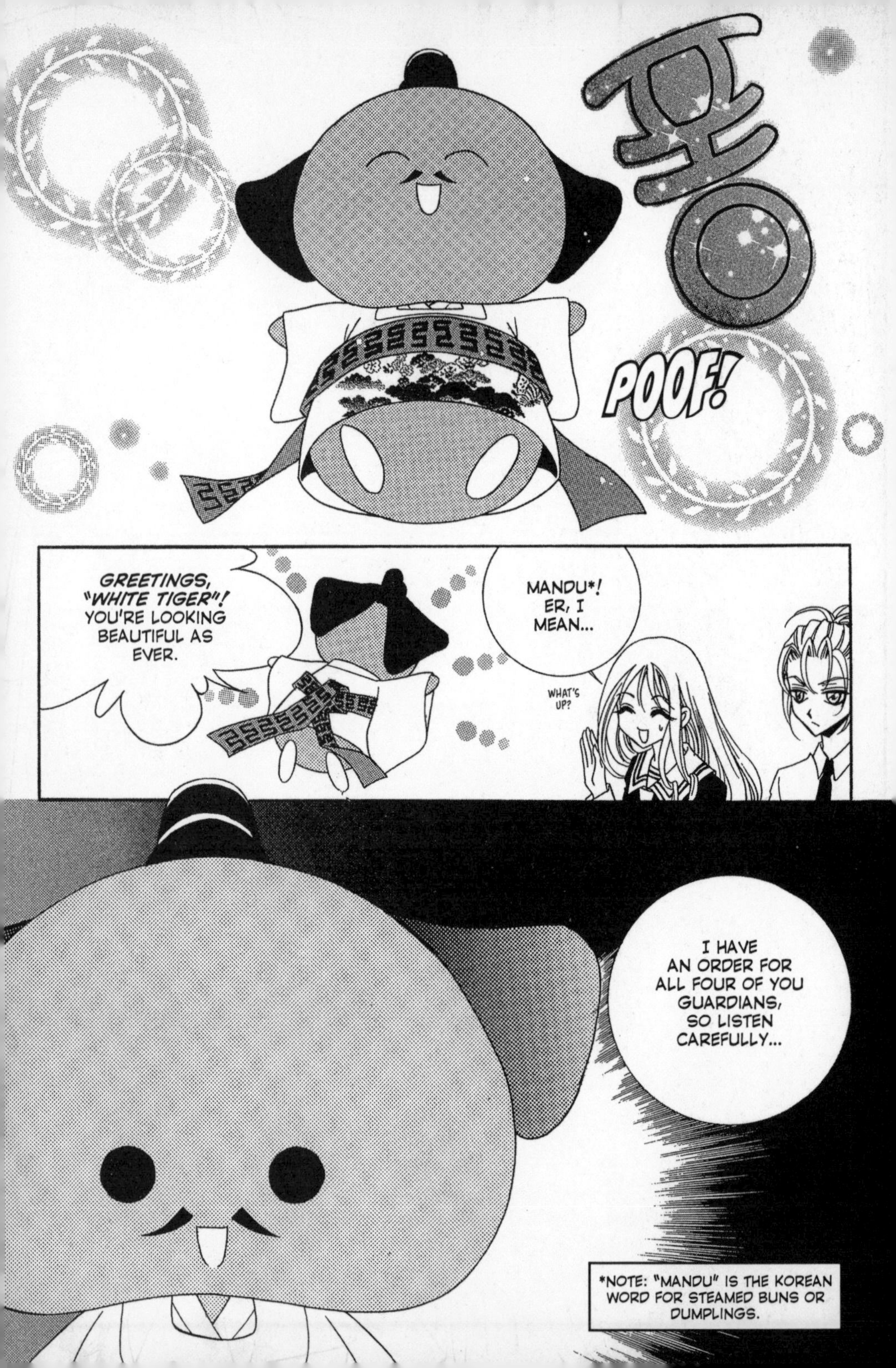
퐁
POOF!
GREETINGS, "WHITE TIGER"! YOU'RE LOOKING BEAUTIFUL AS EVER.
MANDU*! ER, I MEAN...
WHAT'S UP?
I HAVE AN ORDER FOR ALL FOUR OF YOU GUARDIANS, SO LISTEN CAREFULLY...
*NOTE: "MANDU" IS THE KOREAN WORD FOR STEAMED BUNS OR DUMPLINGS.

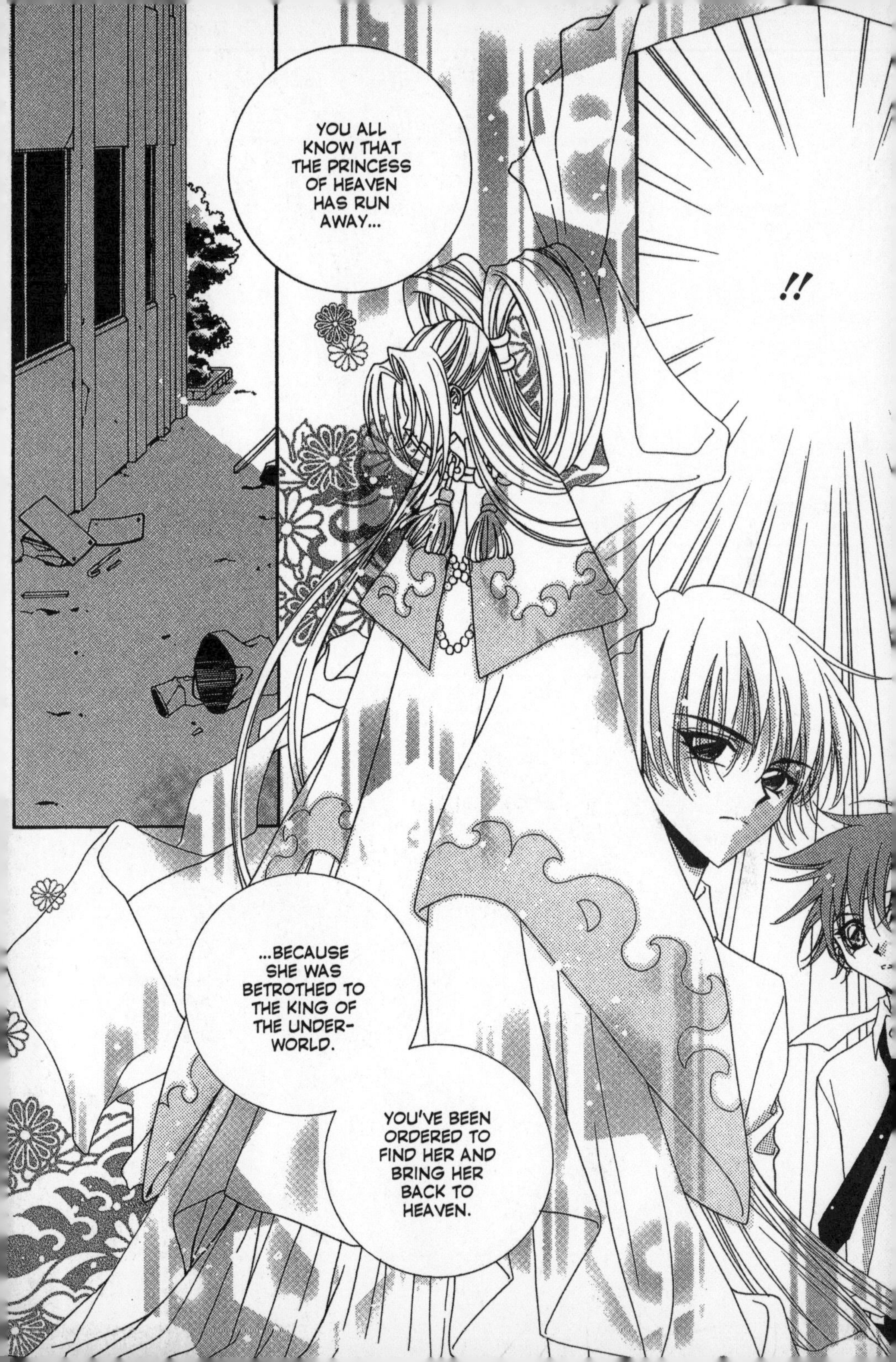
YOU ALL KNOW THAT THE PRINCESS OF HEAVEN HAS RUN AWAY...
!!
...BECAUSE SHE WAS BETROTHED TO THE KING OF THE UNDER-WORLD.
YOU'VE BEEN ORDERED TO FIND HER AND BRING HER BACK TO HEAVEN.

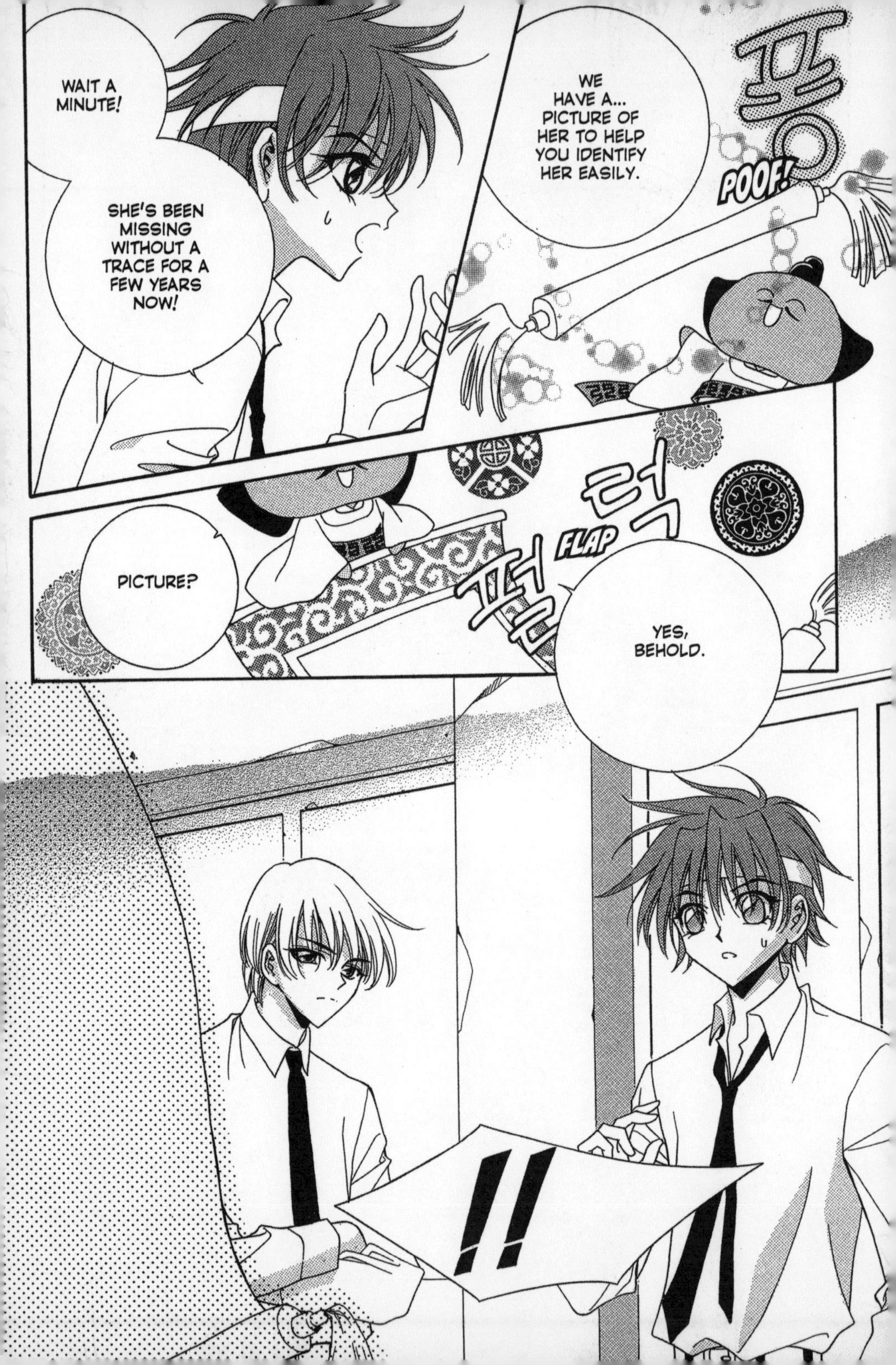
WAIT A MINUTE!
SHE'S BEEN MISSING WITHOUT A TRACE FOR A FEW YEARS NOW!
WE HAVE A... PICTURE OF HER TO HELP YOU IDENTIFY HER EASILY.
퐁
POOF!
PICTURE?
펄럭
FLAP
YES, BEHOLD.
!!

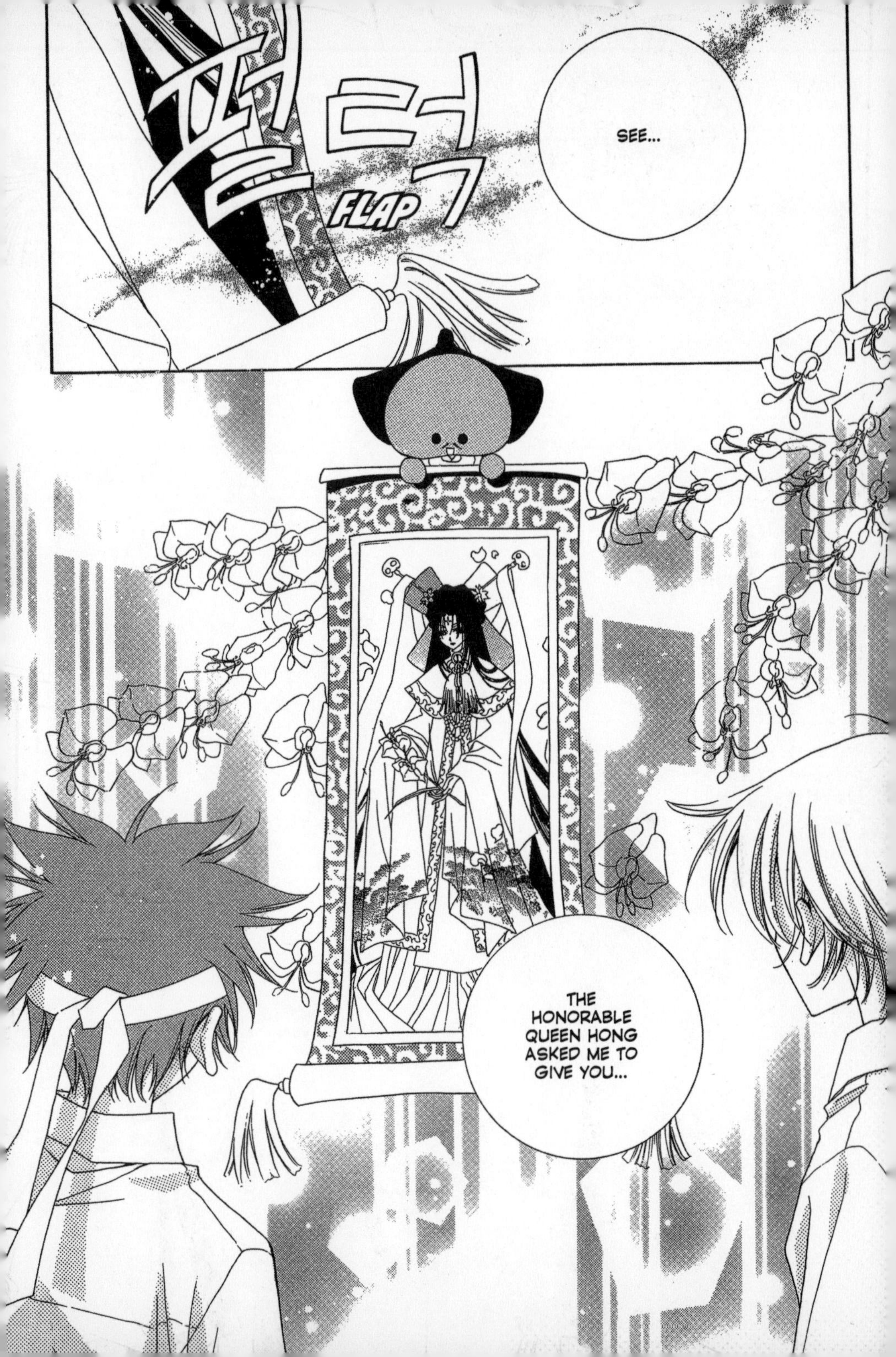

펄럭
FLAP
SEE...
THE HONORABLE QUEEN HONG ASKED ME TO GIVE YOU...

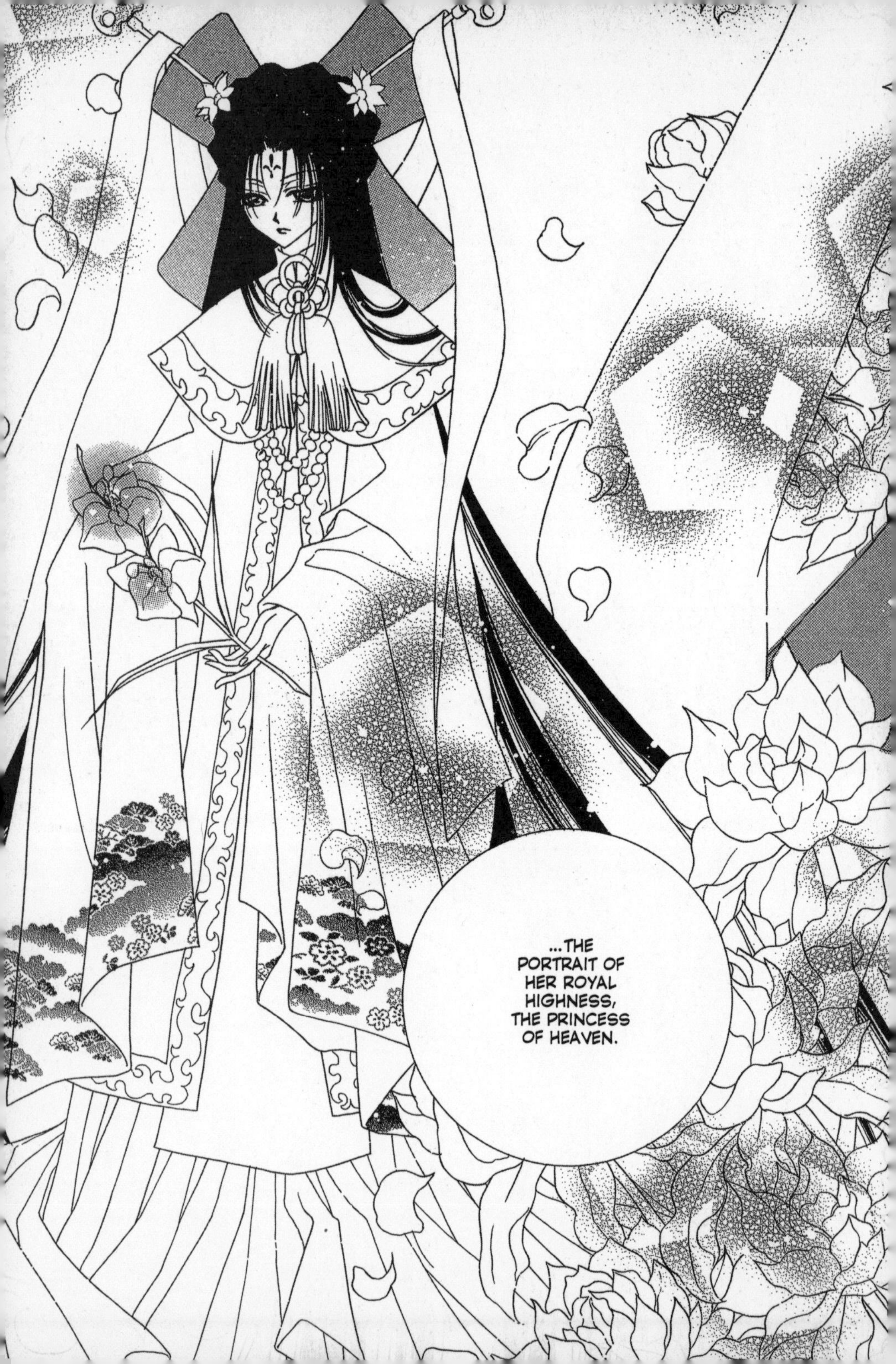
...THE PORTRAIT OF HER ROYAL HIGHNESS, THE PRINCESS OF HEAVEN.

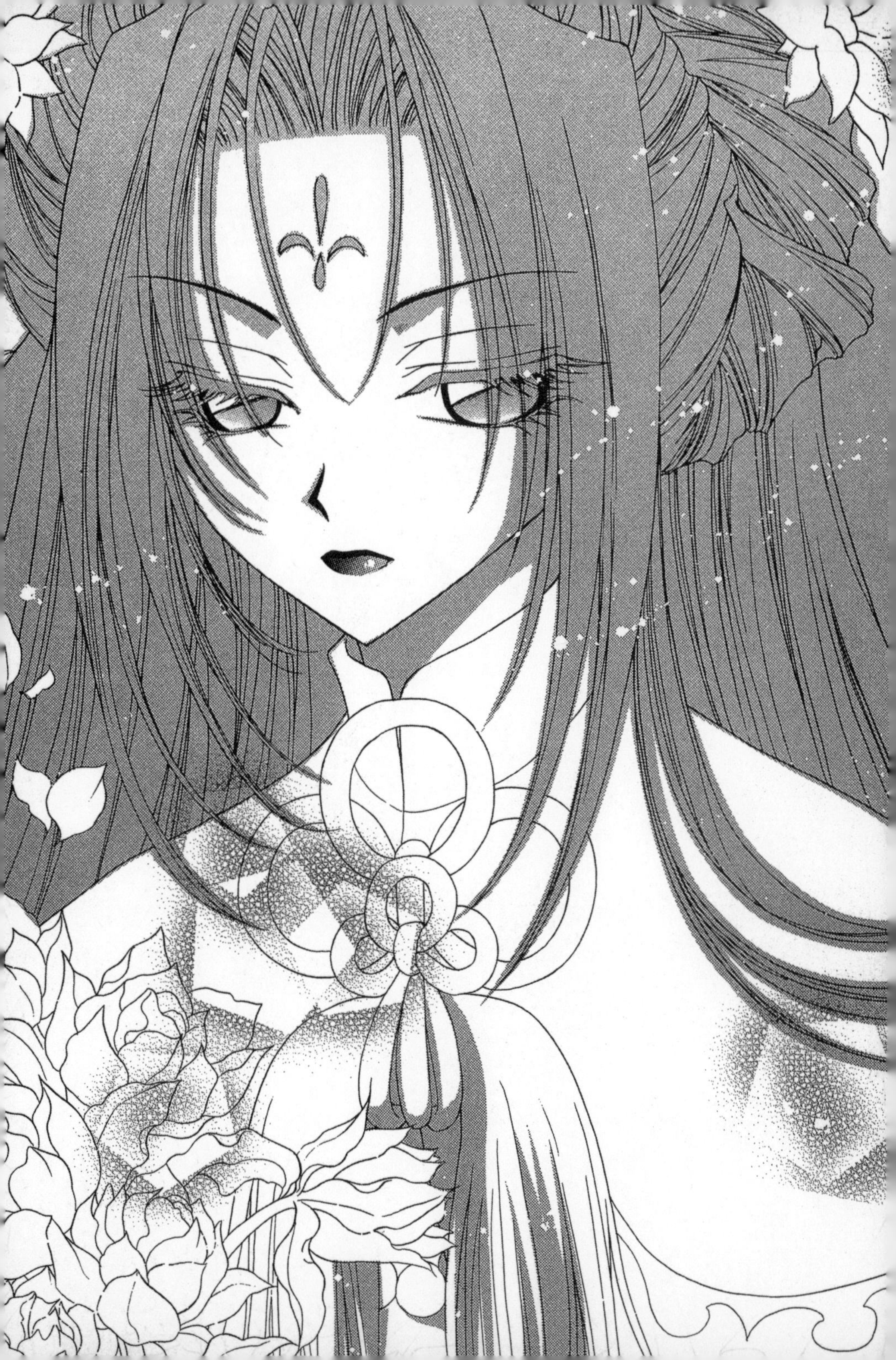

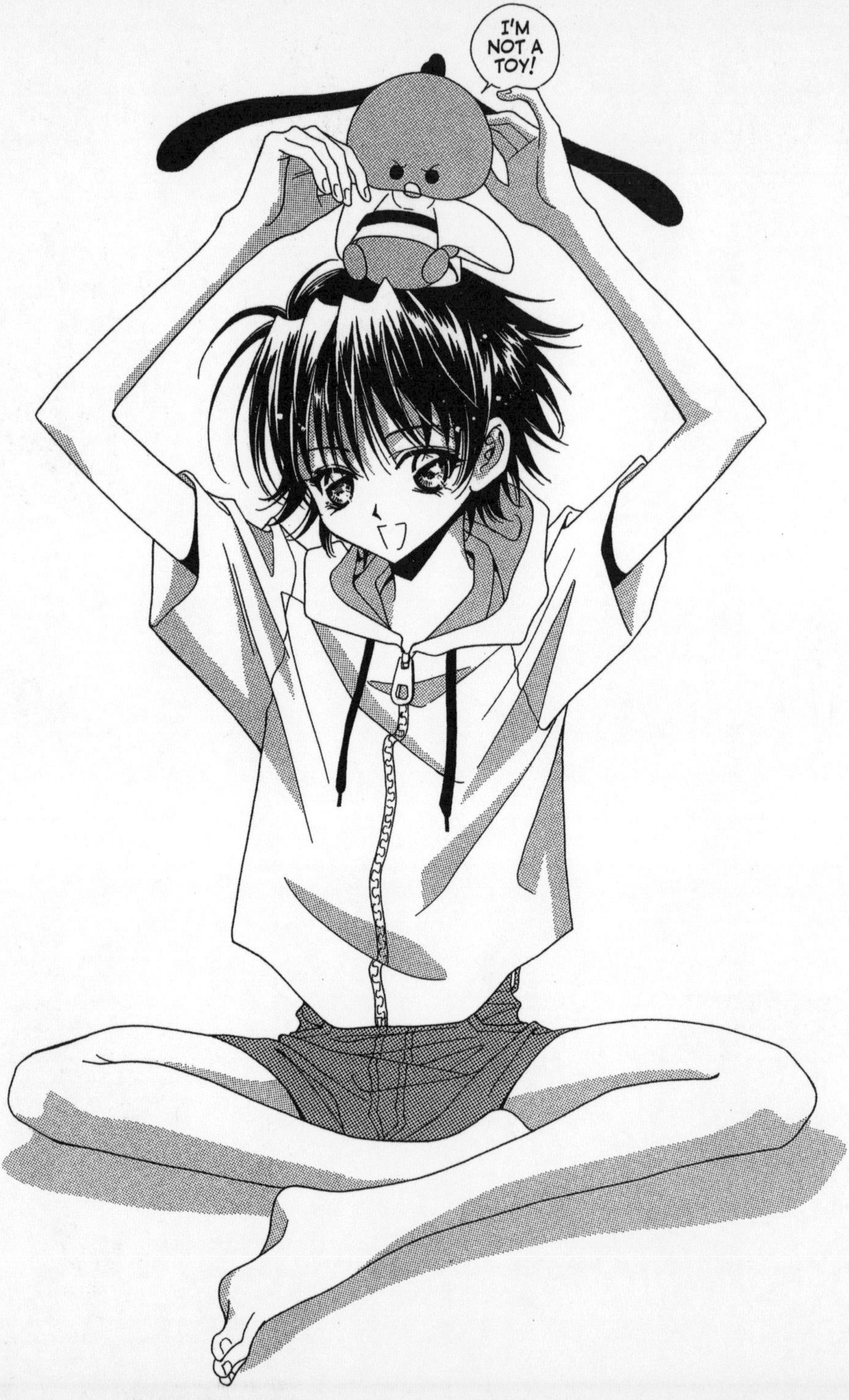
I'M NOT A TOY!

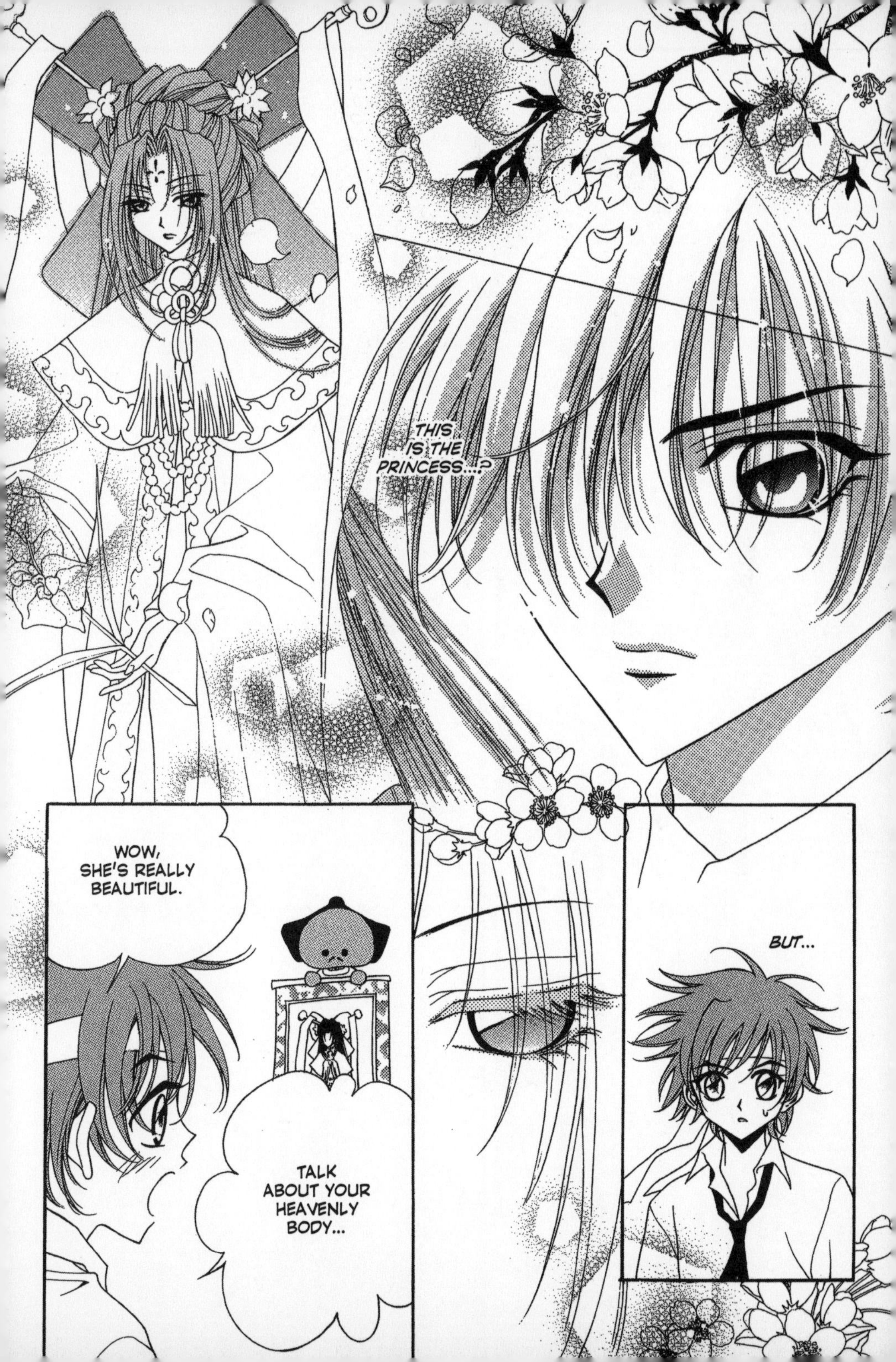
THIS IS THE PRINCESS...?
WOW, SHE'S REALLY BEAUTIFUL.
TALK ABOUT YOUR HEAVENLY BODY...
BUT...

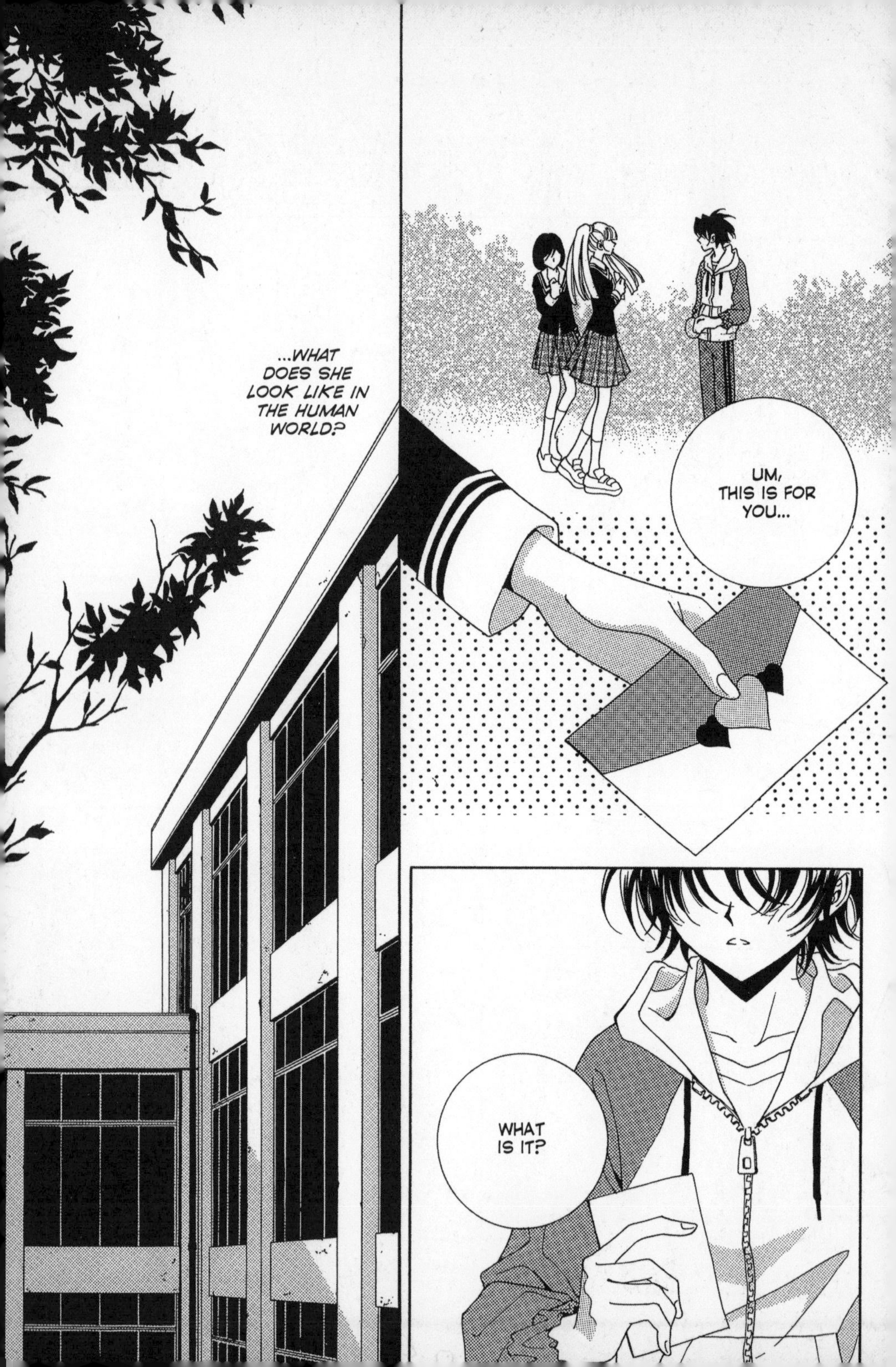
...WHAT DOES SHE LOOK LIKE IN THE HUMAN WORLD?
UM, THIS IS FOR YOU...
WHAT IS IT?

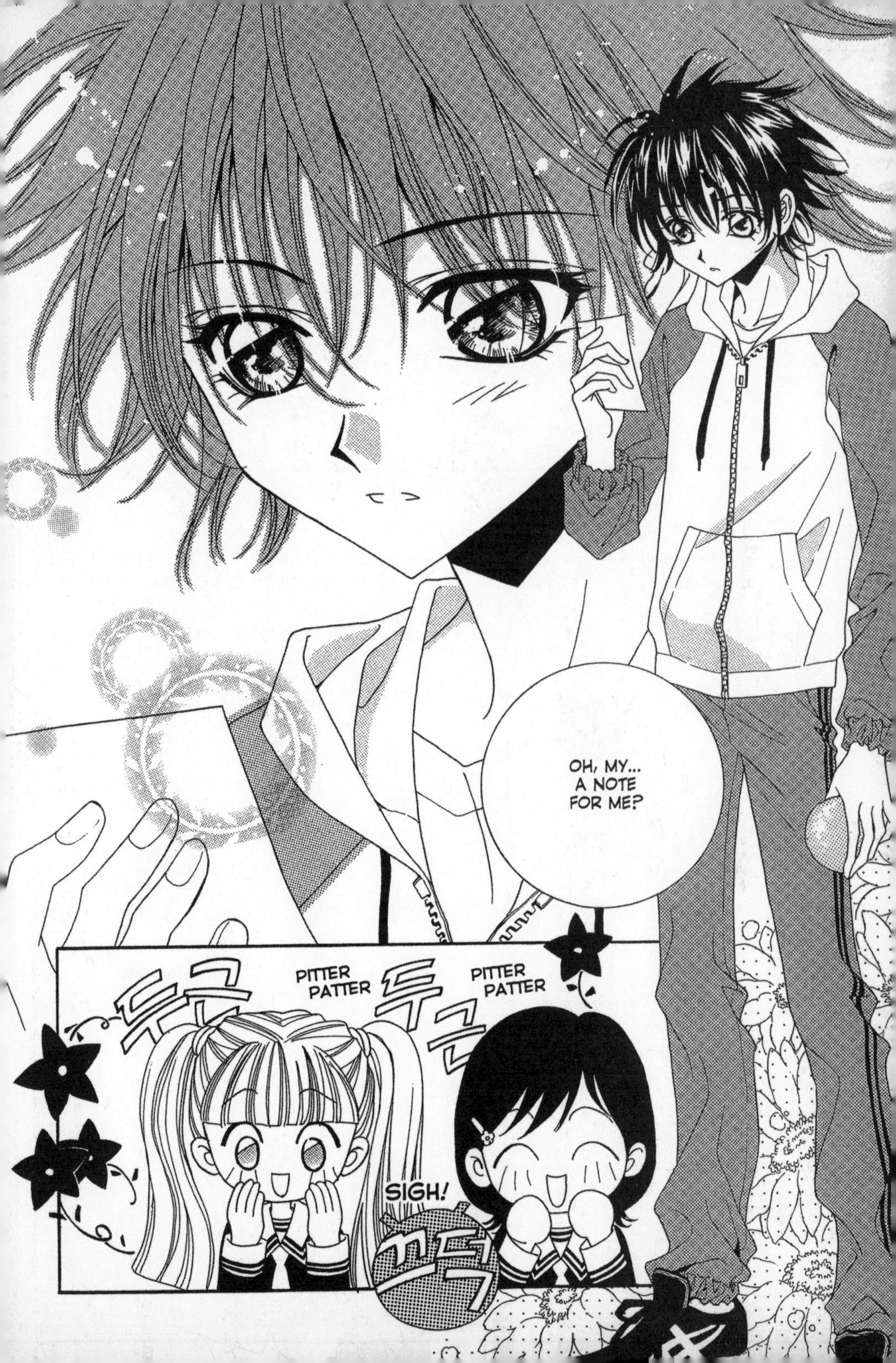
OH, MY... A NOTE FOR ME?
PITTER PATTER
PITTER PATTER
SIGH!

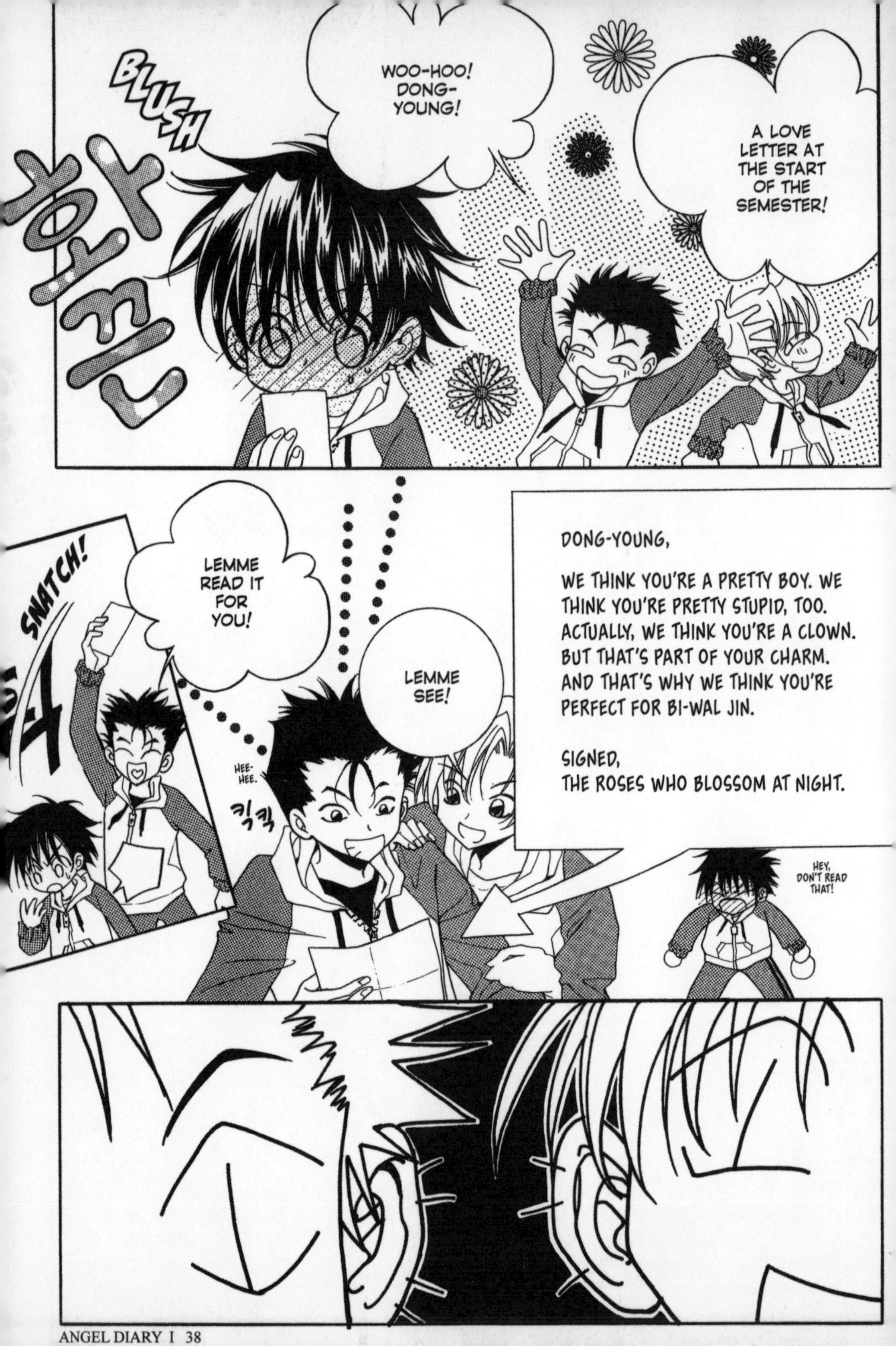
BLUSH
화끈
WOO-HOO! DONG-YOUNG!
A LOVE LETTER AT THE START OF THE SEMESTER!
SNATCH!
LEMME READ IT FOR YOU!
LEMME SEE!
HEE-HEE.
킥킥
DONG-YOUNG,
WE THINK YOU'RE A PRETTY BOY. WE THINK YOU'RE PRETTY STUPID, TOO. ACTUALLY, WE THINK YOU'RE A CLOWN. BUT THAT'S PART OF YOUR CHARM. AND THAT'S WHY WE THINK YOU'RE PERFECT FOR BI-WAL JIN.
SIGNED,
THE ROSES WHO BLOSSOM AT NIGHT.
HEY, DON'T READ THAT!

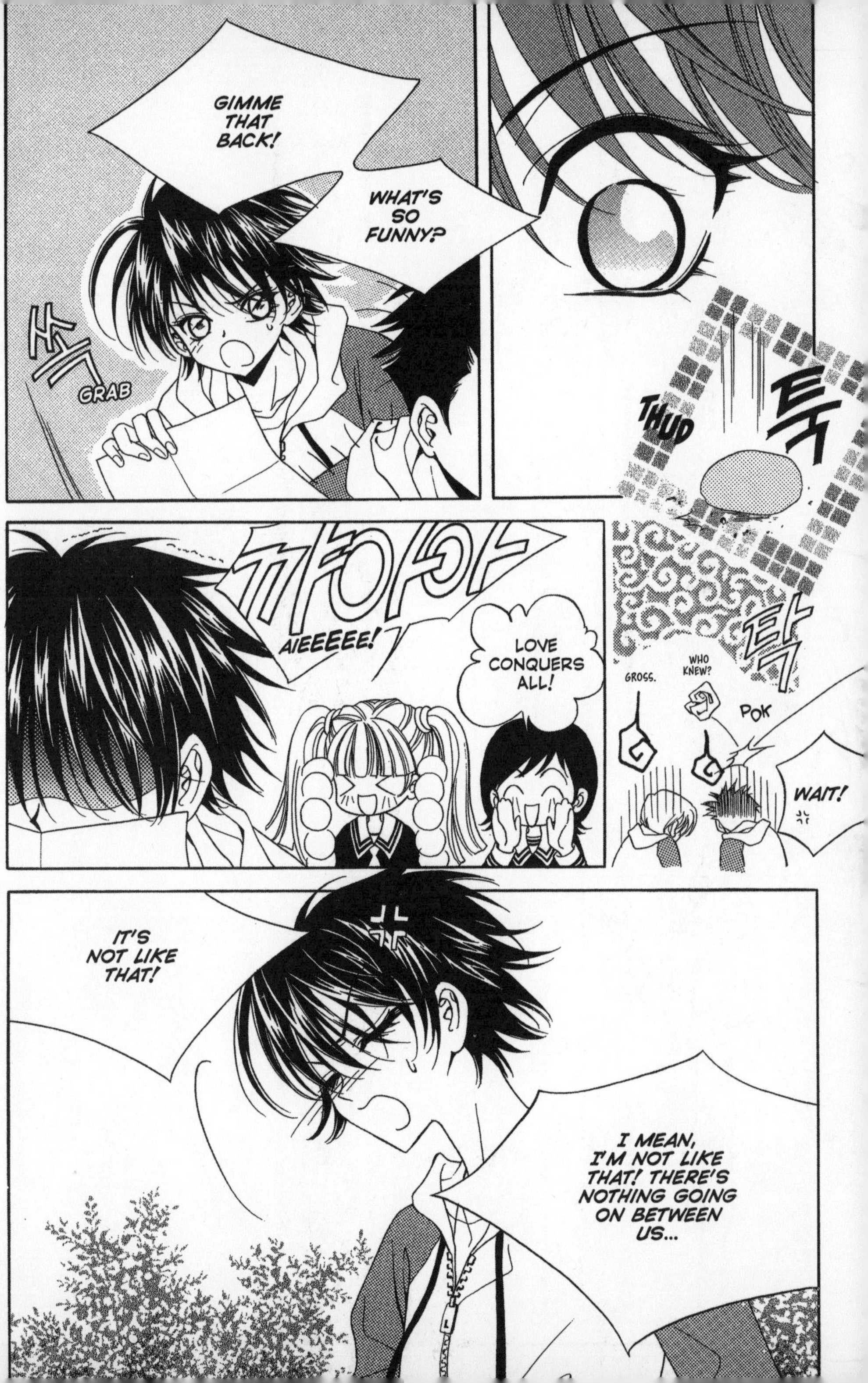
GIMME THAT BACK!
WHAT'S SO FUNNY?
GRAB
THUD
AIEEEEE!
LOVE CONQUERS ALL!
GROSS.
WHO KNEW?
POK
WAIT!
IT'S NOT LIKE THAT!
I MEAN, I'M NOT LIKE THAT! THERE'S NOTHING GOING ON BETWEEN US...

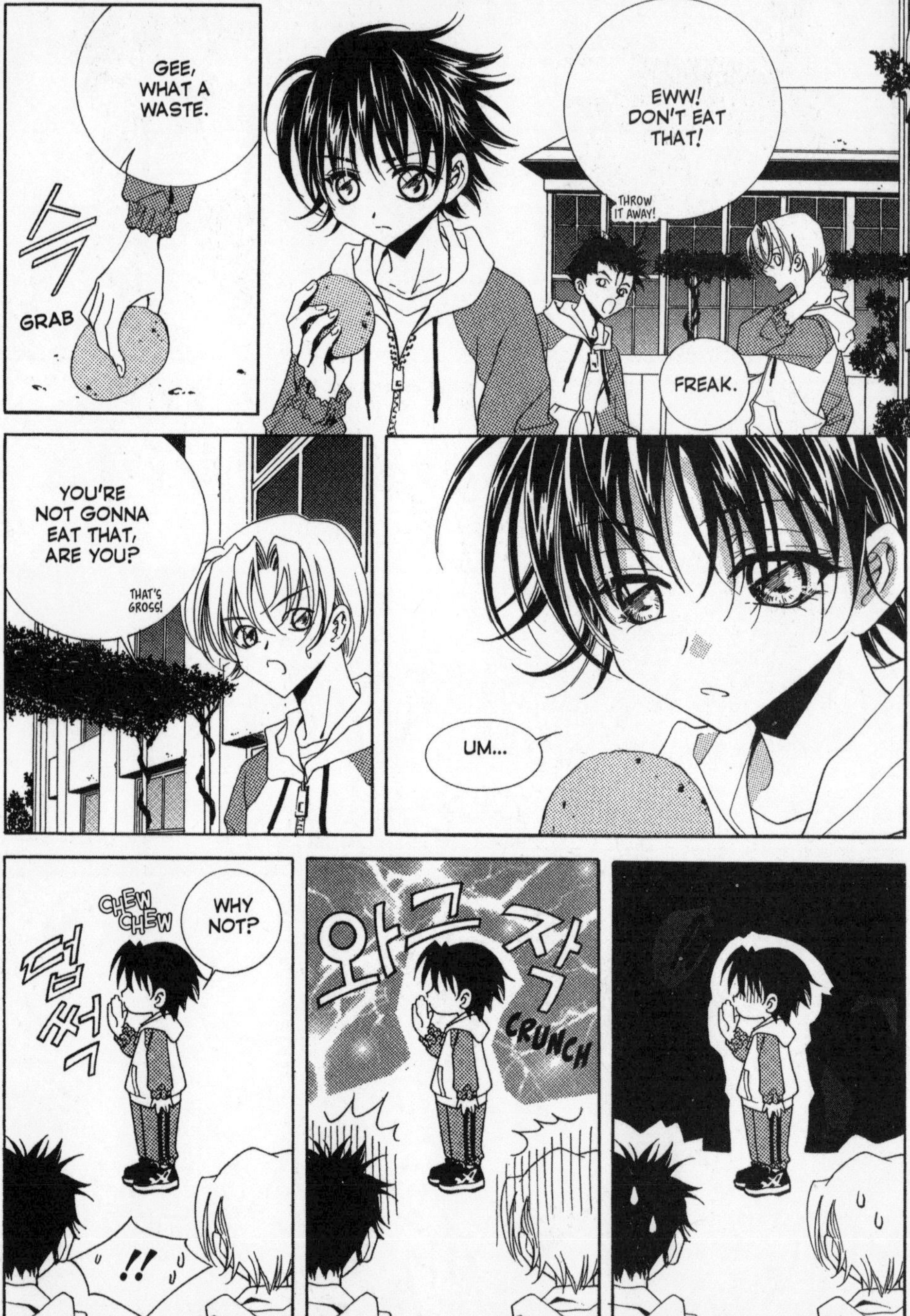
GEE, WHAT A WASTE.
GRAB
EWW! DON'T EAT THAT!
THROW IT AWAY!
FREAK.
YOU'RE NOT GONNA EAT THAT, ARE YOU?
THAT'S GROSS!
UM...
CHEW CHEW
WHY NOT?
!!
와그작
CRUNCH

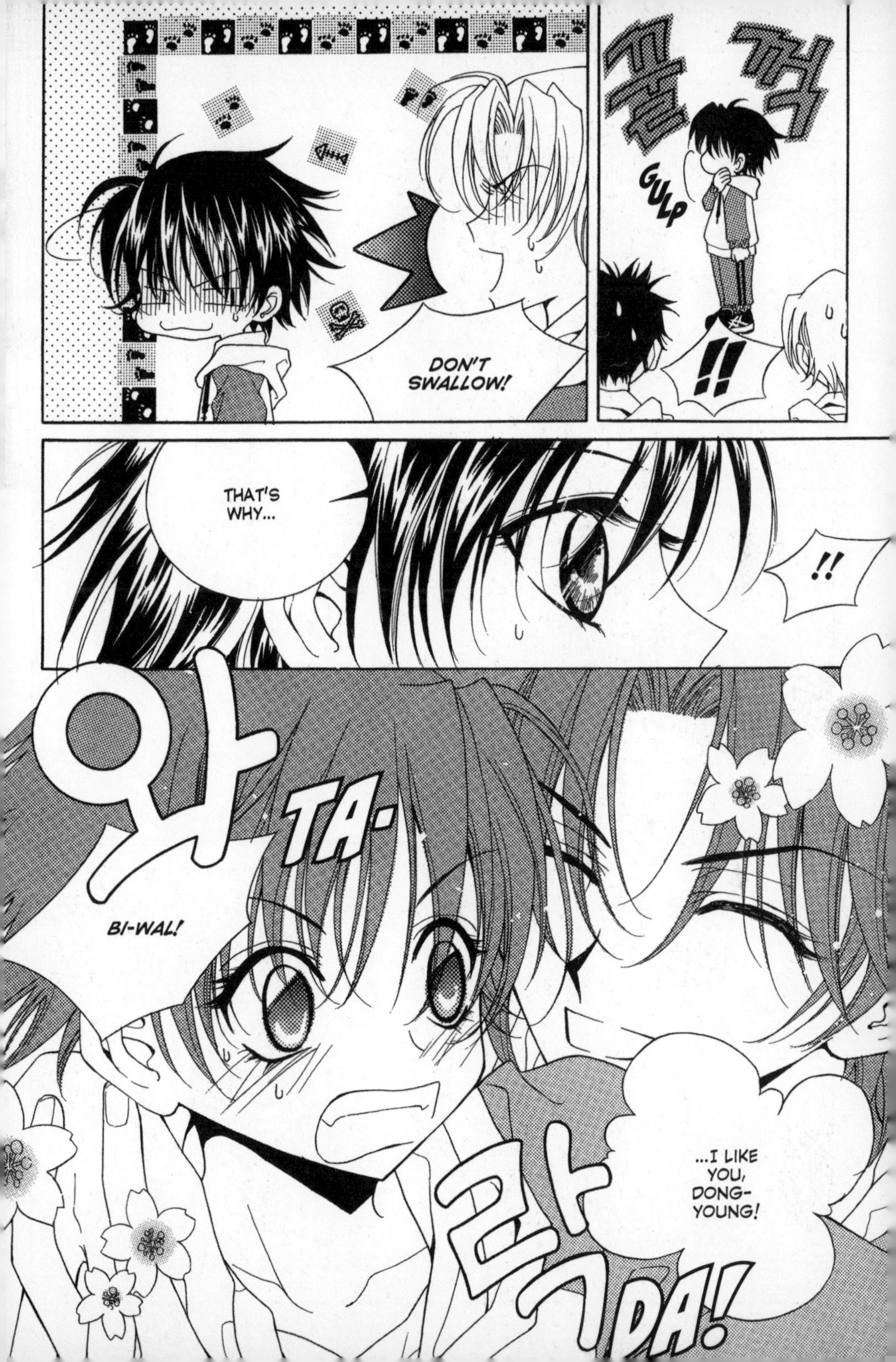
DON'T SWALLOW!
꿀꺽
GULP
!!
THAT'S WHY...
!!
TA-
BI-WAL!
...I LIKE YOU, DONG-YOUNG!
DA!

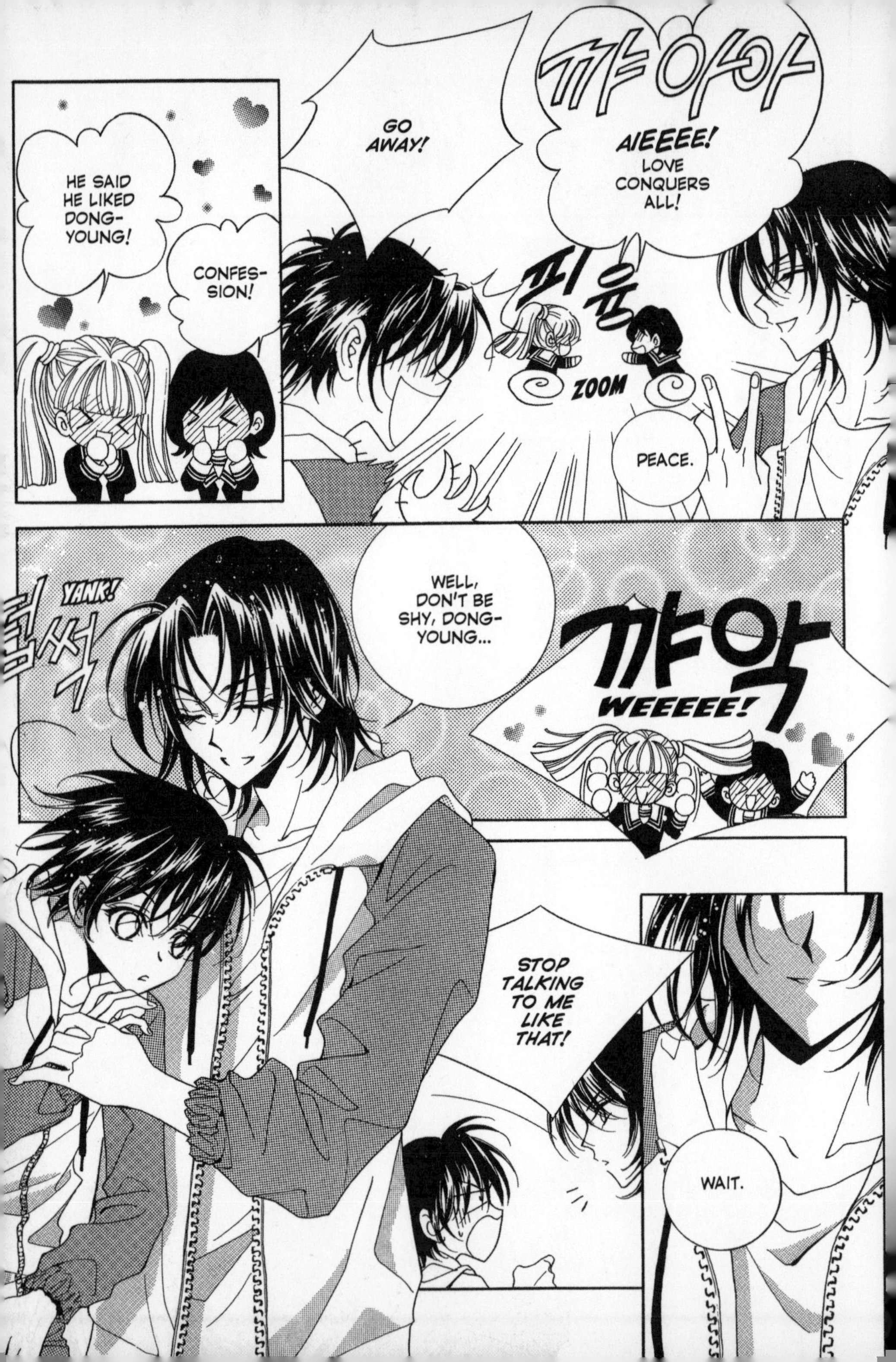
HE SAID HE LIKED DONG-YOUNG!
CONFES-SION!
GO AWAY!
까아아아
AIEEEE!
LOVE CONQUERS ALL!
피융
ZOOM
PEACE.
덥석
YANK!
WELL, DON'T BE SHY, DONG-YOUNG...
까악
WEEEEE!
STOP TALKING TO ME LIKE THAT!
WAIT.

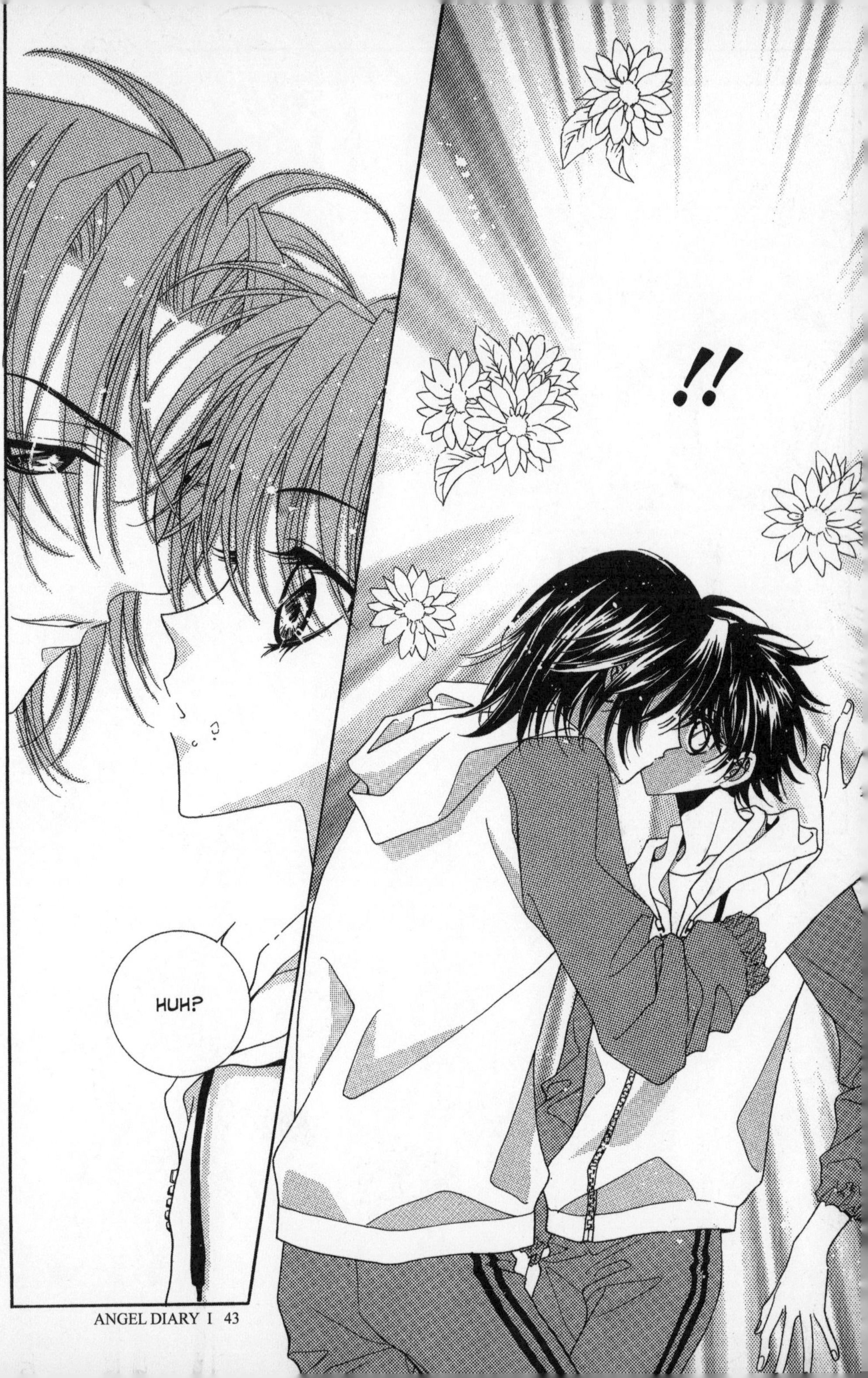
!!
HUH?

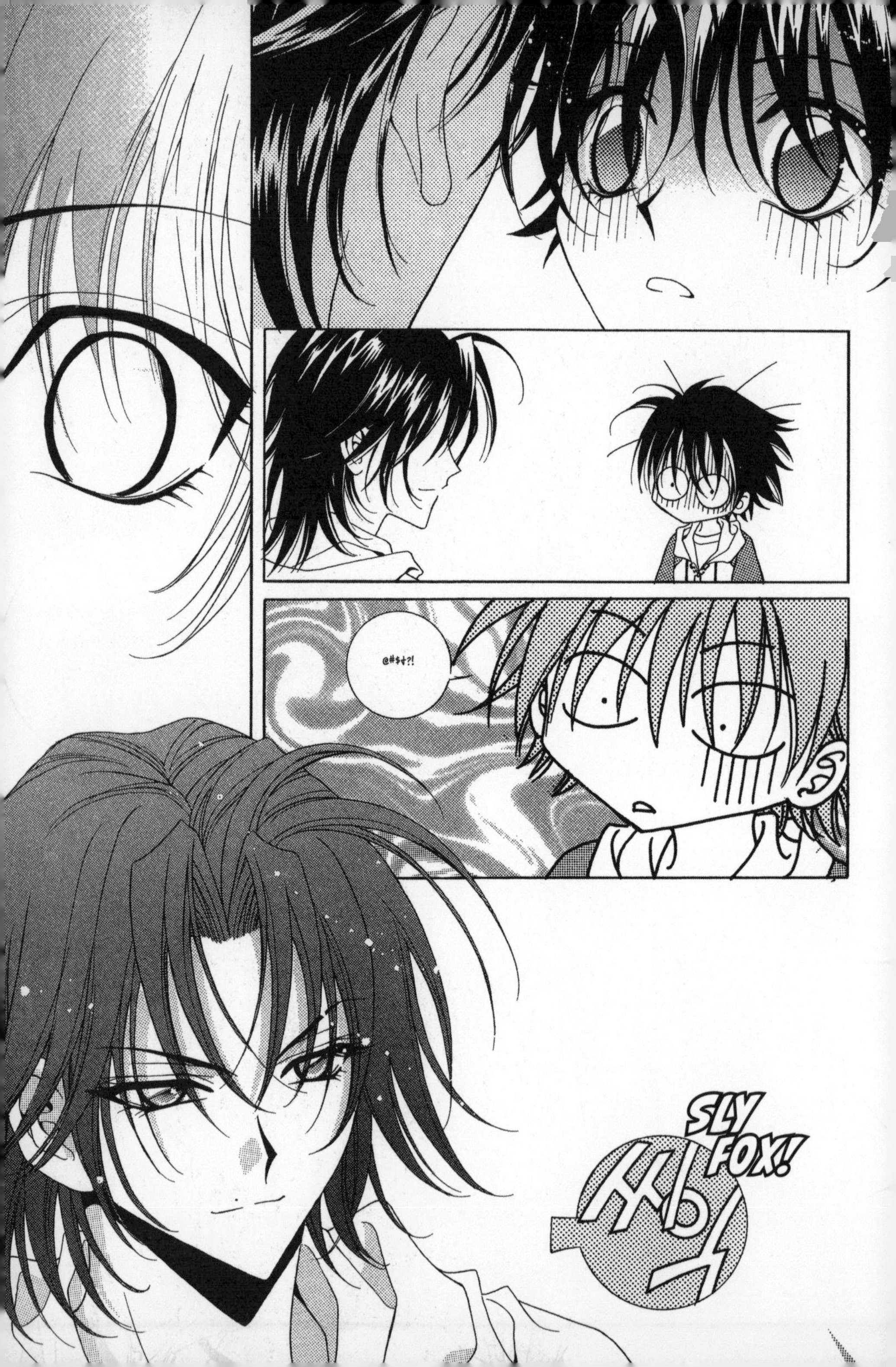
@#$‡?!
SLY FOX!

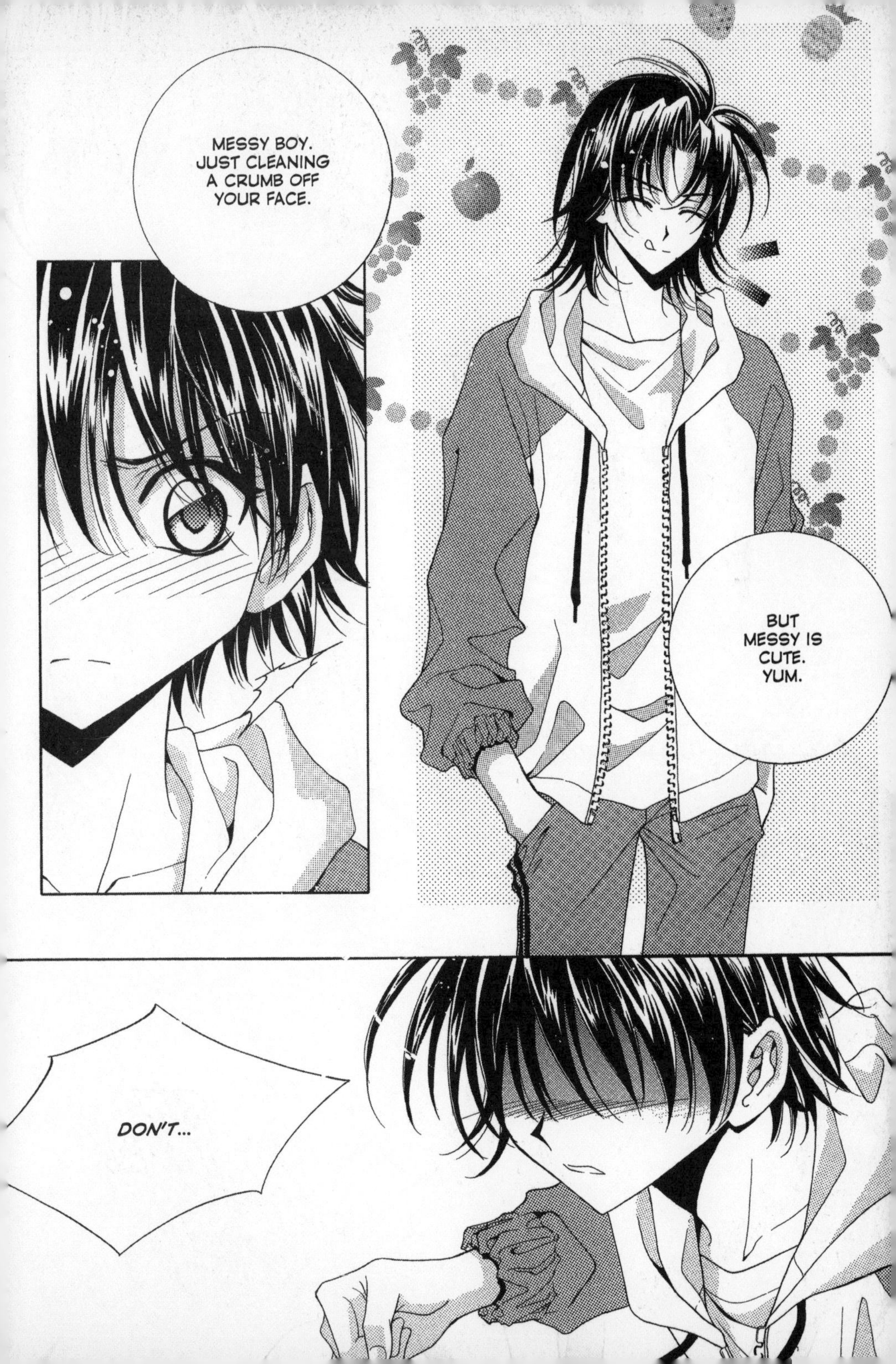
MESSY BOY. JUST CLEANING A CRUMB OFF YOUR FACE.
BUT MESSY IS CUTE. YUM.
DON'T...

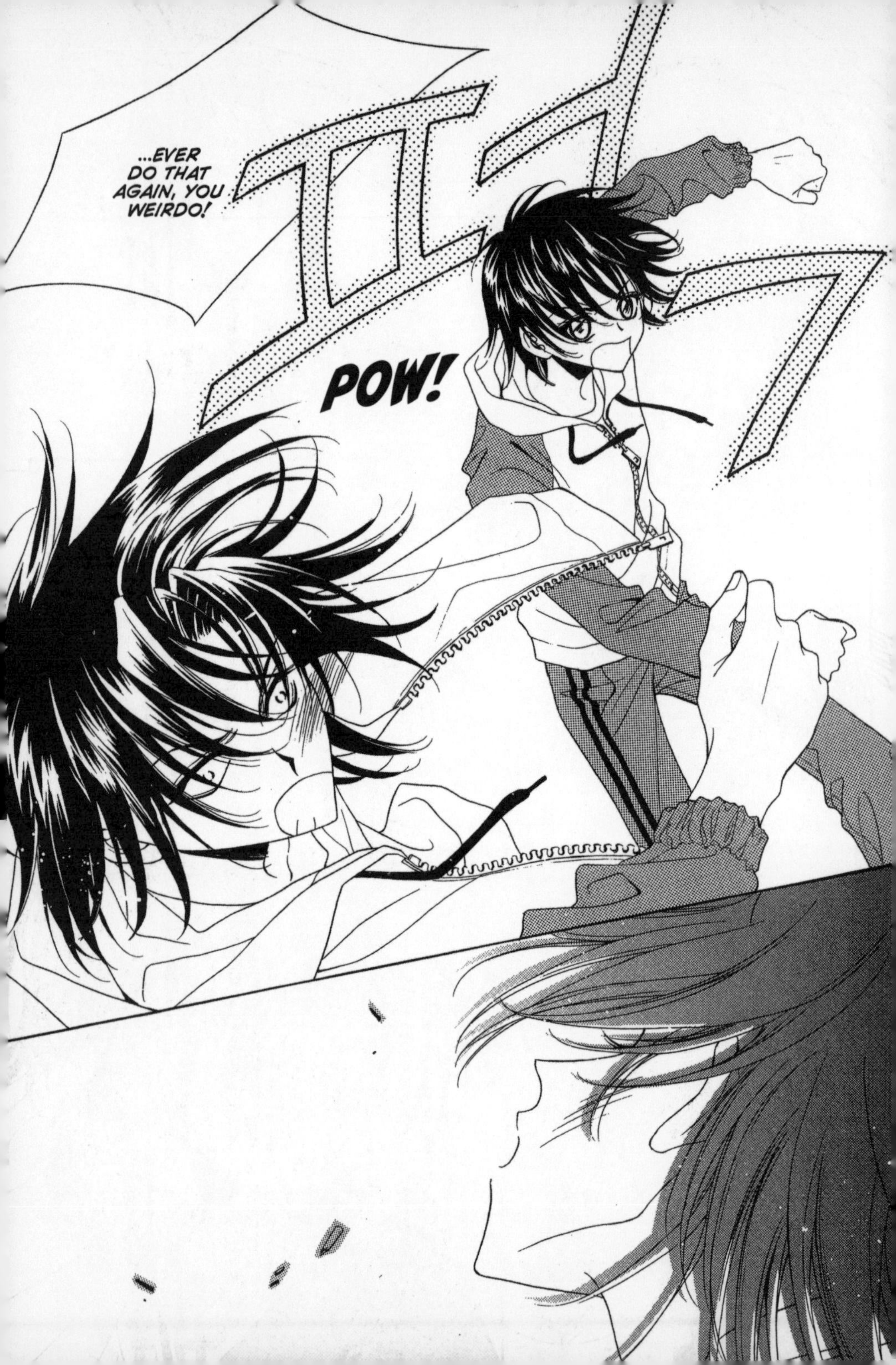
...EVER DO THAT AGAIN, YOU WEIRDO!
POW!

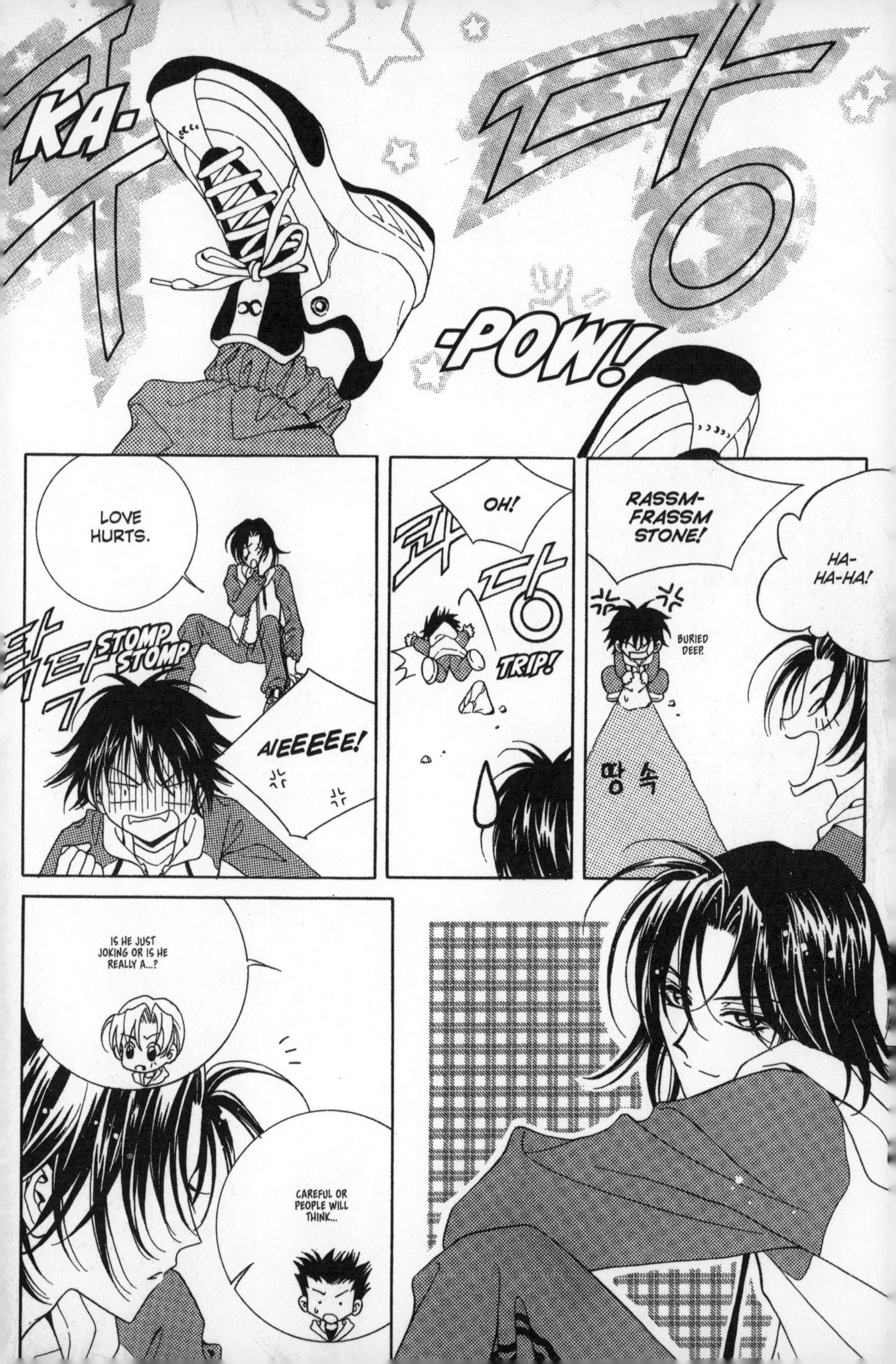
KA-
-POW!
LOVE HURTS.
STOMP STOMP
AIEEEEE!
OH!
TRIP!
RASSM-FRASSM STONE!
BURIED DEEP.
HA-HA-HA!
IS HE JUST JOKING OR IS HE REALLY A...?
CAREFUL OR PEOPLE WILL THINK...

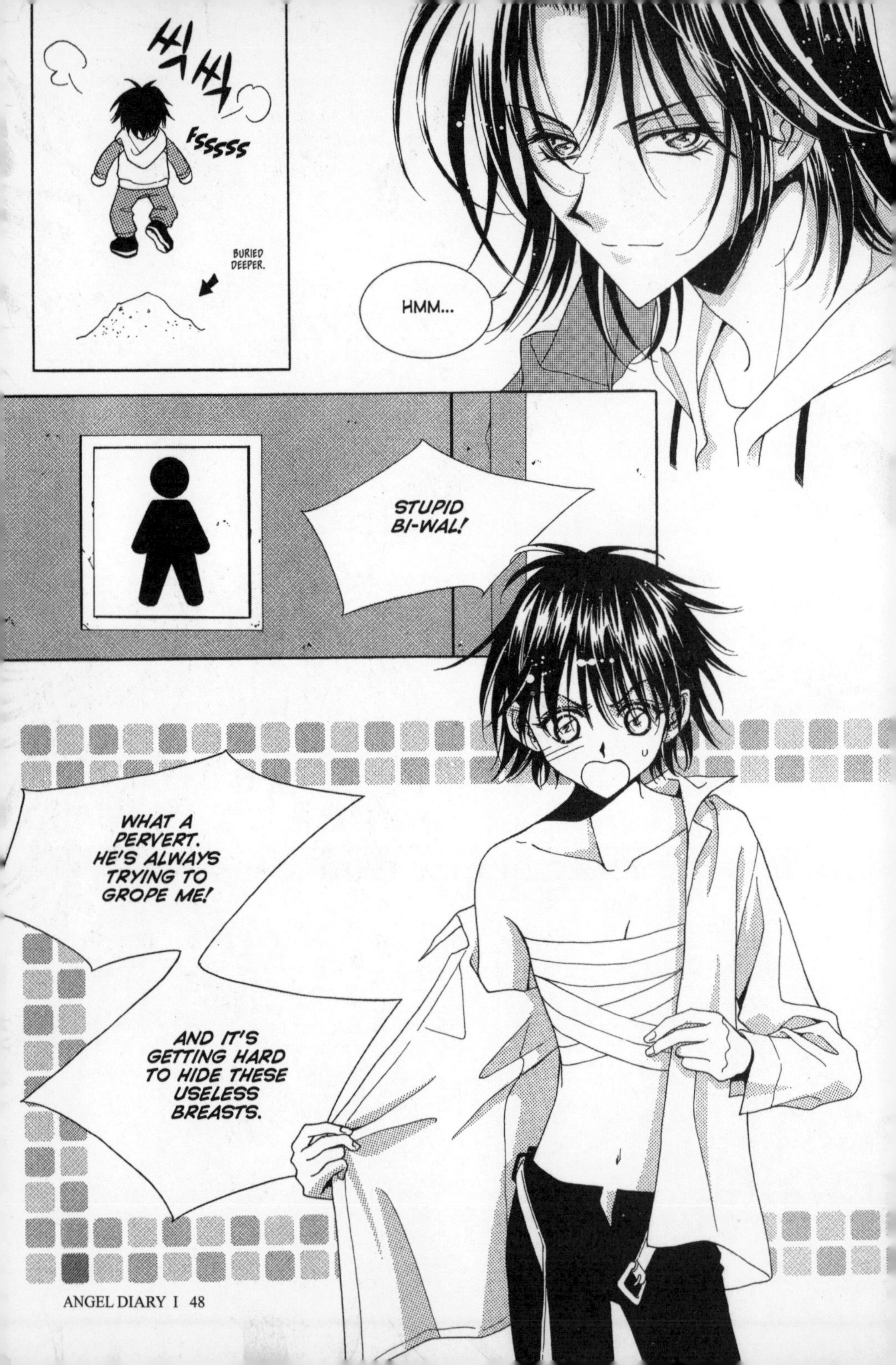

FSSSSS
BURIED DEEPER.
HMM...
STUPID BI-WAL!
WHAT A PERVERT. HE'S ALWAYS TRYING TO GROPE ME!
AND IT'S GETTING HARD TO HIDE THESE USELESS BREASTS.

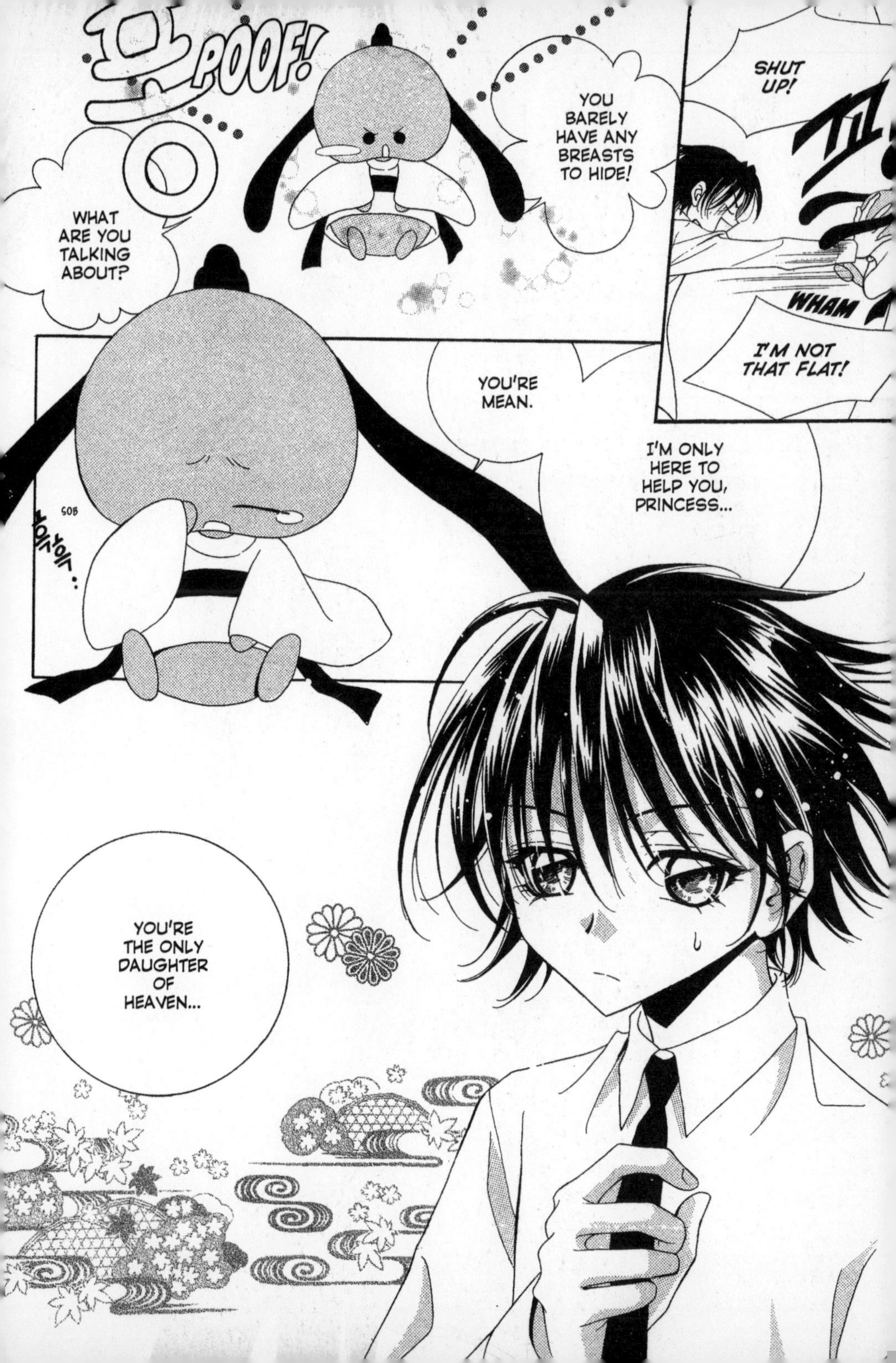
POOF!
WHAT ARE YOU TALKING ABOUT?
YOU BARELY HAVE ANY BREASTS TO HIDE!
SHUT UP!
WHAM
I'M NOT THAT FLAT!
SOB
YOU'RE MEAN.
I'M ONLY HERE TO HELP YOU, PRINCESS...
YOU'RE THE ONLY DAUGHTER OF HEAVEN...

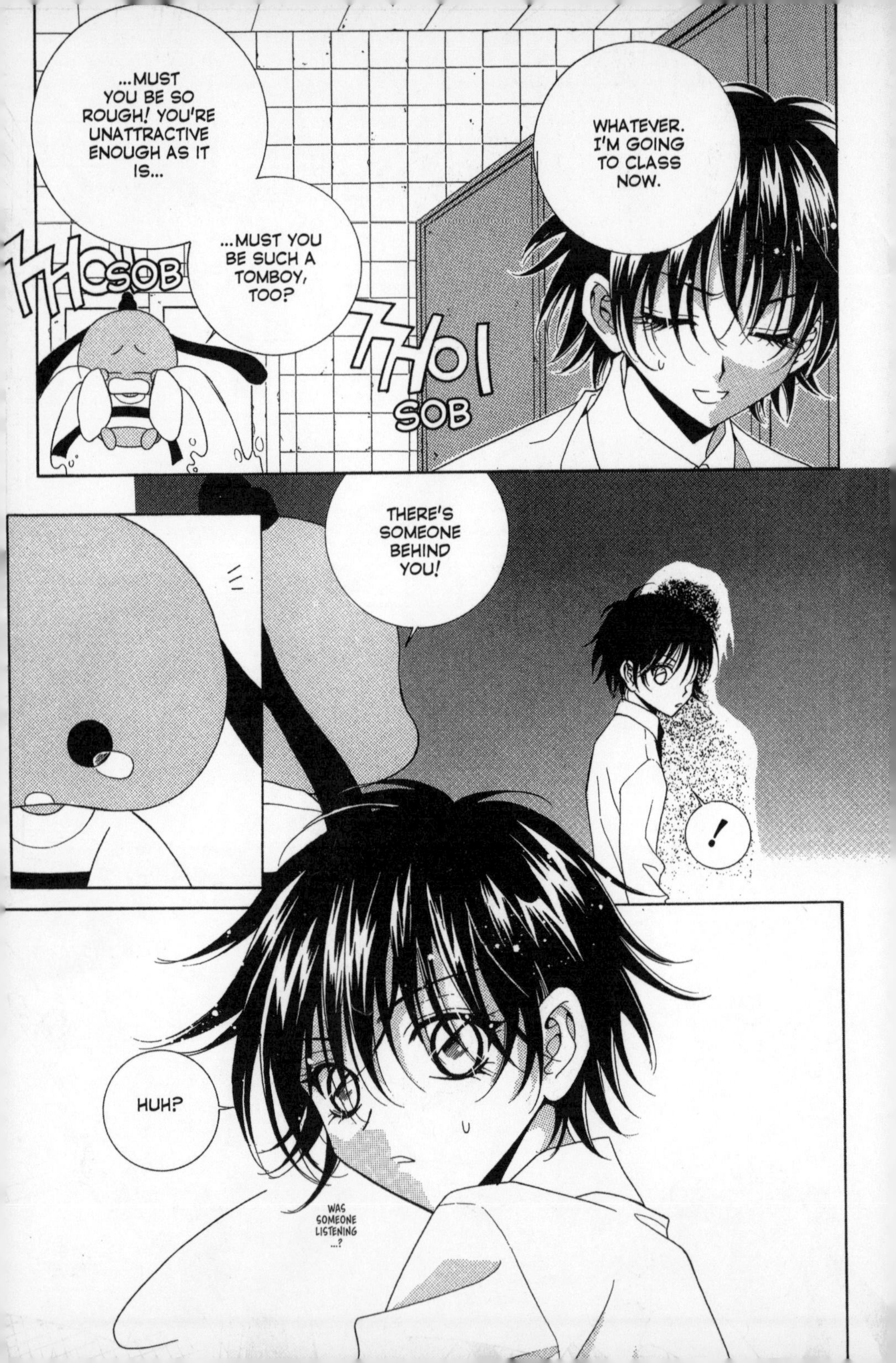
...MUST YOU BE SO ROUGH! YOU'RE UNATTRACTIVE ENOUGH AS IT IS...
HIC SOB
...MUST YOU BE SUCH A TOMBOY, TOO?
HIC SOB
WHATEVER. I'M GOING TO CLASS NOW.
THERE'S SOMEONE BEHIND YOU!
!
HUH?
WAS SOMEONE LISTENING ...?

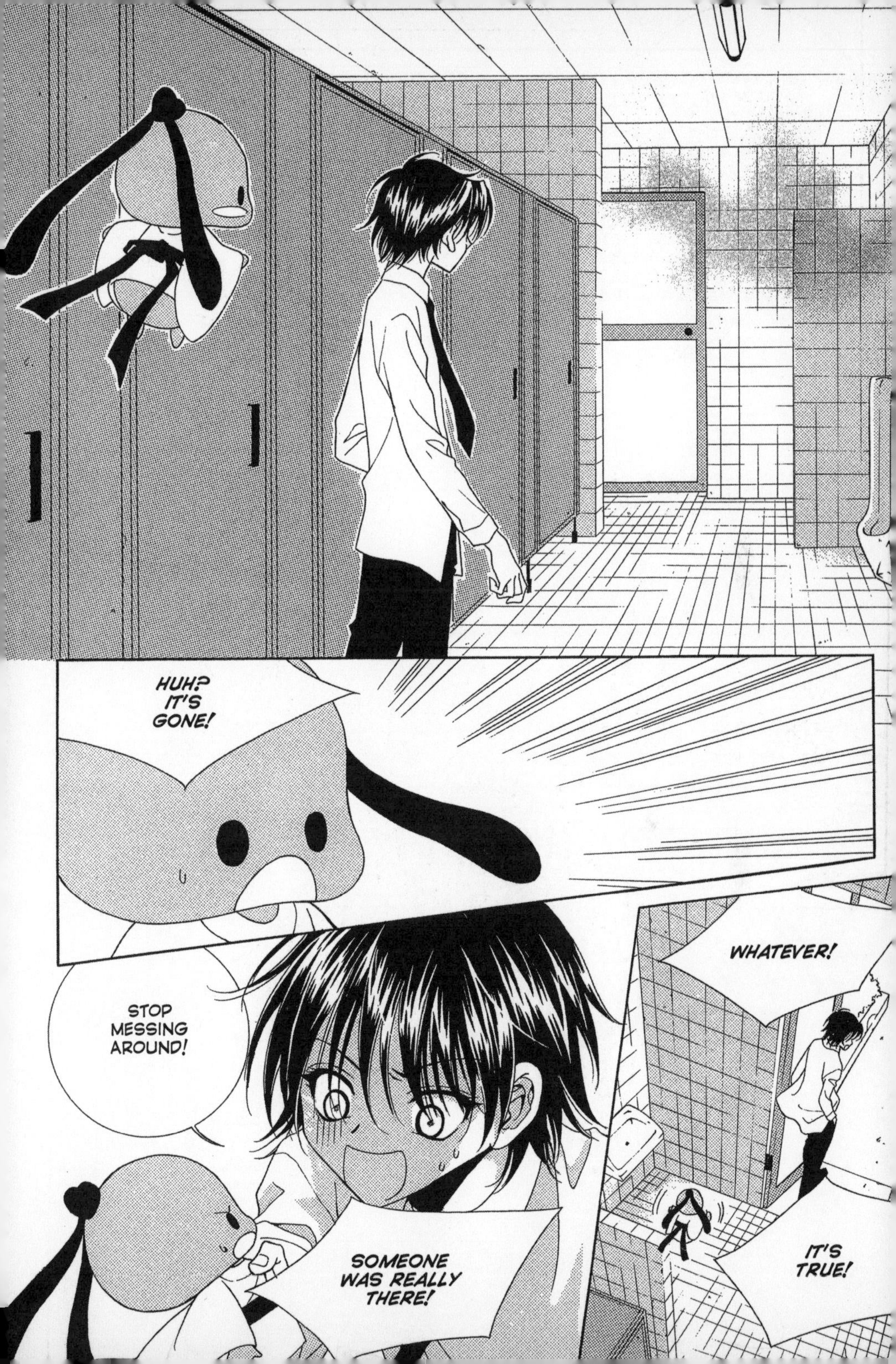
HUH? IT'S GONE!
STOP MESSING AROUND!
SOMEONE WAS REALLY THERE!
WHATEVER!
IT'S TRUE!

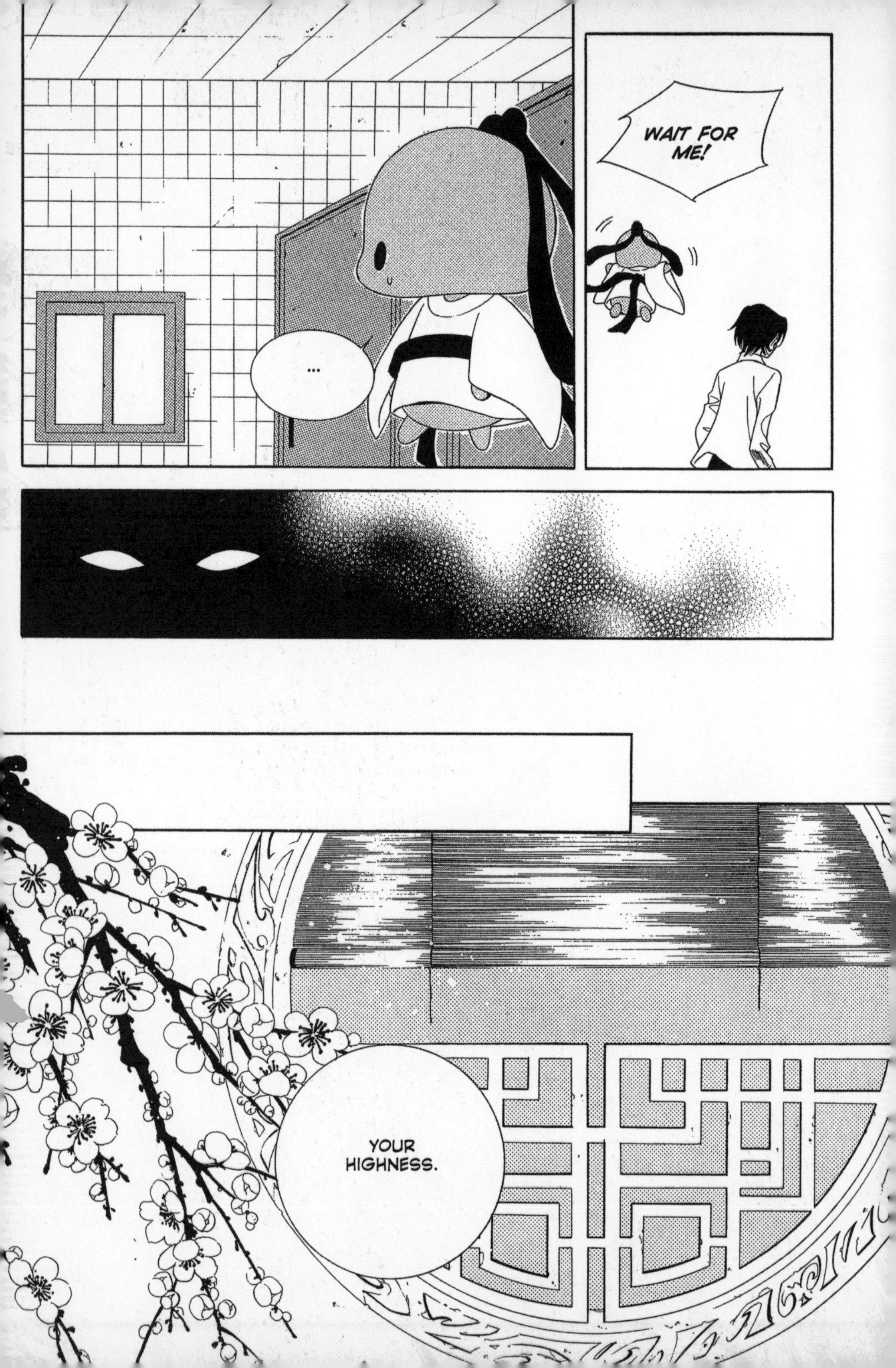

...
WAIT FOR ME!
YOUR HIGHNESS.

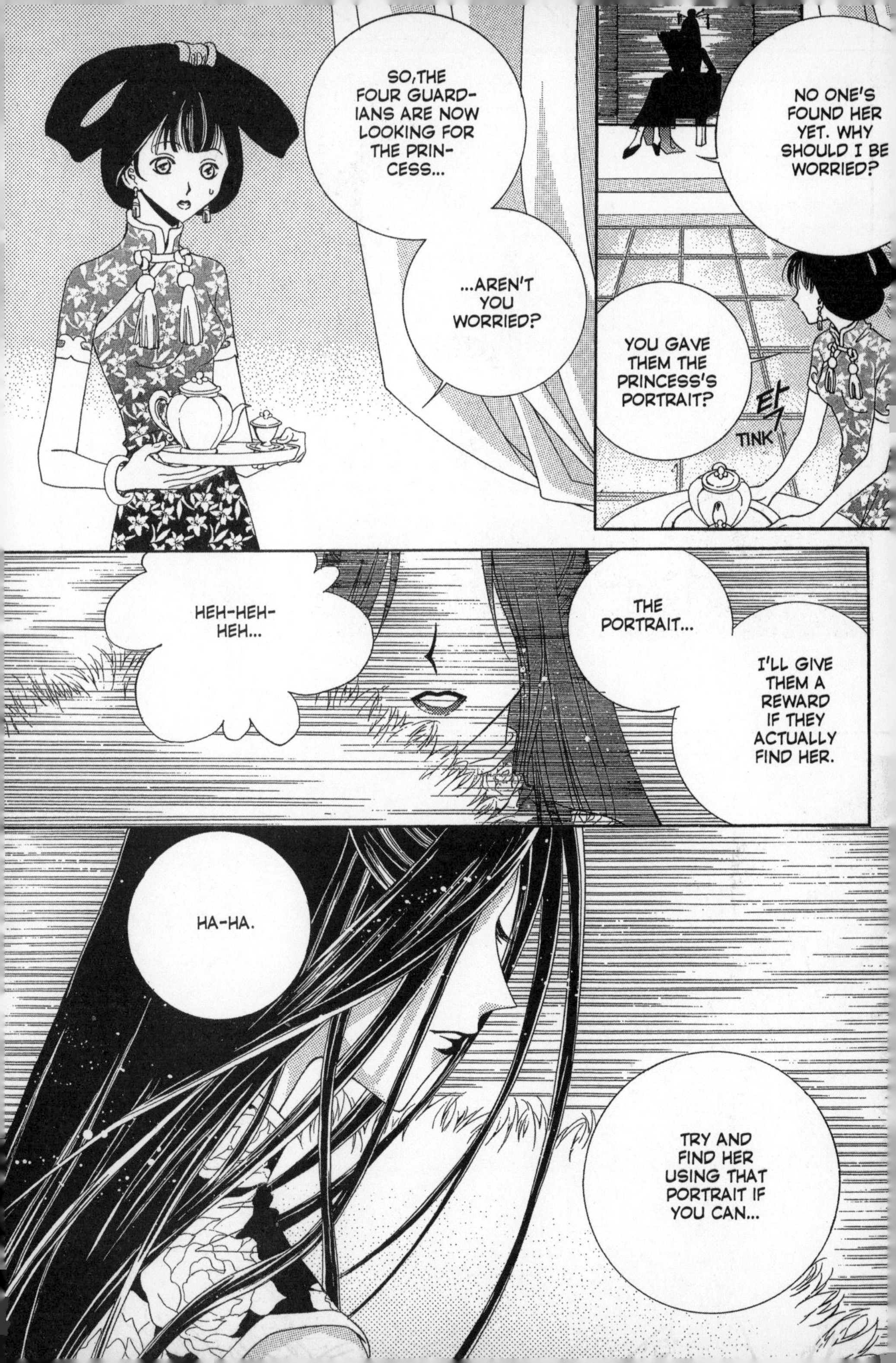
SO, THE FOUR GUARDIANS ARE NOW LOOKING FOR THE PRINCESS...
...AREN'T YOU WORRIED?
NO ONE'S FOUND HER YET. WHY SHOULD I BE WORRIED?
YOU GAVE THEM THE PRINCESS'S PORTRAIT?
틱
TINK
HEH-HEH-HEH...
THE PORTRAIT...
I'LL GIVE THEM A REWARD IF THEY ACTUALLY FIND HER.
HA-HA.
TRY AND FIND HER USING THAT PORTRAIT IF YOU CAN...

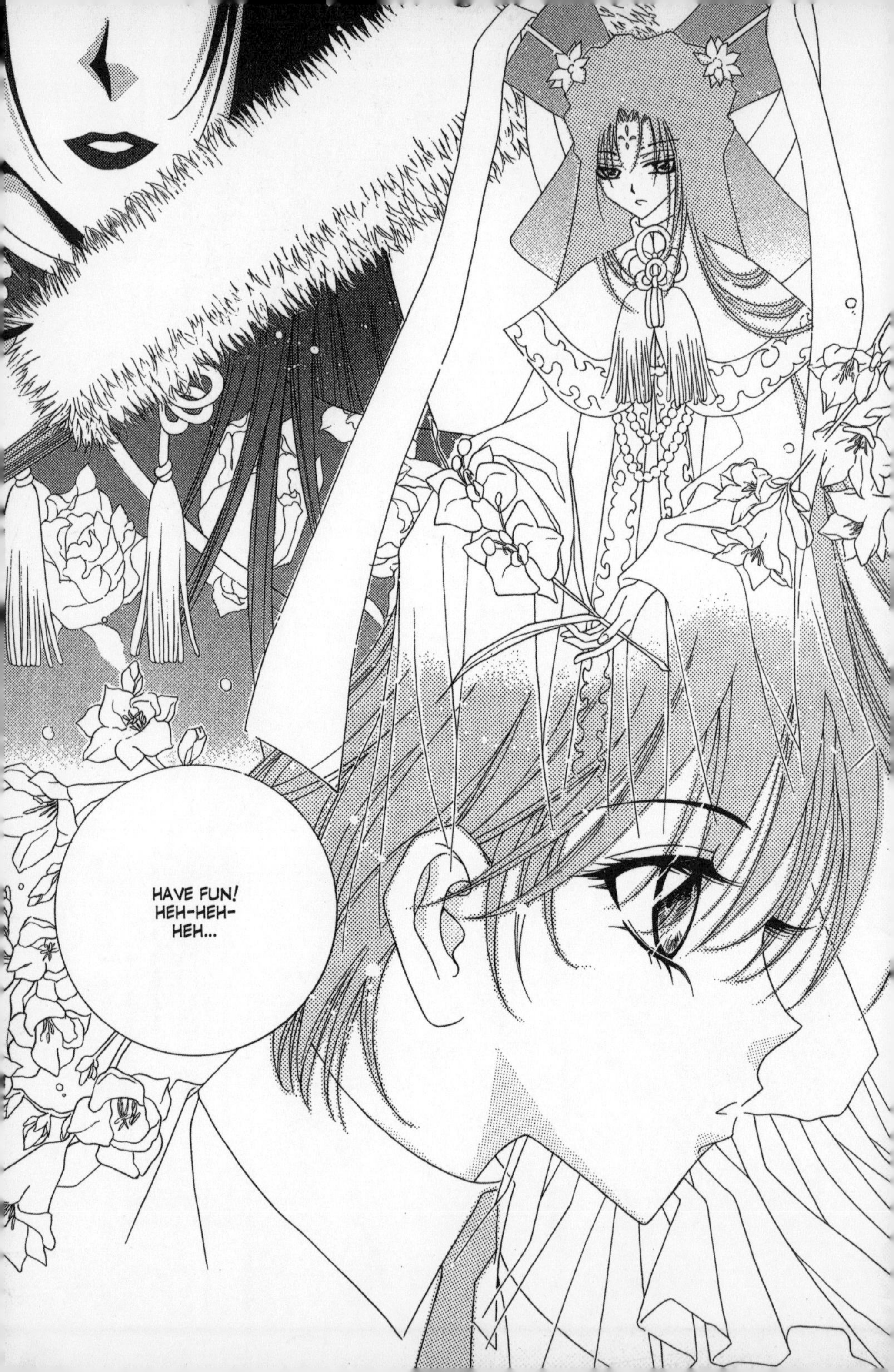
HAVE FUN! HEH-HEH-HEH...

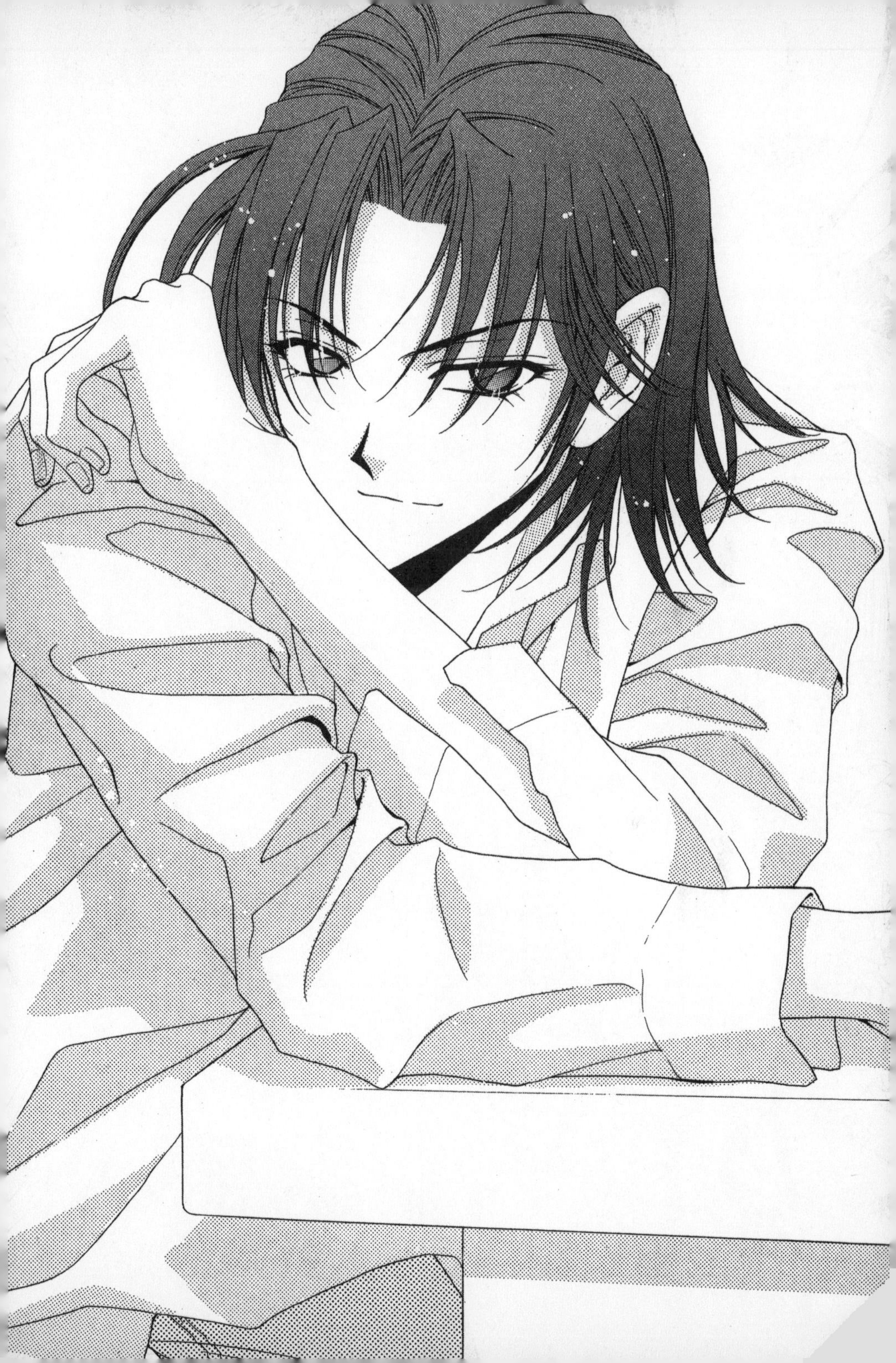

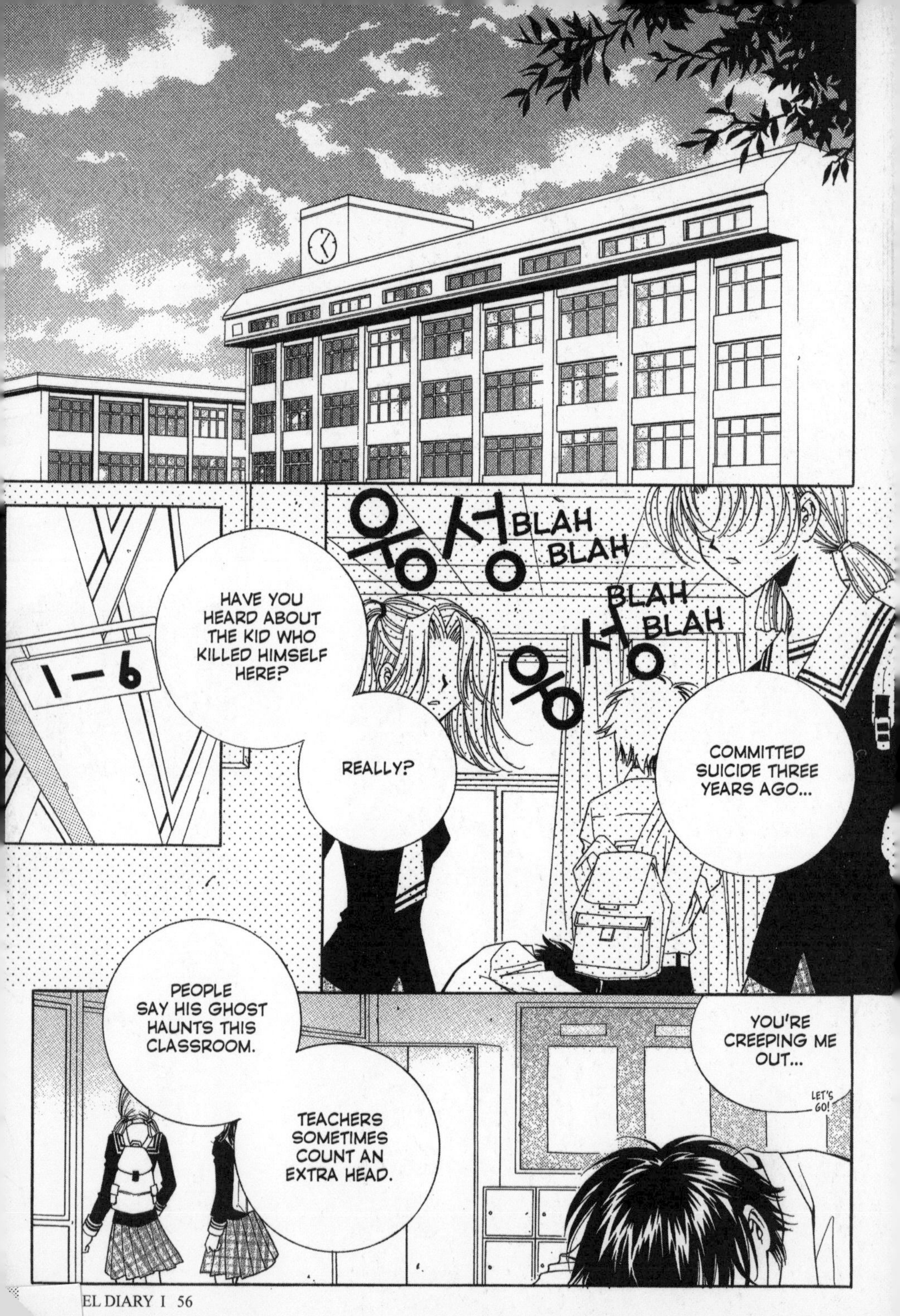
1-6
HAVE YOU HEARD ABOUT THE KID WHO KILLED HIMSELF HERE?
REALLY?
웅성 BLAH BLAH
웅성 BLAH BLAH
COMMITTED SUICIDE THREE YEARS AGO...
PEOPLE SAY HIS GHOST HAUNTS THIS CLASSROOM.
TEACHERS SOMETIMES COUNT AN EXTRA HEAD.
YOU'RE CREEPING ME OUT...
LET'S GO!

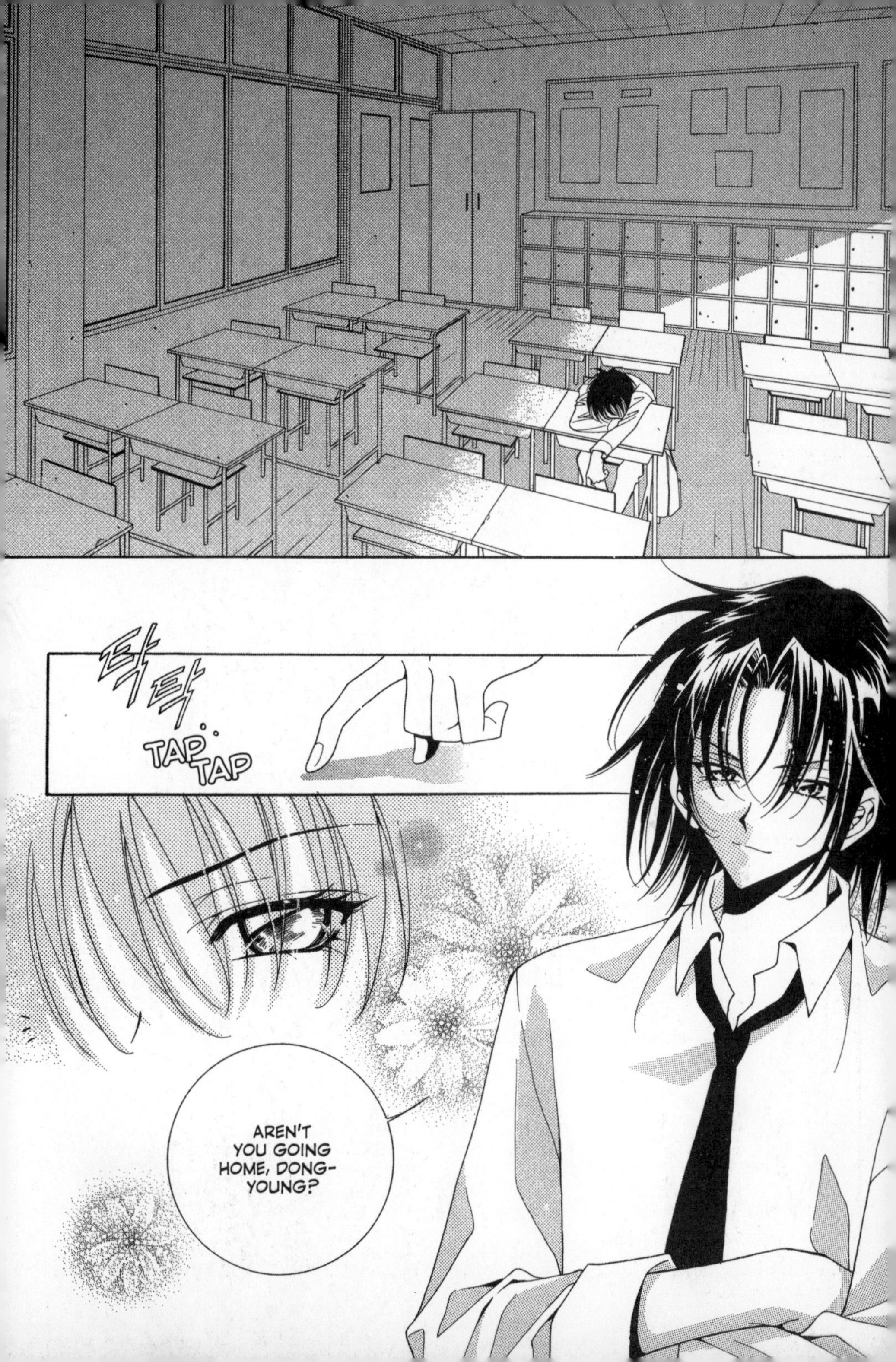

탁 탁
TAP TAP
AREN'T YOU GOING HOME, DONG-YOUNG?

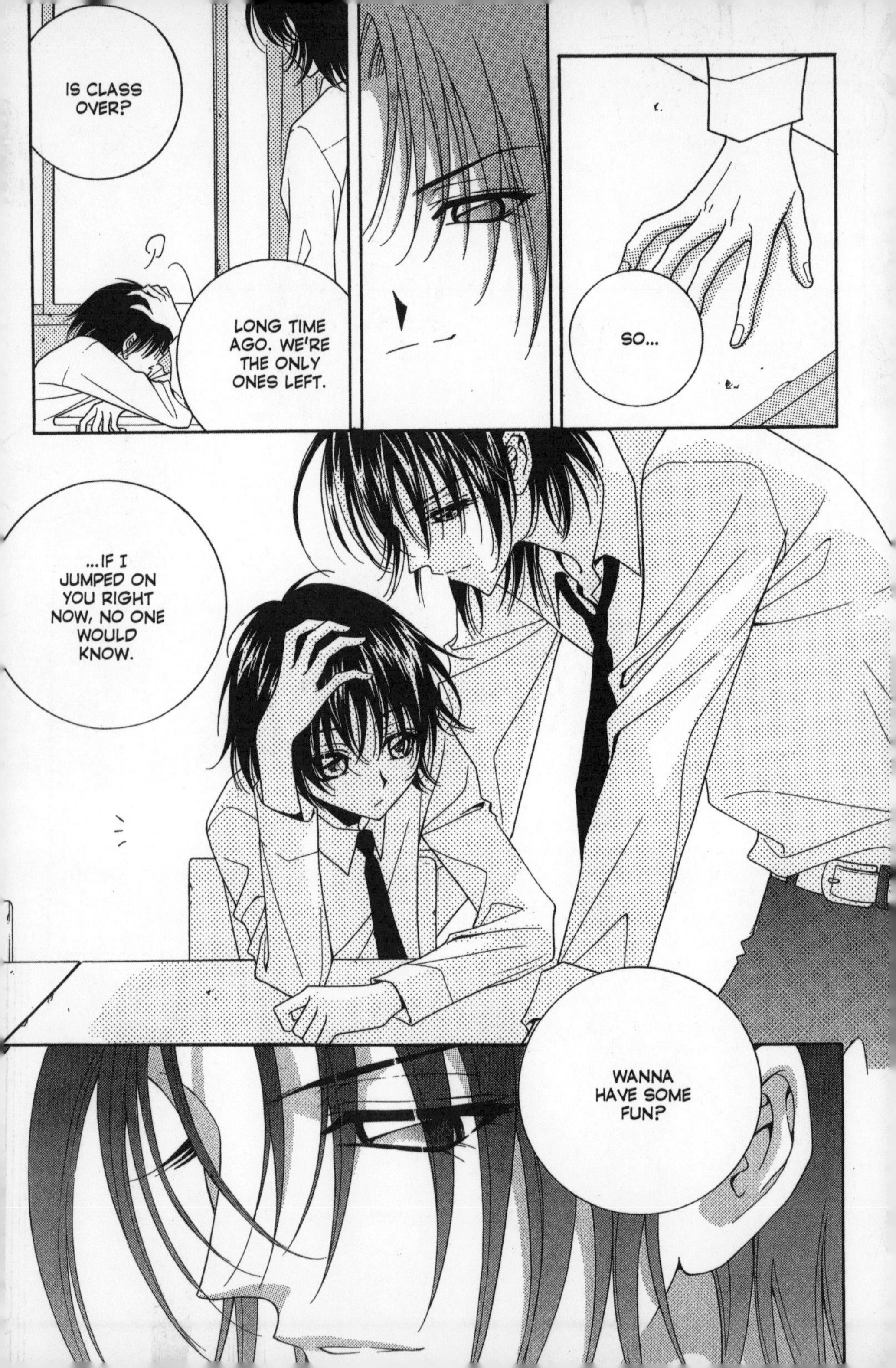
IS CLASS OVER?
LONG TIME AGO. WE'RE THE ONLY ONES LEFT.
SO...
...IF I JUMPED ON YOU RIGHT NOW, NO ONE WOULD KNOW.
WANNA HAVE SOME FUN?

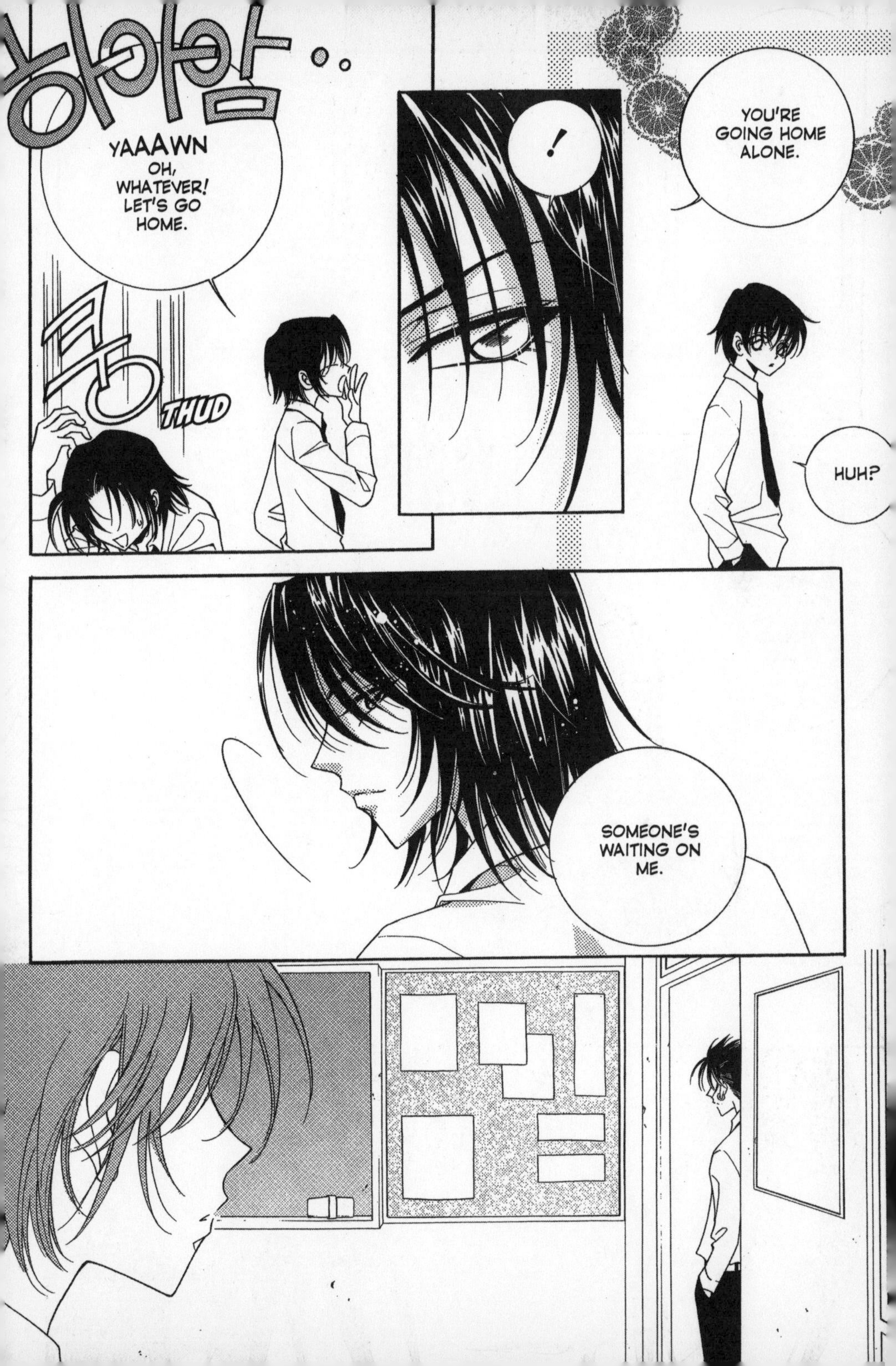
하아암..
YAAAWN
OH, WHATEVER! LET'S GO HOME.
툭
THUD
!
YOU'RE GOING HOME ALONE.
HUH?
SOMEONE'S WAITING ON ME.

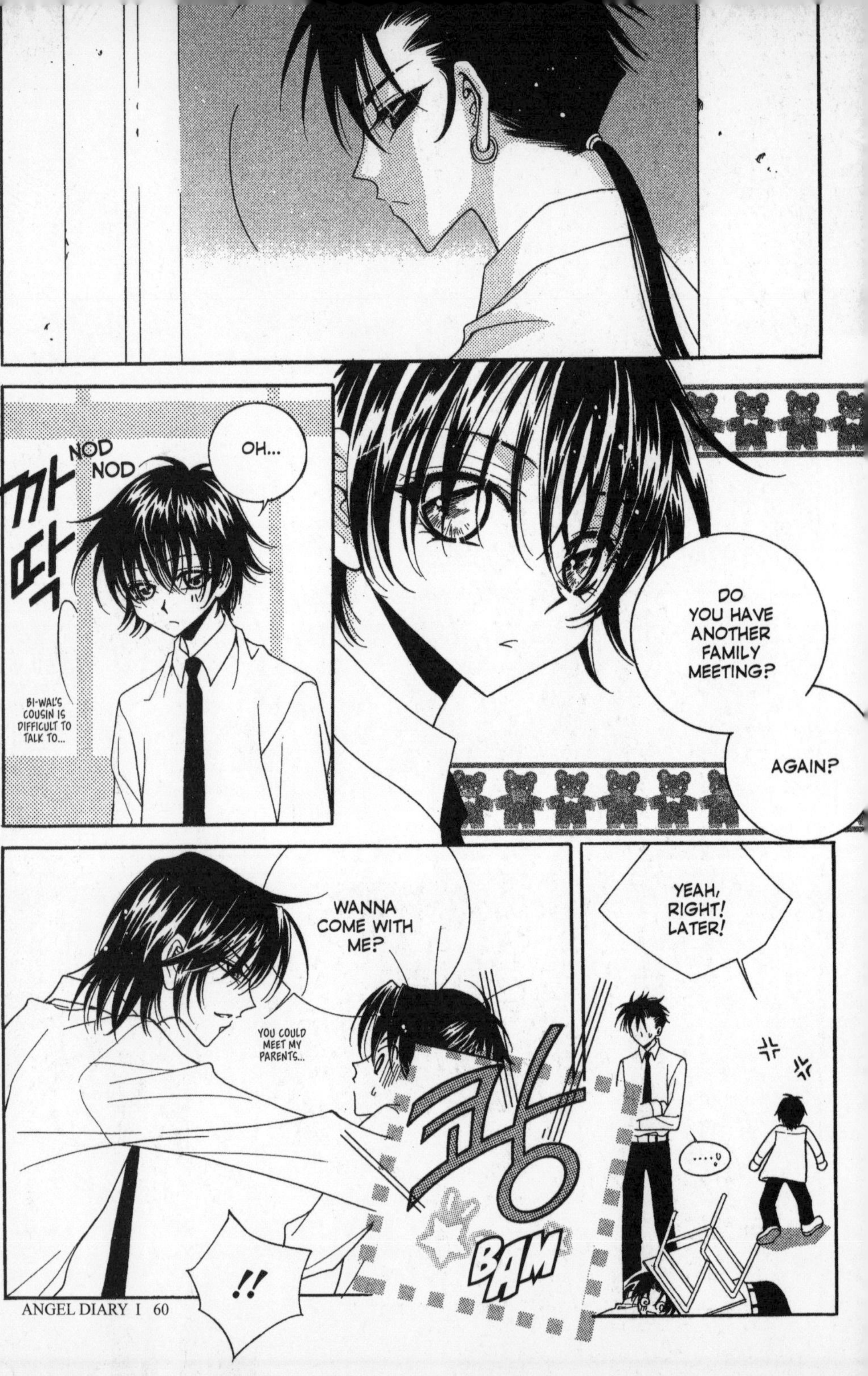

NOD NOD
까딱
OH...
BI-WAL'S COUSIN IS DIFFICULT TO TALK TO...
DO YOU HAVE ANOTHER FAMILY MEETING?
AGAIN?
WANNA COME WITH ME?
YOU COULD MEET MY PARENTS...
쾅
BAM
!!
YEAH, RIGHT! LATER!
.....

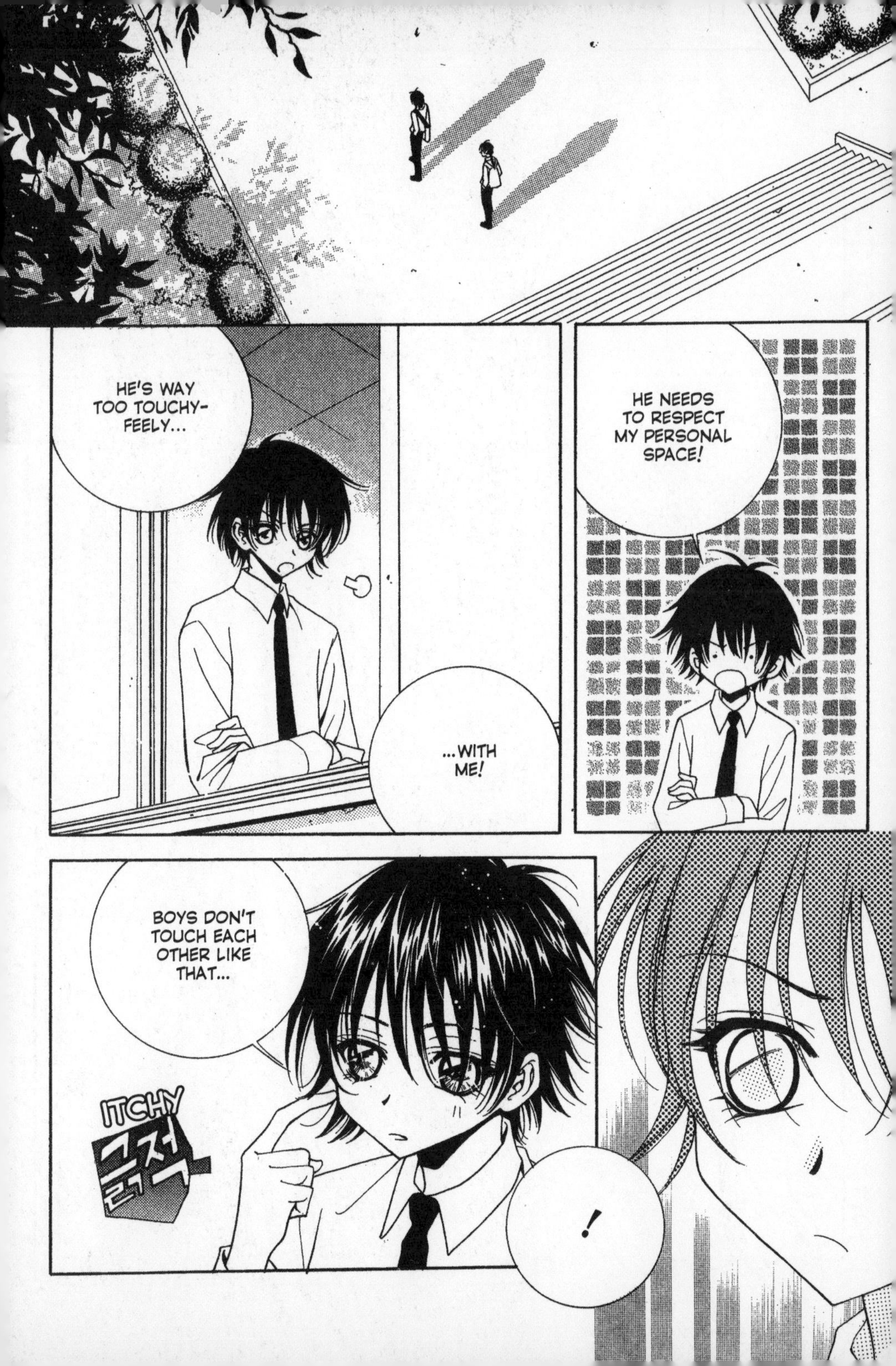
HE'S WAY TOO TOUCHY-FEELY...
...WITH ME!
HE NEEDS TO RESPECT MY PERSONAL SPACE!
BOYS DON'T TOUCH EACH OTHER LIKE THAT...
ITCHY
!

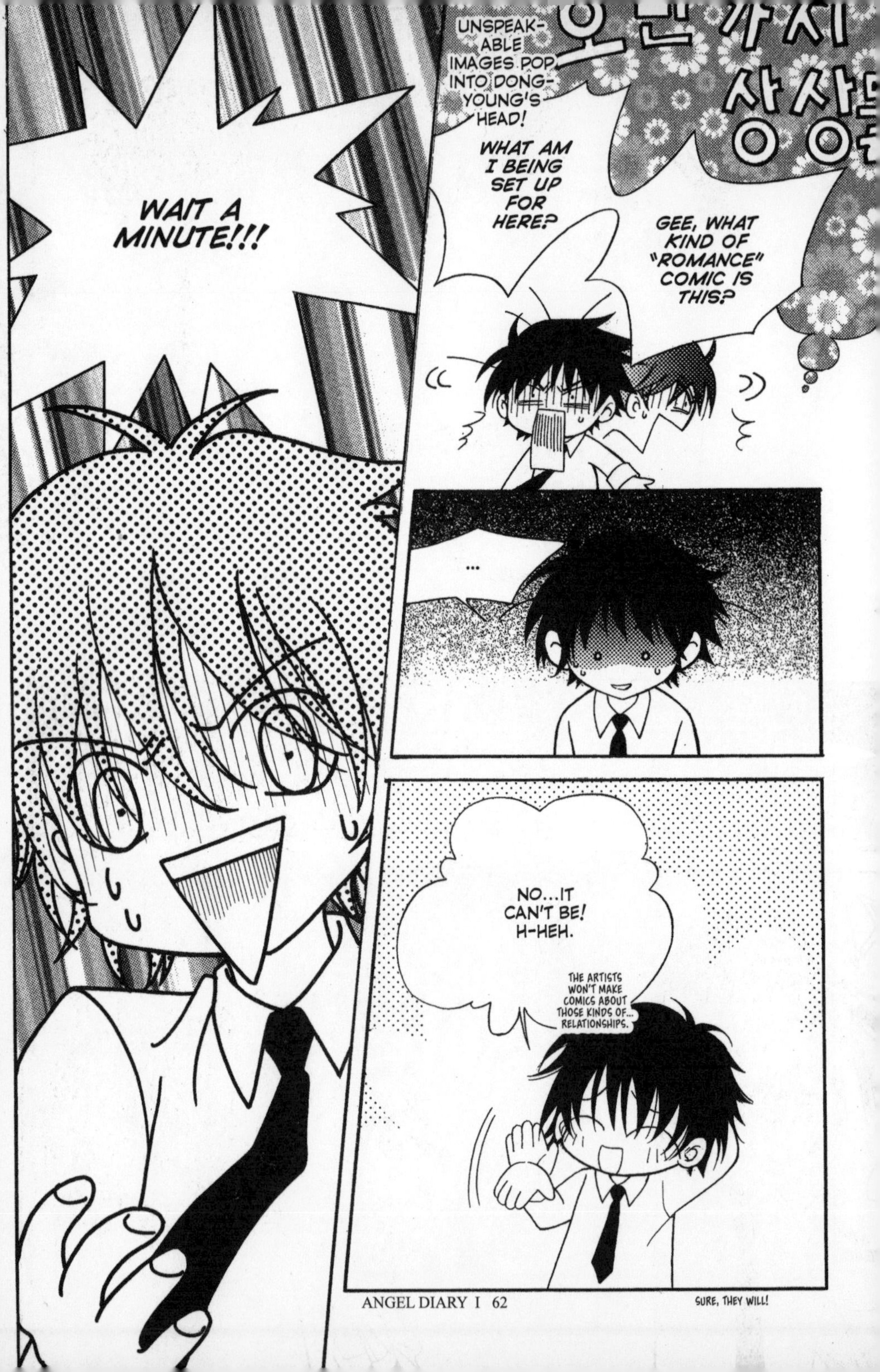
WAIT A MINUTE!!!
UNSPEAKABLE IMAGES POP INTO DONG-YOUNG'S HEAD!
WHAT AM I BEING SET UP FOR HERE?
GEE, WHAT KIND OF "ROMANCE" COMIC IS THIS?
...
NO...IT CAN'T BE! H-HEH.
THE ARTISTS WON'T MAKE COMICS ABOUT THOSE KINDS OF... RELATIONSHIPS.
SURE, THEY WILL!

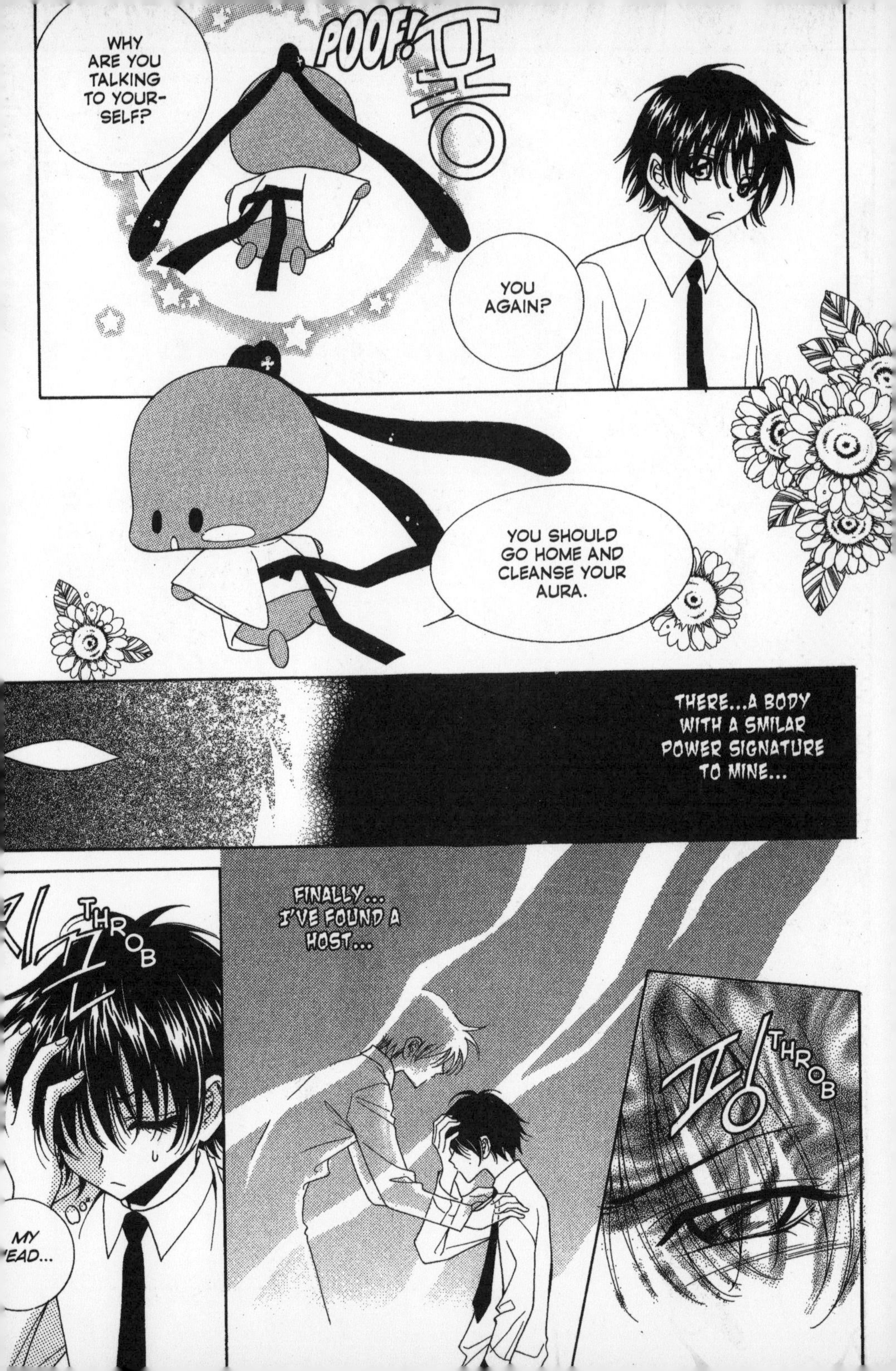
WHY ARE YOU TALKING TO YOURSELF?
POOF!
YOU AGAIN?
YOU SHOULD GO HOME AND CLEANSE YOUR AURA.
THERE...A BODY WITH A SMILAR POWER SIGNATURE TO MINE...
THROB
MY EAD...
FINALLY... I'VE FOUND A HOST...
THROB

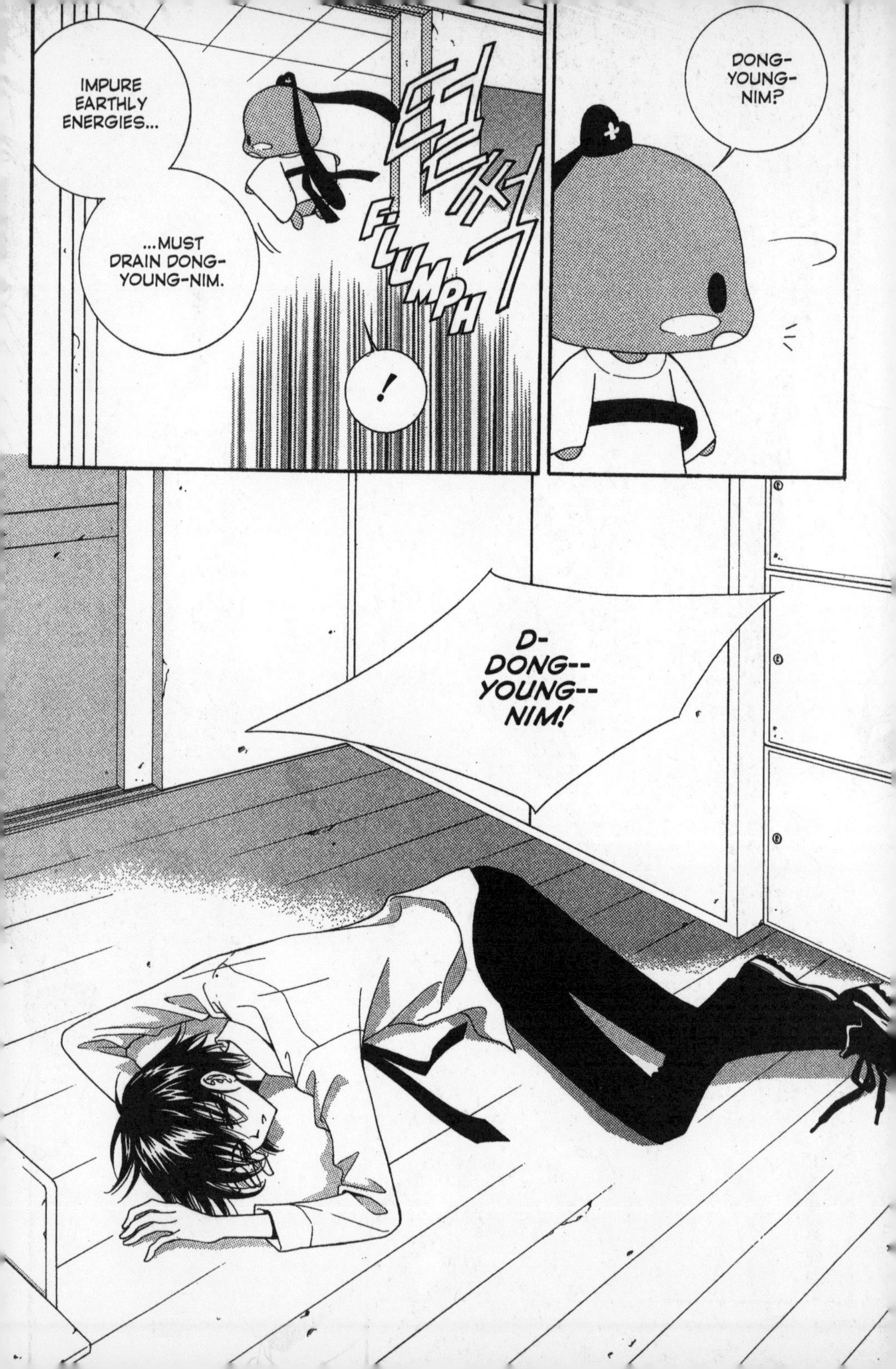
IMPURE EARTHLY ENERGIES...
...MUST DRAIN DONG-YOUNG-NIM.
털썩
FLUMPH
!
DONG-YOUNG-NIM?
D-DONG--YOUNG--NIM!

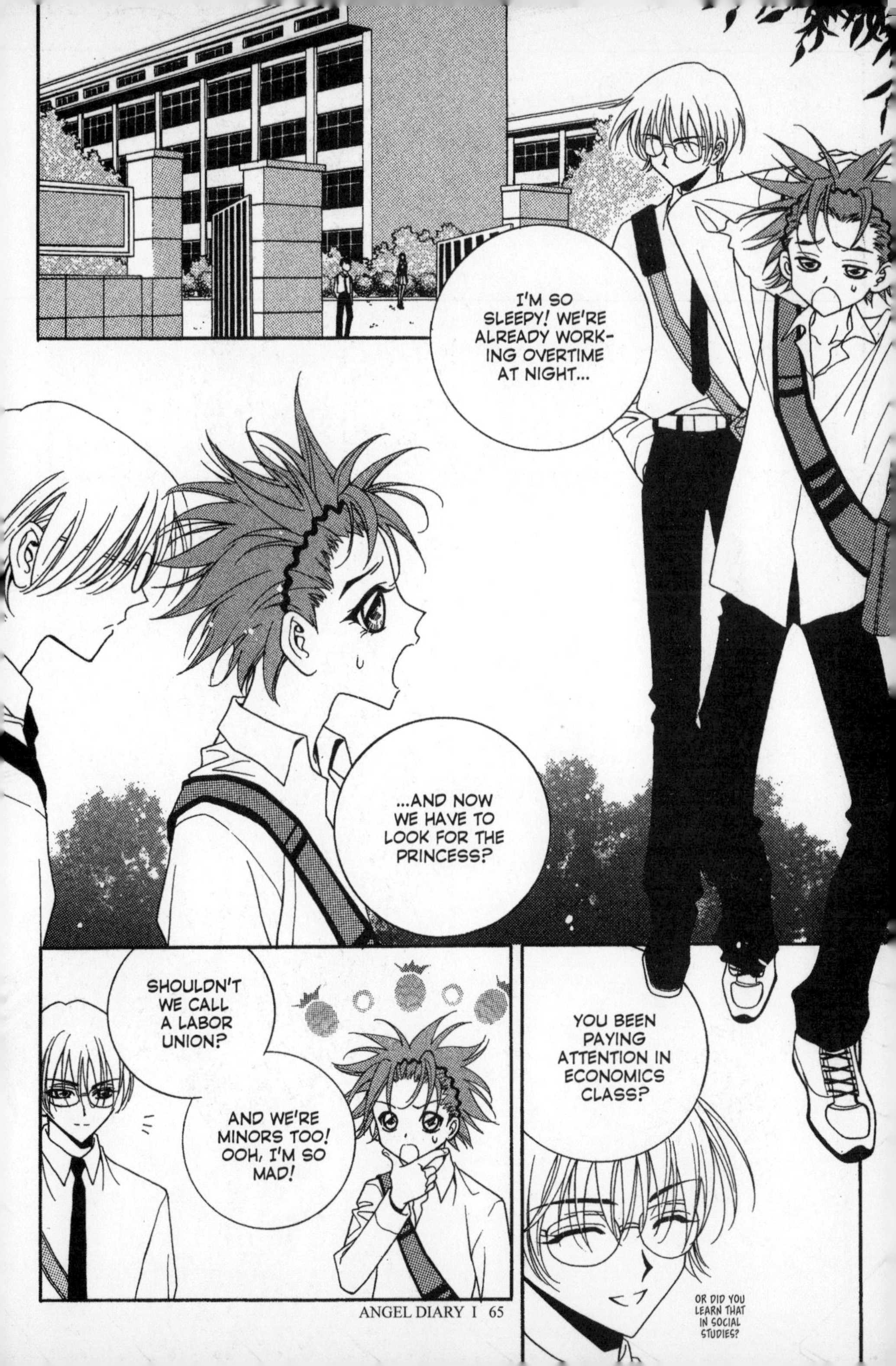
I'M SO SLEEPY! WE'RE ALREADY WORKING OVERTIME AT NIGHT...
...AND NOW WE HAVE TO LOOK FOR THE PRINCESS?
SHOULDN'T WE CALL A LABOR UNION?
AND WE'RE MINORS TOO! OOH, I'M SO MAD!
YOU BEEN PAYING ATTENTION IN ECONOMICS CLASS?
OR DID YOU LEARN THAT IN SOCIAL STUDIES?

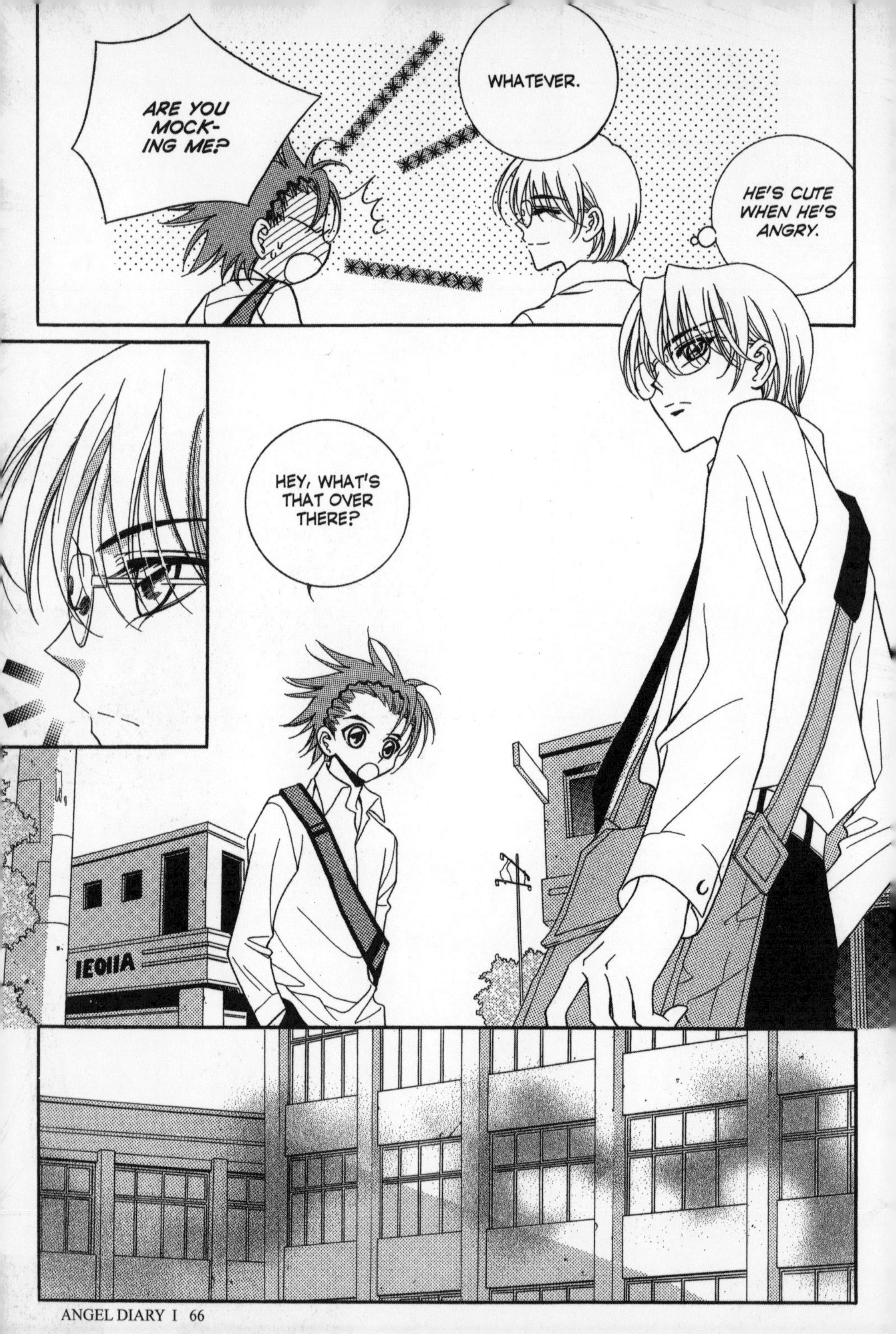
ARE YOU MOCKING-ING ME?
WHATEVER.
HE'S CUTE WHEN HE'S ANGRY.
HEY, WHAT'S THAT OVER THERE?
IEOIIA

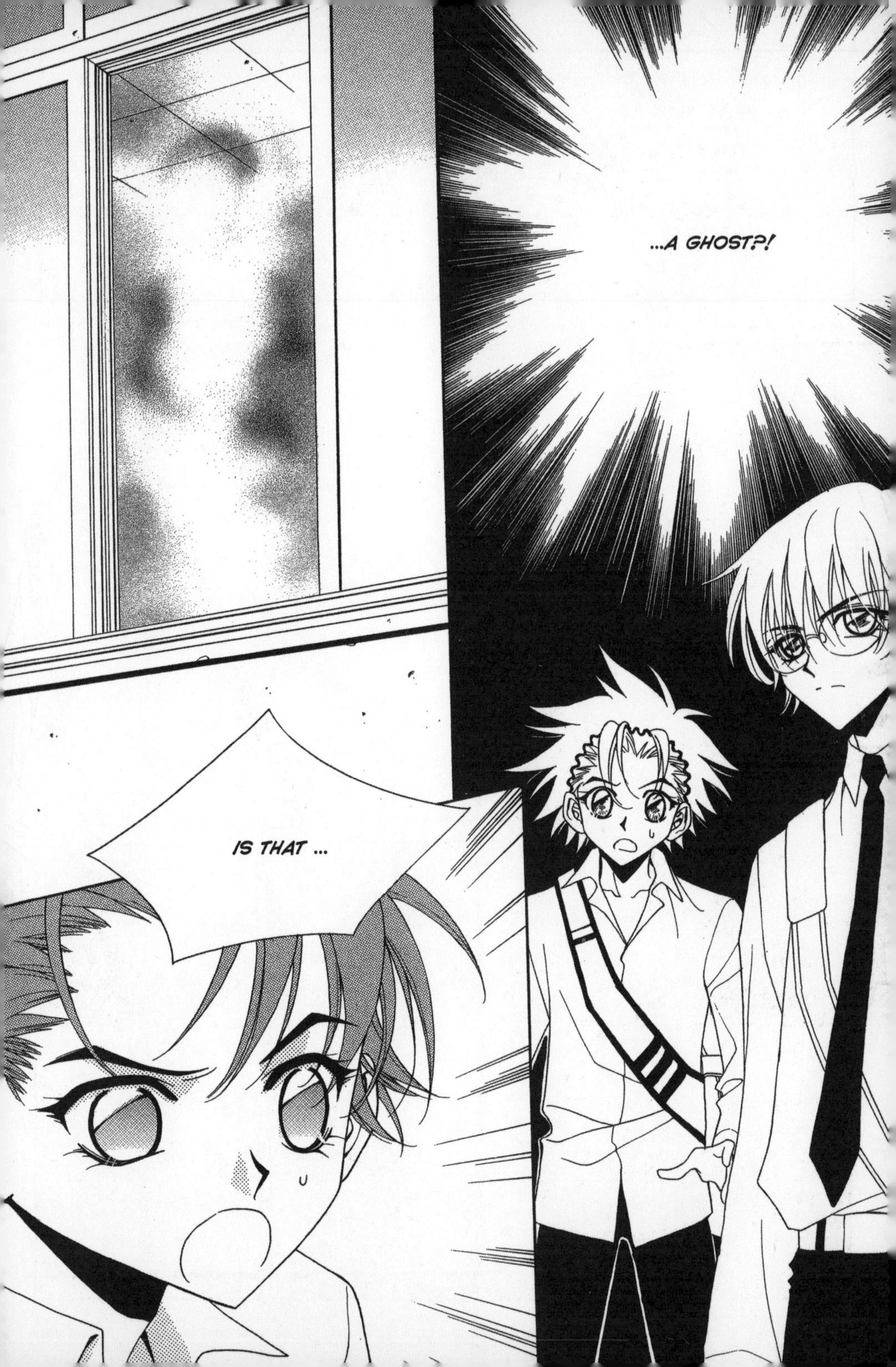
...A GHOST?!
IS THAT ...

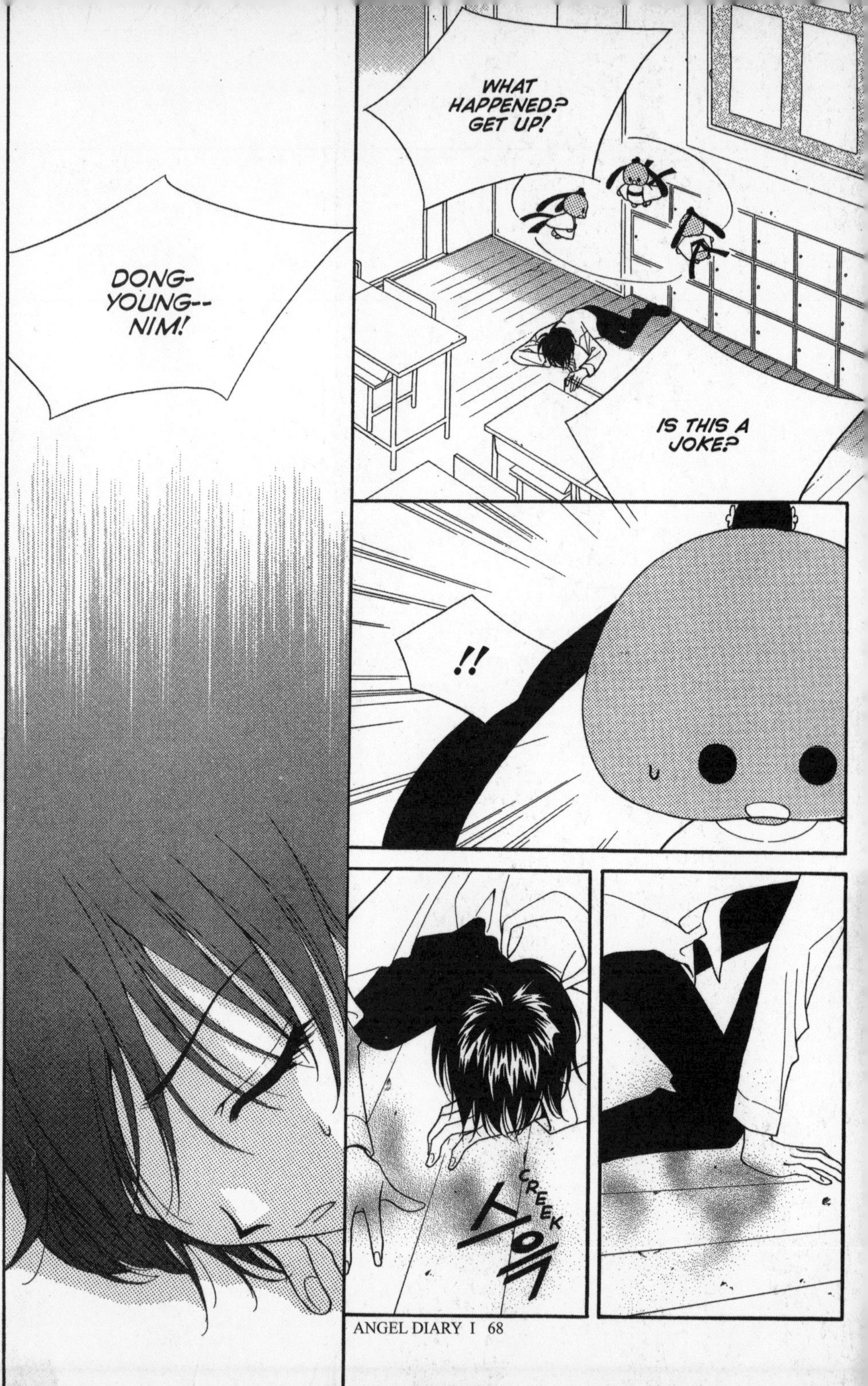
DONG-YOUNG--NIM!
WHAT HAPPENED? GET UP!
IS THIS A JOKE?
!!
CREEK

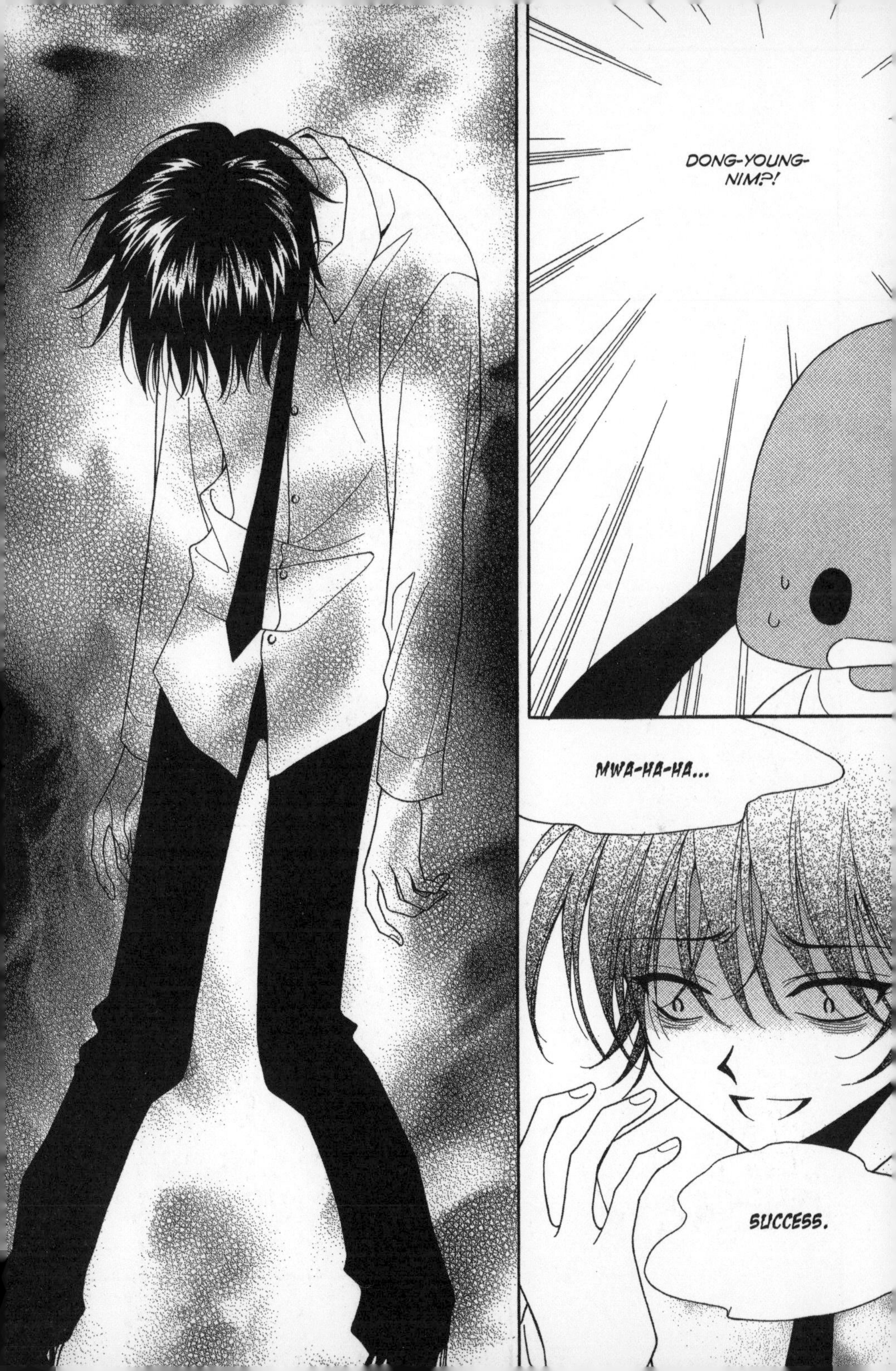
DONG-YOUNG-NIM?!
MWA-HA-HA...
SUCCESS.

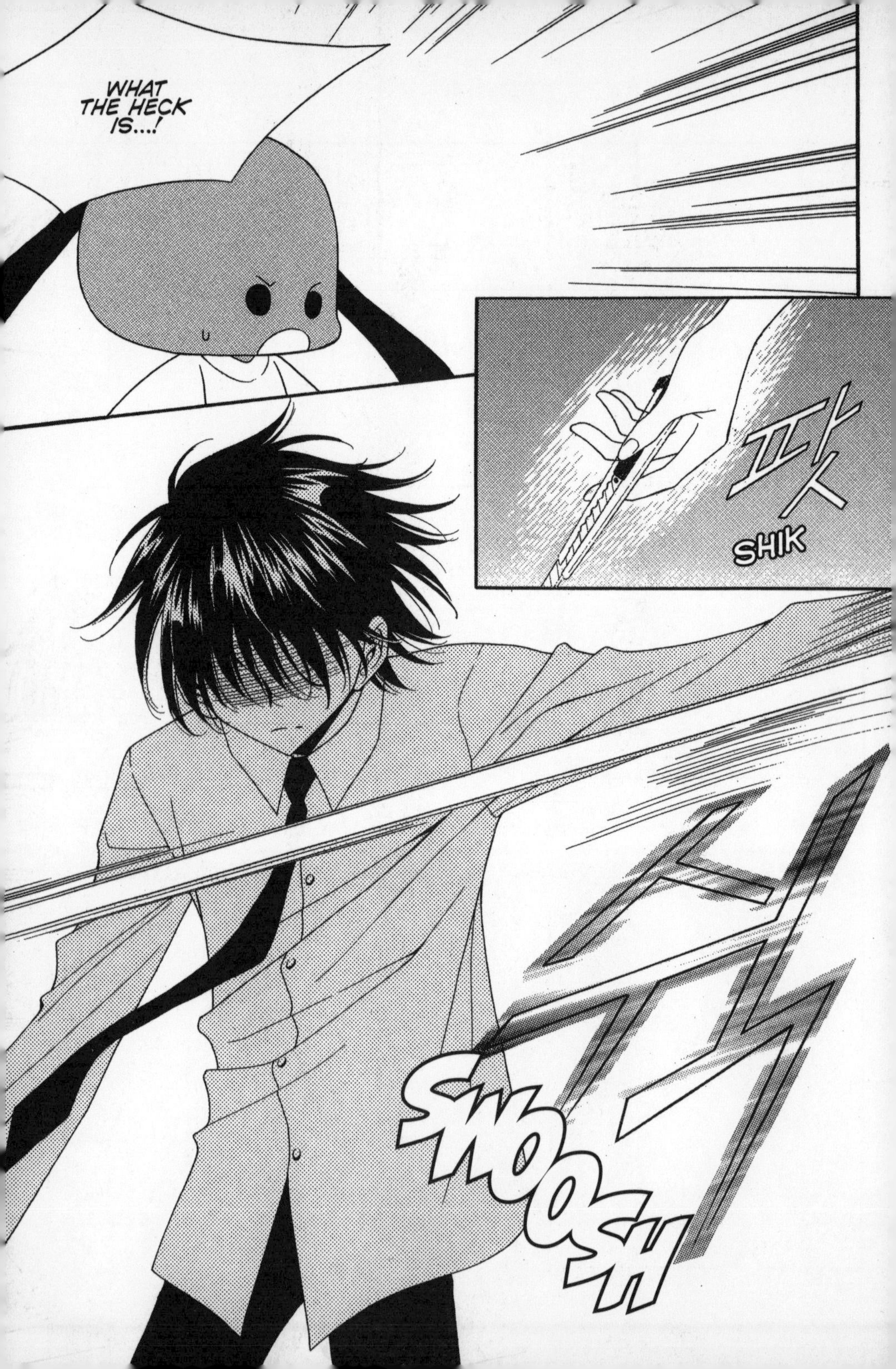
WHAT THE HECK IS...!
SHIK
SWOOSH

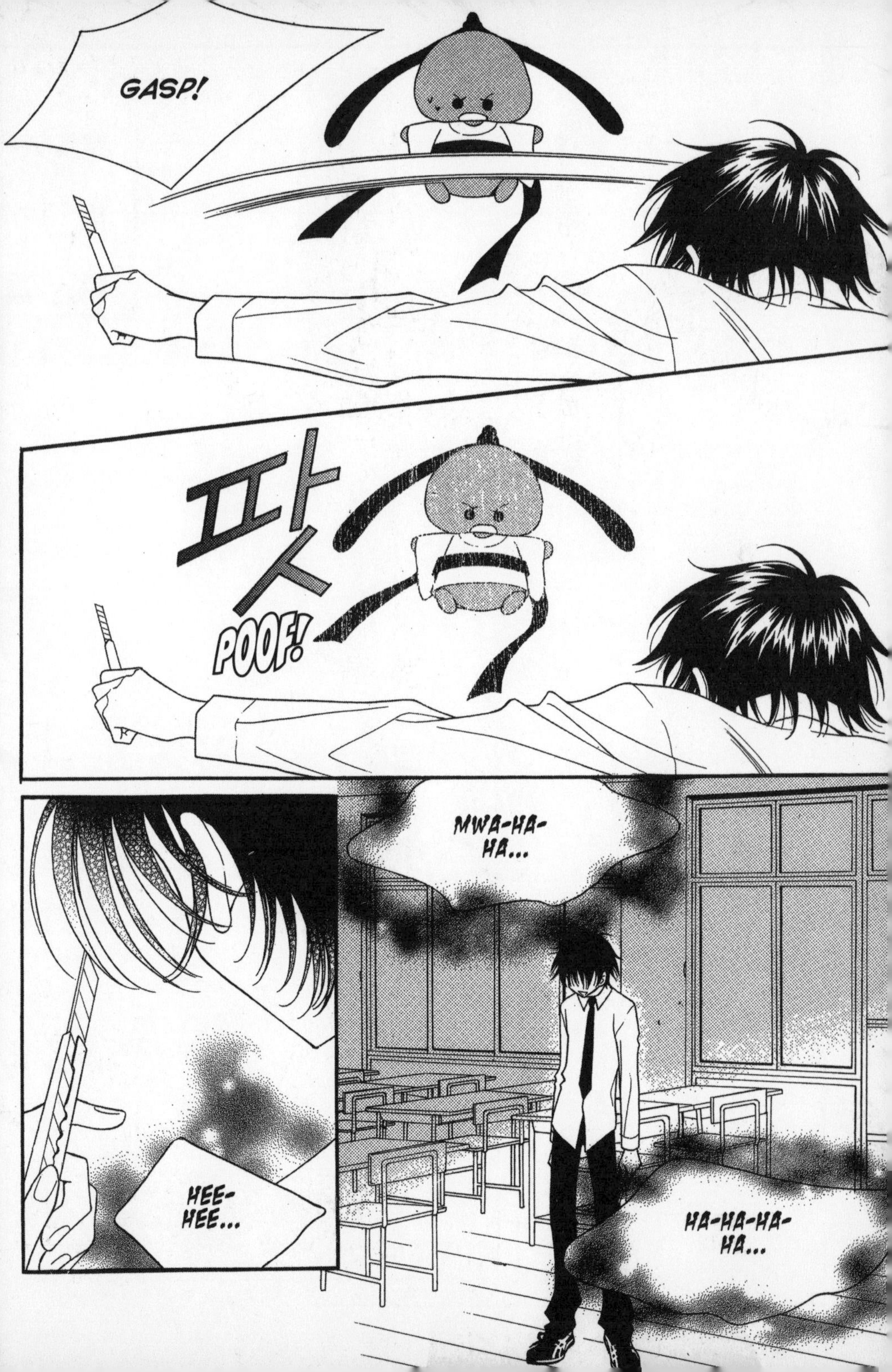
GASP!
팟
POOF!
HEE-HEE...
MWA-HA-HA...
HA-HA-HA-HA...

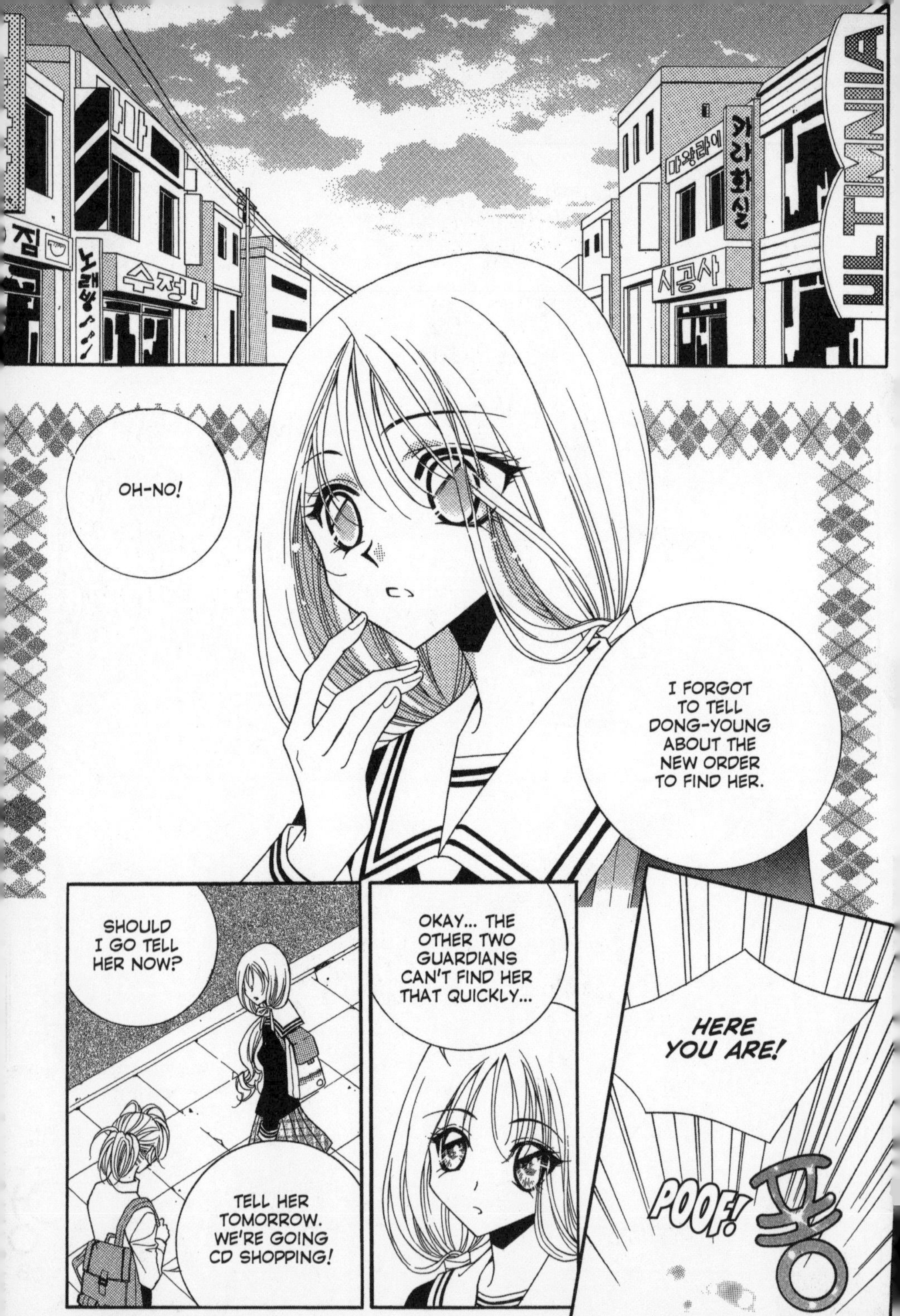
집
노래방
수정!
카라화실
시공사
OH-NO!
I FORGOT TO TELL DONG-YOUNG ABOUT THE NEW ORDER TO FIND HER.
SHOULD I GO TELL HER NOW?
TELL HER TOMORROW. WE'RE GOING CD SHOPPING!
OKAY... THE OTHER TWO GUARDIANS CAN'T FIND HER THAT QUICKLY...
HERE YOU ARE!
POOF!
퐁

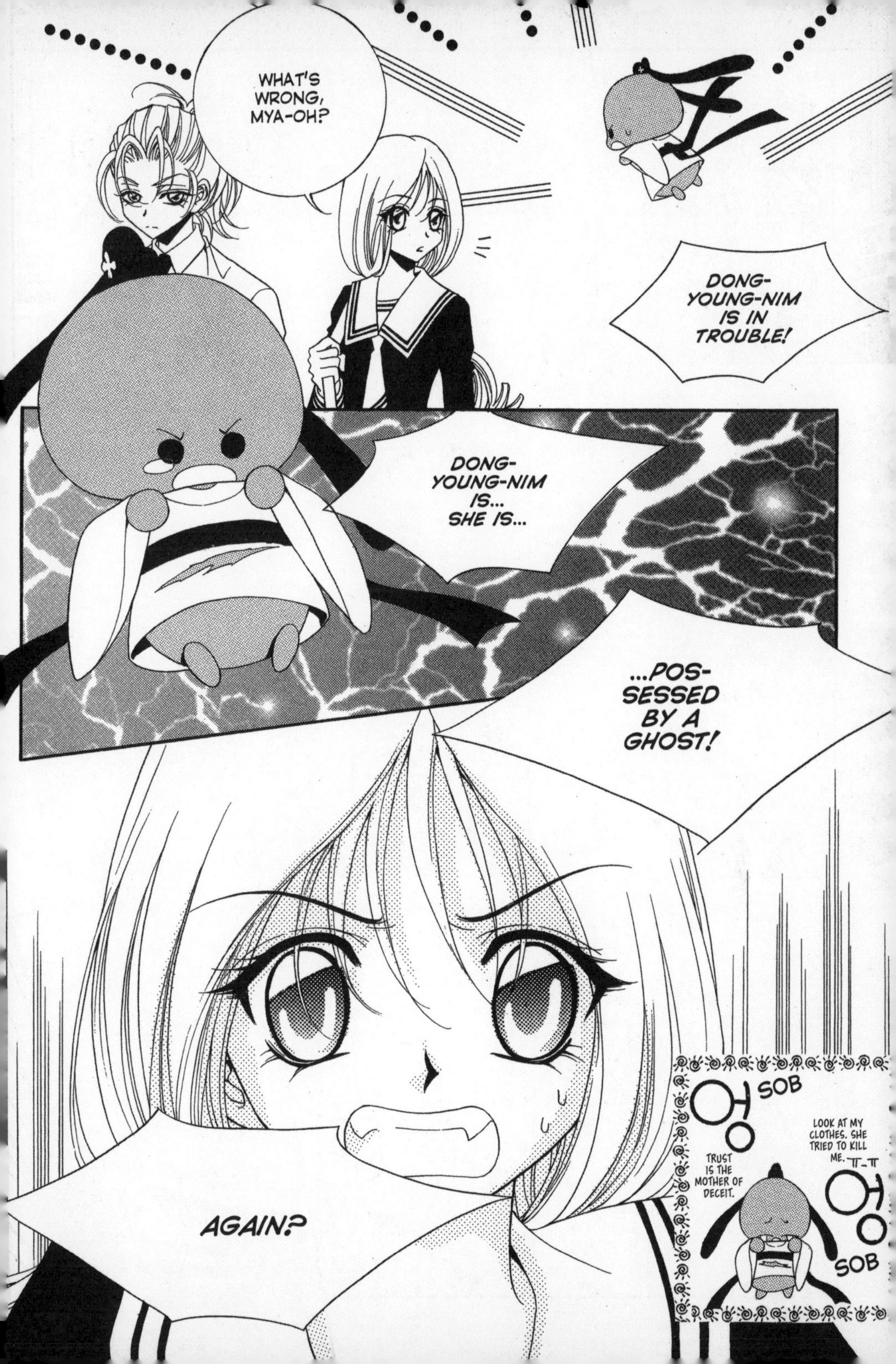
WHAT'S WRONG, MYA-OH?
DONG-YOUNG-NIM IS IN TROUBLE!
DONG-YOUNG-NIM IS... SHE IS...
...POS-SESSED BY A GHOST!
AGAIN?
SOB
TRUST IS THE MOTHER OF DECEIT.
LOOK AT MY CLOTHES. SHE TRIED TO KILL ME. ㅠ_ㅠ
SOB

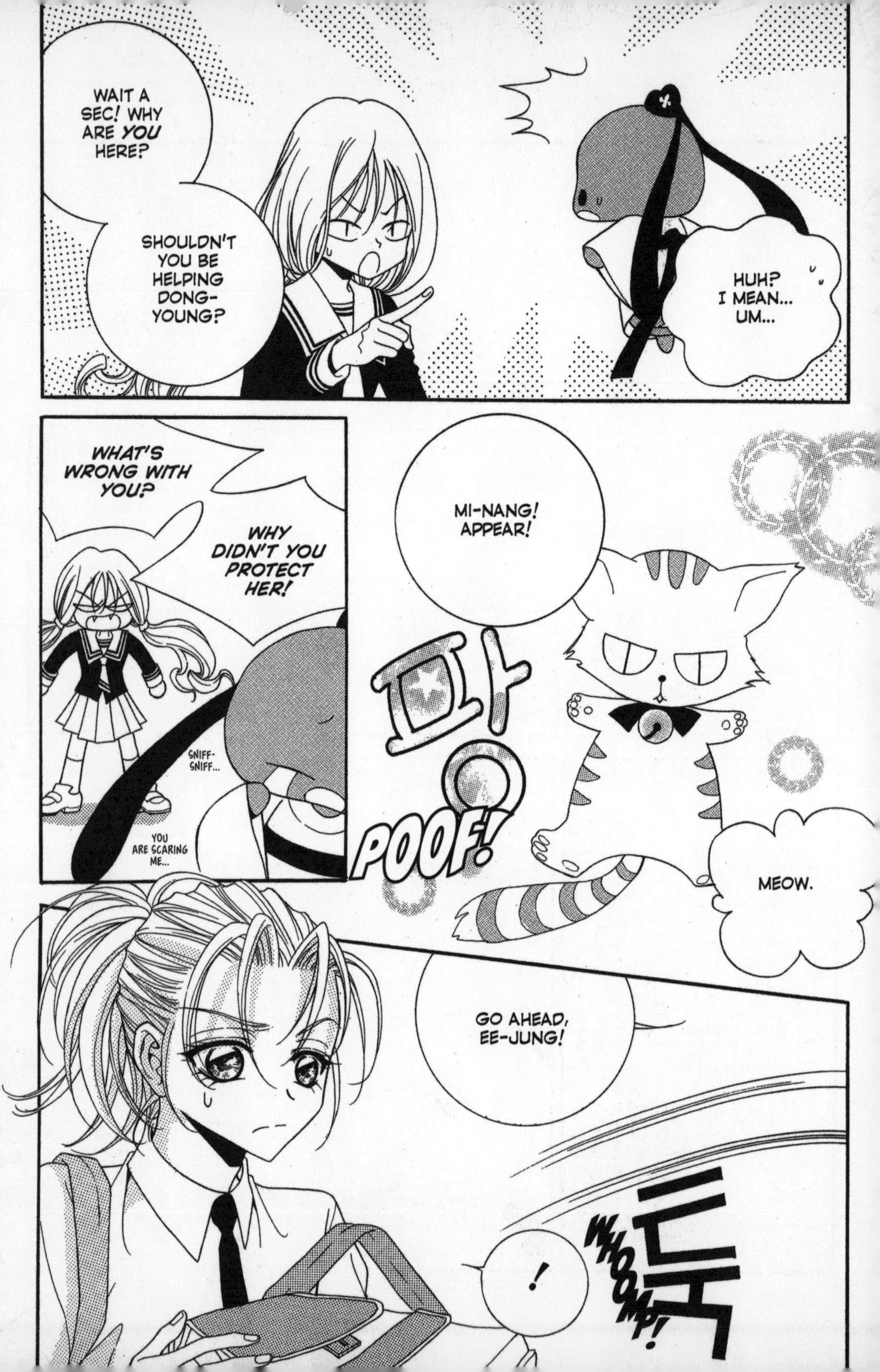
WAIT A SEC! WHY ARE YOU HERE?
SHOULDN'T YOU BE HELPING DONG-YOUNG?
HUH? I MEAN... UM...
WHAT'S WRONG WITH YOU?
WHY DIDN'T YOU PROTECT HER!
SNIFF-SNIFF...
YOU ARE SCARING ME...
MI-NANG! APPEAR!
팡
POOF!
MEOW.
GO AHEAD, EE-JUNG!
!
WHOOMP!

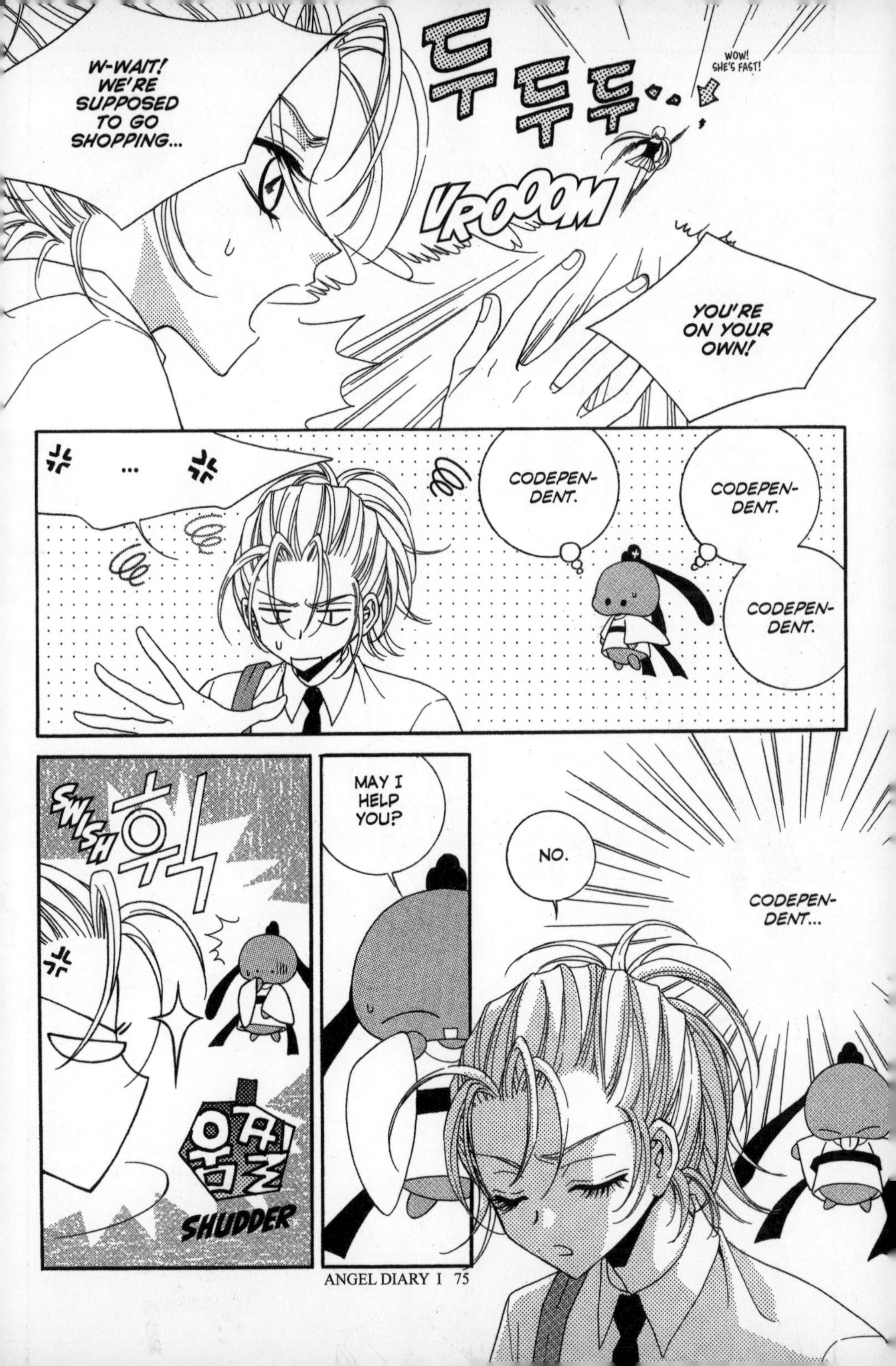
W-WAIT! WE'RE SUPPOSED TO GO SHOPPING...
두두두
WOW! SHE'S FAST!
VROOOM
YOU'RE ON YOUR OWN!
...
CODEPEN-DENT.
CODEPEN-DENT.
CODEPEN-DENT.
SWISH
훅
움찔
SHUDDER
MAY I HELP YOU?
NO.
CODEPEN-DENT...

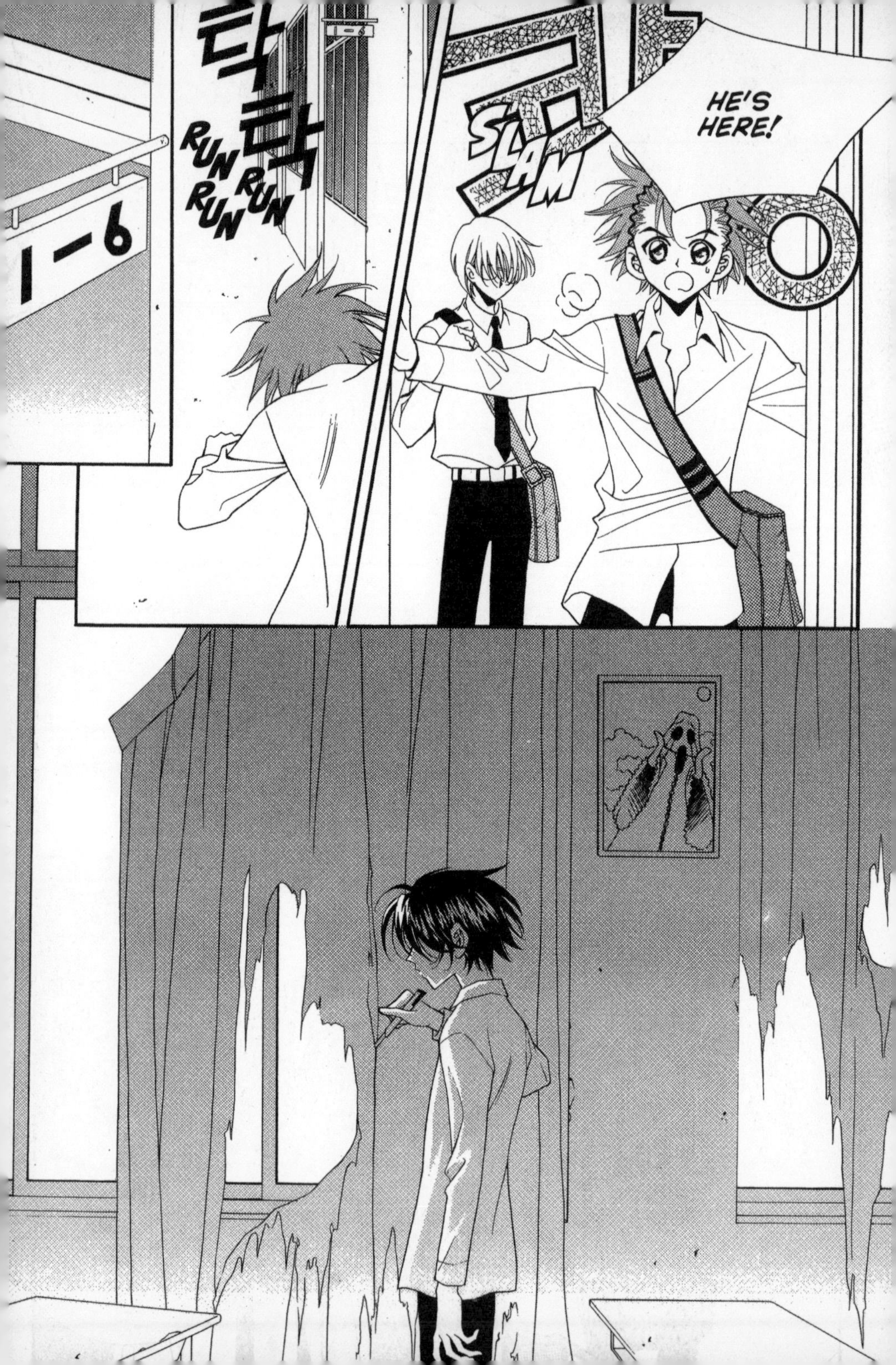
RUN RUN RUN
SLAM
HE'S HERE!

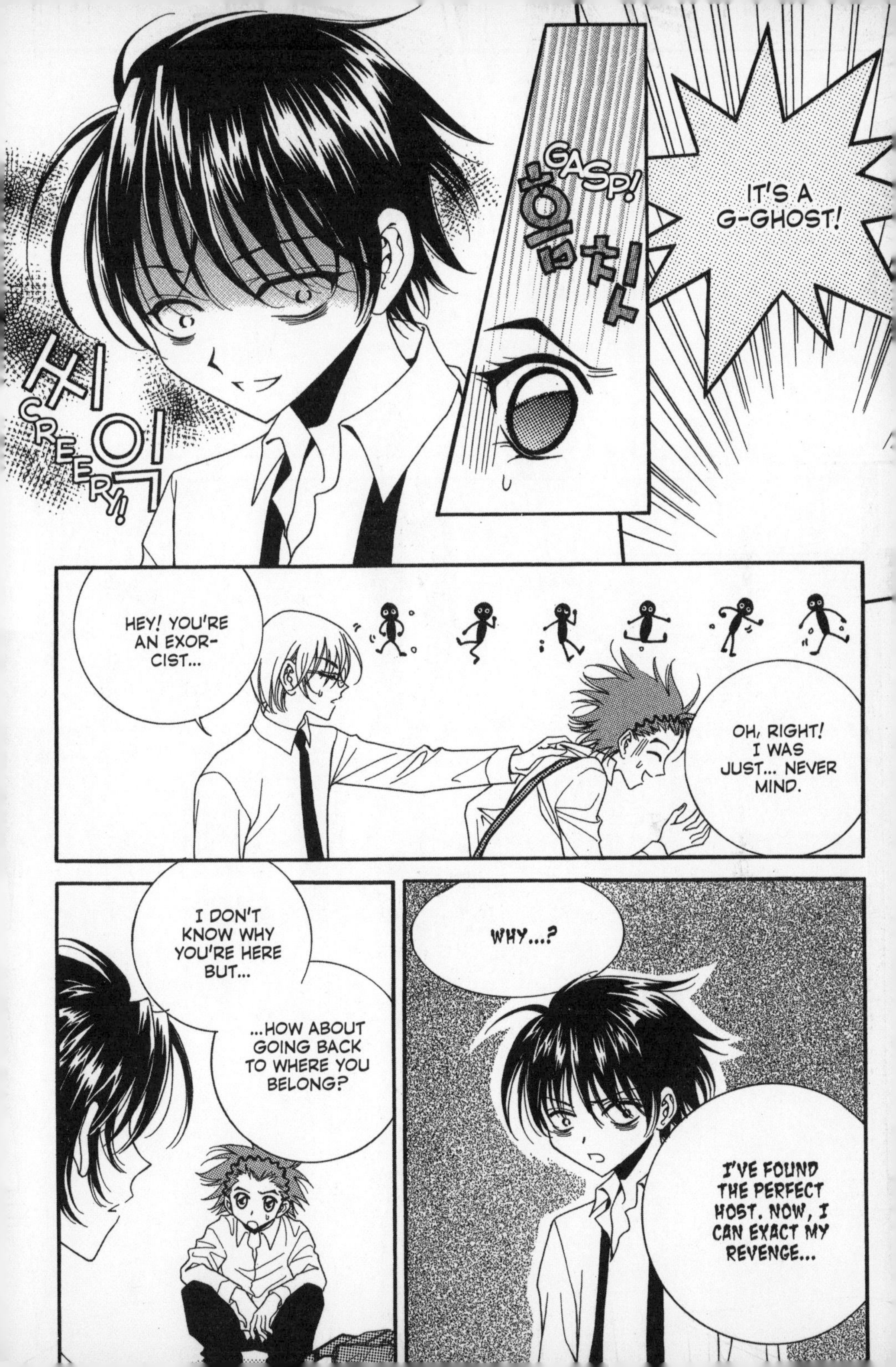
히익
CREEPY!
흠칫!
GASP!
IT'S A G-GHOST!
HEY! YOU'RE AN EXOR-CIST...
OH, RIGHT! I WAS JUST... NEVER MIND.
I DON'T KNOW WHY YOU'RE HERE BUT...
...HOW ABOUT GOING BACK TO WHERE YOU BELONG?
WHY...?
I'VE FOUND THE PERFECT HOST. NOW, I CAN EXACT MY REVENGE...

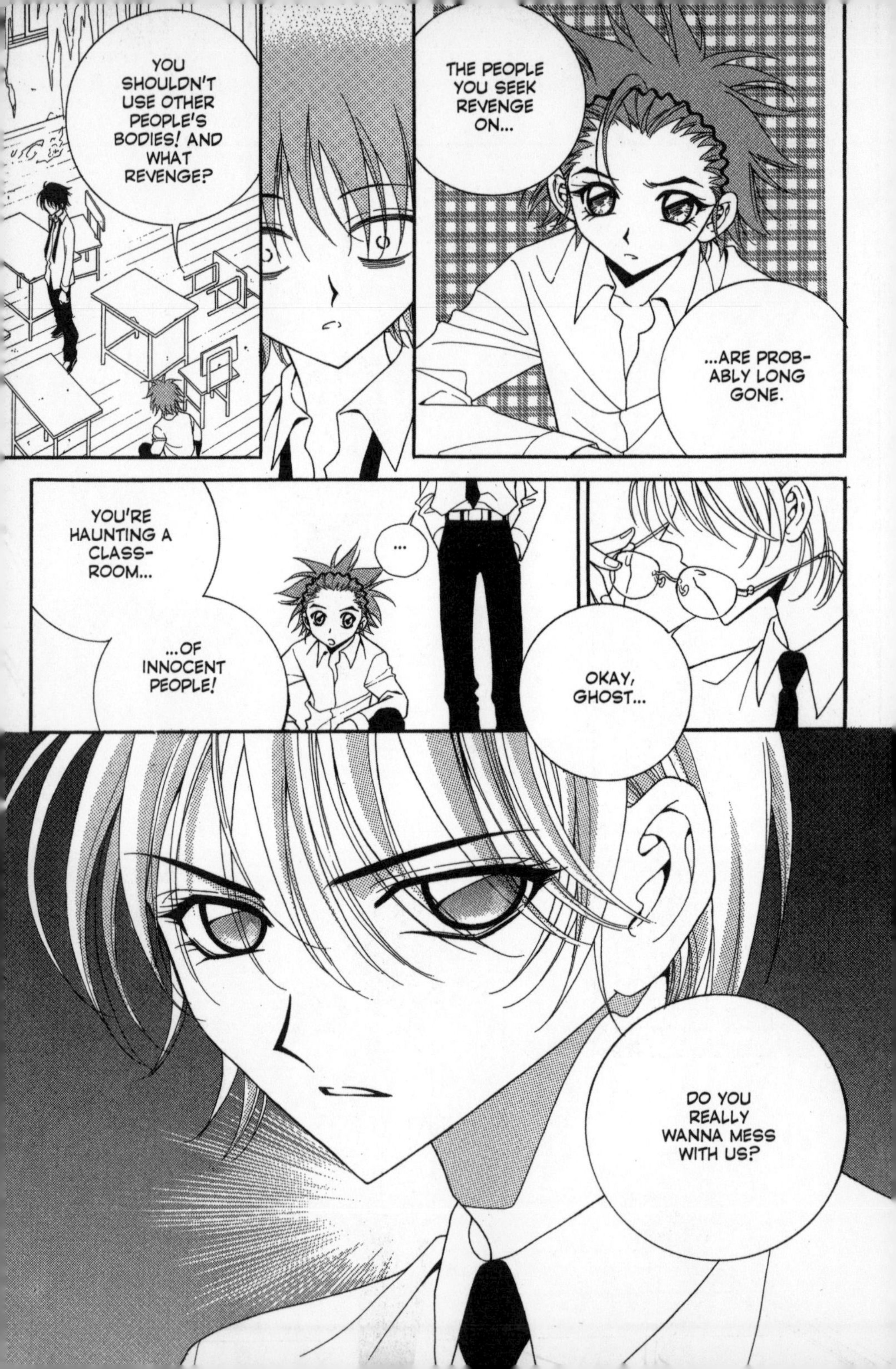
YOU SHOULDN'T USE OTHER PEOPLE'S BODIES! AND WHAT REVENGE?
THE PEOPLE YOU SEEK REVENGE ON...
...ARE PROB-ABLY LONG GONE.
YOU'RE HAUNTING A CLASS-ROOM...
...OF INNOCENT PEOPLE!
...
OKAY, GHOST...
DO YOU REALLY WANNA MESS WITH US?

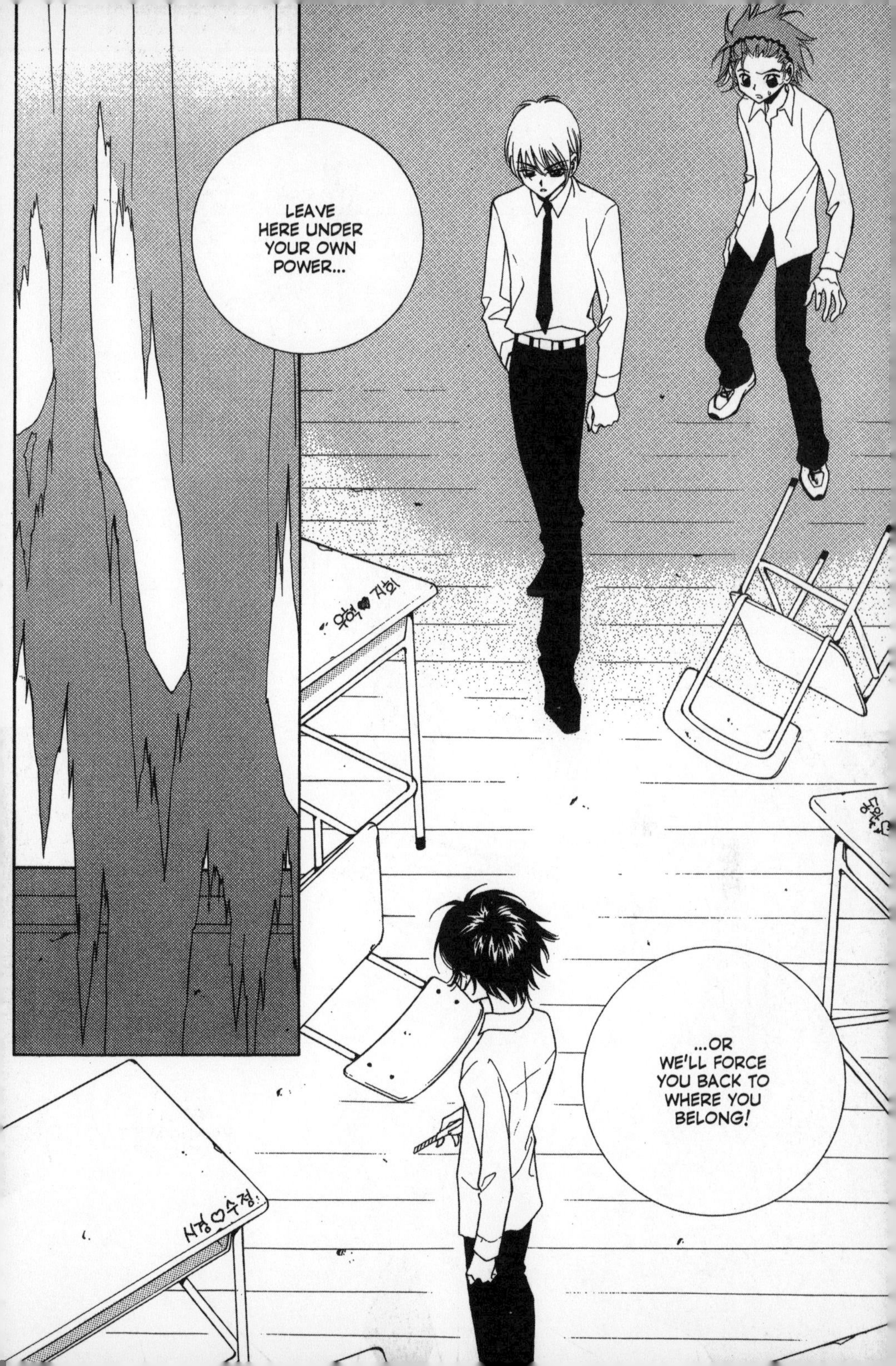
LEAVE HERE UNDER YOUR OWN POWER...
...OR WE'LL FORCE YOU BACK TO WHERE YOU BELONG!

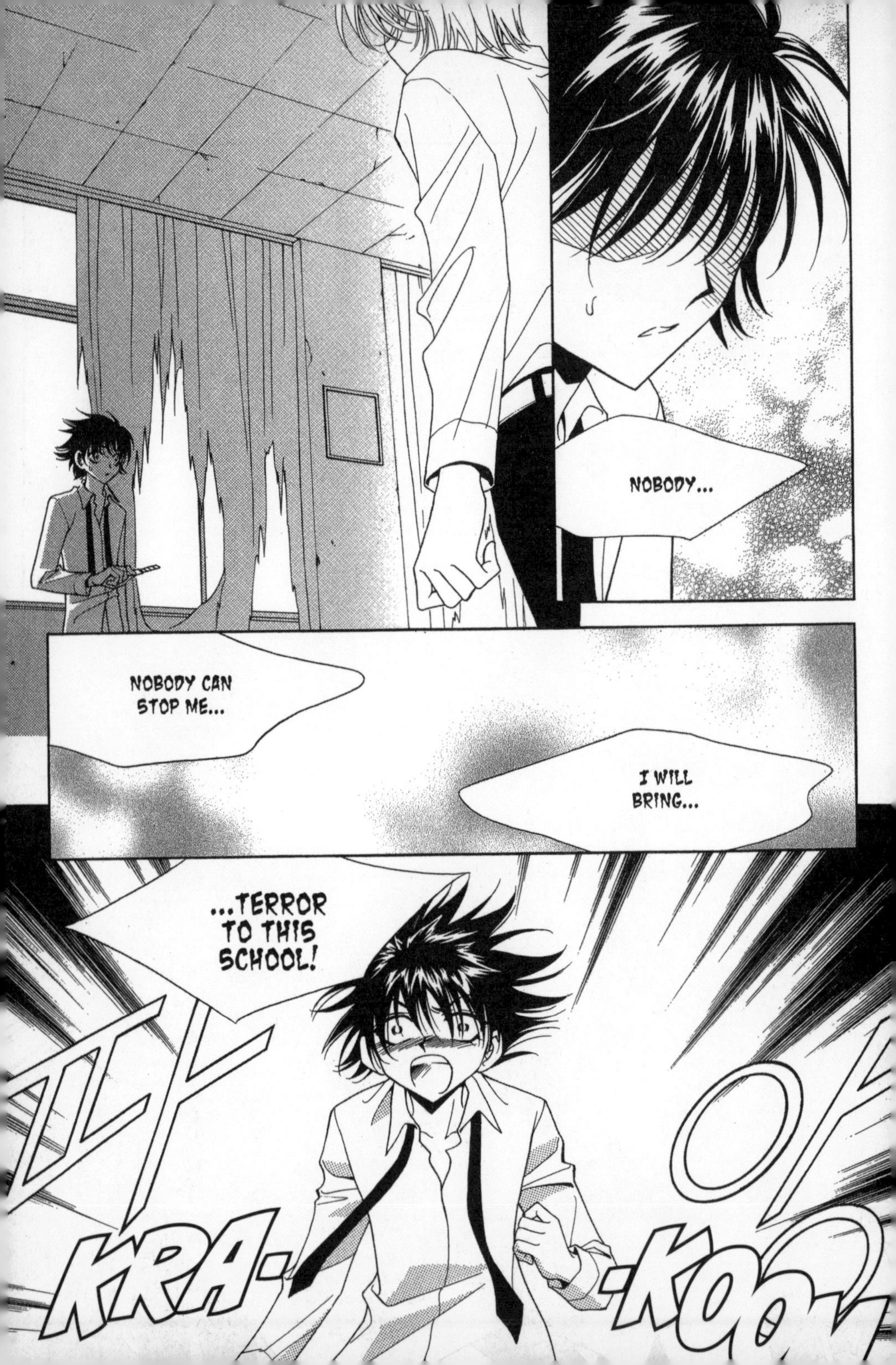
NOBODY...
NOBODY CAN STOP ME...
I WILL BRING...
...TERROR TO THIS SCHOOL!
KRA-
-KOO

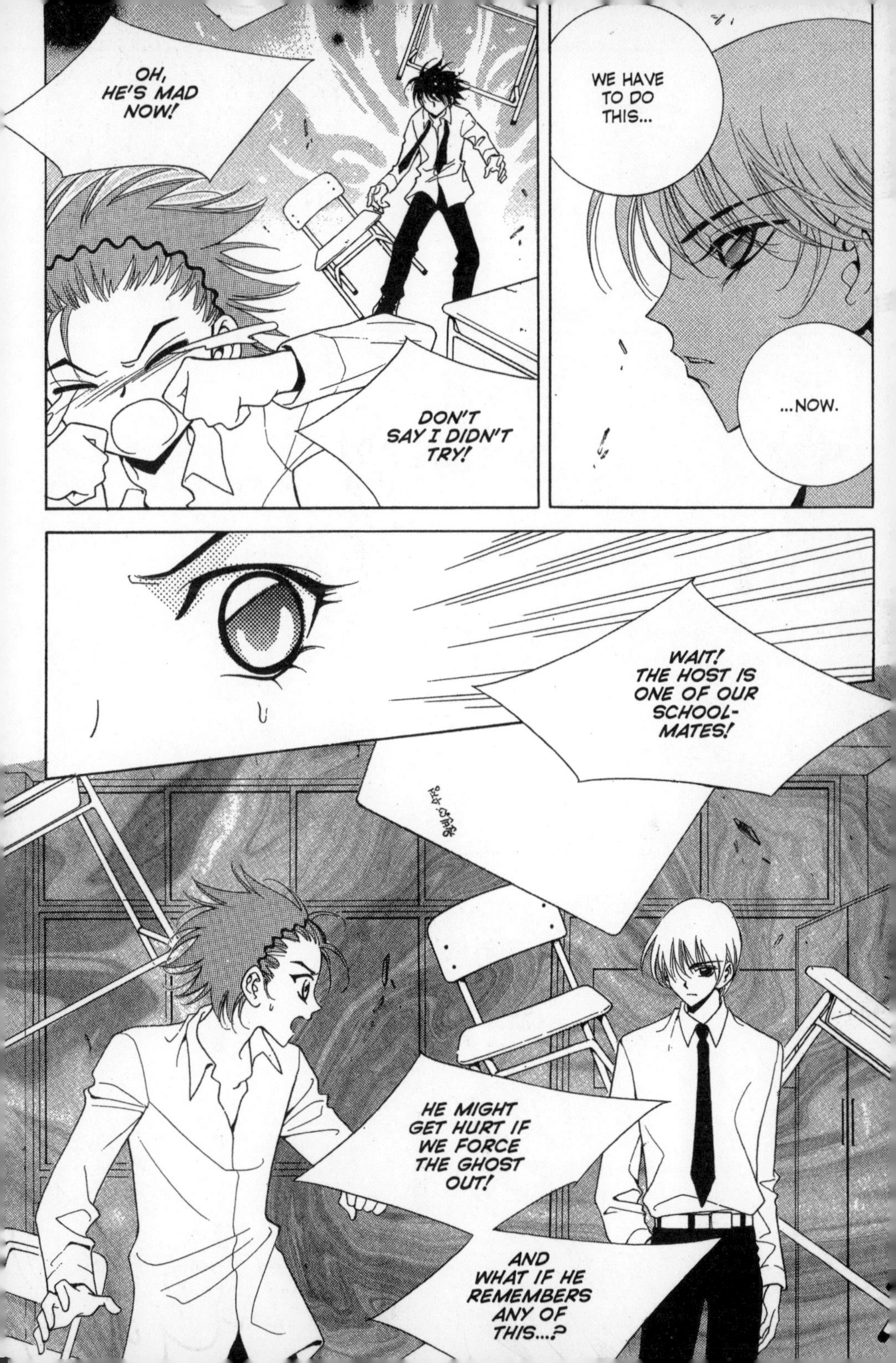
OH, HE'S MAD NOW!
DON'T SAY I DIDN'T TRY!
WE HAVE TO DO THIS...
...NOW.
WAIT! THE HOST IS ONE OF OUR SCHOOL-MATES!
HE MIGHT GET HURT IF WE FORCE THE GHOST OUT!
AND WHAT IF HE REMEMBERS ANY OF THIS...?

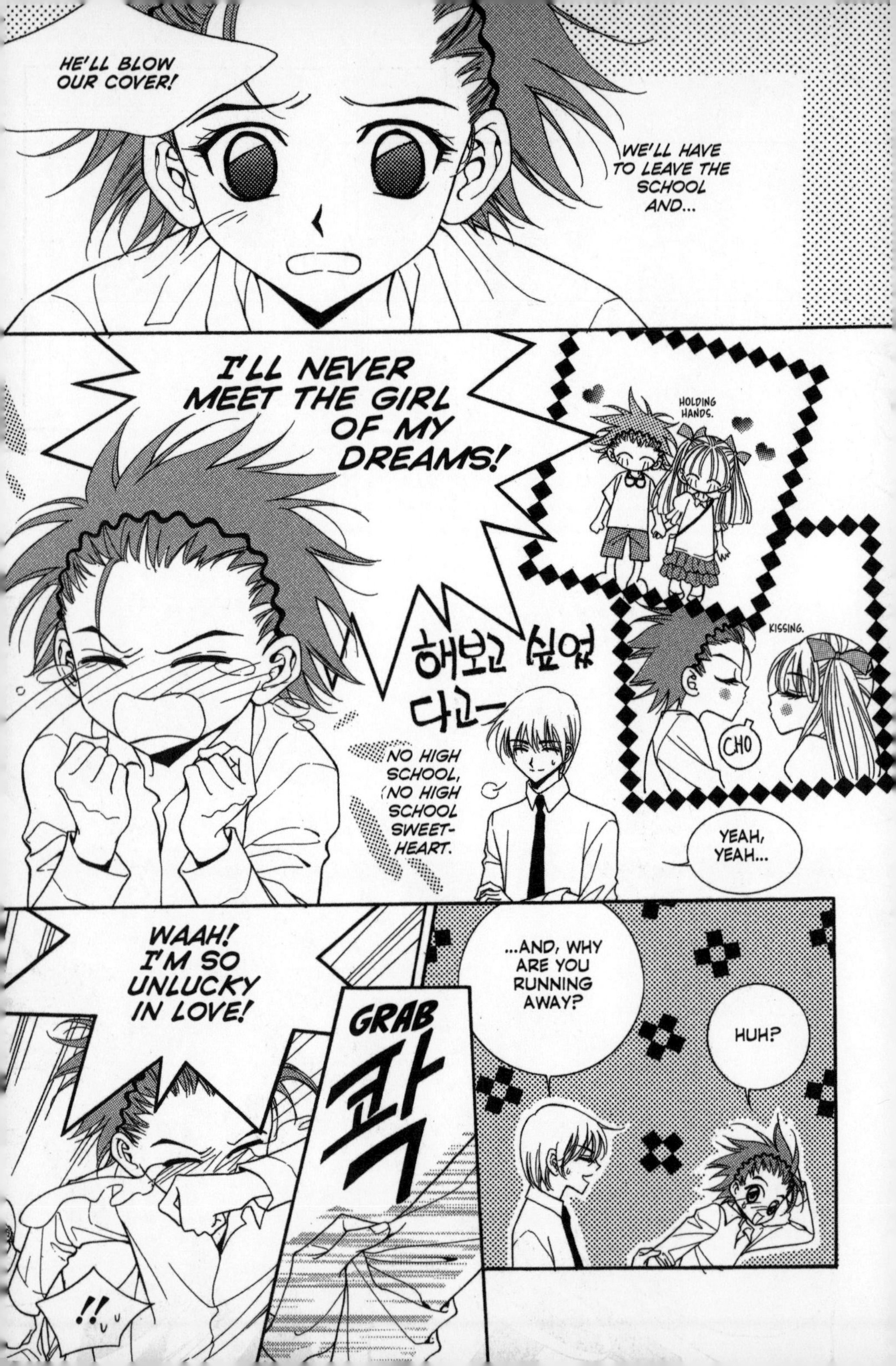
HE'LL BLOW OUR COVER!
WE'LL HAVE TO LEAVE THE SCHOOL AND...
I'LL NEVER MEET THE GIRL OF MY DREAMS!
해보고 싶었다고—
HOLDING HANDS.
KISSING.
CHO
NO HIGH SCHOOL, NO HIGH SCHOOL SWEET-HEART.
YEAH, YEAH...
WAAH! I'M SO UNLUCKY IN LOVE!
GRAB
콰
!!
...AND, WHY ARE YOU RUNNING AWAY?
HUH?

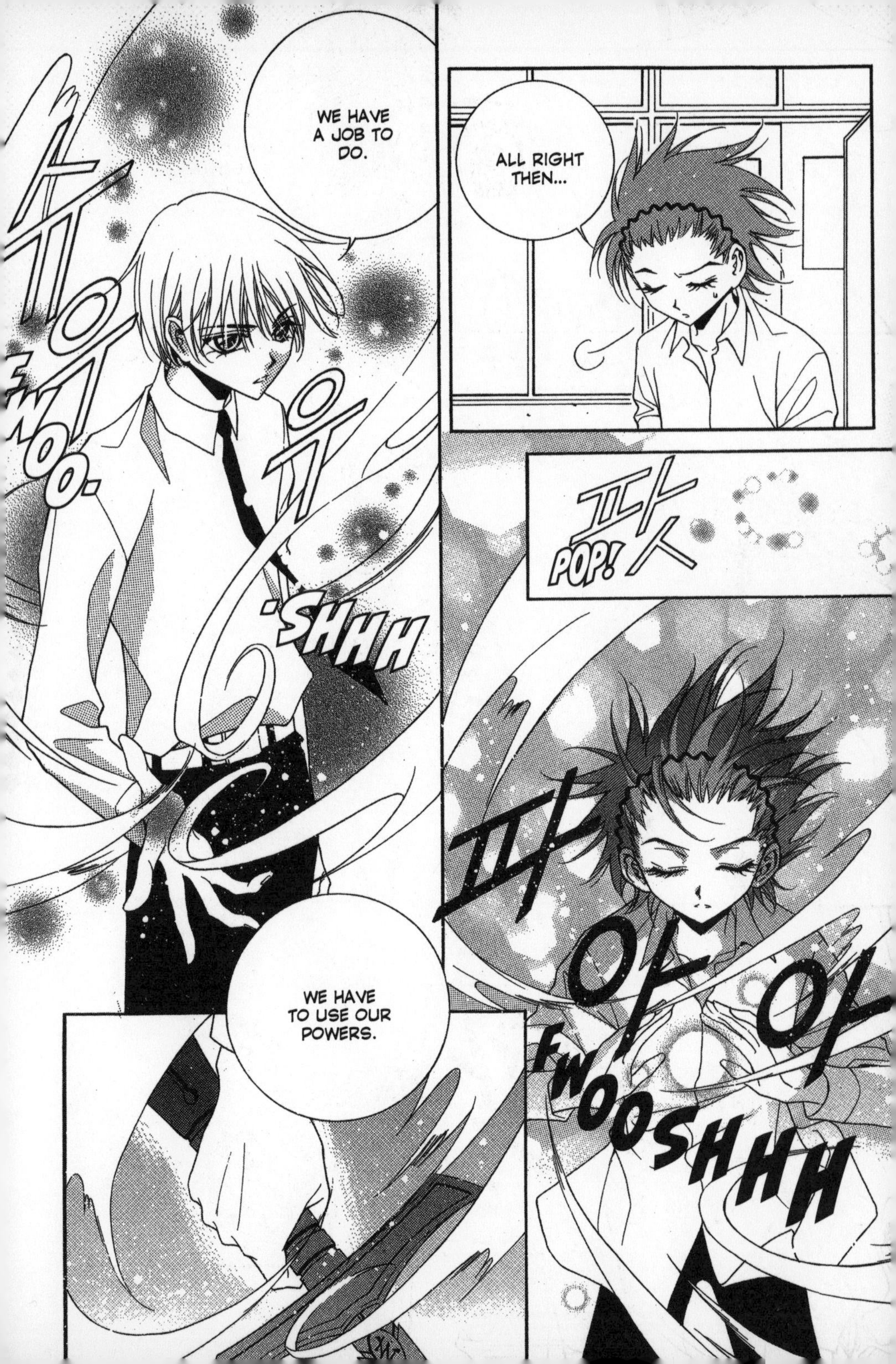
WE HAVE A JOB TO DO.
FWOO-
SHHH
WE HAVE TO USE OUR POWERS.
ALL RIGHT THEN...
팟
POP!
FWOOSHHH

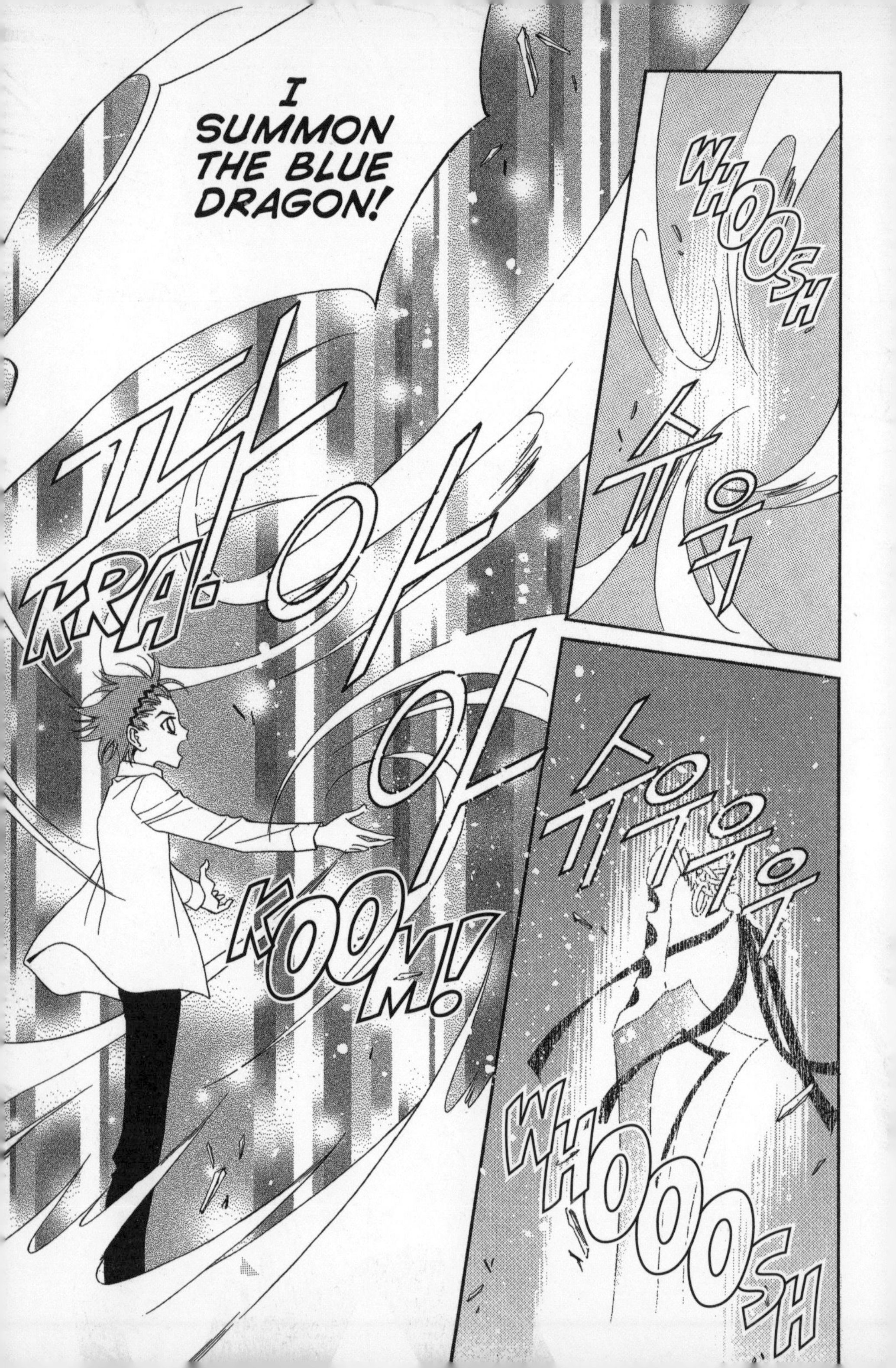
I SUMMON THE BLUE DRAGON!
KRA!
KOOM!
WHOOSH
WHOOOOSH

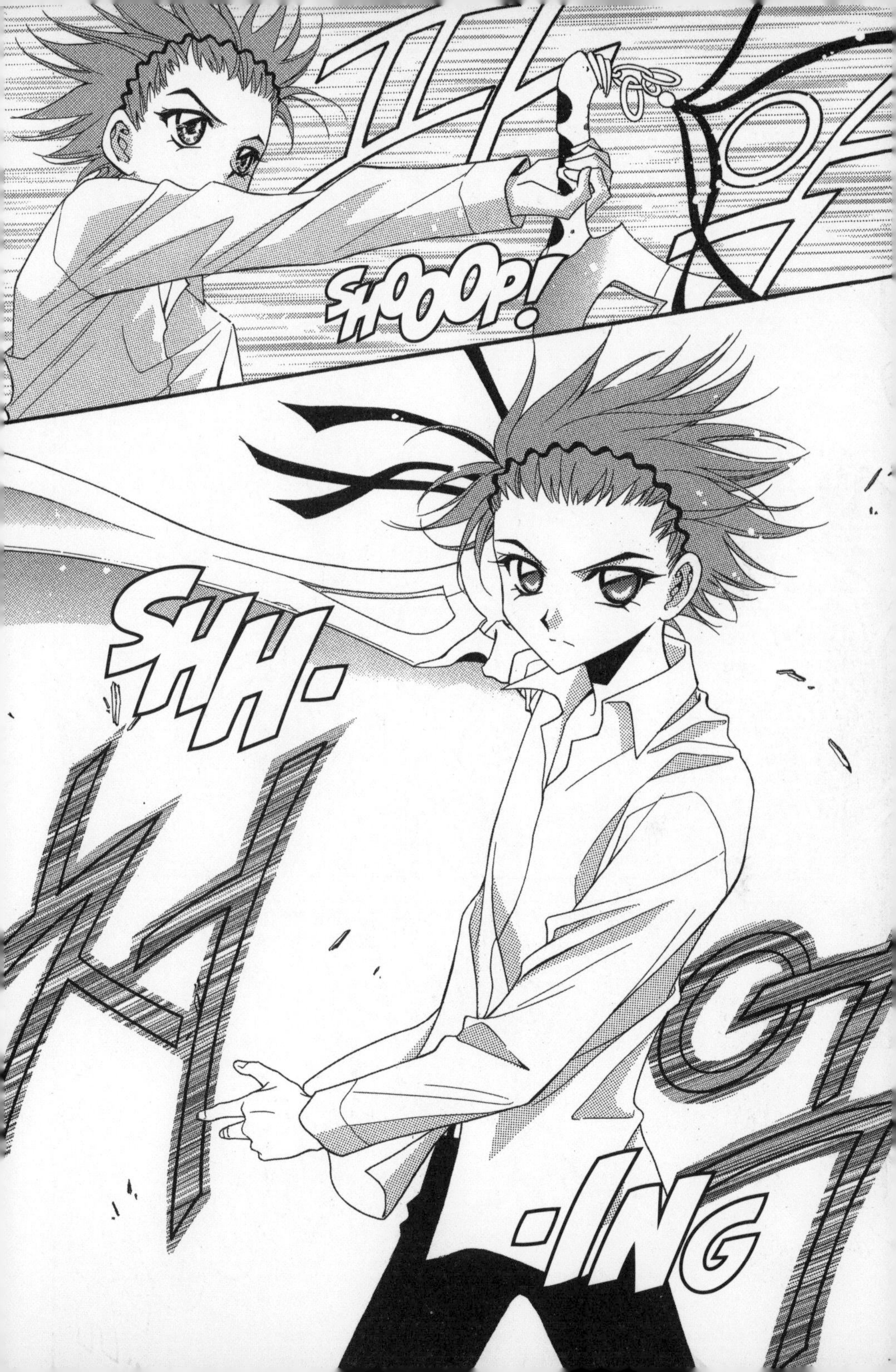
SHOOOP!
SHH-
-ING

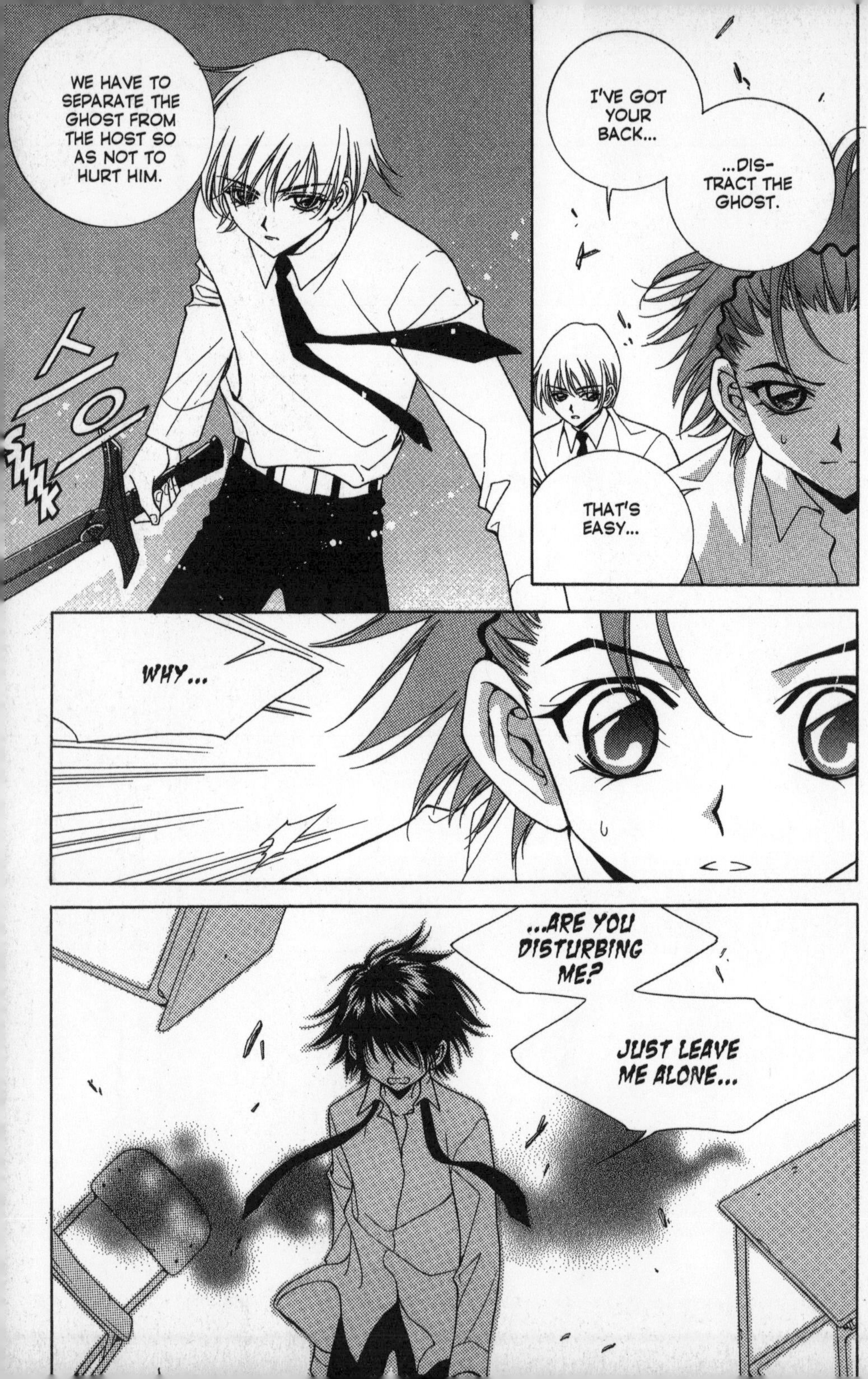
WE HAVE TO SEPARATE THE GHOST FROM THE HOST SO AS NOT TO HURT HIM.
SHHK
I'VE GOT YOUR BACK...
...DIS-TRACT THE GHOST.
THAT'S EASY...
WHY...
...ARE YOU DISTURBING ME?
JUST LEAVE ME ALONE...

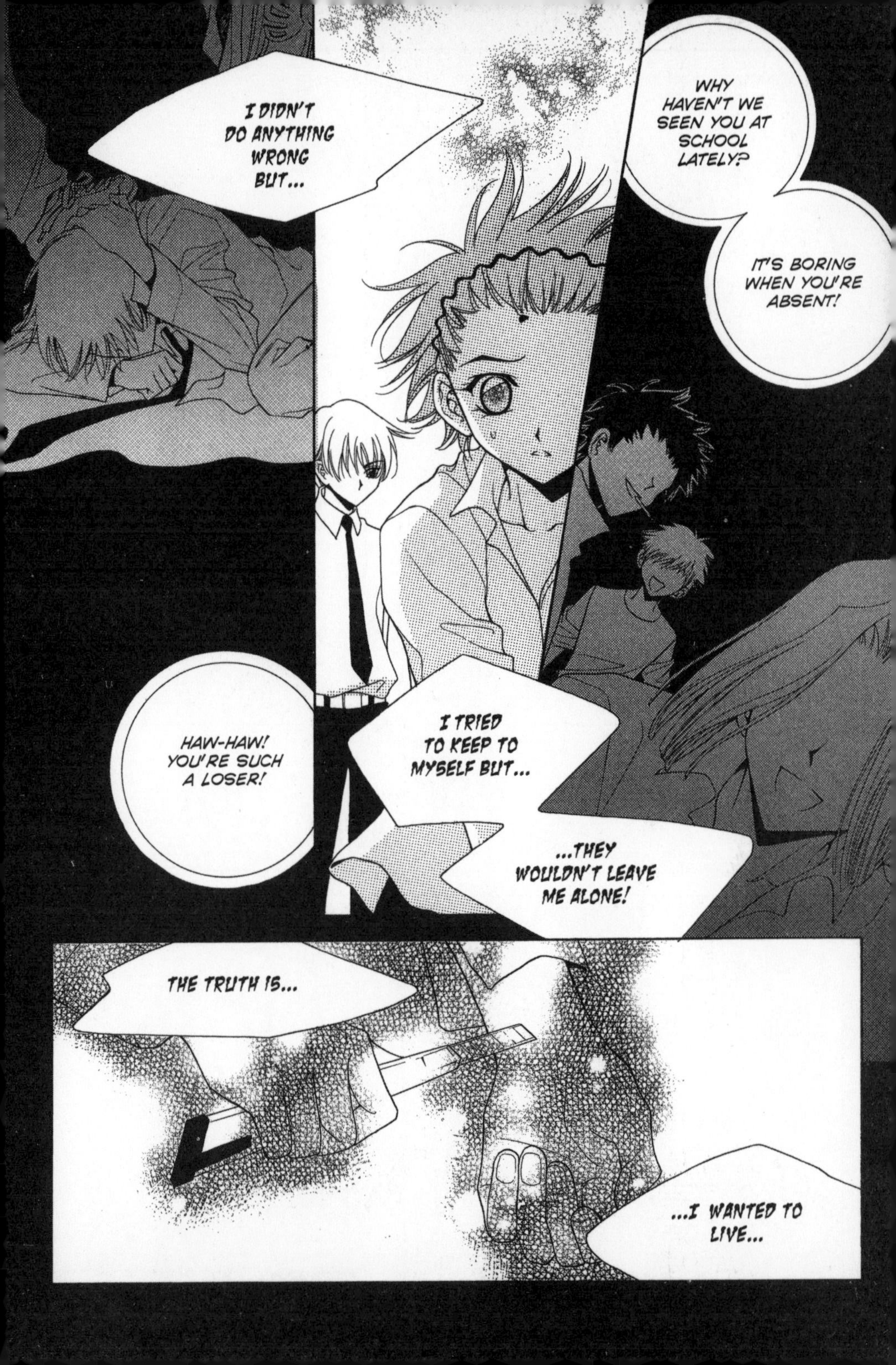
WHY HAVEN'T WE SEEN YOU AT SCHOOL LATELY?
IT'S BORING WHEN YOU'RE ABSENT!
I DIDN'T DO ANYTHING WRONG BUT...
I TRIED TO KEEP TO MYSELF BUT...
HAW-HAW! YOU'RE SUCH A LOSER!
...THEY WOULDN'T LEAVE ME ALONE!
THE TRUTH IS...
...I WANTED TO LIVE...

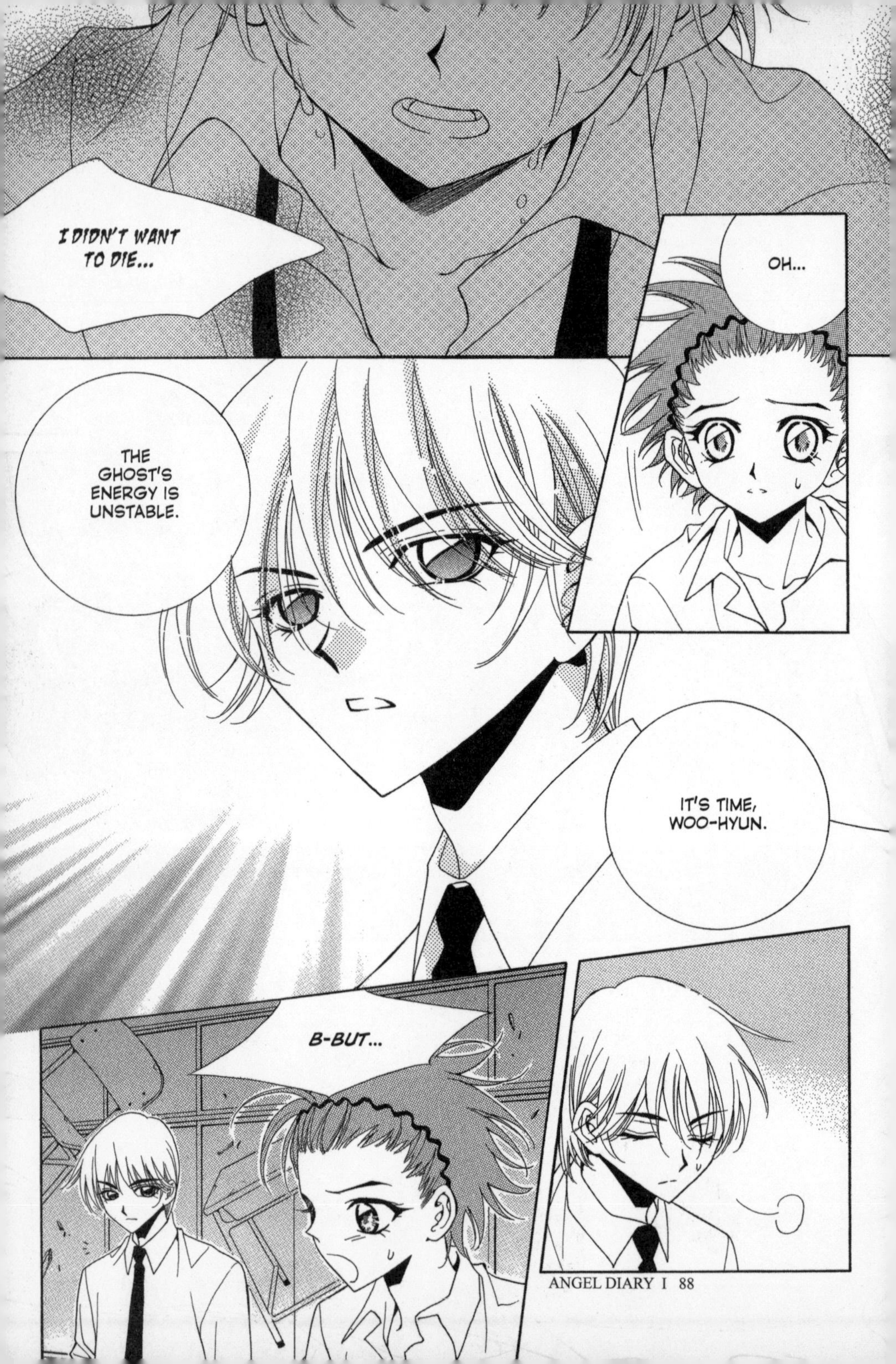
I DIDN'T WANT TO DIE...
OH...
THE GHOST'S ENERGY IS UNSTABLE.
IT'S TIME, WOO-HYUN.
B-BUT...

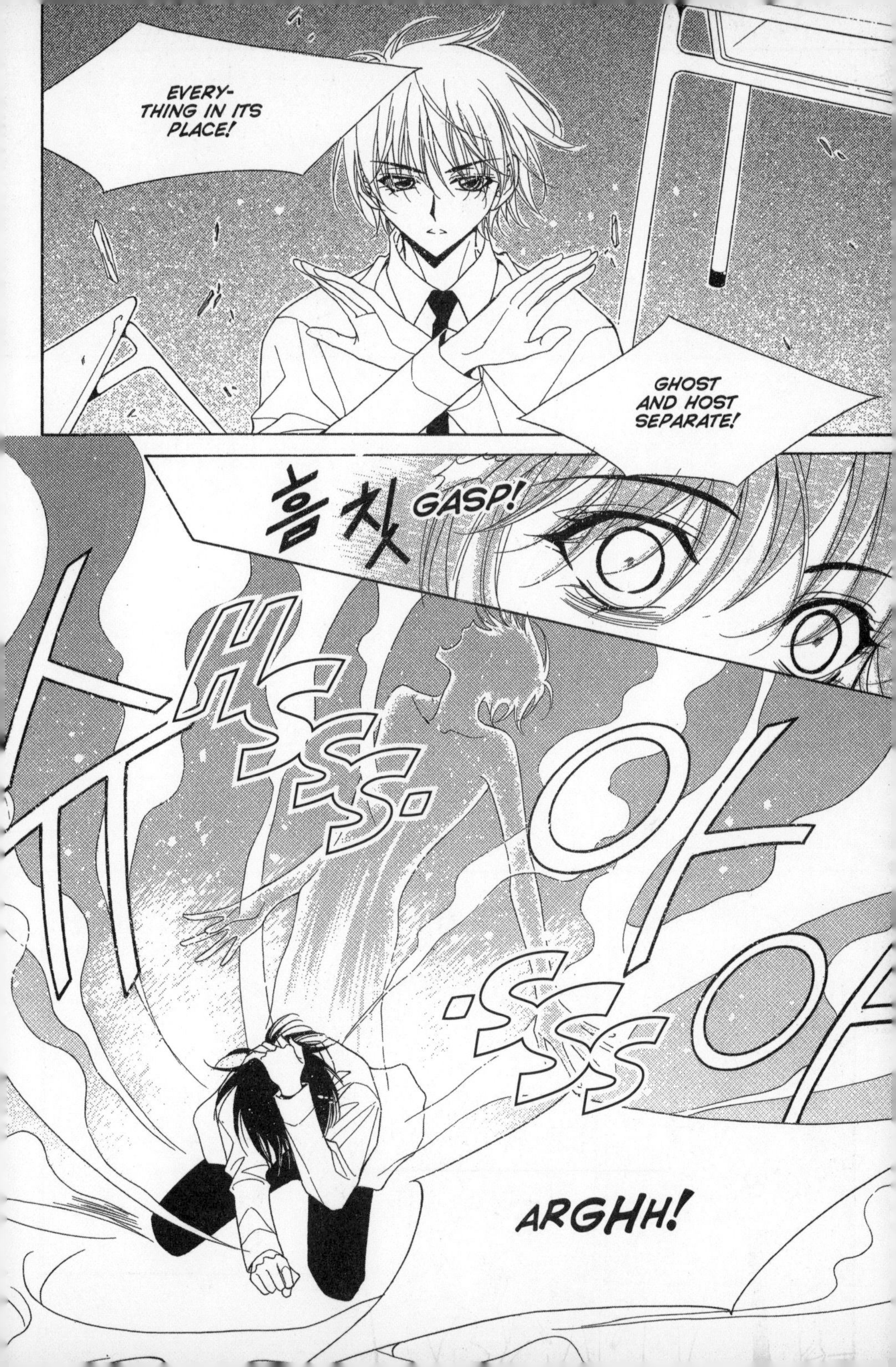
EVERY-
THING IN ITS
PLACE!
GHOST
AND HOST
SEPARATE!
흠칫 GASP!
HSSS.
SSS
ARGHH!

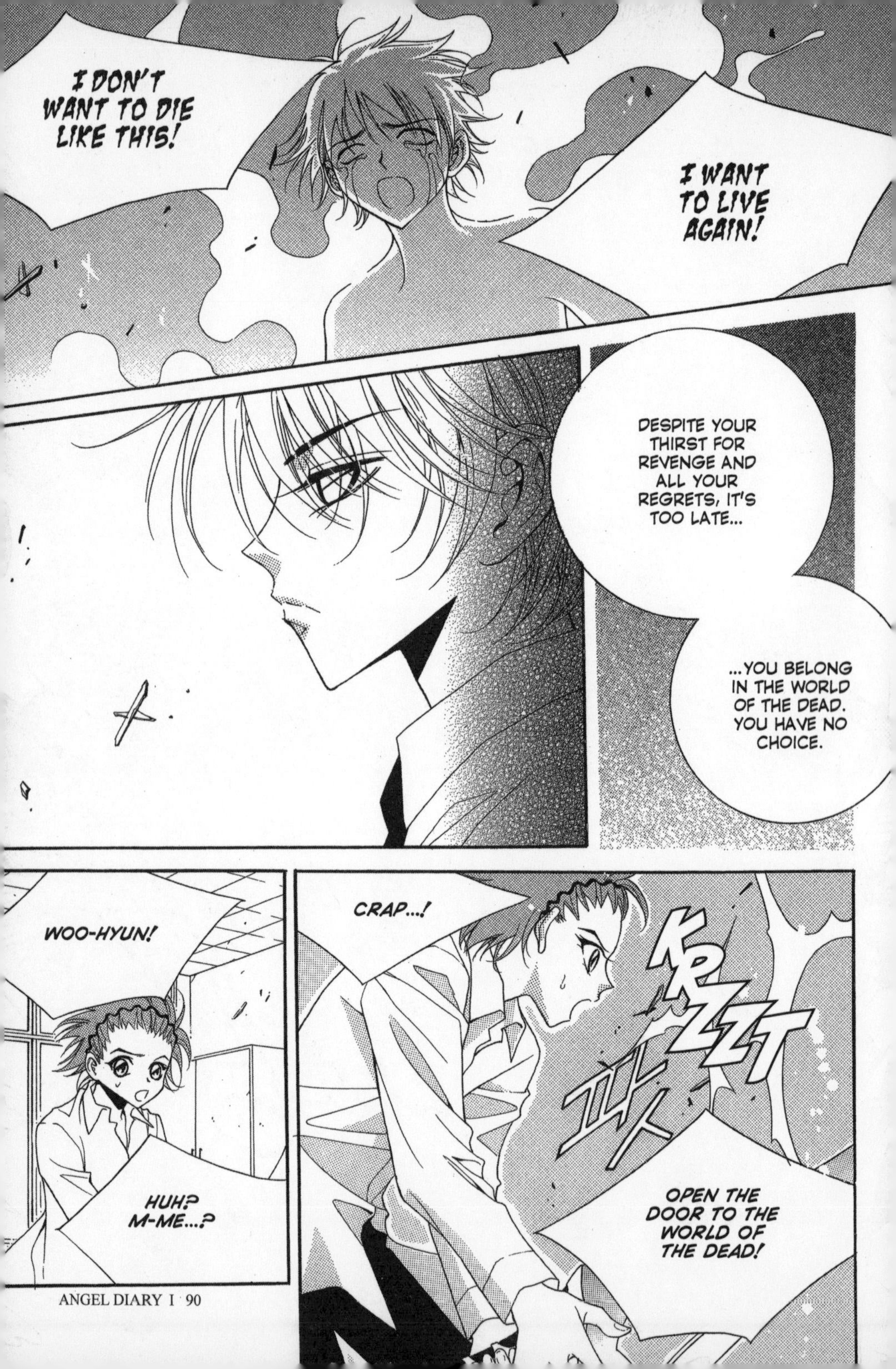
I DON'T WANT TO DIE LIKE THIS!
I WANT TO LIVE AGAIN!
DESPITE YOUR THIRST FOR REVENGE AND ALL YOUR REGRETS, IT'S TOO LATE...
...YOU BELONG IN THE WORLD OF THE DEAD. YOU HAVE NO CHOICE.
WOO-HYUN!
HUH? M-ME...?
CRAP...!
KRZZZT
OPEN THE DOOR TO THE WORLD OF THE DEAD!

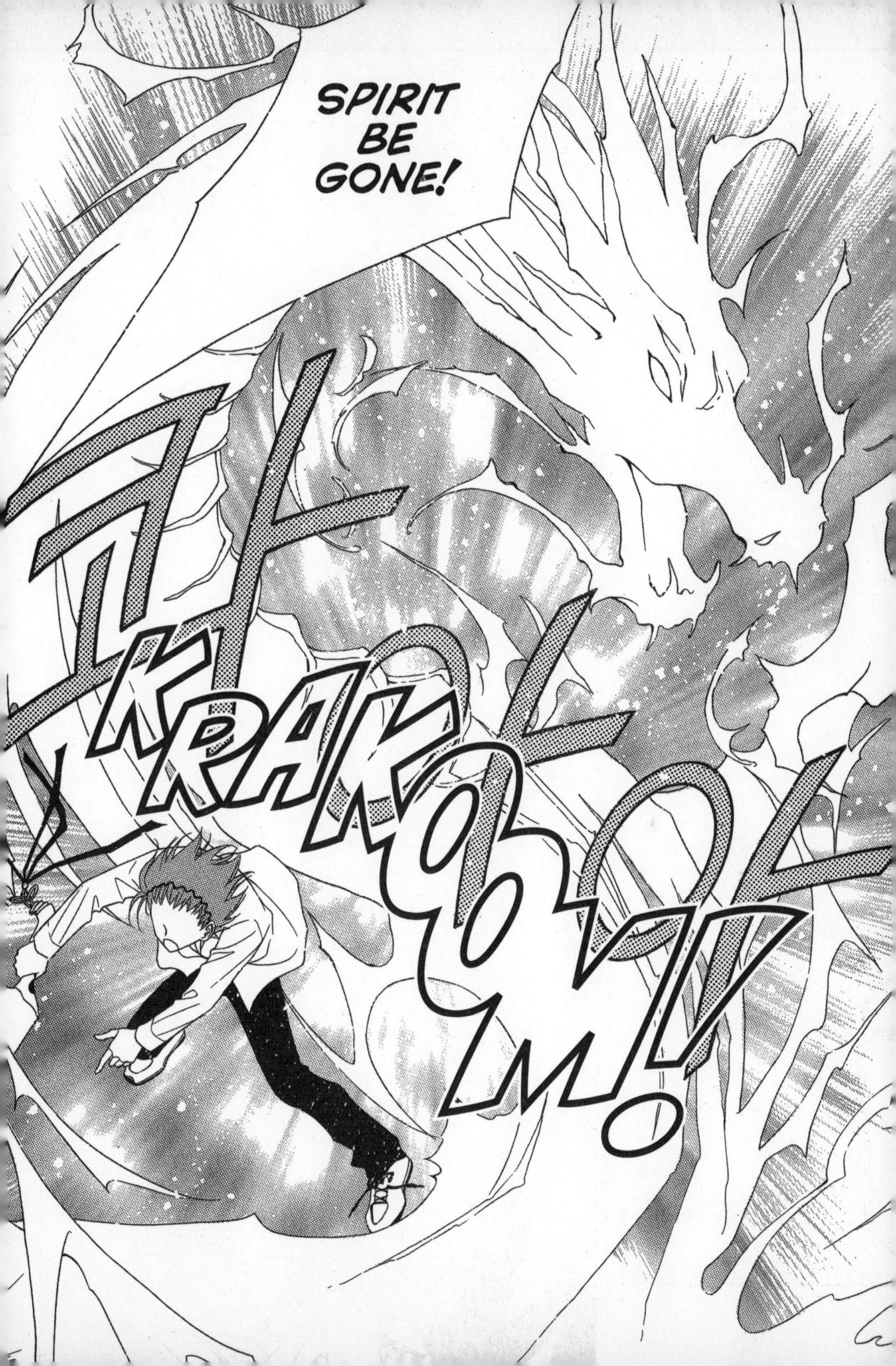
SPIRIT BE GONE!
KRAKOOOM!!

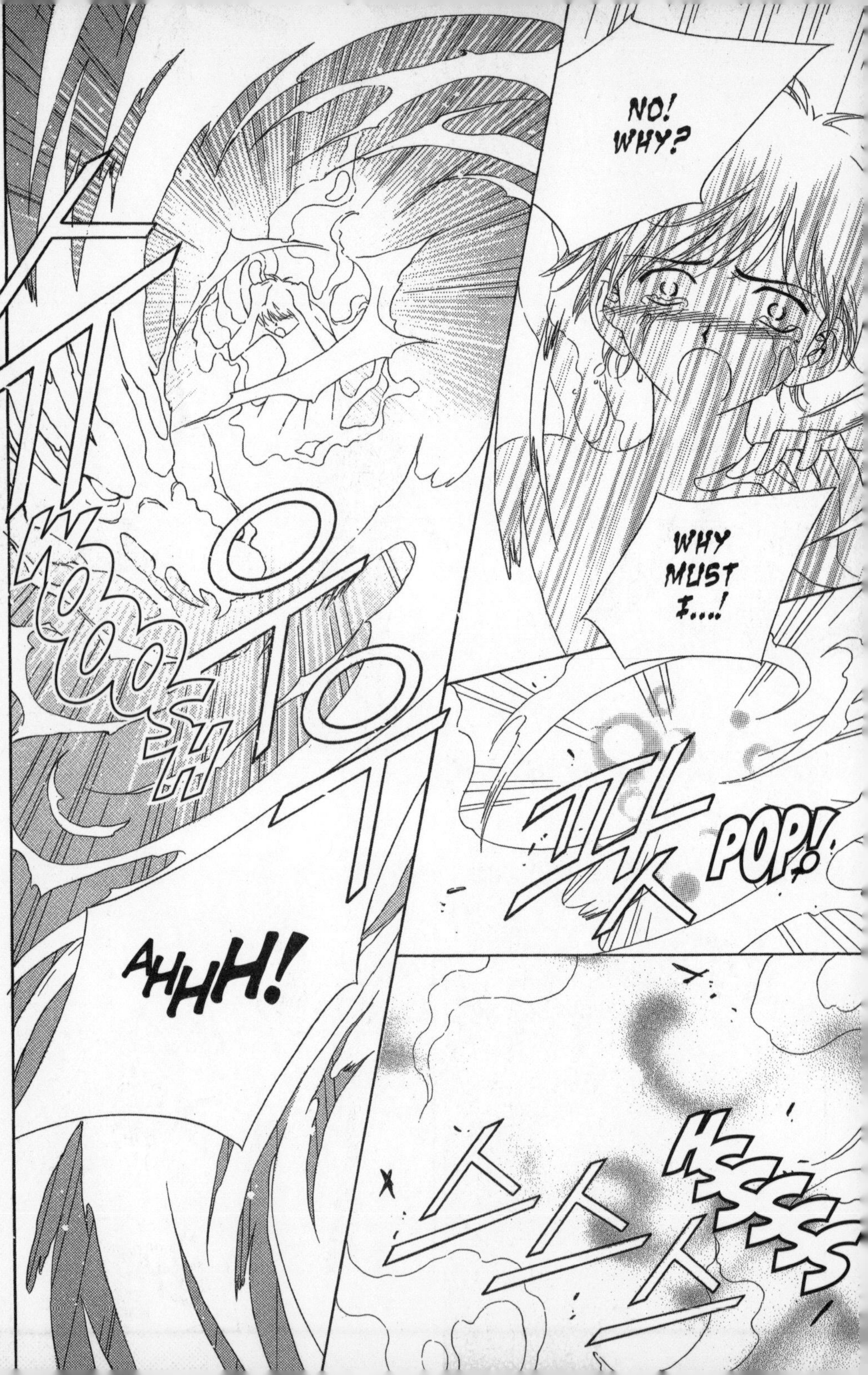
WHOOOOSH
AHHH!
NO! WHY?
WHY MUST I...!
POP!
HSSSS

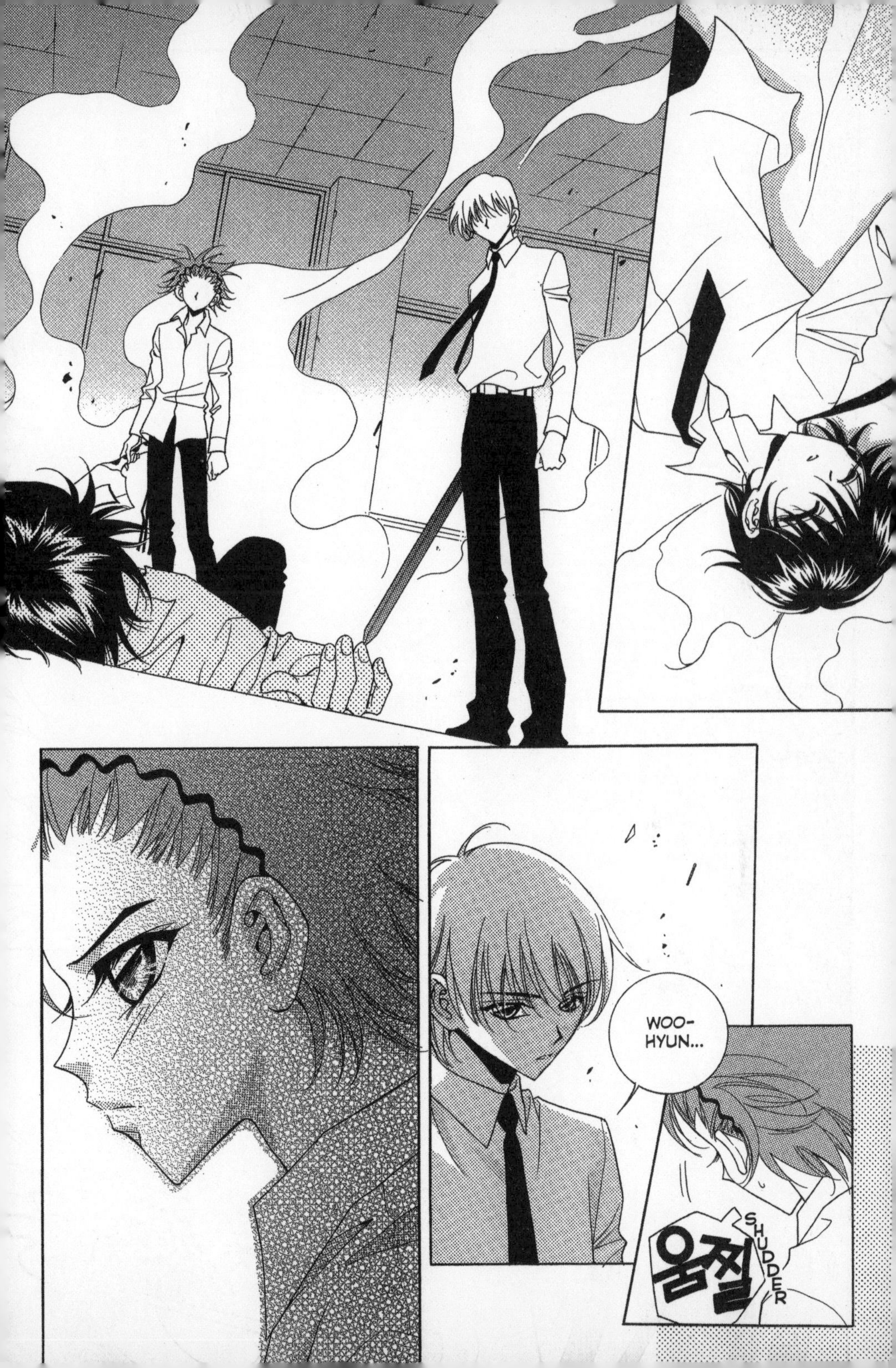
WOO-
HYUN...
움찔
SHUDDER

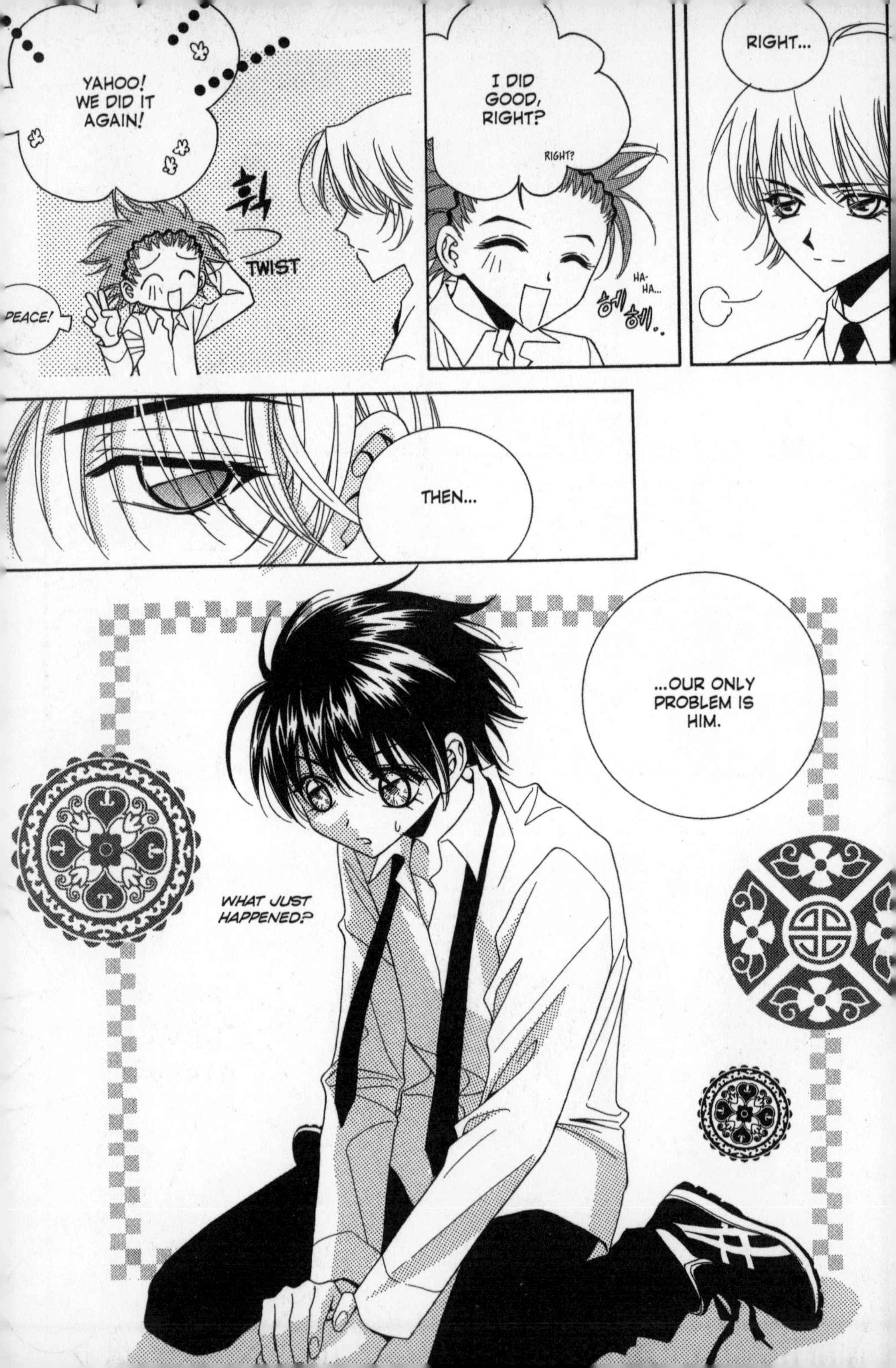
YAHOO! WE DID IT AGAIN!
휙
TWIST
PEACE!
I DID GOOD, RIGHT?
RIGHT?
HA-HA...
헤헤..
RIGHT...
THEN...
...OUR ONLY PROBLEM IS HIM.
WHAT JUST HAPPENED?

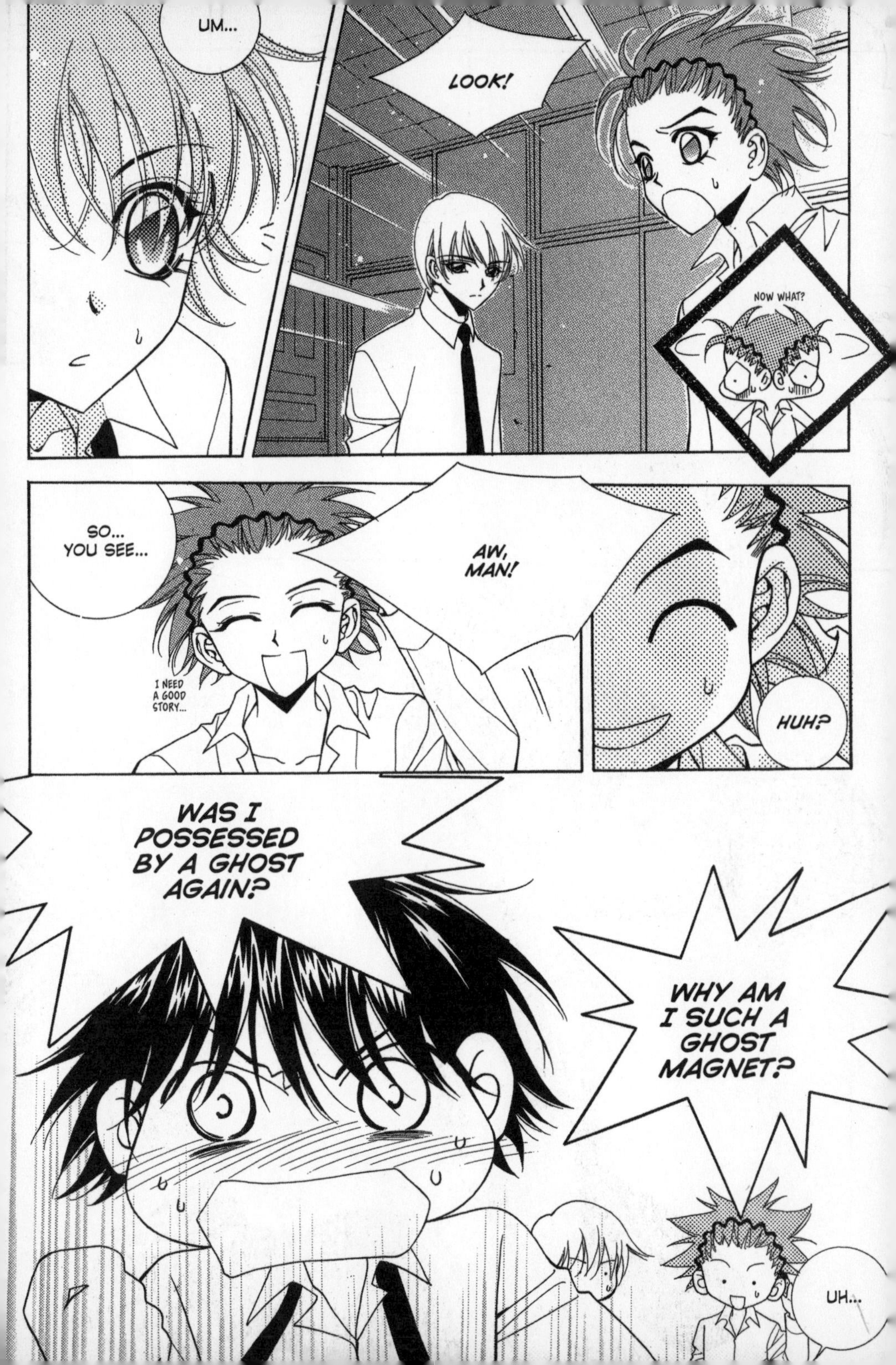
UM...
LOOK!
NOW WHAT?
SO... YOU SEE...
AW, MAN!
I NEED A GOOD STORY...
HUH?
WAS I POSSESSED BY A GHOST AGAIN?
WHY AM I SUCH A GHOST MAGNET?
UH...

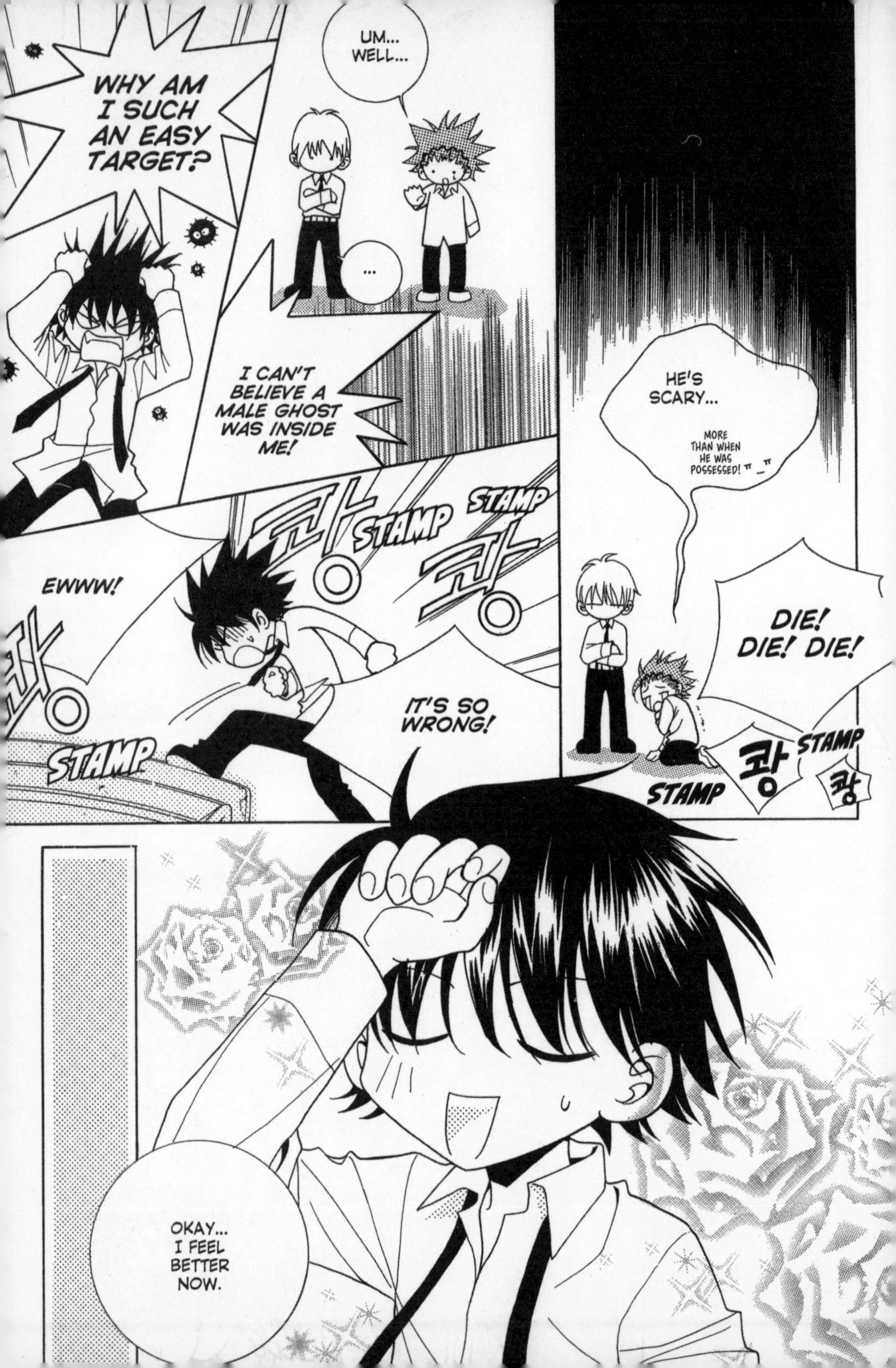
WHY AM I SUCH AN EASY TARGET?
UM... WELL...
...
I CAN'T BELIEVE A MALE GHOST WAS INSIDE ME!
EWWW!
쾅
쾅
STAMP
STAMP
쾅
쾅
STAMP
IT'S SO WRONG!
HE'S SCARY...
MORE THAN WHEN HE WAS POSSESSED! ㅠ_ㅠ
DIE! DIE! DIE!
STAMP
쾅
STAMP
쾅
OKAY... I FEEL BETTER NOW.

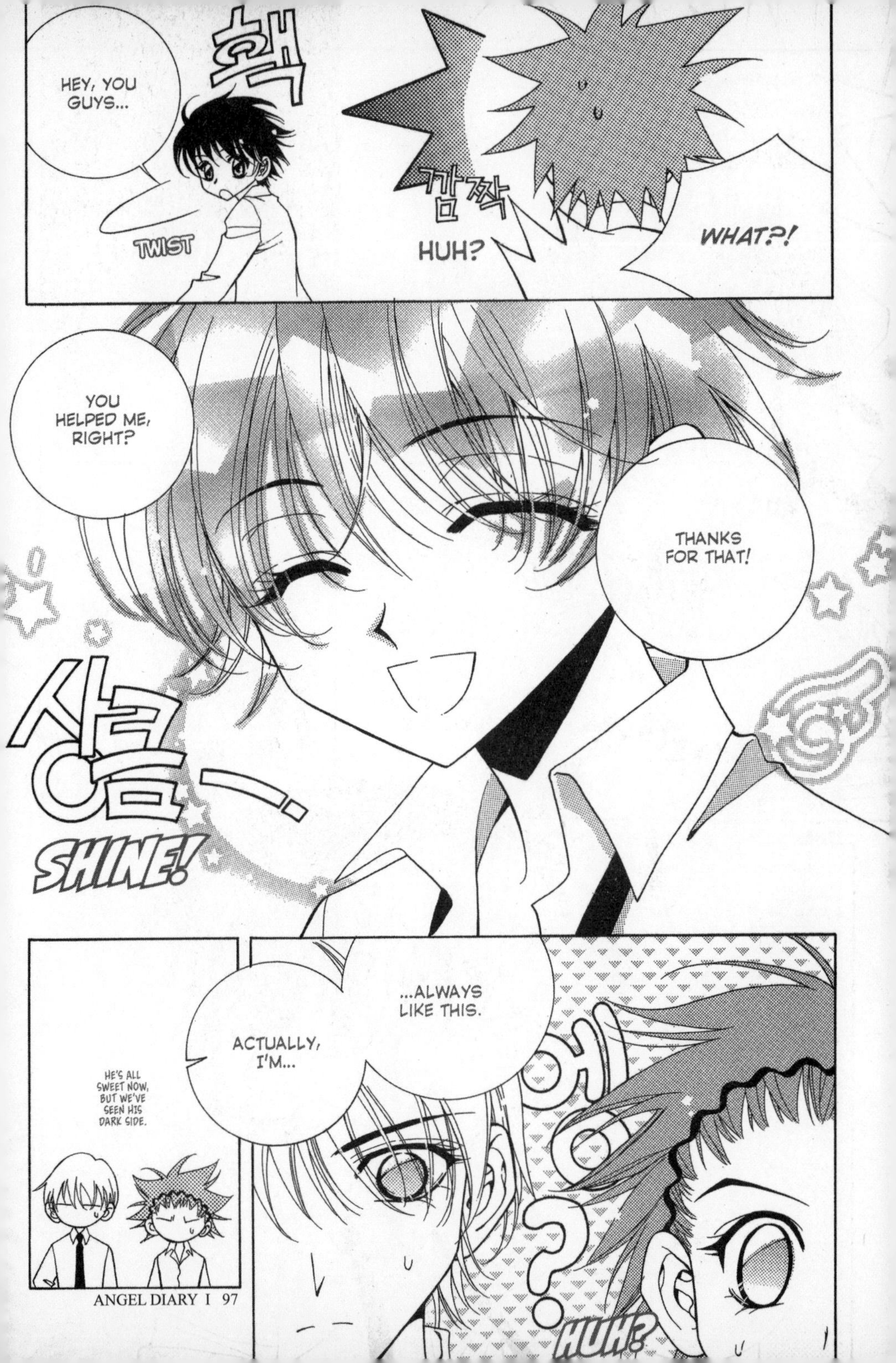
HEY, YOU GUYS...
홱
TWIST
깜짝
HUH?
WHAT?!
YOU HELPED ME, RIGHT?
THANKS FOR THAT!
SHINE!
HE'S ALL SWEET NOW, BUT WE'VE SEEN HIS DARK SIDE.
ACTUALLY, I'M...
...ALWAYS LIKE THIS.
에?
HUH?

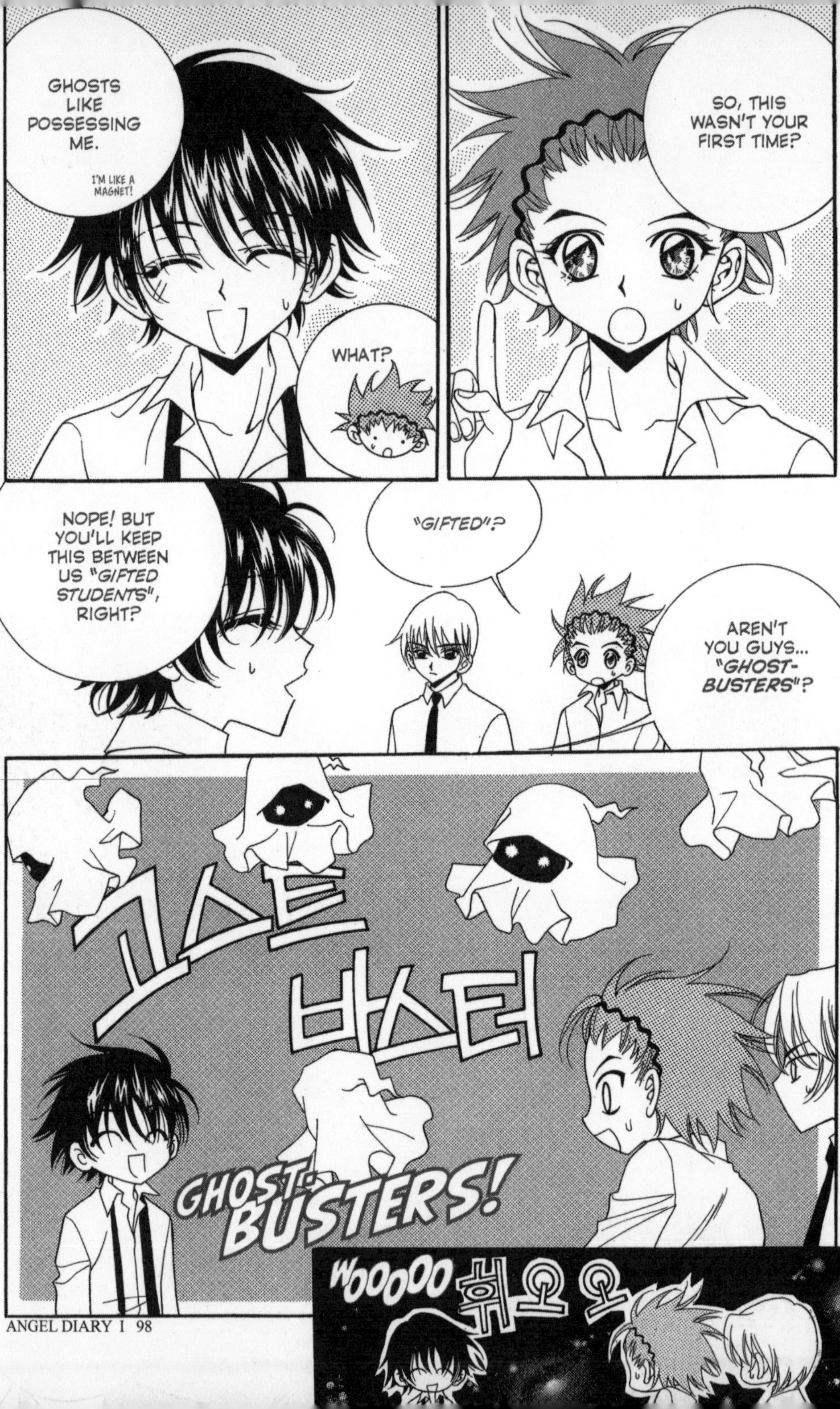
GHOSTS LIKE POSSESSING ME.
I'M LIKE A MAGNET!
WHAT?
SO, THIS WASN'T YOUR FIRST TIME?
NOPE! BUT YOU'LL KEEP THIS BETWEEN US "GIFTED STUDENTS", RIGHT?
"GIFTED"?
AREN'T YOU GUYS... "GHOST-BUSTERS"?
고스트 바스터
GHOST-BUSTERS!
WOOOOO 휘오오

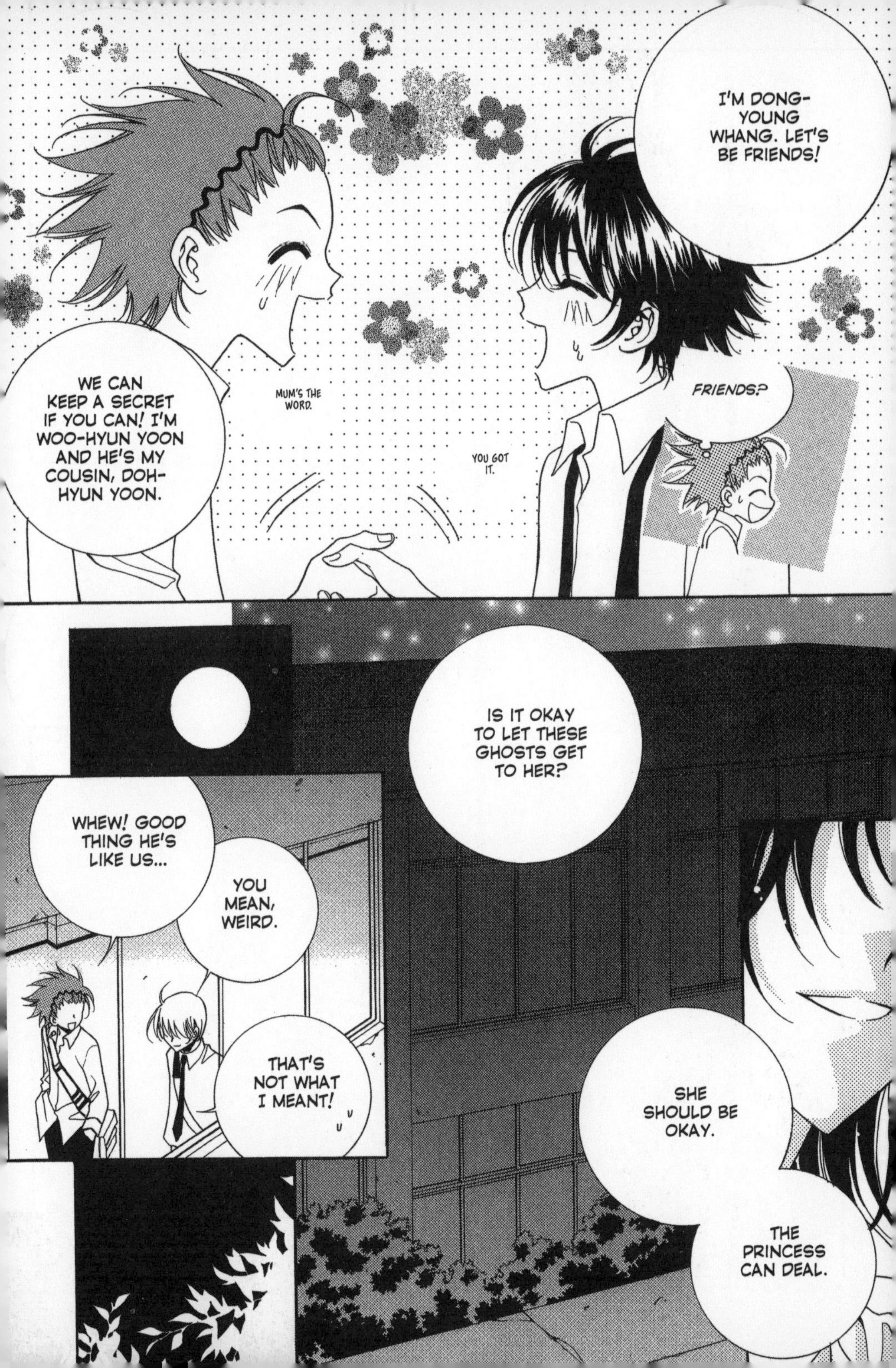
I'M DONG-YOUNG WHANG. LET'S BE FRIENDS!
WE CAN KEEP A SECRET IF YOU CAN! I'M WOO-HYUN YOON AND HE'S MY COUSIN, DOH-HYUN YOON.
MUM'S THE WORD.
YOU GOT IT.
FRIENDS?
WHEW! GOOD THING HE'S LIKE US...
YOU MEAN, WEIRD.
THAT'S NOT WHAT I MEANT!
IS IT OKAY TO LET THESE GHOSTS GET TO HER?
SHE SHOULD BE OKAY.
THE PRINCESS CAN DEAL.

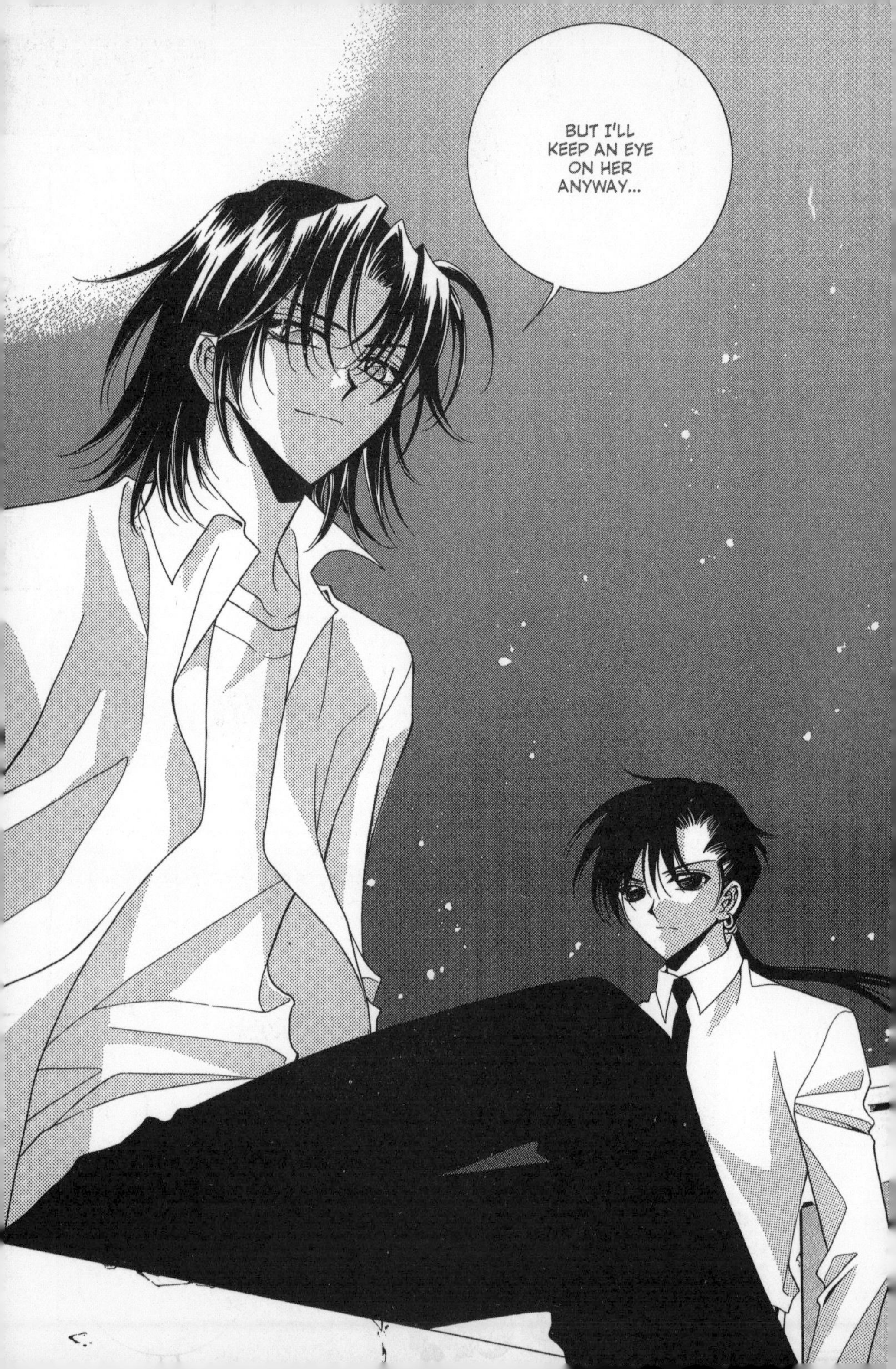
BUT I'LL KEEP AN EYE ON HER ANYWAY...

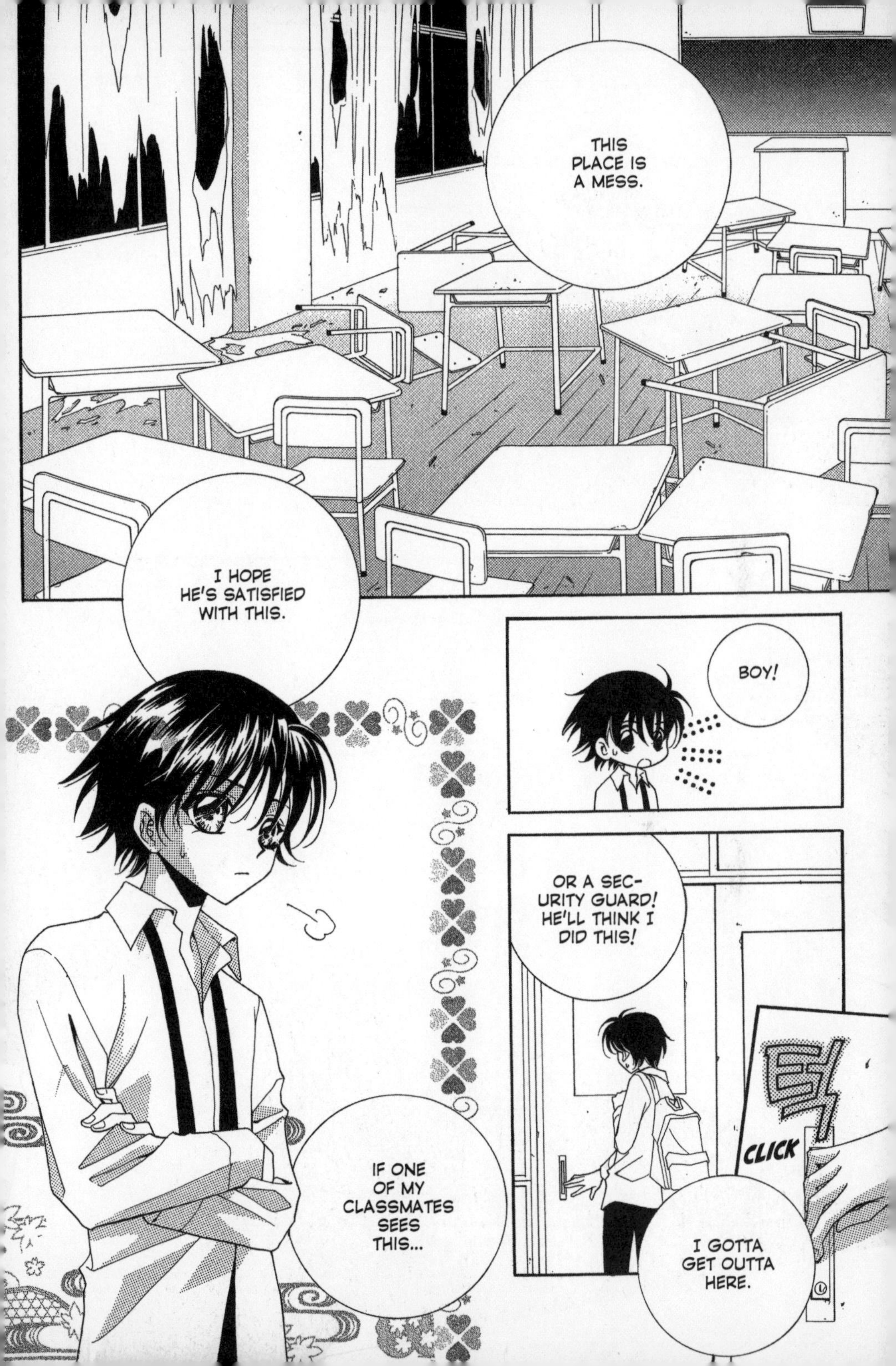
THIS PLACE IS A MESS.
I HOPE HE'S SATISFIED WITH THIS.
IF ONE OF MY CLASSMATES SEES THIS...
BOY!
OR A SEC-URITY GUARD! HE'LL THINK I DID THIS!
CLICK
I GOTTA GET OUTTA HERE.

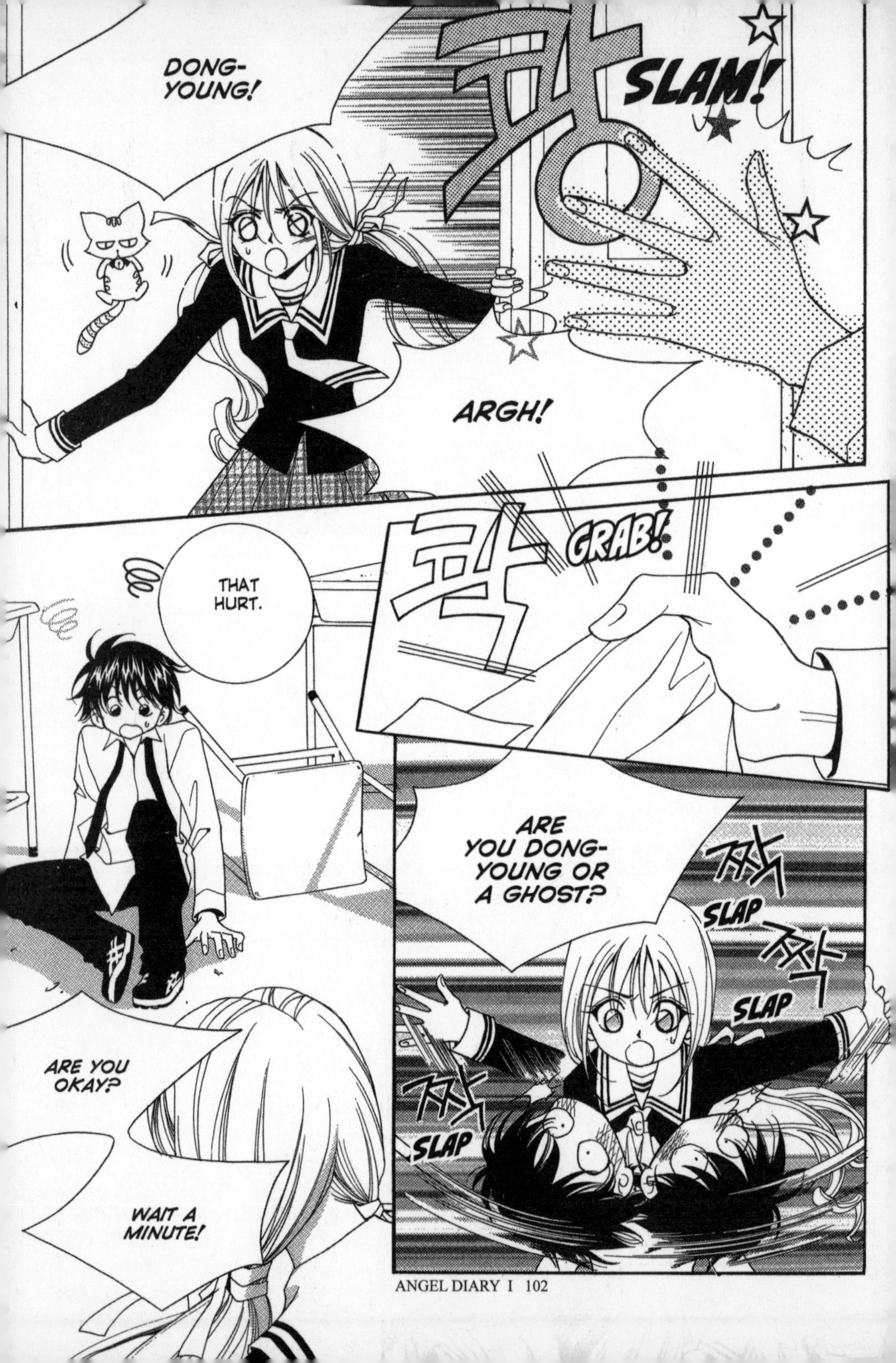
DONG-YOUNG!
SLAM!
ARGH!
THAT HURT.
ARE YOU OKAY?
WAIT A MINUTE!
GRAB!
ARE YOU DONG-YOUNG OR A GHOST?
SLAP
SLAP
SLAP

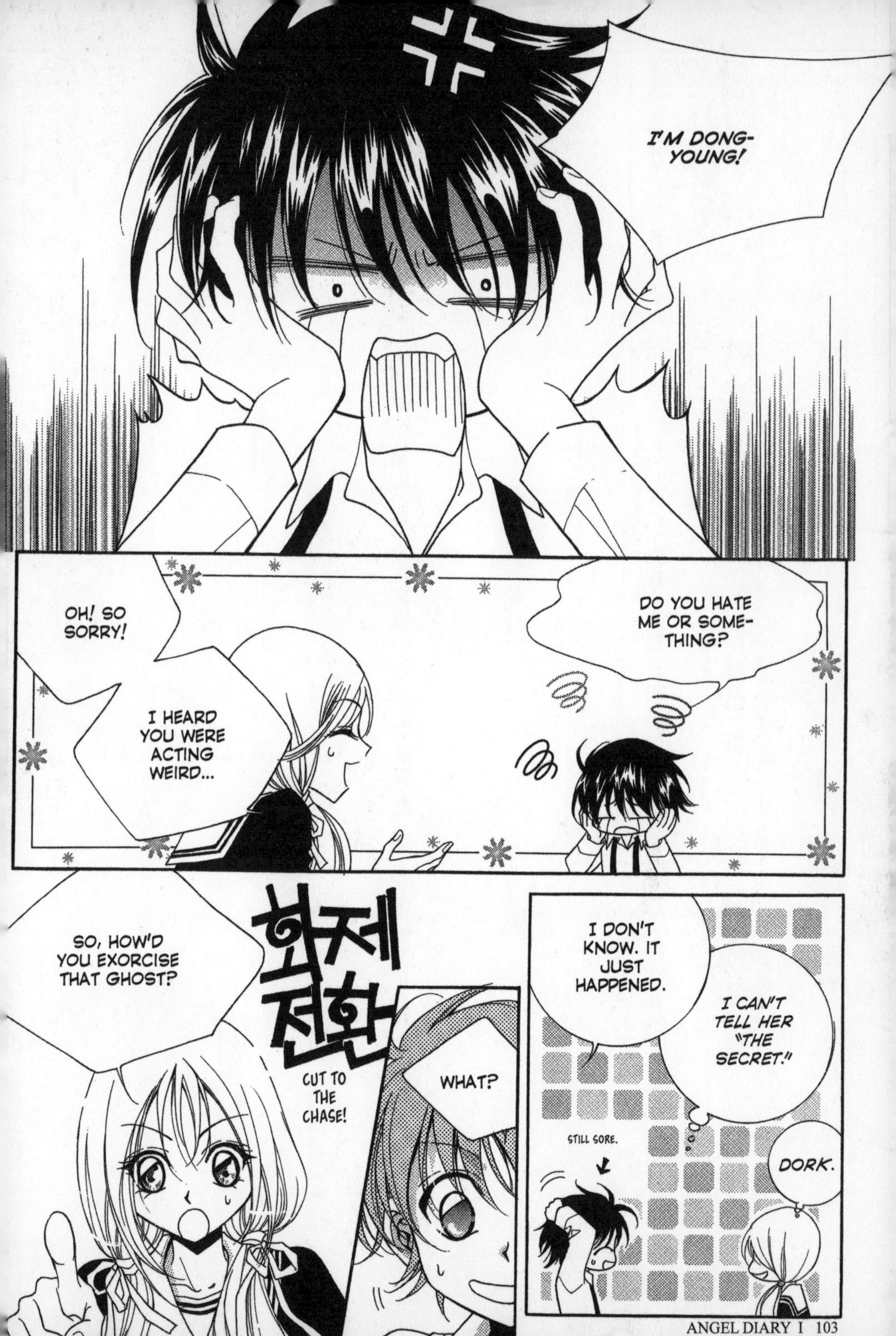
I'M DONG-YOUNG!
OH! SO SORRY!
I HEARD YOU WERE ACTING WEIRD...
DO YOU HATE ME OR SOME-THING?
SO, HOW'D YOU EXORCISE THAT GHOST?
화제 전환
CUT TO THE CHASE!
WHAT?
I DON'T KNOW. IT JUST HAPPENED.
I CAN'T TELL HER "THE SECRET."
STILL SORE.
DORK.

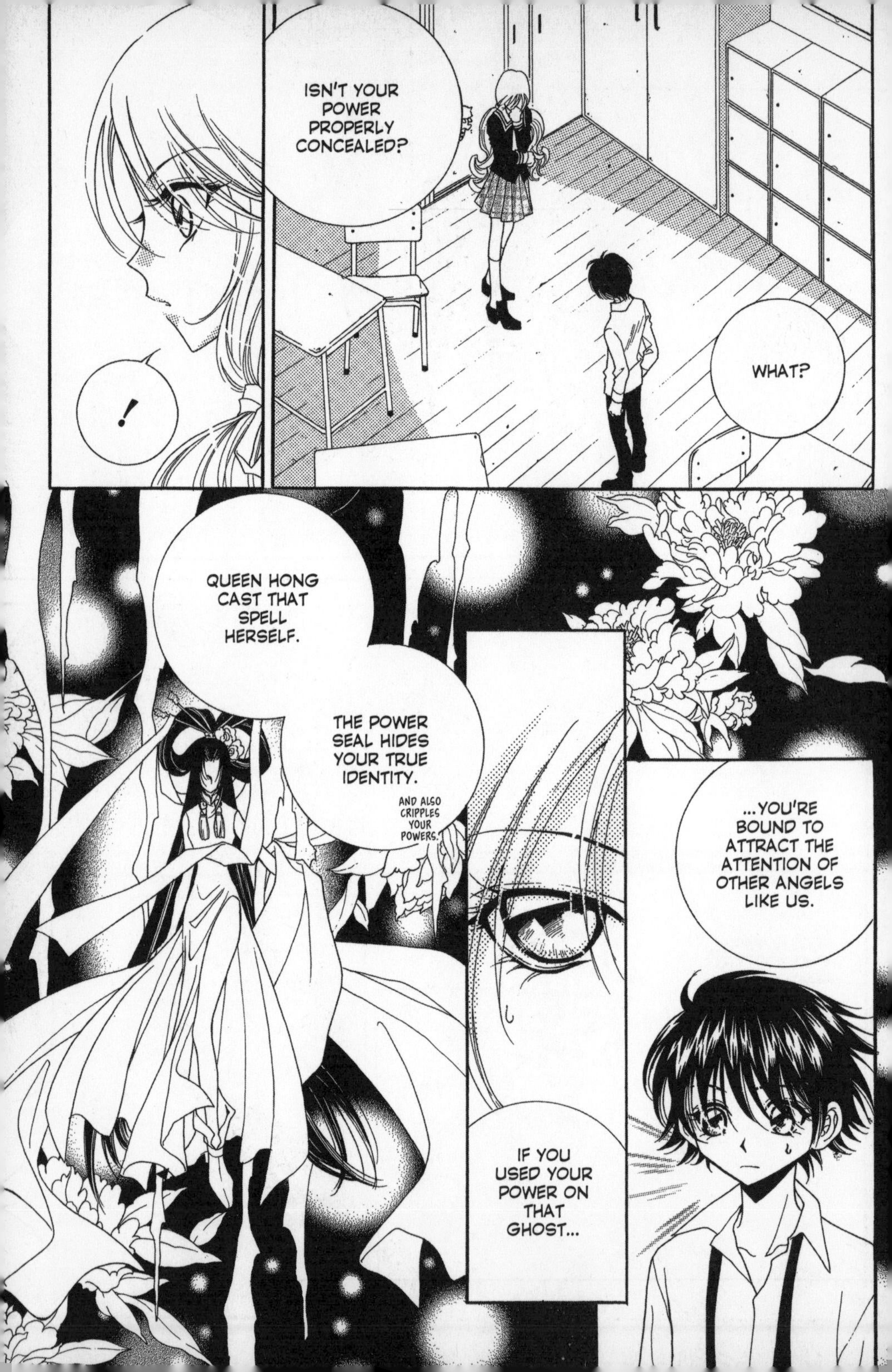
!
ISN'T YOUR POWER PROPERLY CONCEALED?
WHAT?
QUEEN HONG CAST THAT SPELL HERSELF.
THE POWER SEAL HIDES YOUR TRUE IDENTITY.
AND ALSO CRIPPLES YOUR POWERS.
IF YOU USED YOUR POWER ON THAT GHOST...
...YOU'RE BOUND TO ATTRACT THE ATTENTION OF OTHER ANGELS LIKE US.

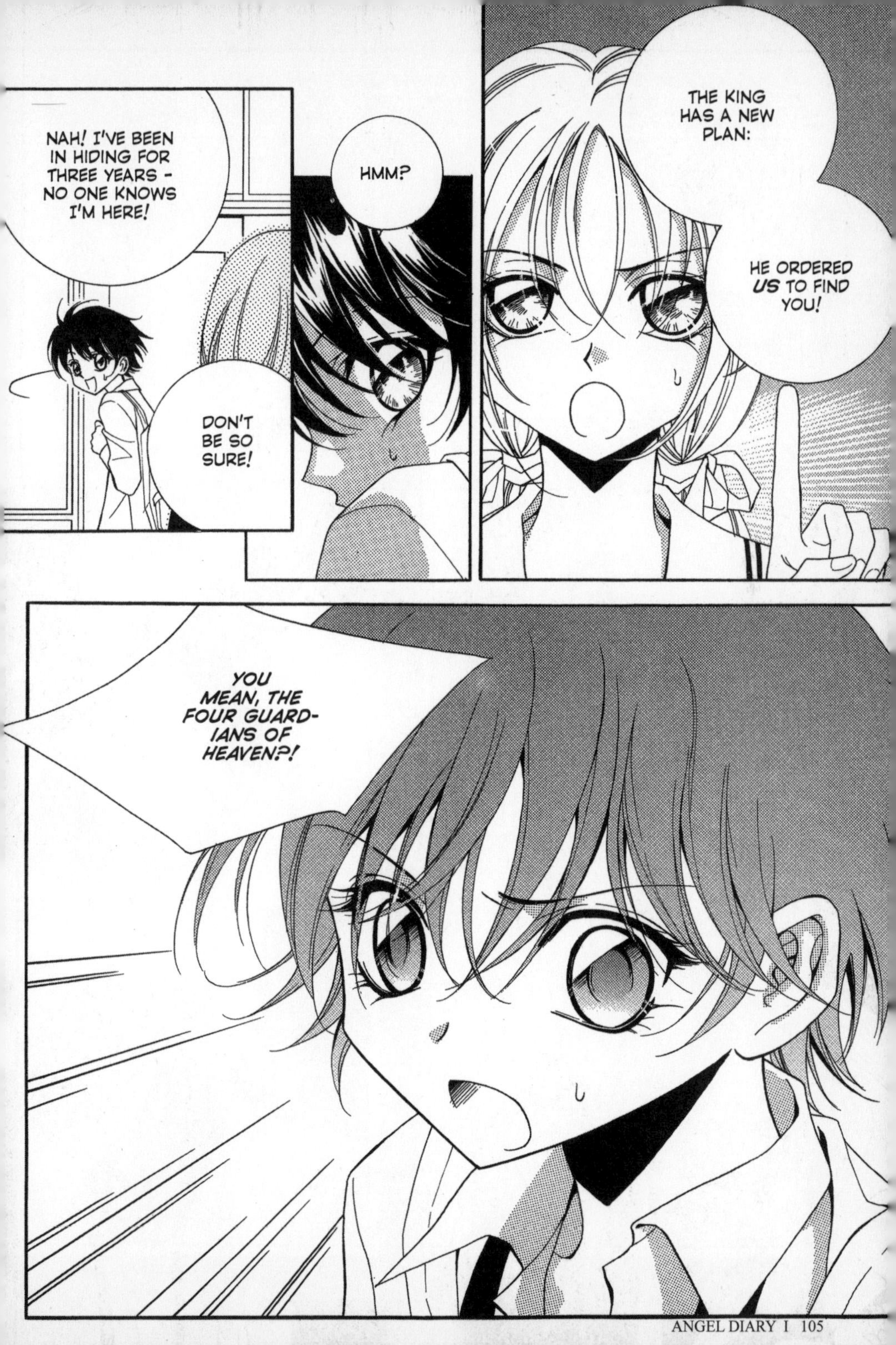

NAH! I'VE BEEN IN HIDING FOR THREE YEARS - NO ONE KNOWS I'M HERE!
HMM?
DON'T BE SO SURE!
THE KING HAS A NEW PLAN:
HE ORDERED *US* TO FIND YOU!
YOU MEAN, THE FOUR GUARDIANS OF HEAVEN?!

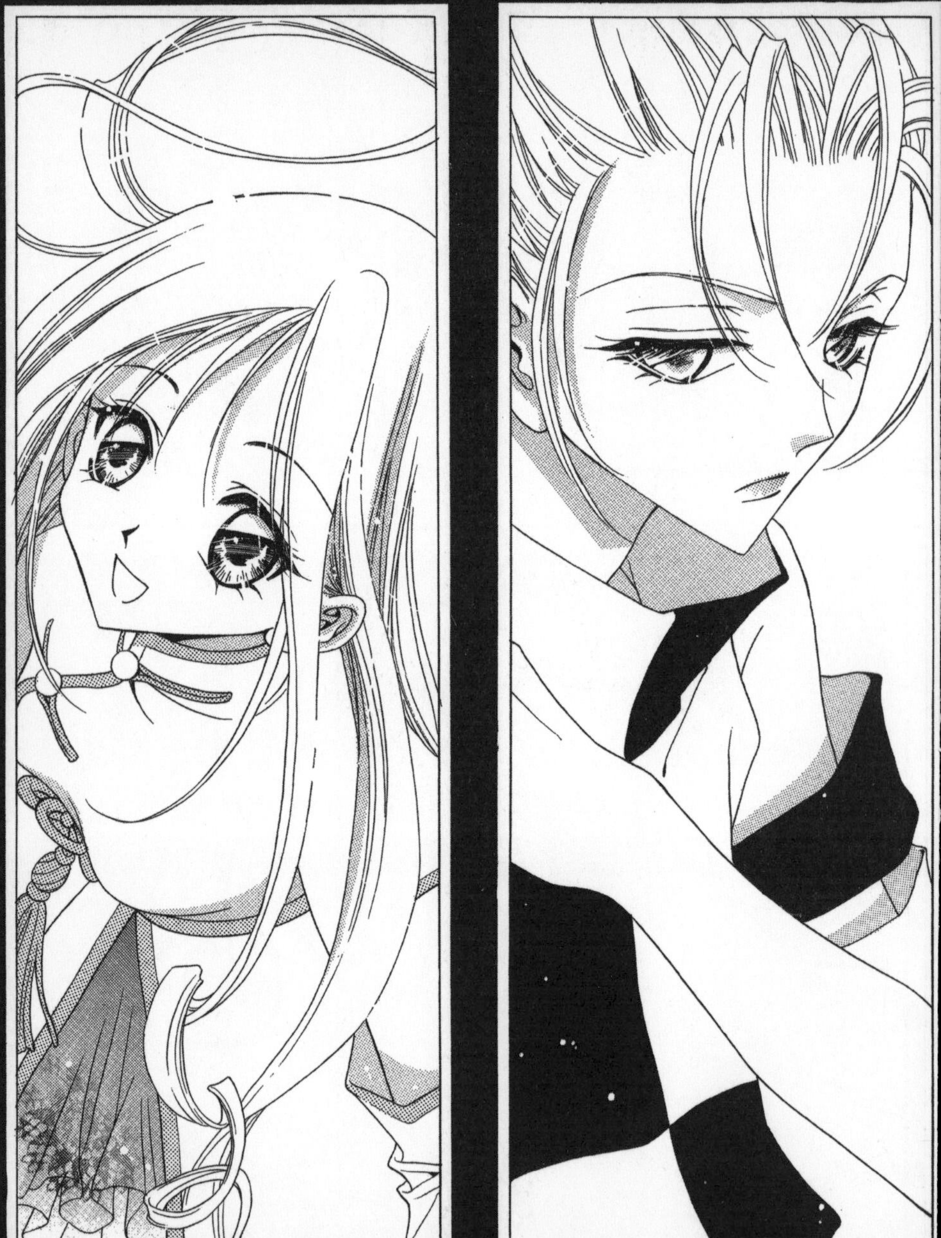

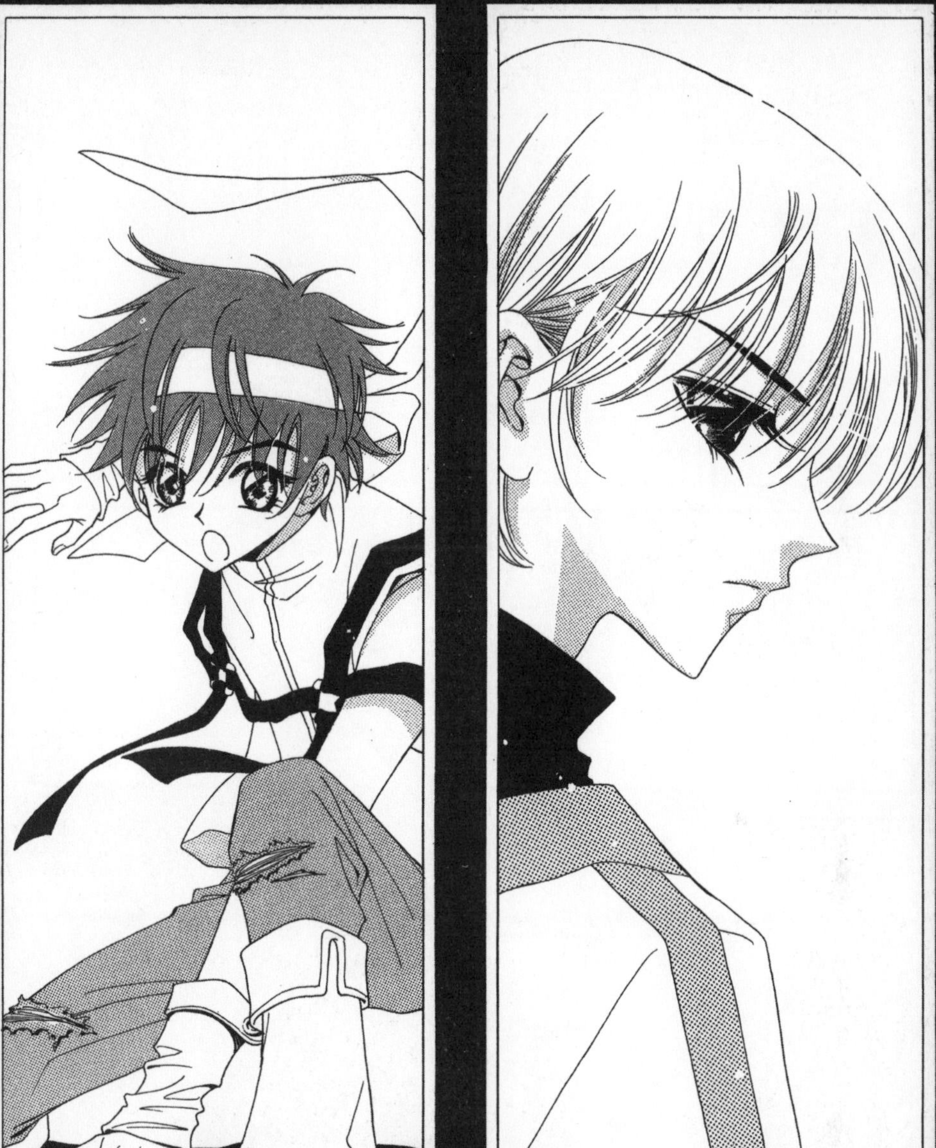

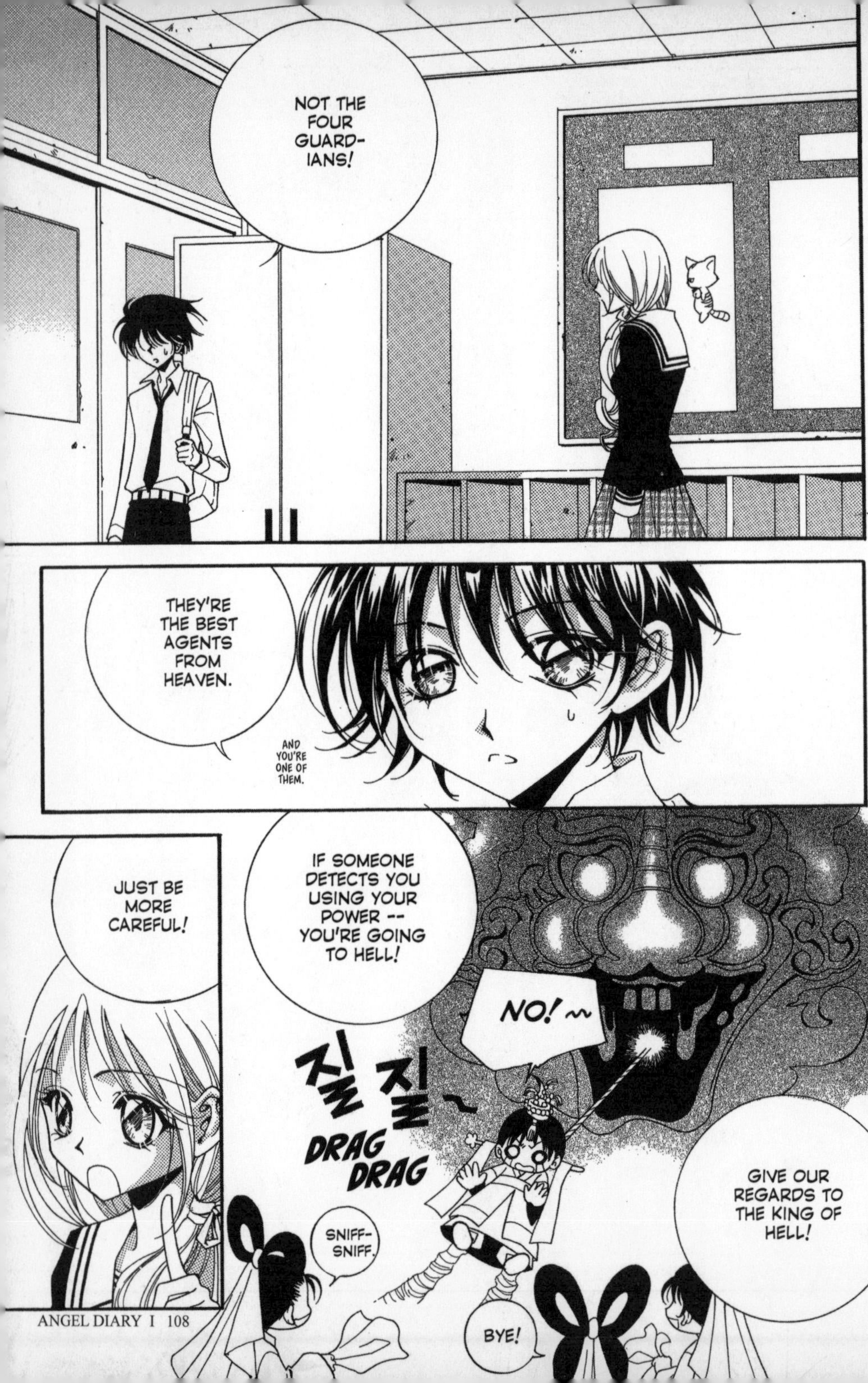
NOT THE FOUR GUARD-IANS!
THEY'RE THE BEST AGENTS FROM HEAVEN.
AND YOU'RE ONE OF THEM.
JUST BE MORE CAREFUL!
IF SOMEONE DETECTS YOU USING YOUR POWER -- YOU'RE GOING TO HELL!
NO!~
질질~
DRAG DRAG
SNIFF-SNIFF.
GIVE OUR REGARDS TO THE KING OF HELL!
BYE!

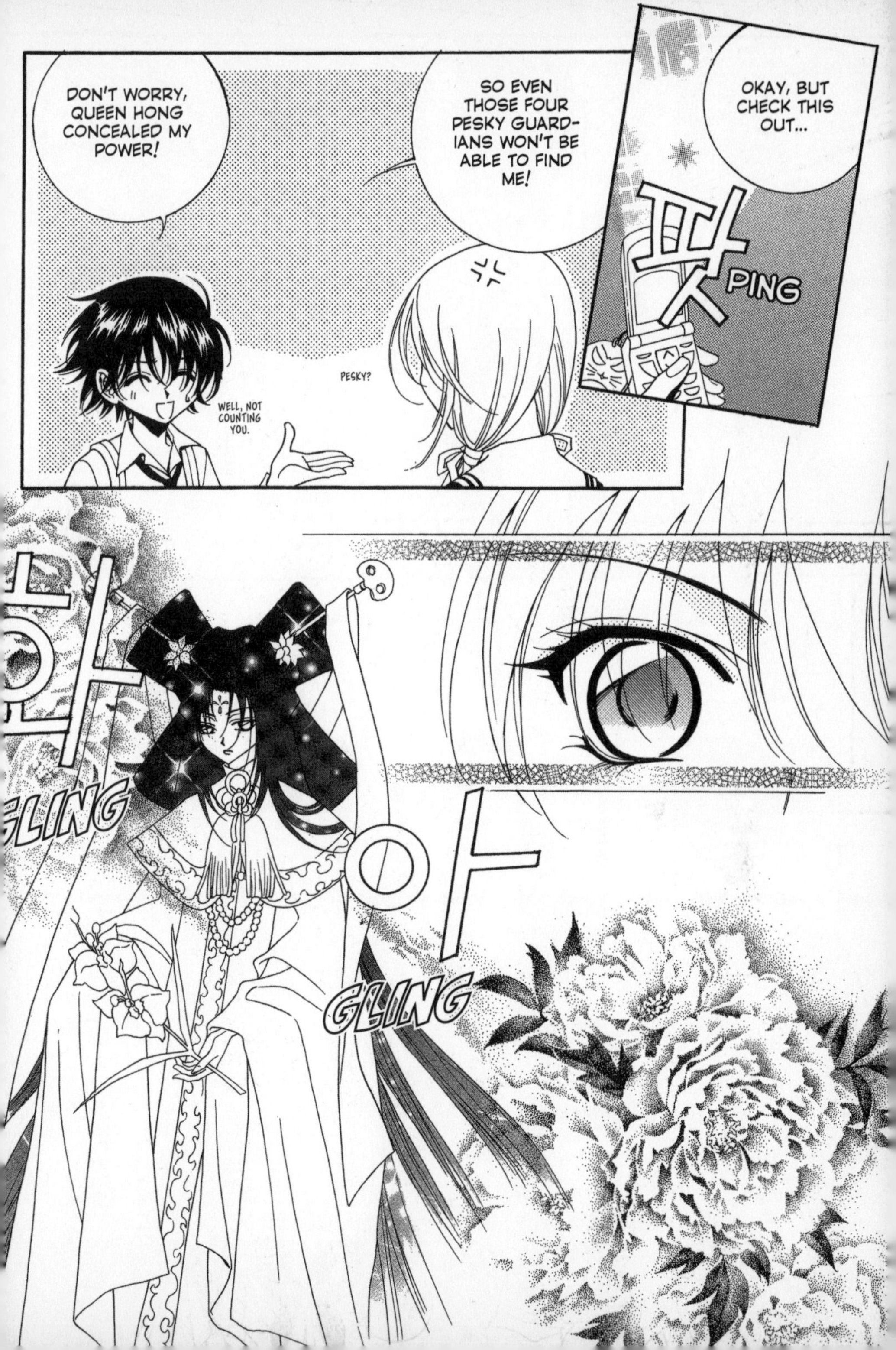
DON'T WORRY, QUEEN HONG CONCEALED MY POWER!
SO EVEN THOSE FOUR PESKY GUARDIANS WON'T BE ABLE TO FIND ME!
PESKY?
WELL, NOT COUNTING YOU.
OKAY, BUT CHECK THIS OUT...
팍
PING
GLING
아
GLING

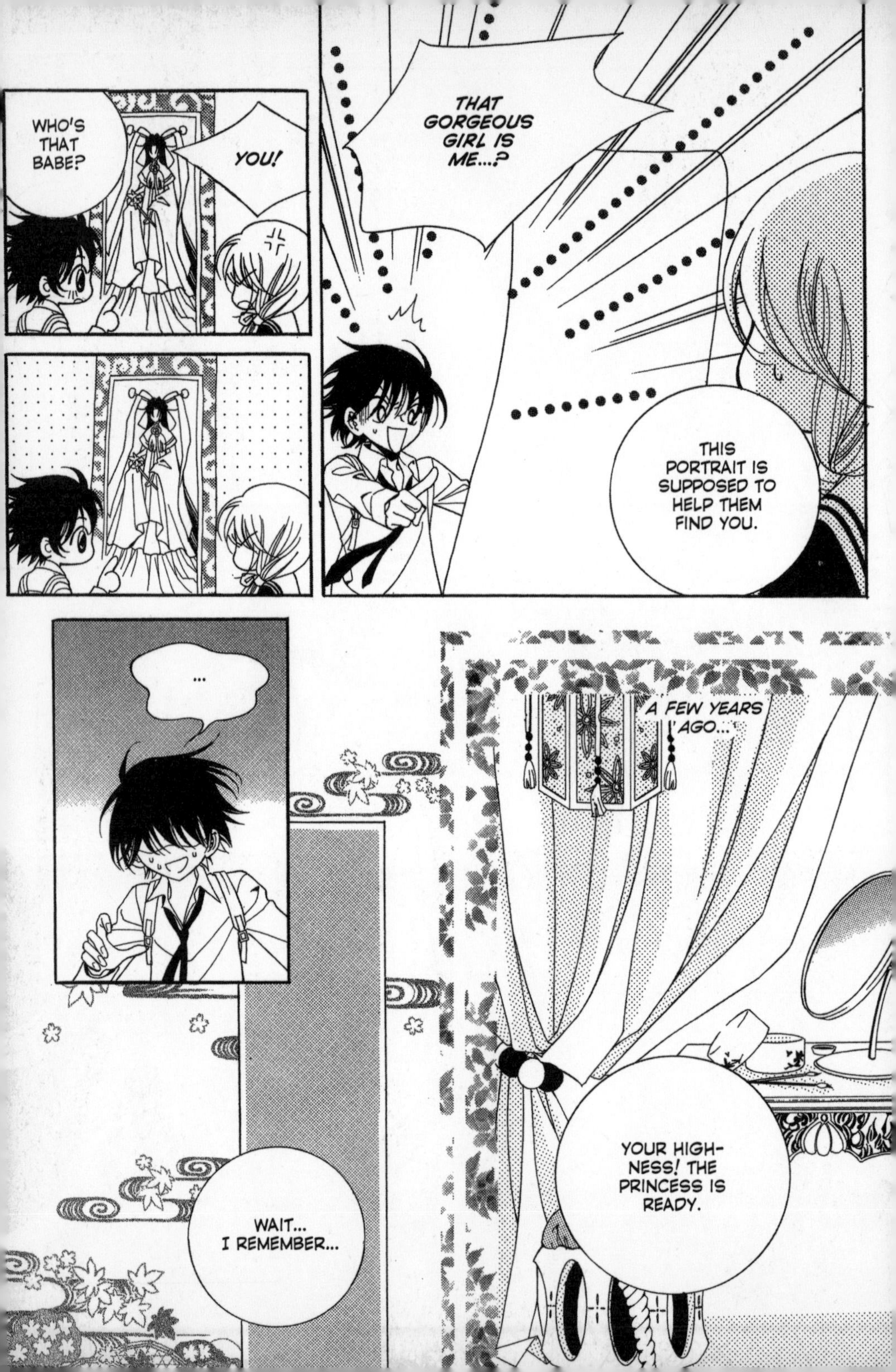
WHO'S THAT BABE?
YOU!
THAT GORGEOUS GIRL IS ME...?
THIS PORTRAIT IS SUPPOSED TO HELP THEM FIND YOU.
...
WAIT... I REMEMBER...
A FEW YEARS AGO...
YOUR HIGH-NESS! THE PRINCESS IS READY.

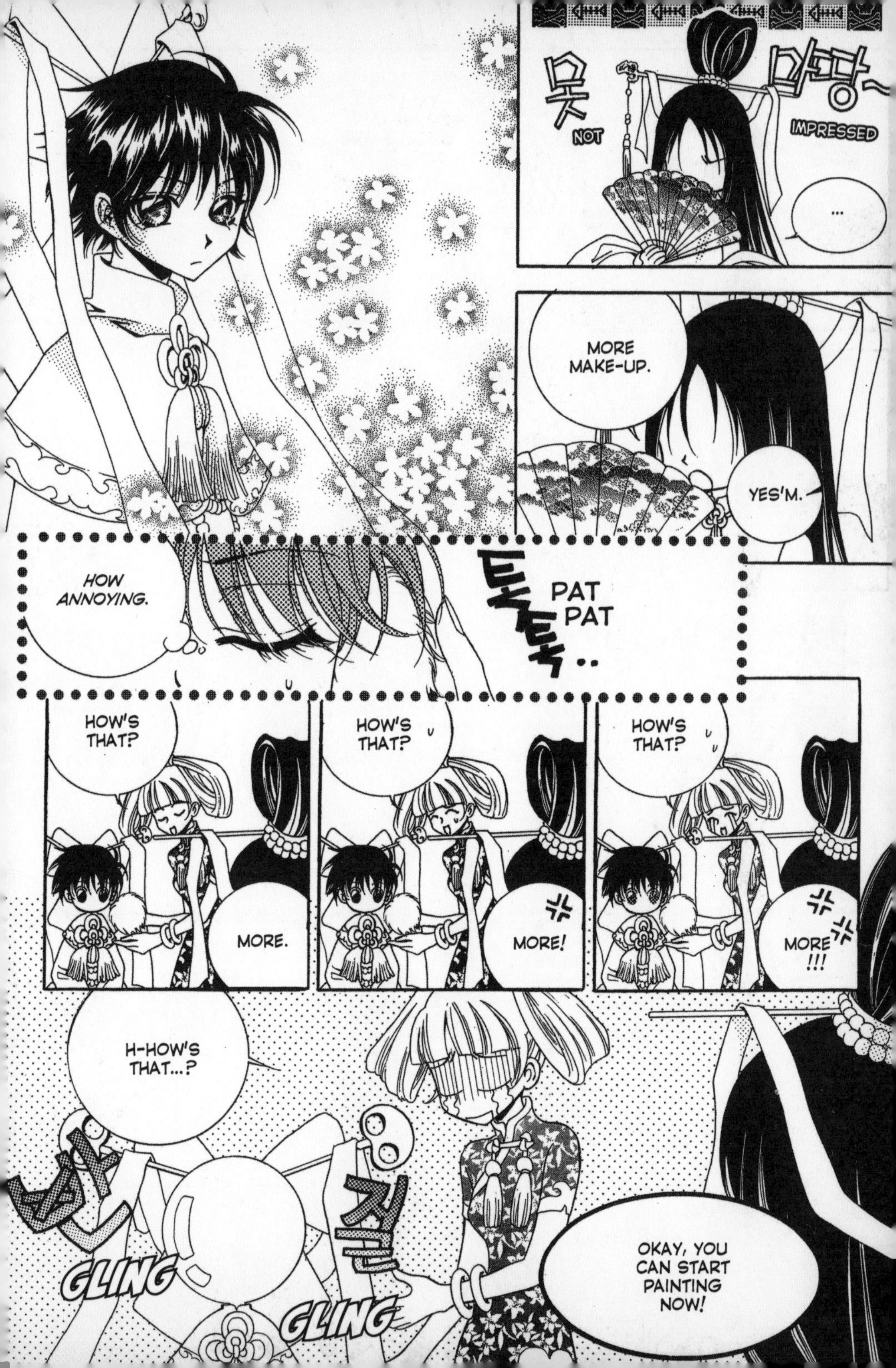
못
NOT
마땅~
IMPRESSED
...
MORE MAKE-UP.
YES'M.
HOW ANNOYING.
PAT PAT..
HOW'S THAT?
MORE.
HOW'S THAT?
MORE!
HOW'S THAT?
MORE !!!
H-HOW'S THAT...?
GLING
GLING
OKAY, YOU CAN START PAINTING NOW!

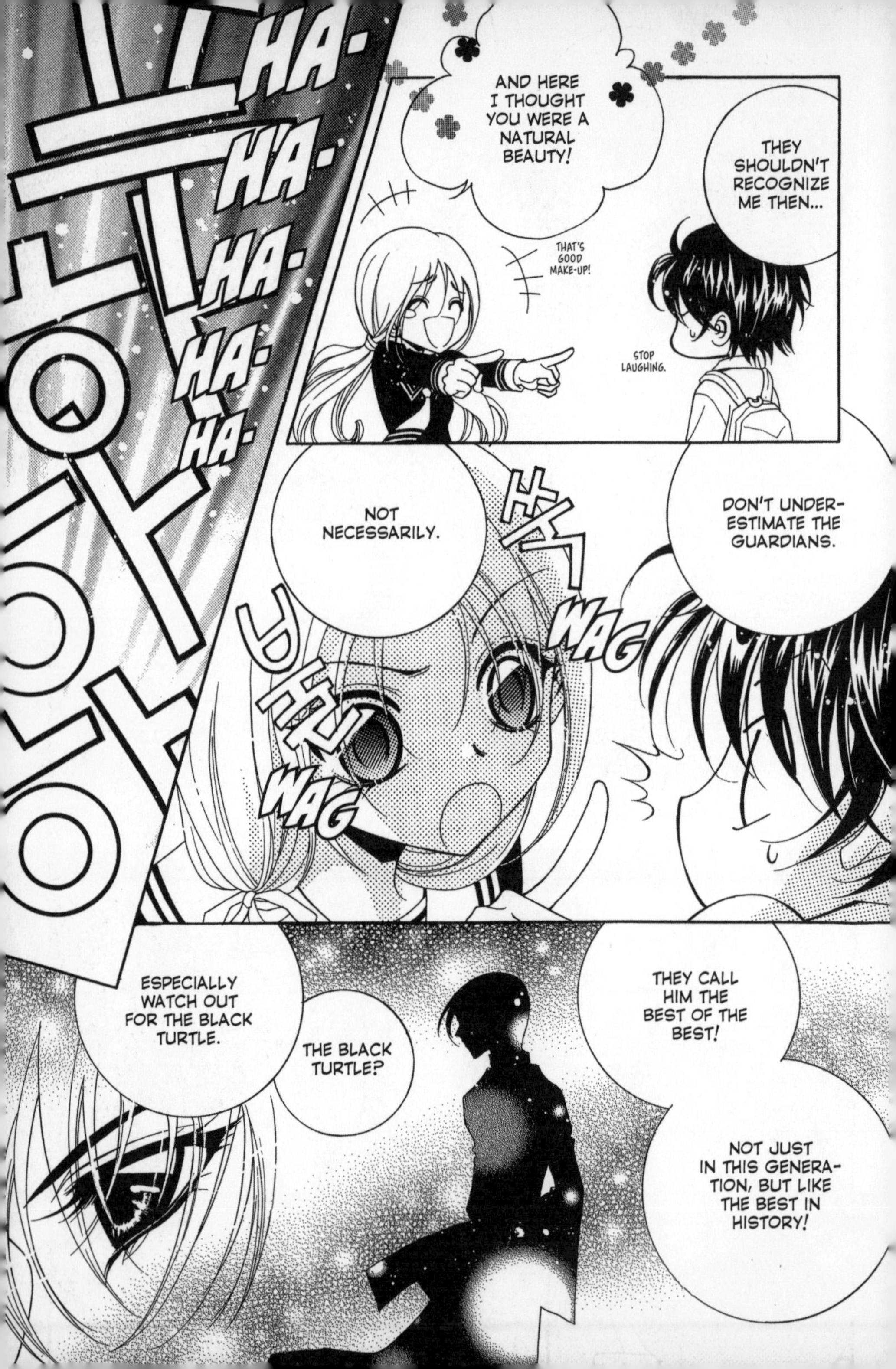
HA-
HA-
HA-
HA-
HA-
AND HERE I THOUGHT YOU WERE A NATURAL BEAUTY!
THAT'S GOOD MAKE-UP!
THEY SHOULDN'T RECOGNIZE ME THEN...
STOP LAUGHING.
NOT NECESSARILY.
WAG
WAG
DON'T UNDER-ESTIMATE THE GUARDIANS.
ESPECIALLY WATCH OUT FOR THE BLACK TURTLE.
THE BLACK TURTLE?
THEY CALL HIM THE BEST OF THE BEST!
NOT JUST IN THIS GENERA-TION, BUT LIKE THE BEST IN HISTORY!

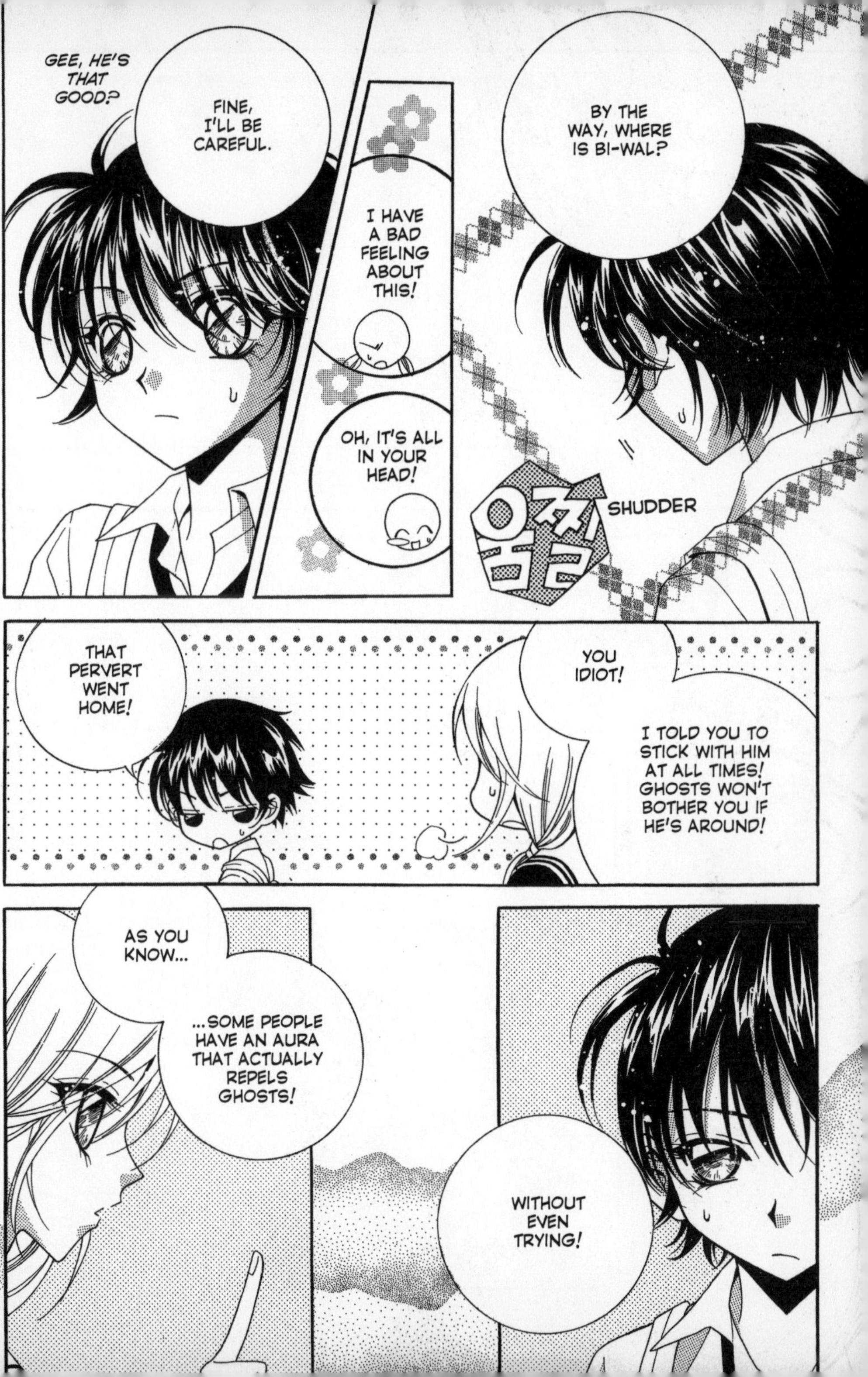
GEE, HE'S THAT GOOD?
FINE, I'LL BE CAREFUL.
I HAVE A BAD FEELING ABOUT THIS!
OH, IT'S ALL IN YOUR HEAD!
BY THE WAY, WHERE IS BI-WAL?
움찔
SHUDDER
THAT PERVERT WENT HOME!
YOU IDIOT!
I TOLD YOU TO STICK WITH HIM AT ALL TIMES! GHOSTS WON'T BOTHER YOU IF HE'S AROUND!
AS YOU KNOW...
...SOME PEOPLE HAVE AN AURA THAT ACTUALLY REPELS GHOSTS!
WITHOUT EVEN TRYING!

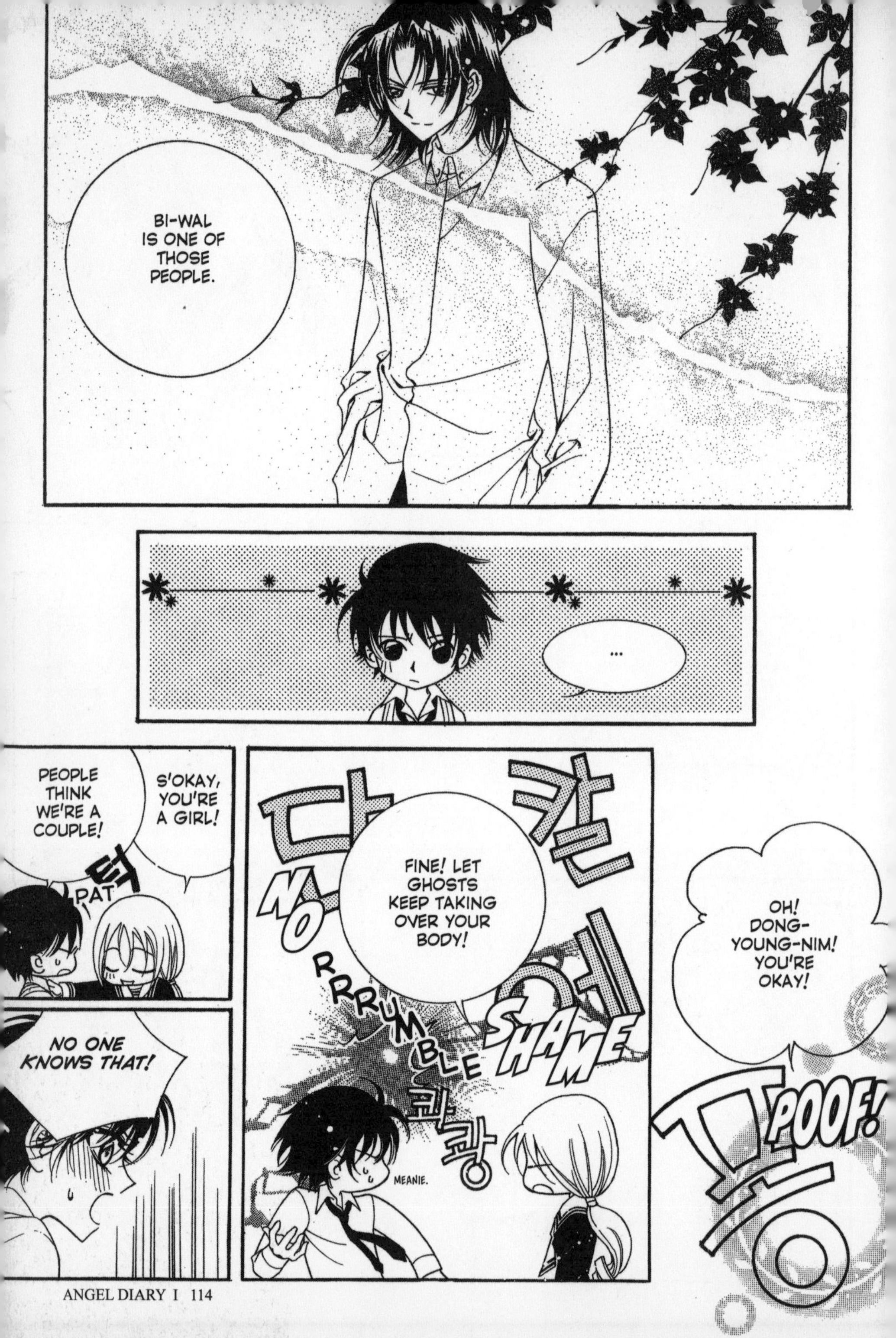
BI-WAL IS ONE OF THOSE PEOPLE.
...
PEOPLE THINK WE'RE A COUPLE!
S'OKAY, YOU'RE A GIRL!
턱
PAT
NO ONE KNOWS THAT!
NO
FINE! LET GHOSTS KEEP TAKING OVER YOUR BODY!
RRRUMBLE
SHAME
콰광
MEANIE.
OH! DONG-YOUNG-NIM! YOU'RE OKAY!
POOF!

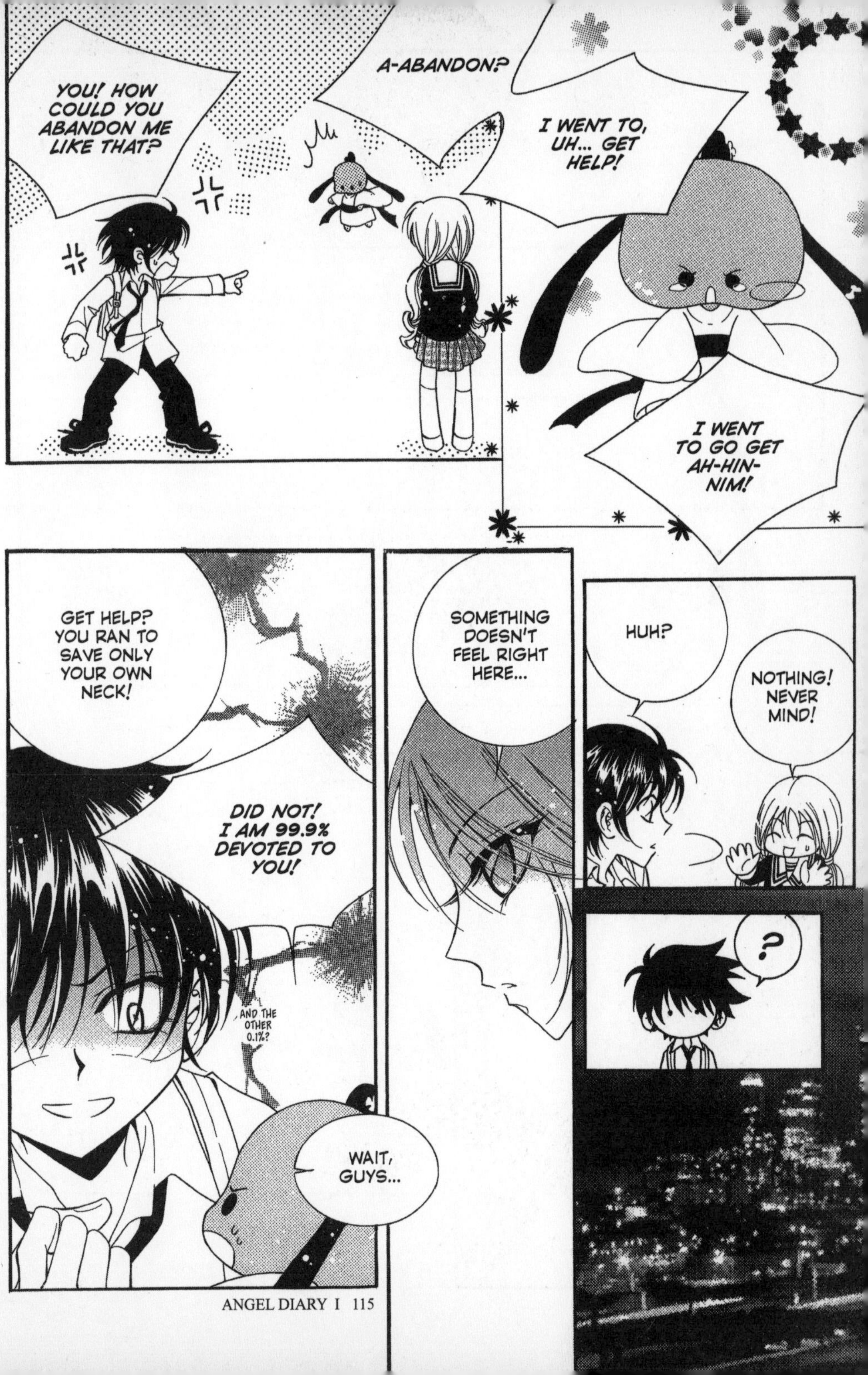
YOU! HOW COULD YOU ABANDON ME LIKE THAT?
A-ABANDON?
I WENT TO, UH... GET HELP!
I WENT TO GO GET AH-HIN-NIM!
GET HELP? YOU RAN TO SAVE ONLY YOUR OWN NECK!
DID NOT! I AM 99.9% DEVOTED TO YOU!
AND THE OTHER 0.1%?
WAIT, GUYS...
SOMETHING DOESN'T FEEL RIGHT HERE...
HUH?
NOTHING! NEVER MIND!
?

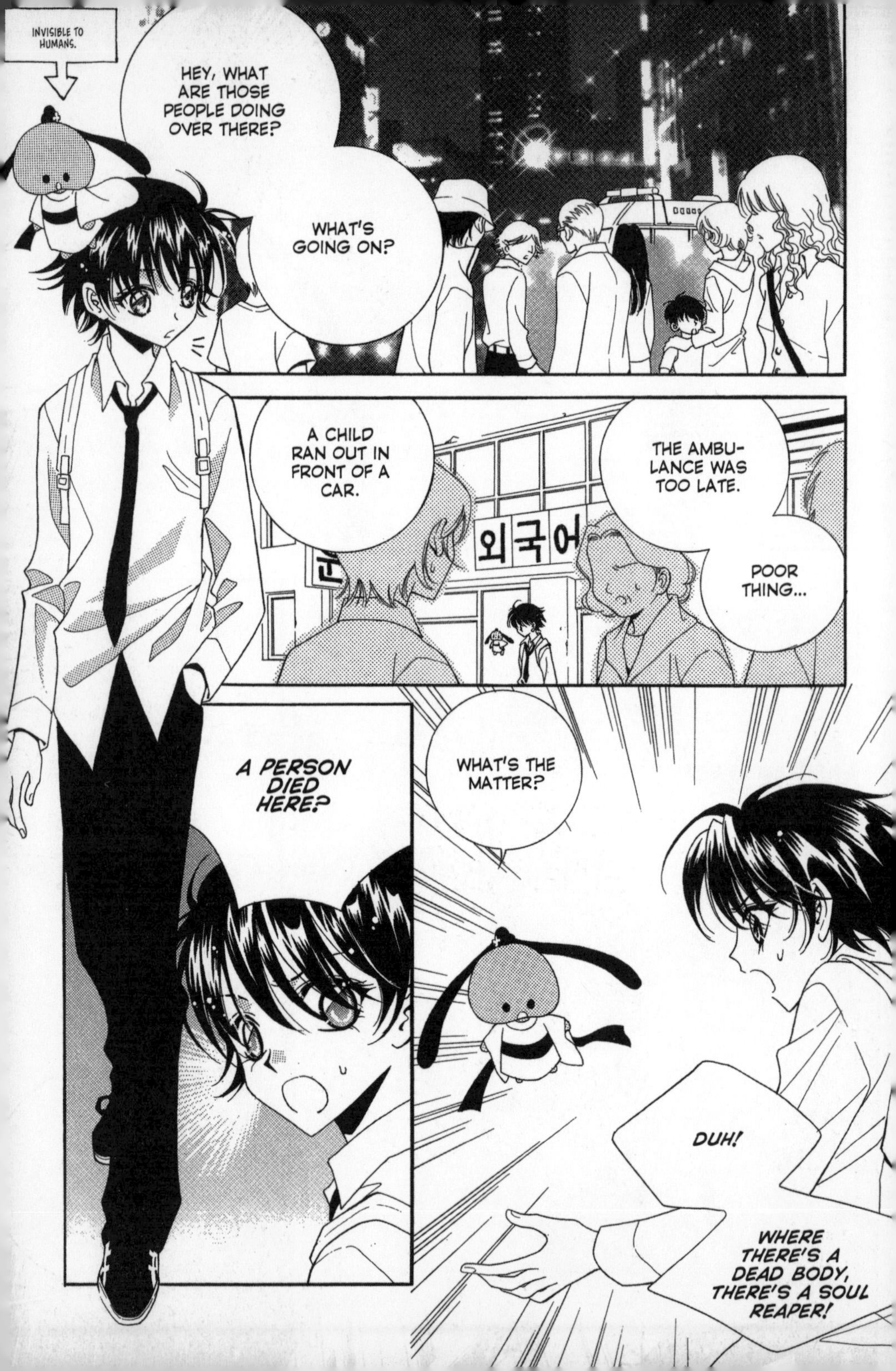

INVISIBLE TO HUMANS.
HEY, WHAT ARE THOSE PEOPLE DOING OVER THERE?
WHAT'S GOING ON?
A CHILD RAN OUT IN FRONT OF A CAR.
THE AMBU-LANCE WAS TOO LATE.
POOR THING...
외국어
A PERSON DIED HERE?
WHAT'S THE MATTER?
DUH!
WHERE THERE'S A DEAD BODY, THERE'S A SOUL REAPER!

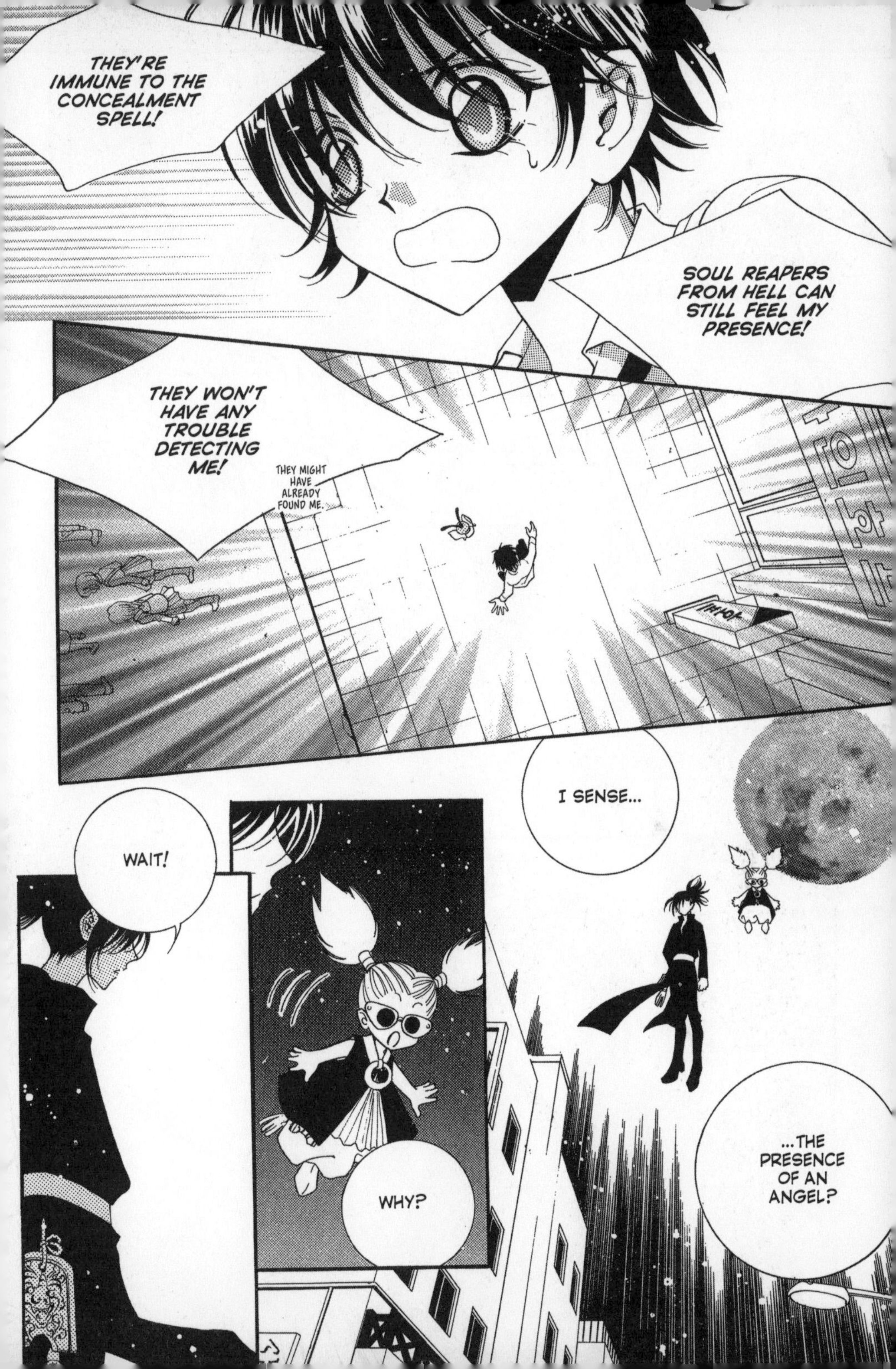
THEY'RE IMMUNE TO THE CONCEALMENT SPELL!
SOUL REAPERS FROM HELL CAN STILL FEEL MY PRESENCE!
THEY WON'T HAVE ANY TROUBLE DETECTING ME!
THEY MIGHT HAVE ALREADY FOUND ME.
WAIT!
WHY?
I SENSE...
...THE PRESENCE OF AN ANGEL?

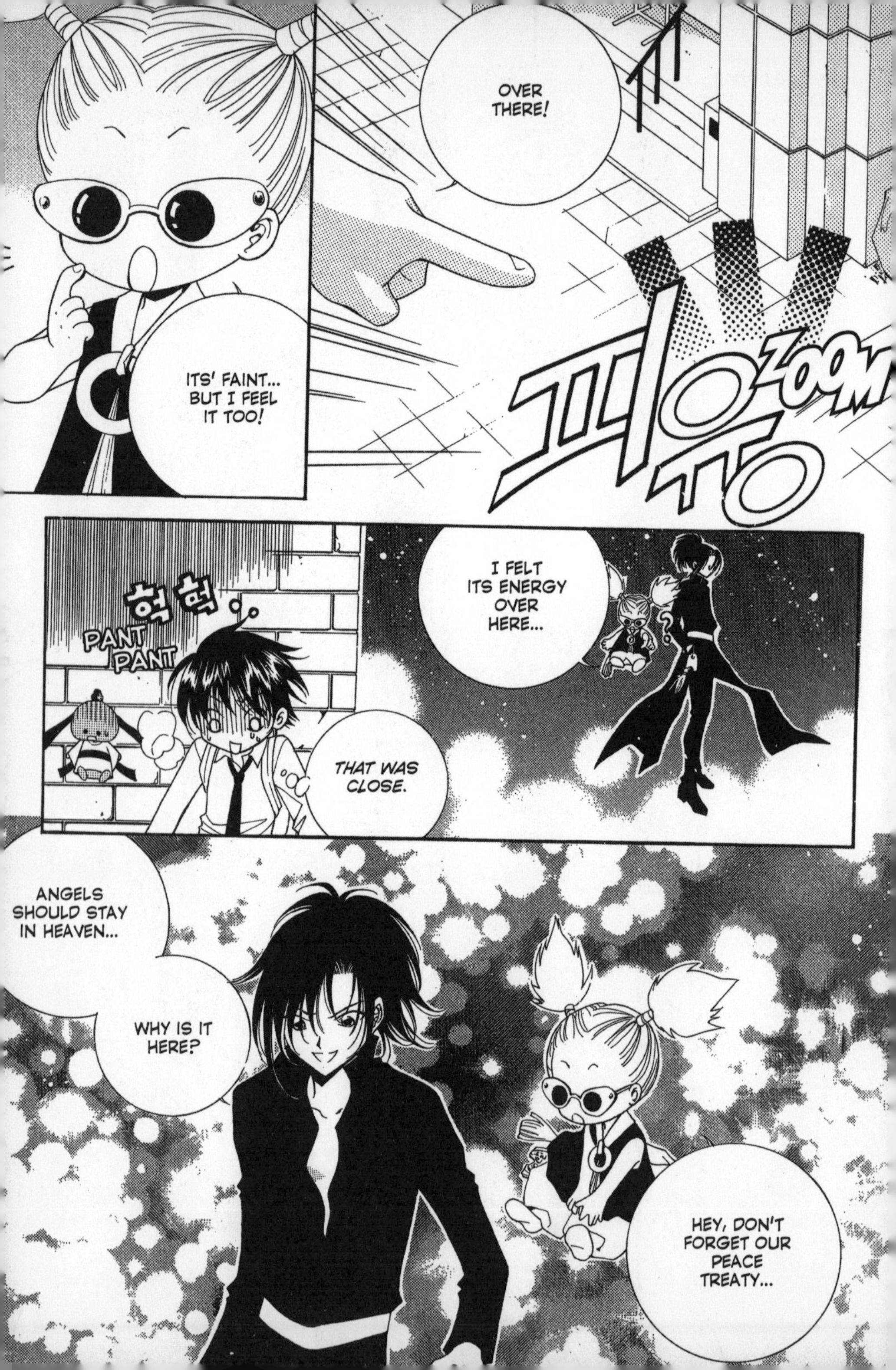
ITS' FAINT... BUT I FEEL IT TOO!
OVER THERE!
ZOOM
헉헉
PANT PANT
THAT WAS CLOSE.
I FELT ITS ENERGY OVER HERE...
ANGELS SHOULD STAY IN HEAVEN...
WHY IS IT HERE?
HEY, DON'T FORGET OUR PEACE TREATY...

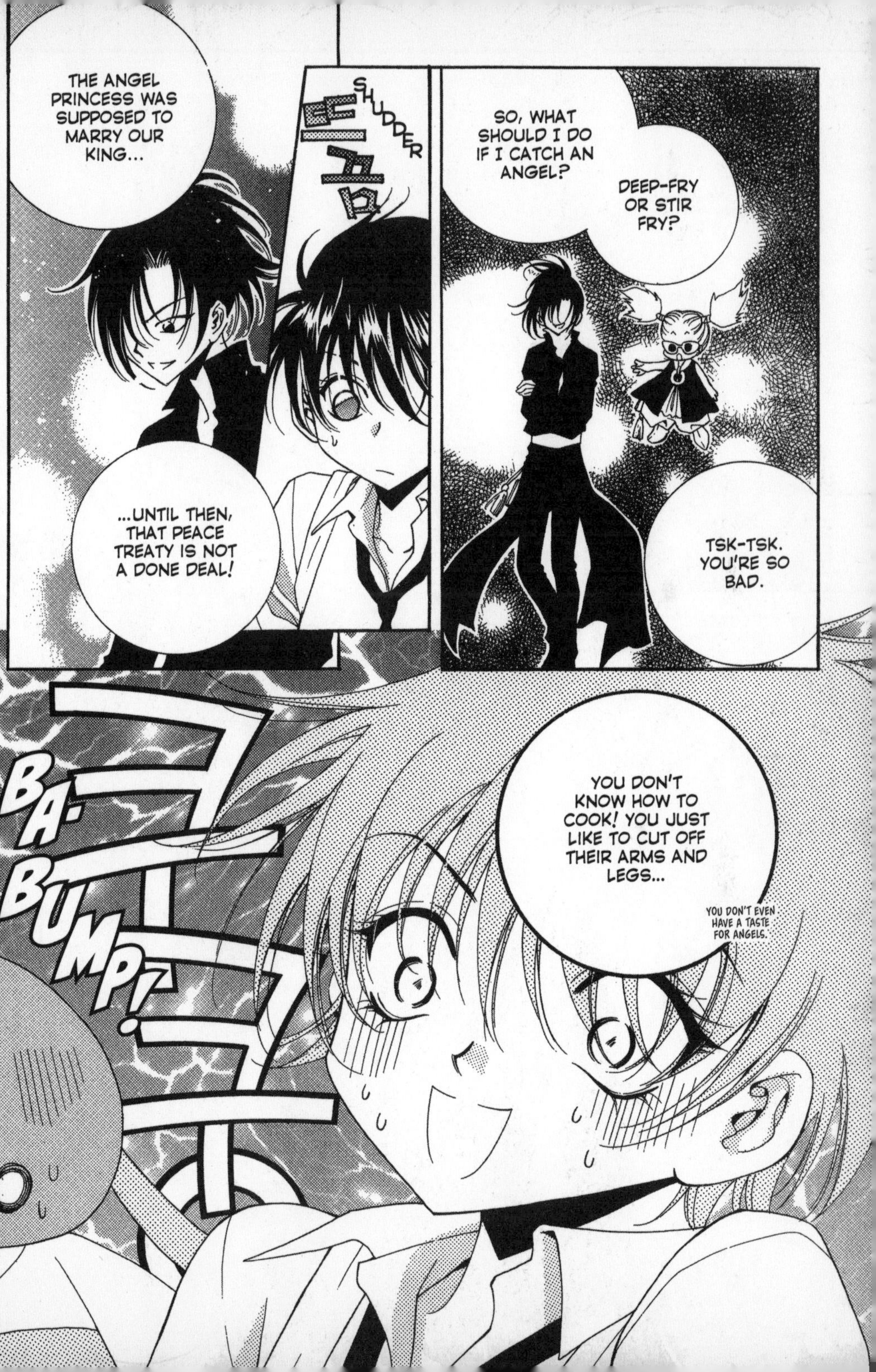
THE ANGEL PRINCESS WAS SUPPOSED TO MARRY OUR KING...
...UNTIL THEN, THAT PEACE TREATY IS NOT A DONE DEAL!
SHUDDER
SO, WHAT SHOULD I DO IF I CATCH AN ANGEL?
DEEP-FRY OR STIR FRY?
TSK-TSK. YOU'RE SO BAD.
BA-BUMP!
YOU DON'T KNOW HOW TO COOK! YOU JUST LIKE TO CUT OFF THEIR ARMS AND LEGS...
YOU DON'T EVEN HAVE A TASTE FOR ANGELS.

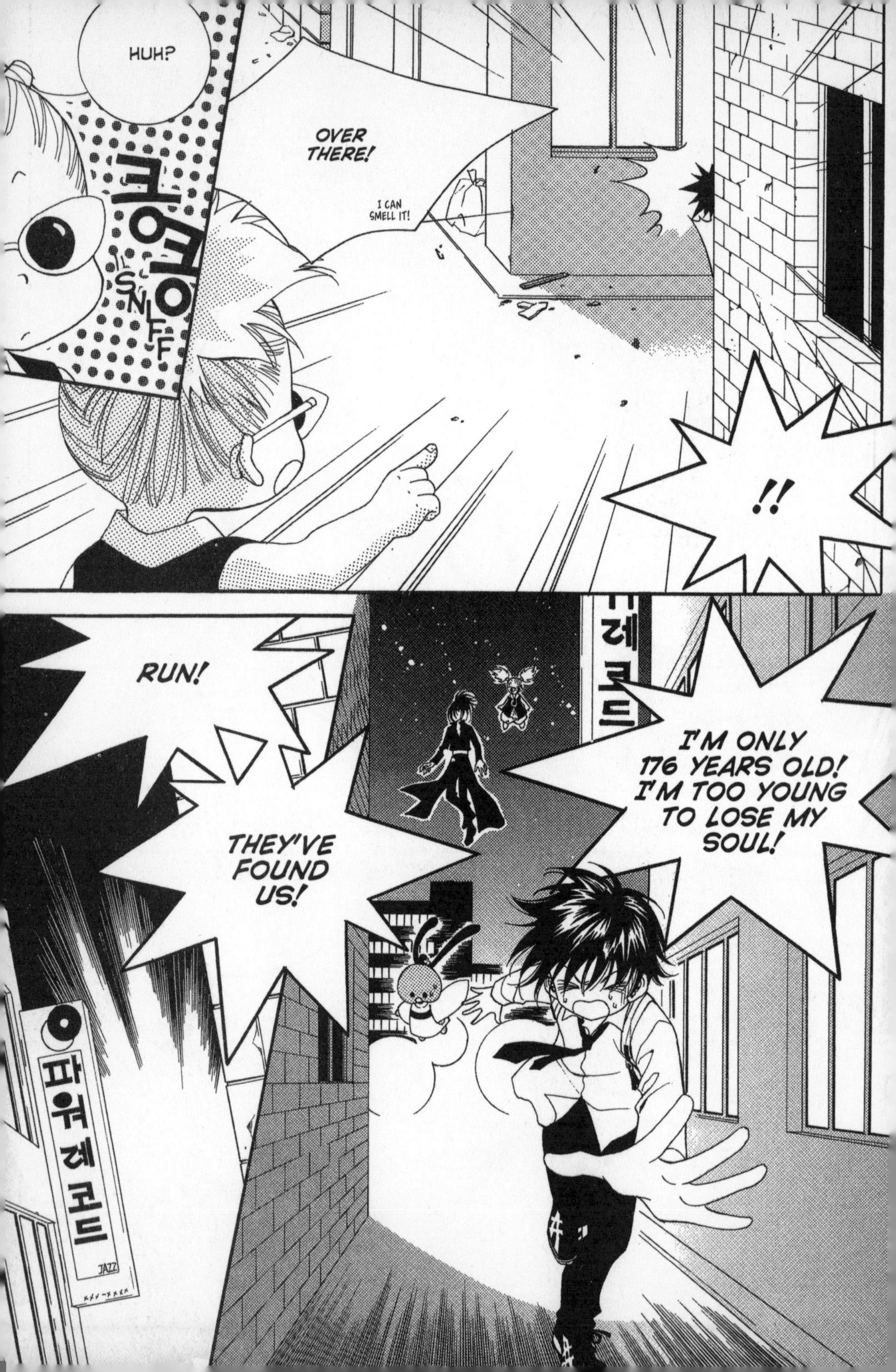
HUH?
킁킁
SNIFF
OVER THERE!
I CAN SMELL IT!
!!
RUN!
THEY'VE FOUND US!
I'M ONLY 176 YEARS OLD! I'M TOO YOUNG TO LOSE MY SOUL!
파워레코드
JAZZ

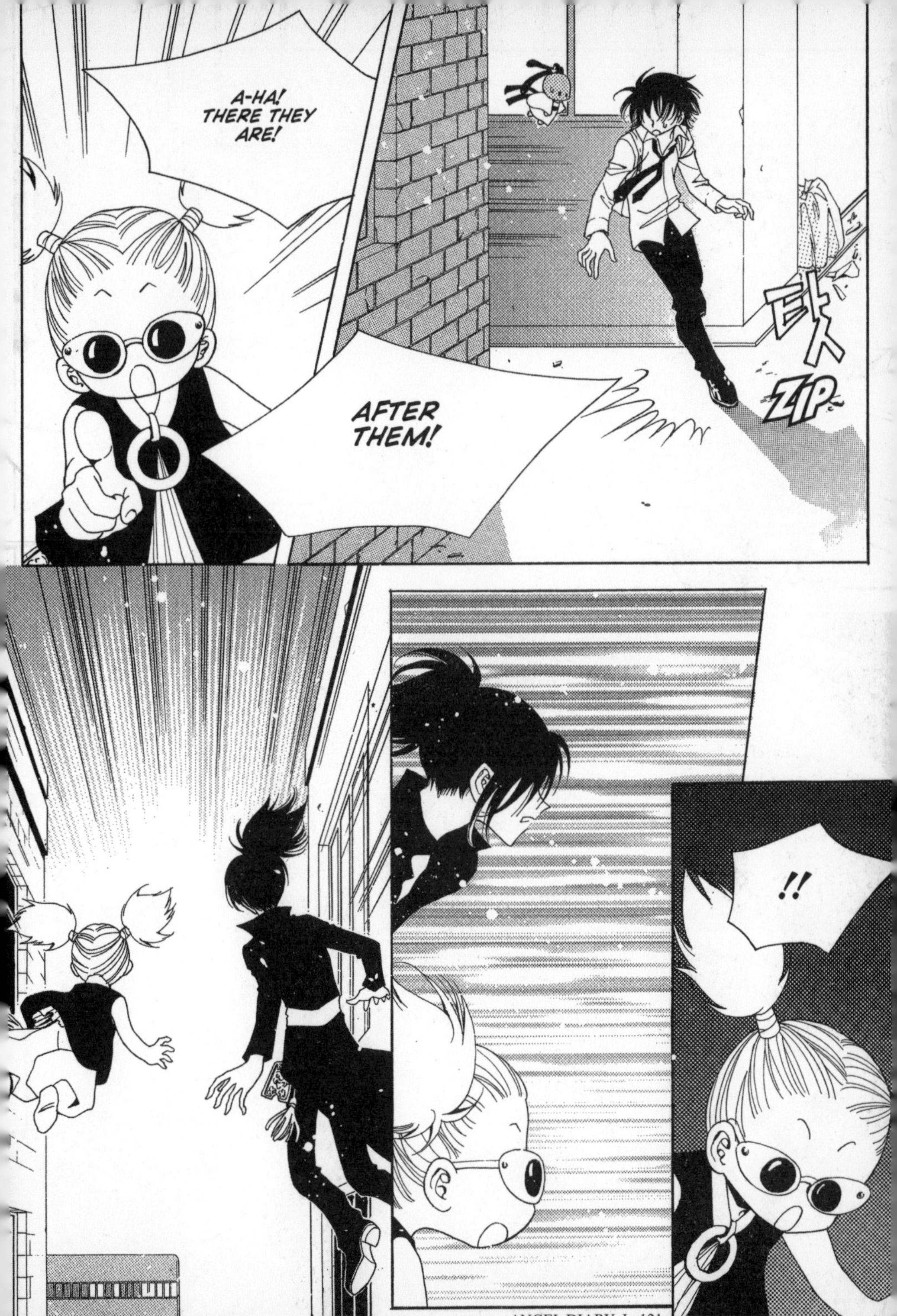
A-HA! THERE THEY ARE!
AFTER THEM!
탓
ZIP
!!

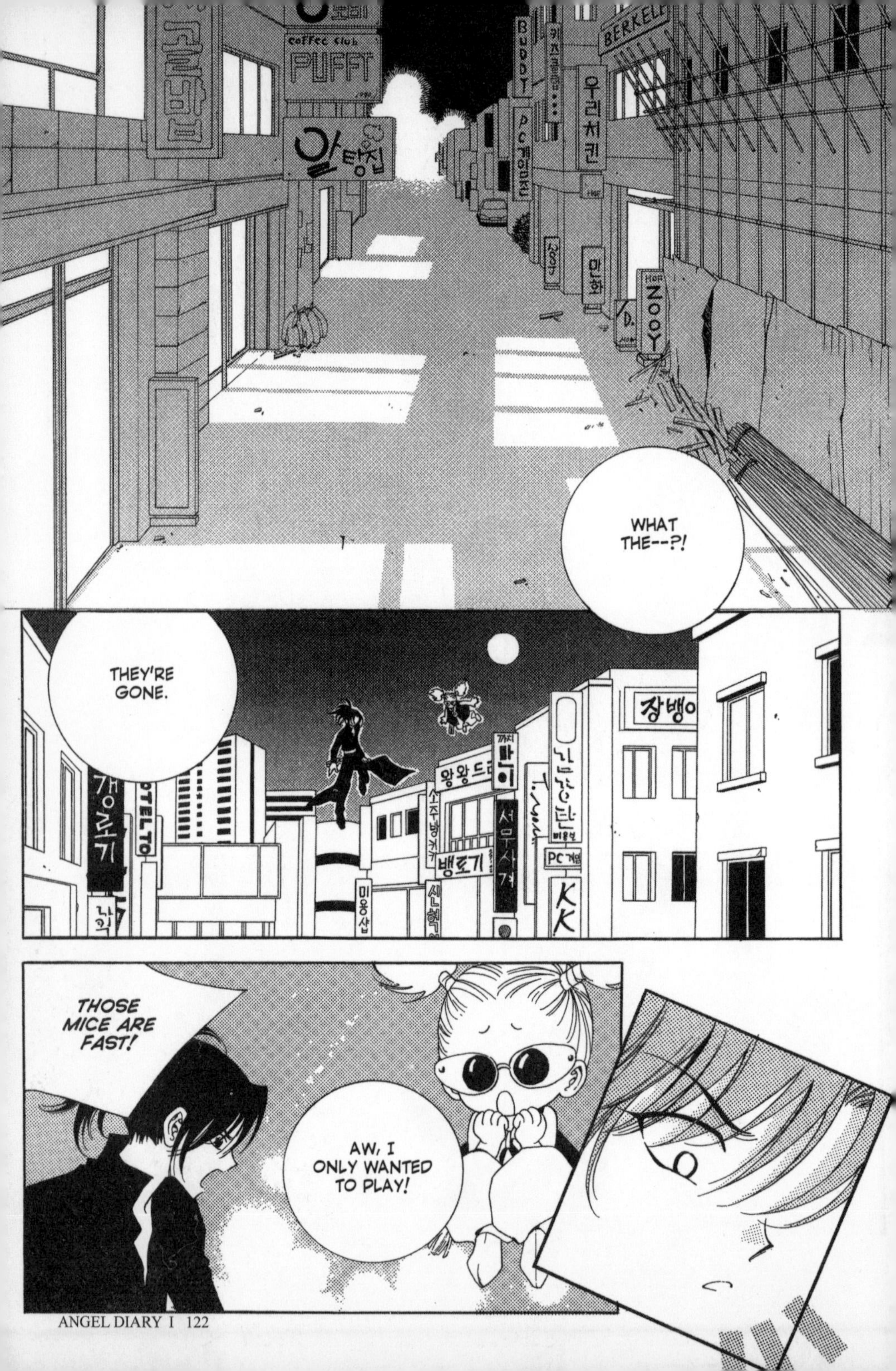
WHAT THE--?!
THEY'RE GONE.
THOSE MICE ARE FAST!
AW, I ONLY WANTED TO PLAY!

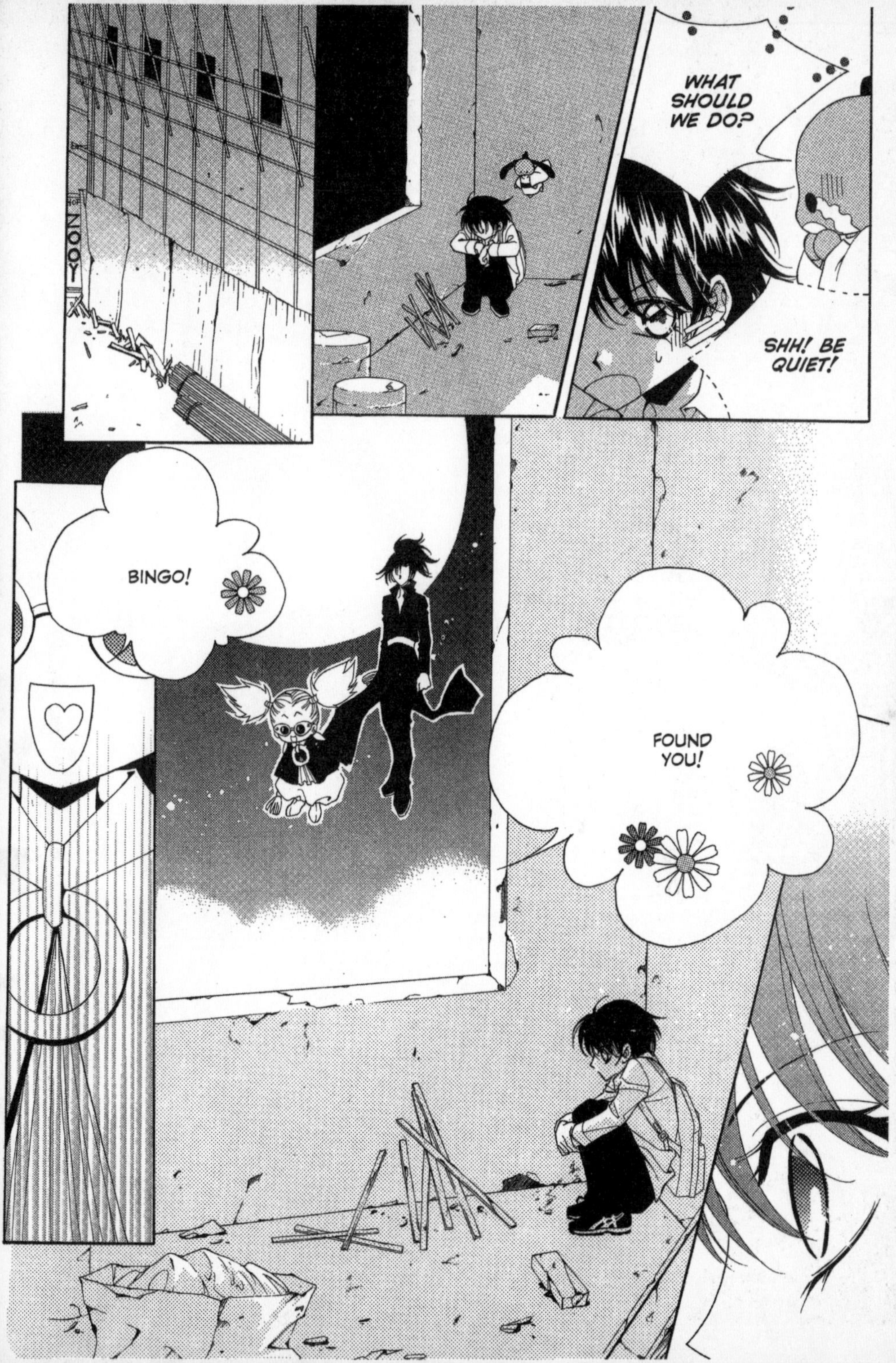
WHAT SHOULD WE DO?
SHH! BE QUIET!
BINGO!
FOUND YOU!

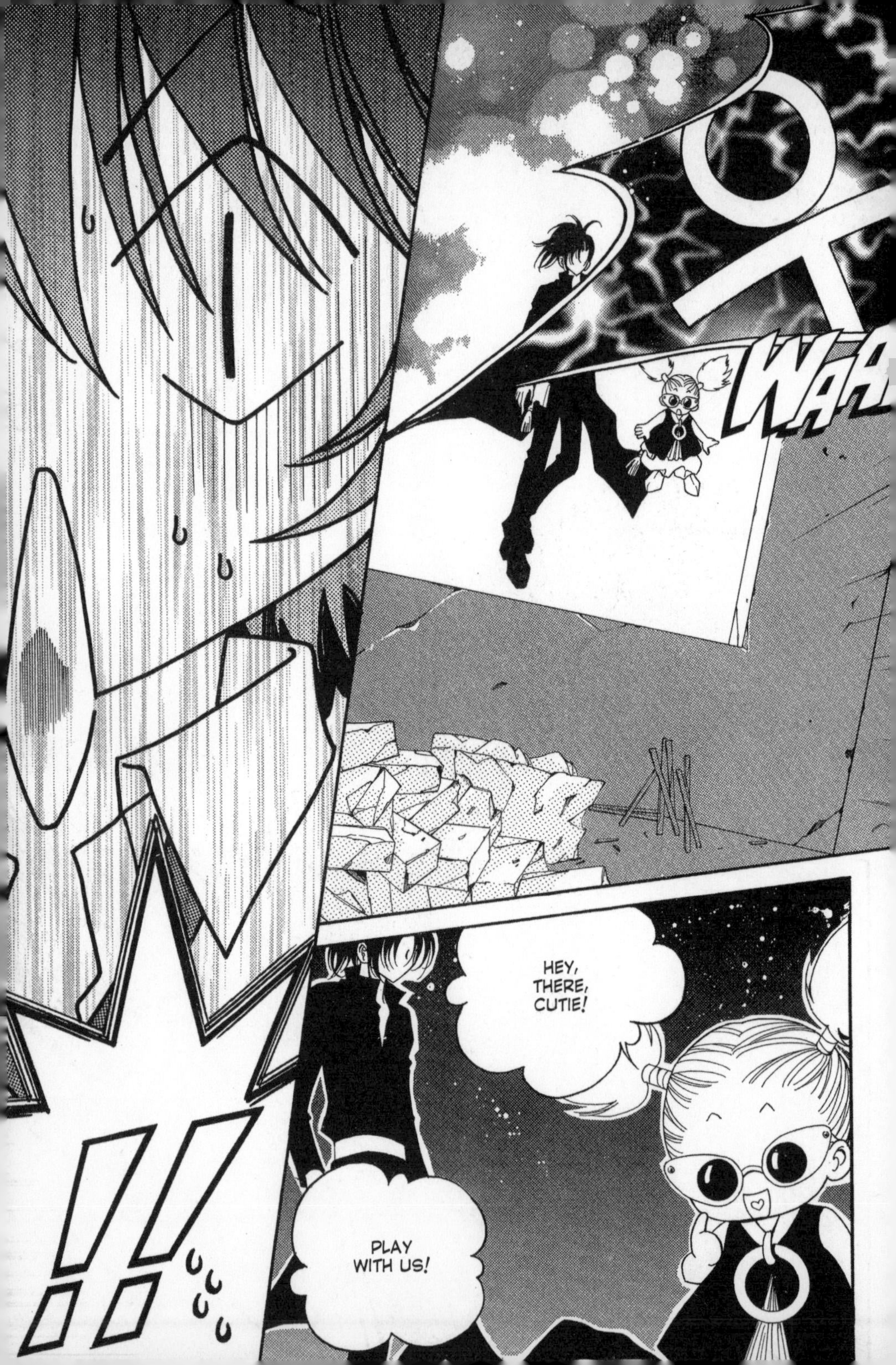
!!
WAA
HEY, THERE, CUTIE!
PLAY WITH US!

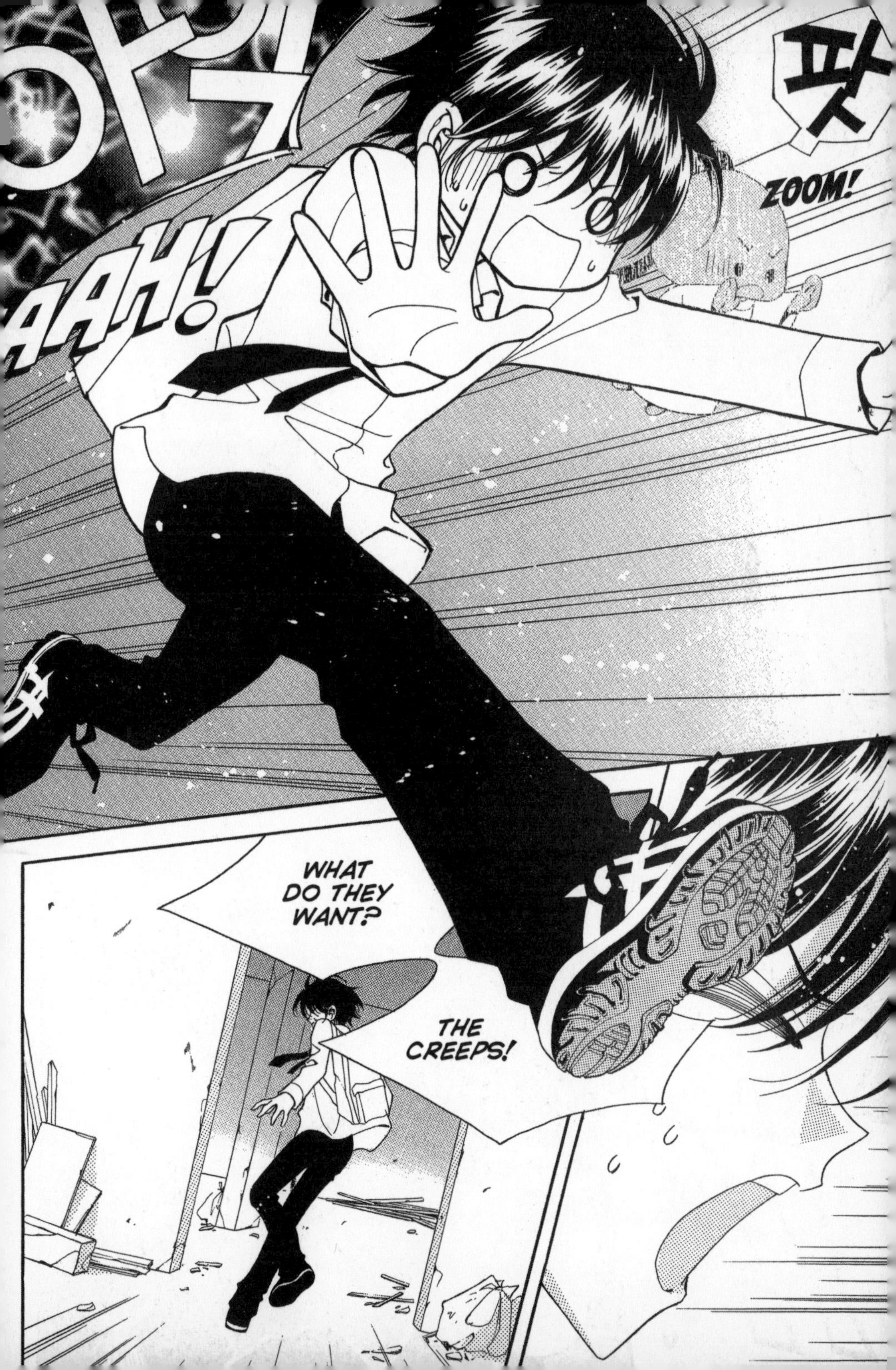
AAH!
팟
ZOOM!
WHAT DO THEY WANT?
THE CREEPS!

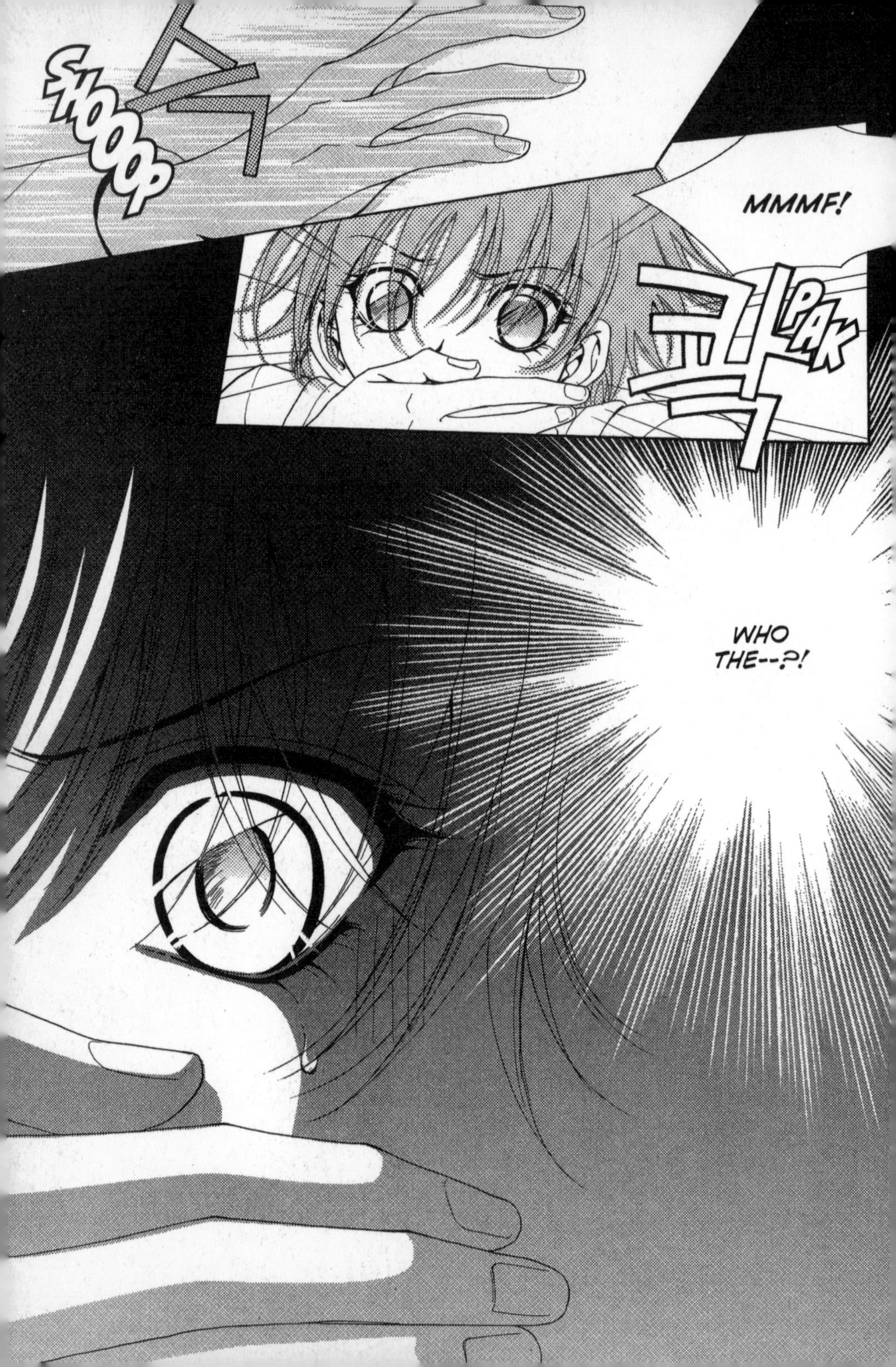
SHOOOP
MMMF!
PAK
WHO THE--?!

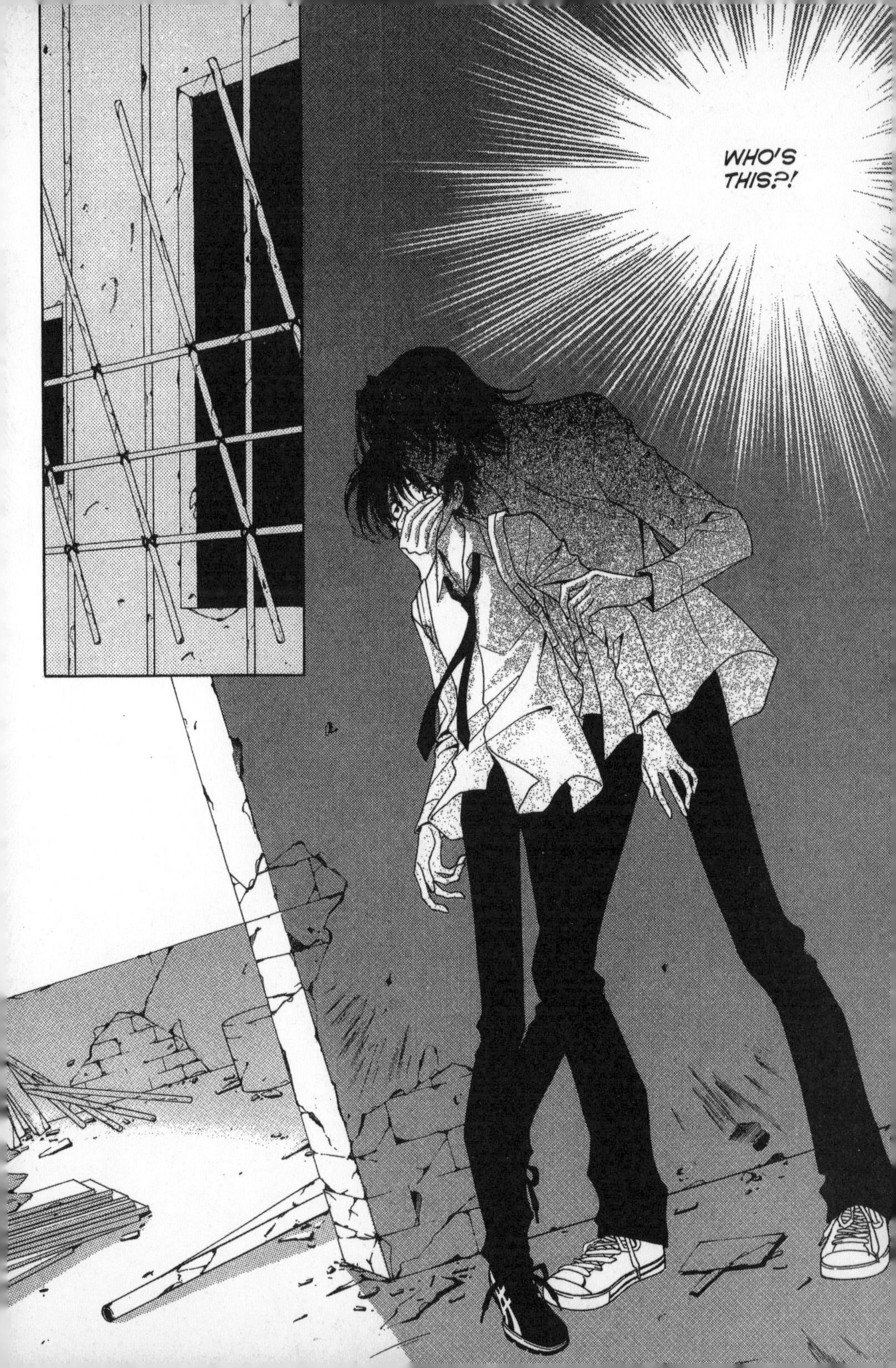
WHO'S THIS?!

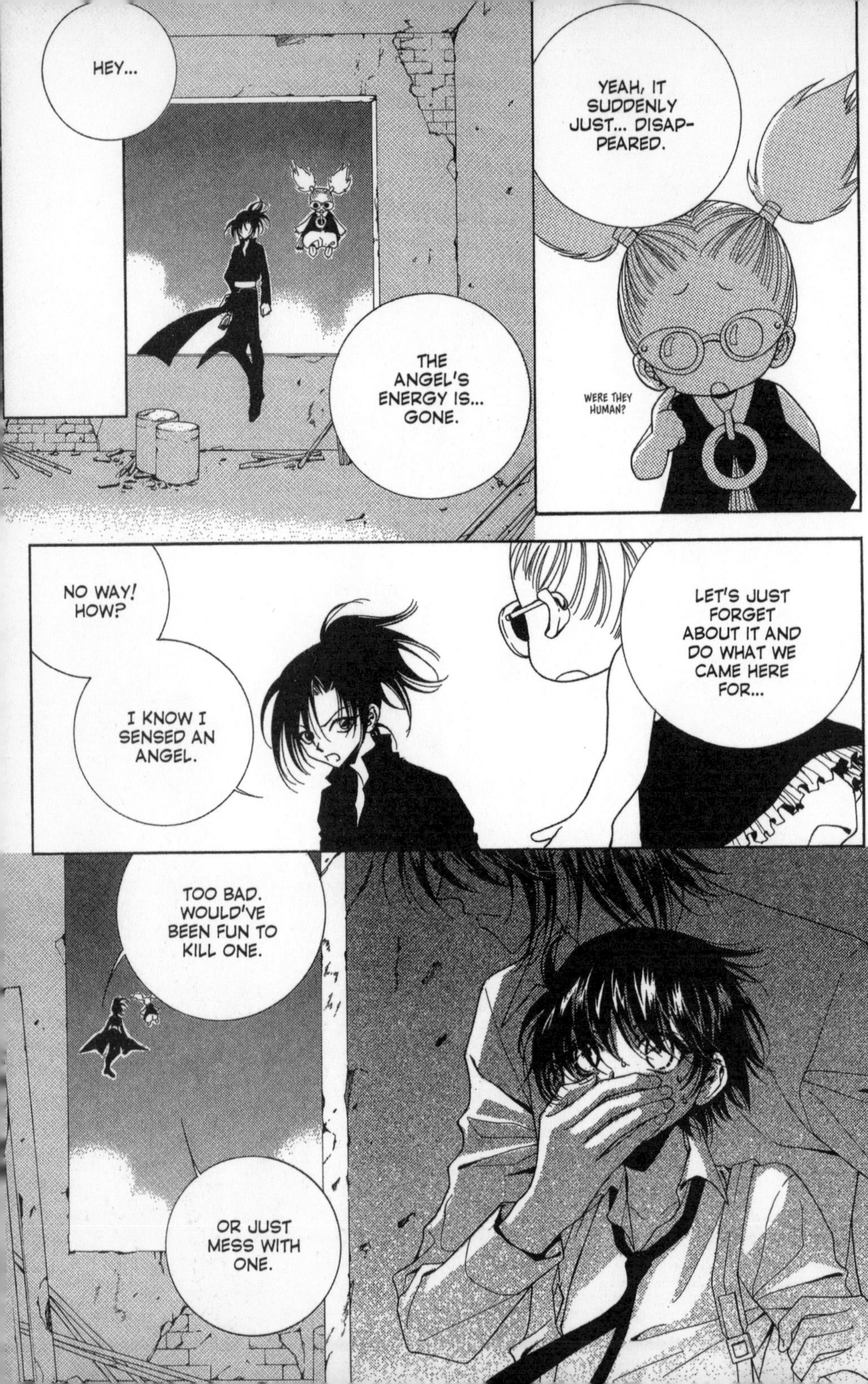
HEY...
THE ANGEL'S ENERGY IS... GONE.
YEAH, IT SUDDENLY JUST... DISAP-PEARED.
WERE THEY HUMAN?
NO WAY! HOW?
I KNOW I SENSED AN ANGEL.
LET'S JUST FORGET ABOUT IT AND DO WHAT WE CAME HERE FOR...
TOO BAD. WOULD'VE BEEN FUN TO KILL ONE.
OR JUST MESS WITH ONE.

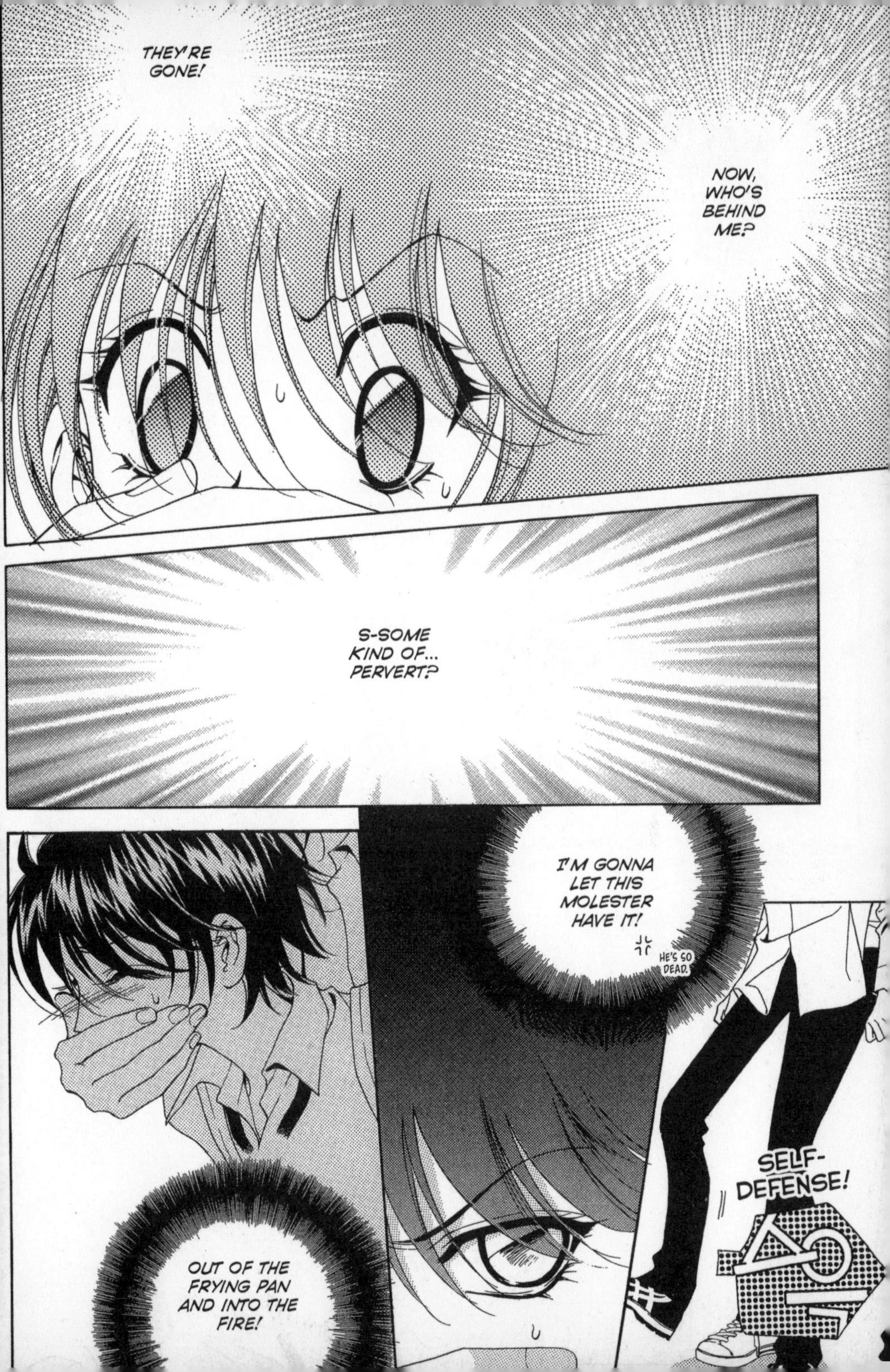
THEY'RE GONE!
NOW, WHO'S BEHIND ME?
S-SOME KIND OF... PERVERT?
OUT OF THE FRYING PAN AND INTO THE FIRE!
I'M GONNA LET THIS MOLESTER HAVE IT!
HE'S SO DEAD.
SELF-DEFENSE!

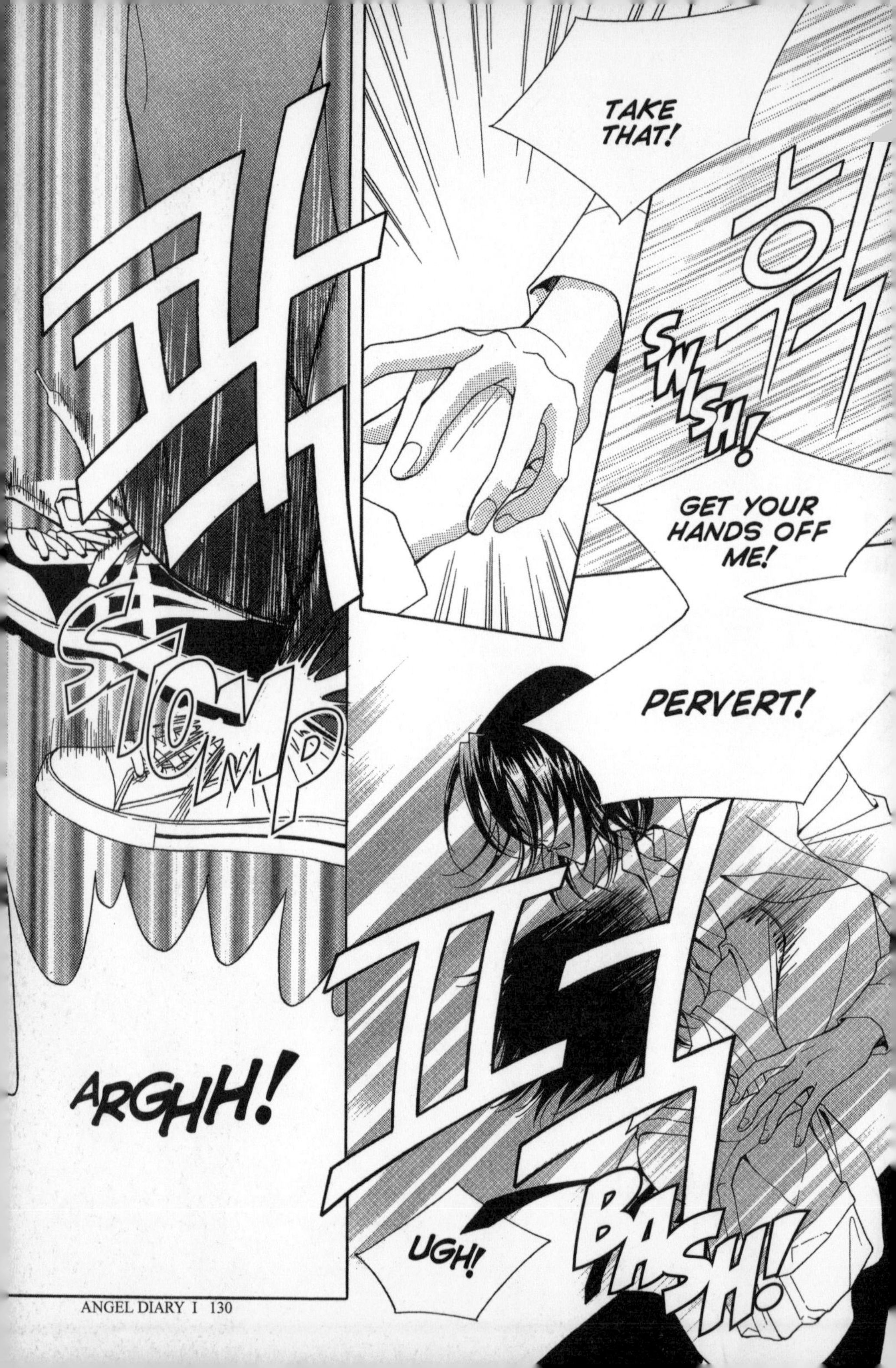
STOMP
ARGHH!
TAKE THAT!
SWISH!
GET YOUR HANDS OFF ME!
PERVERT!
UGH!
BASH!

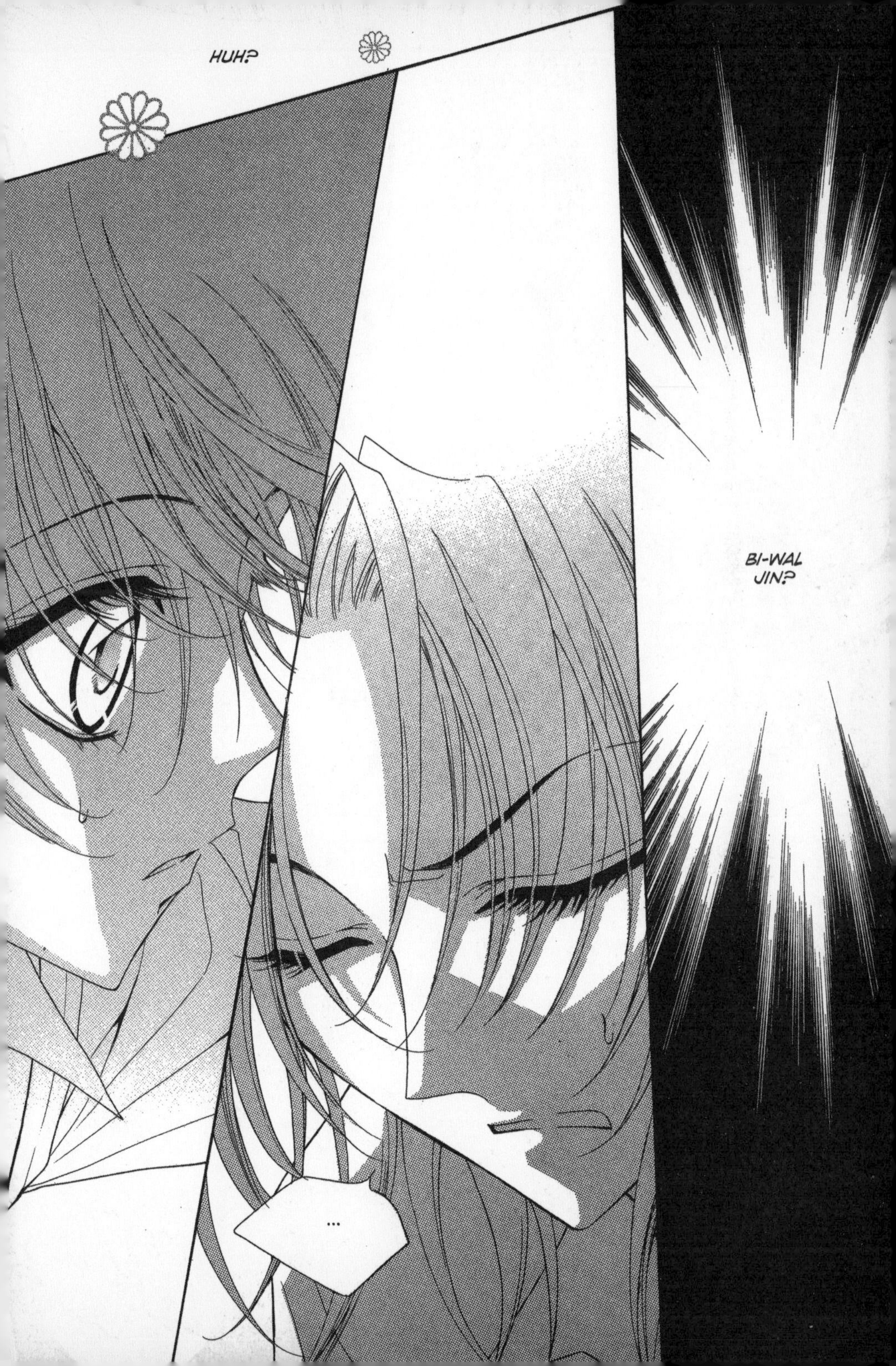
HUH?
BI-WAL JIN?
...

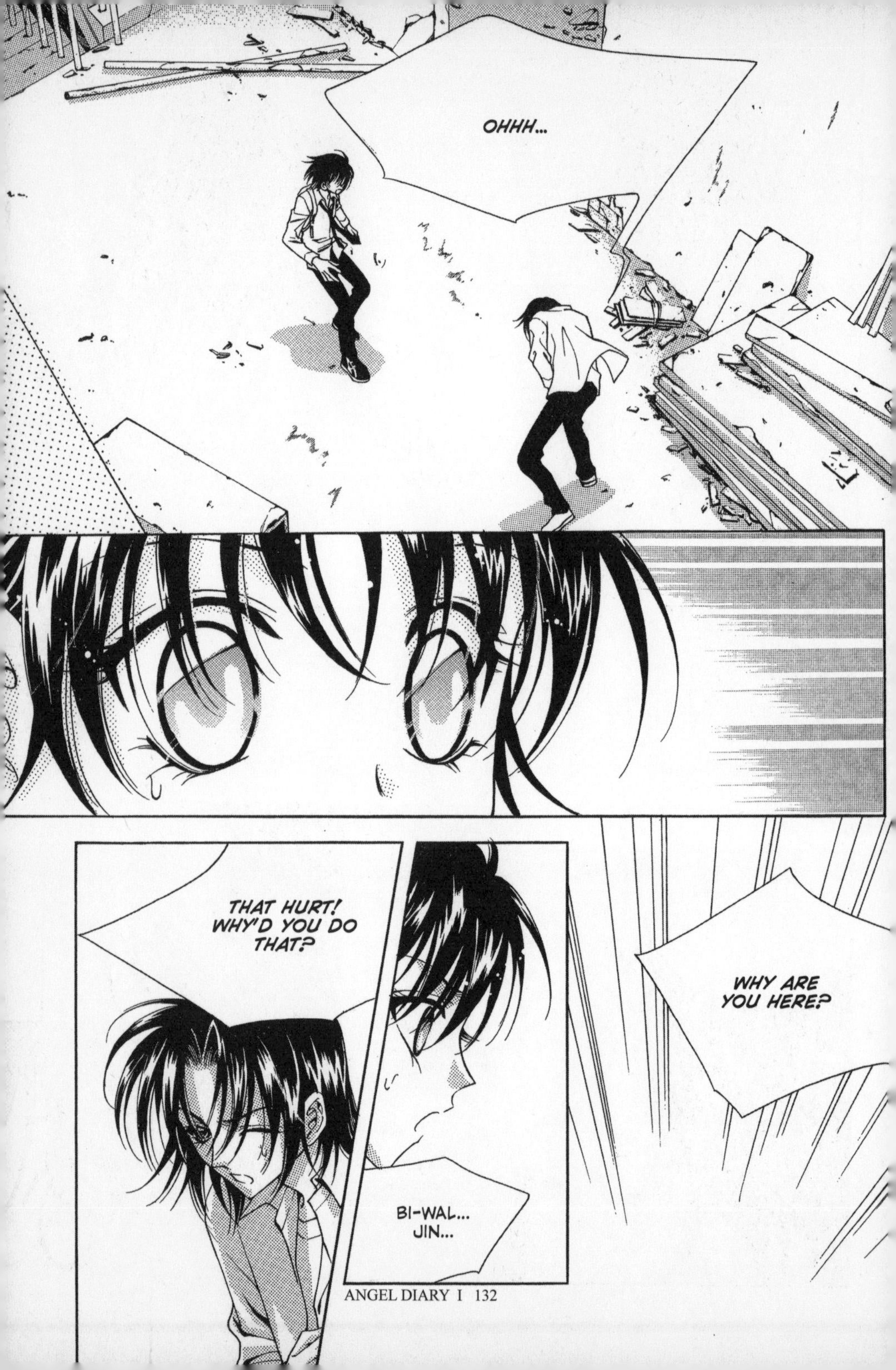
OHHH...
THAT HURT! WHY'D YOU DO THAT?
BI-WAL... JIN...
WHY ARE YOU HERE?

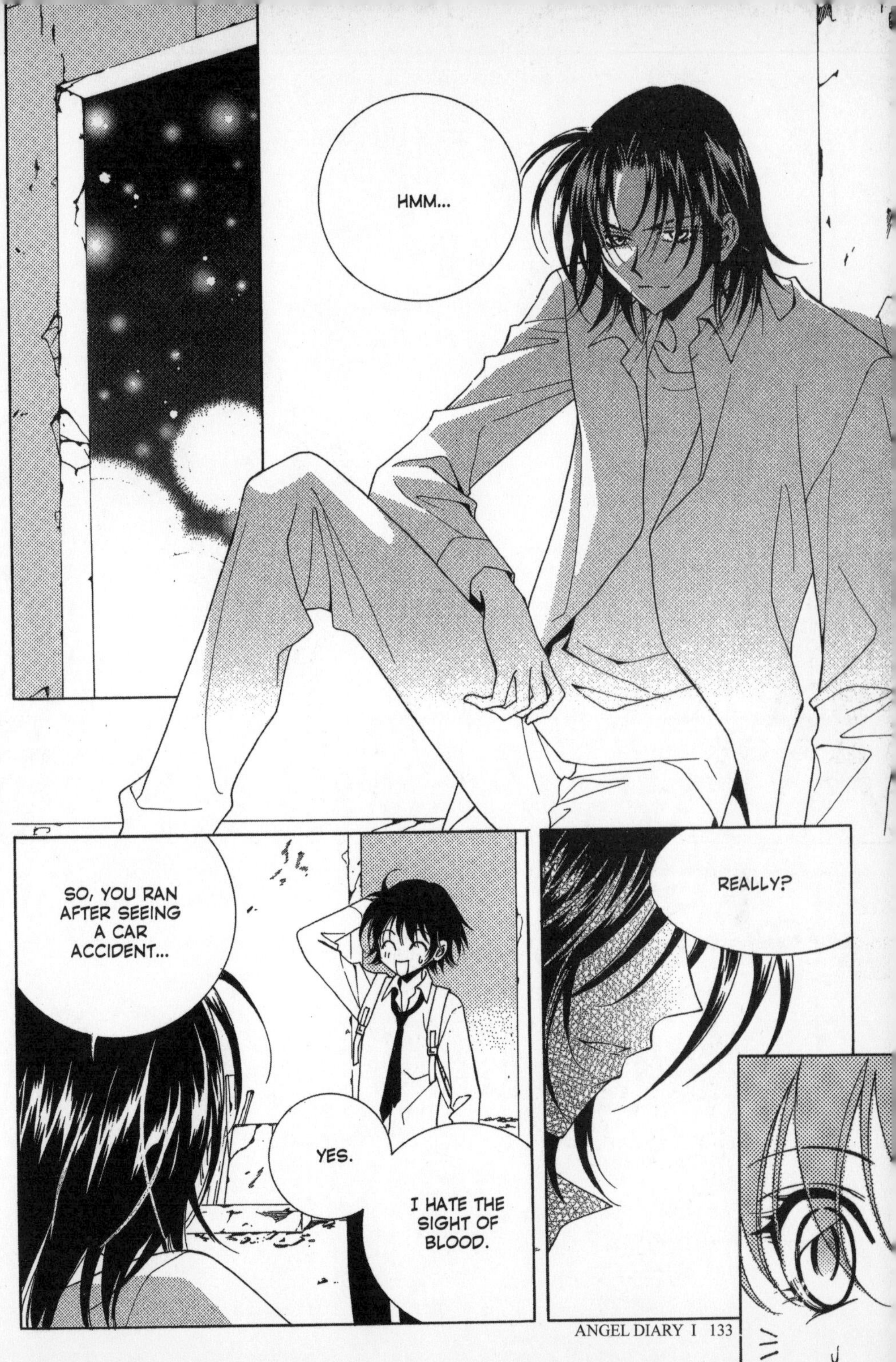
HMM...
SO, YOU RAN AFTER SEEING A CAR ACCIDENT...
YES.
I HATE THE SIGHT OF BLOOD.
REALLY?

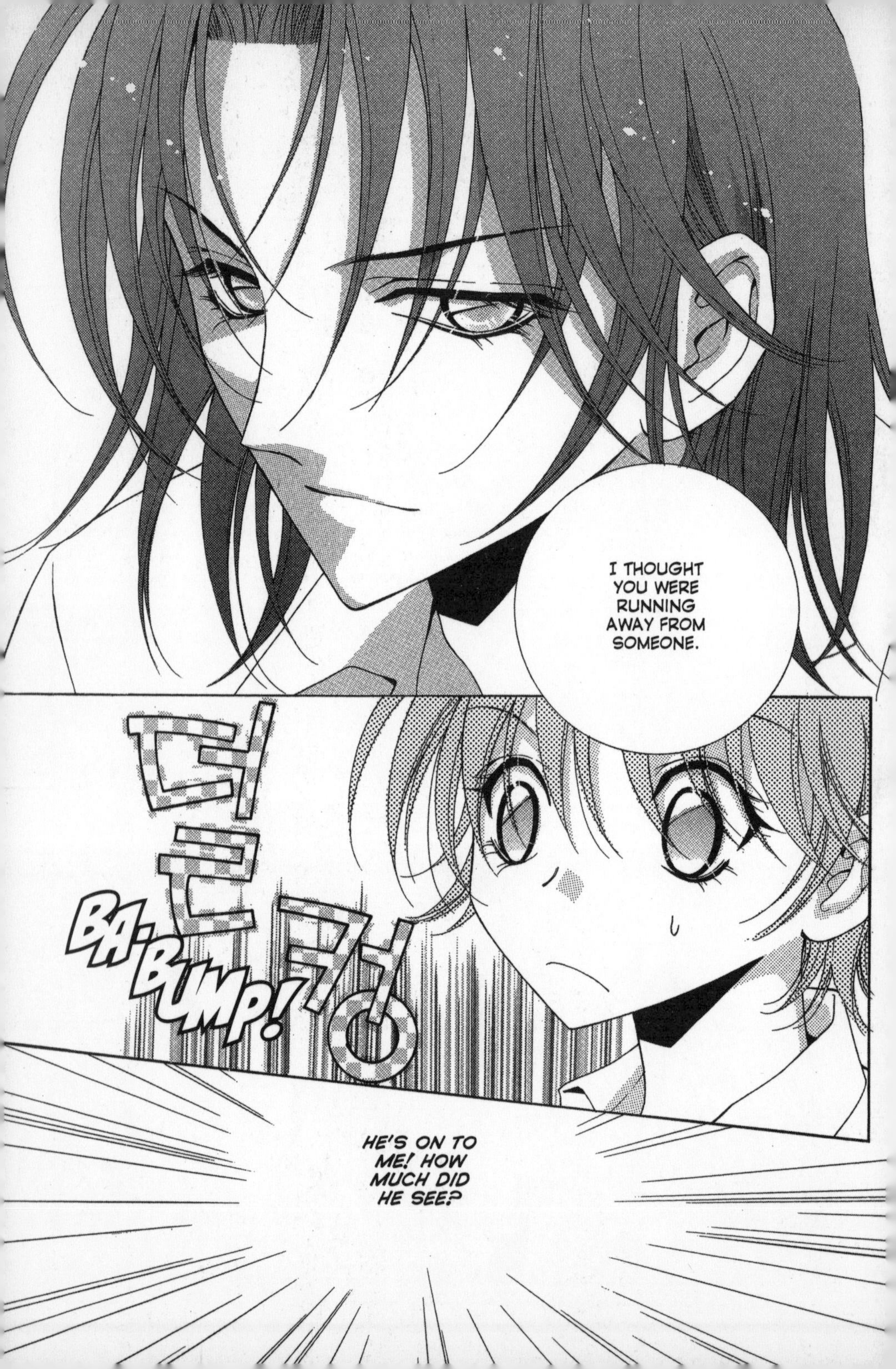
I THOUGHT YOU WERE RUNNING AWAY FROM SOMEONE.
BA-BUMP!
HE'S ON TO ME! HOW MUCH DID HE SEE?

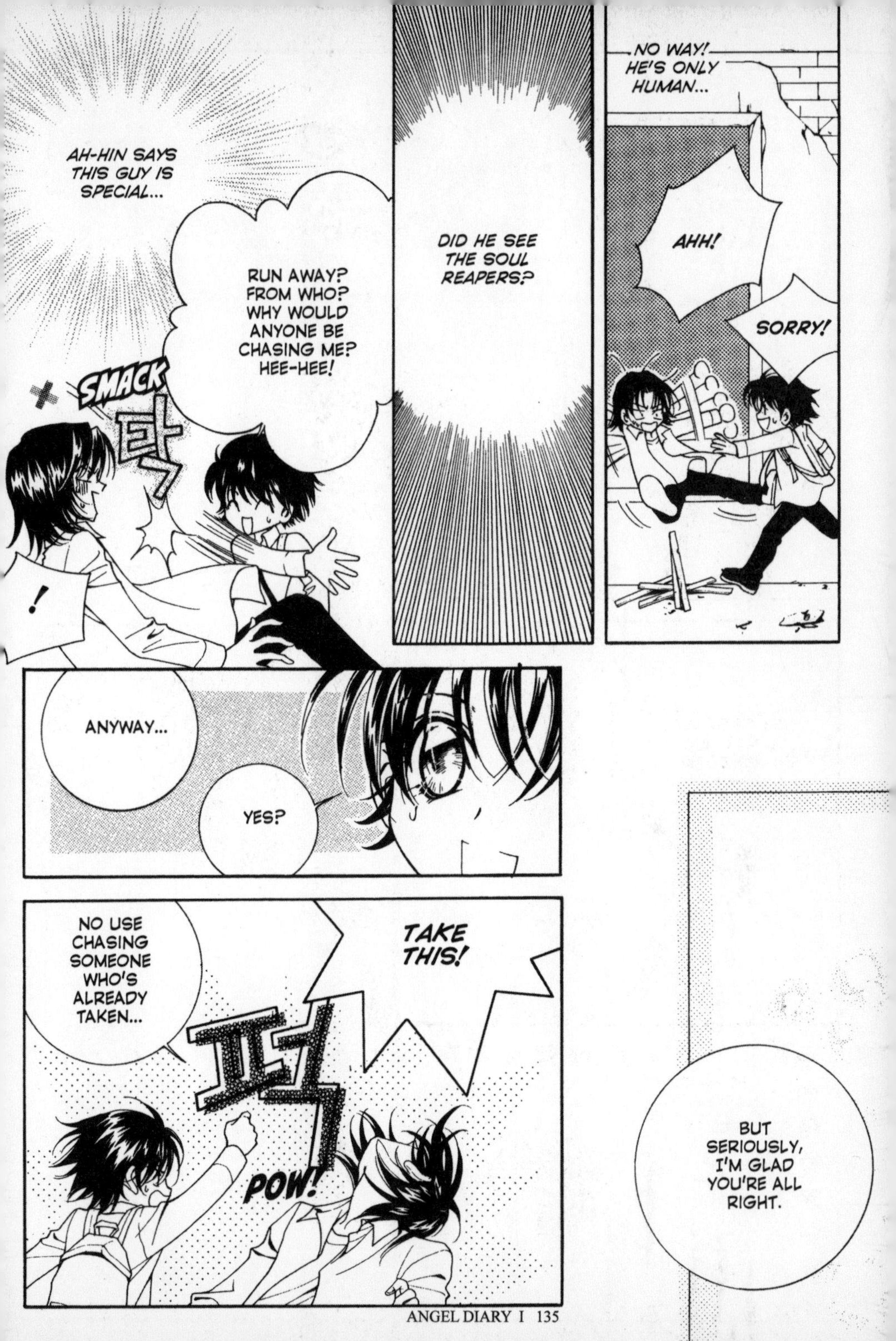
AH-HIN SAYS THIS GUY IS SPECIAL...
RUN AWAY? FROM WHO? WHY WOULD ANYONE BE CHASING ME? HEE-HEE!
SMACK
탁
!
DID HE SEE THE SOUL REAPERS?
NO WAY! HE'S ONLY HUMAN...
AHH!
SORRY!
ANYWAY...
YES?
NO USE CHASING SOMEONE WHO'S ALREADY TAKEN...
TAKE THIS!
퍽
POW!
BUT SERIOUSLY, I'M GLAD YOU'RE ALL RIGHT.

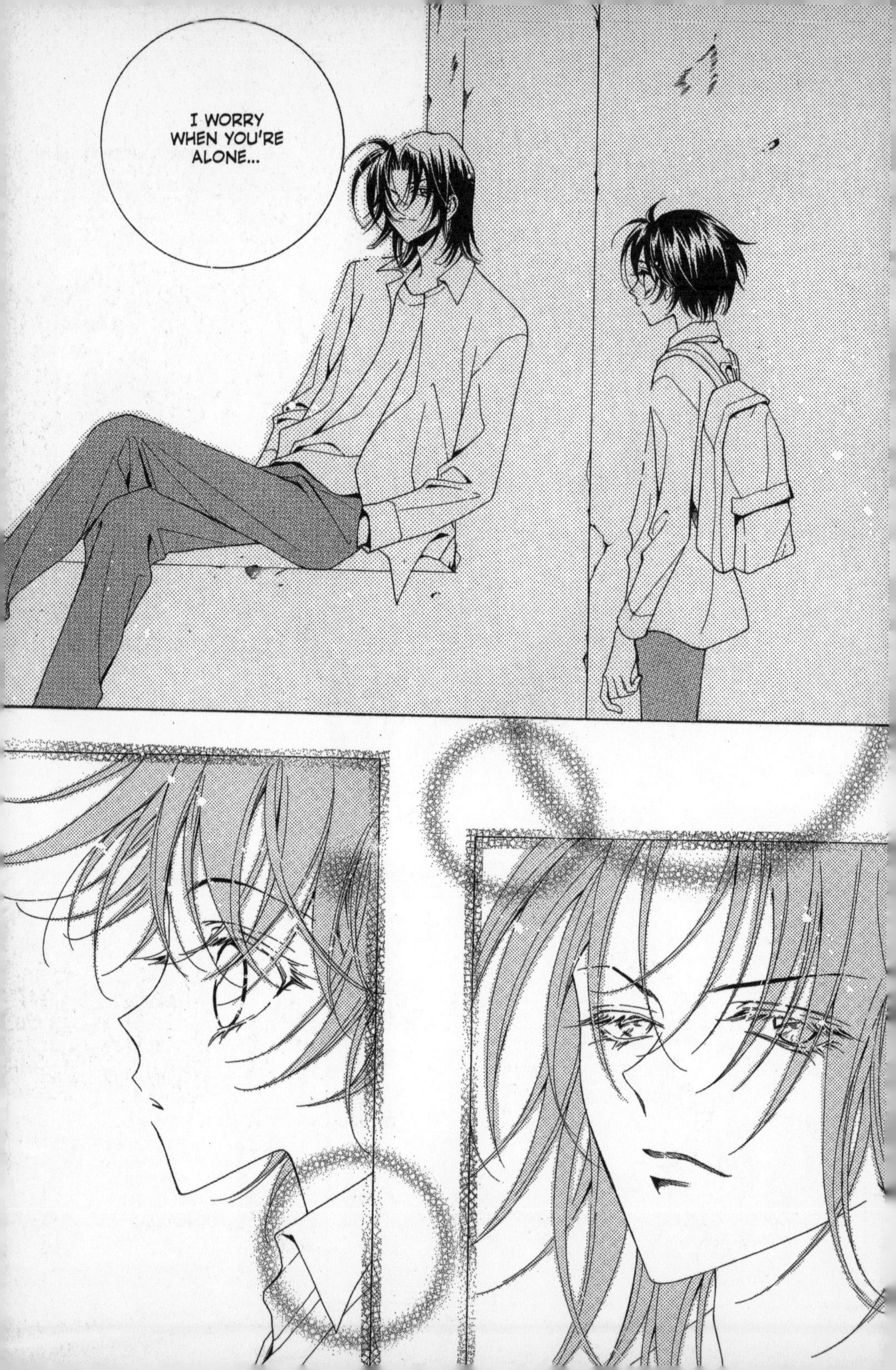
I WORRY WHEN YOU'RE ALONE...

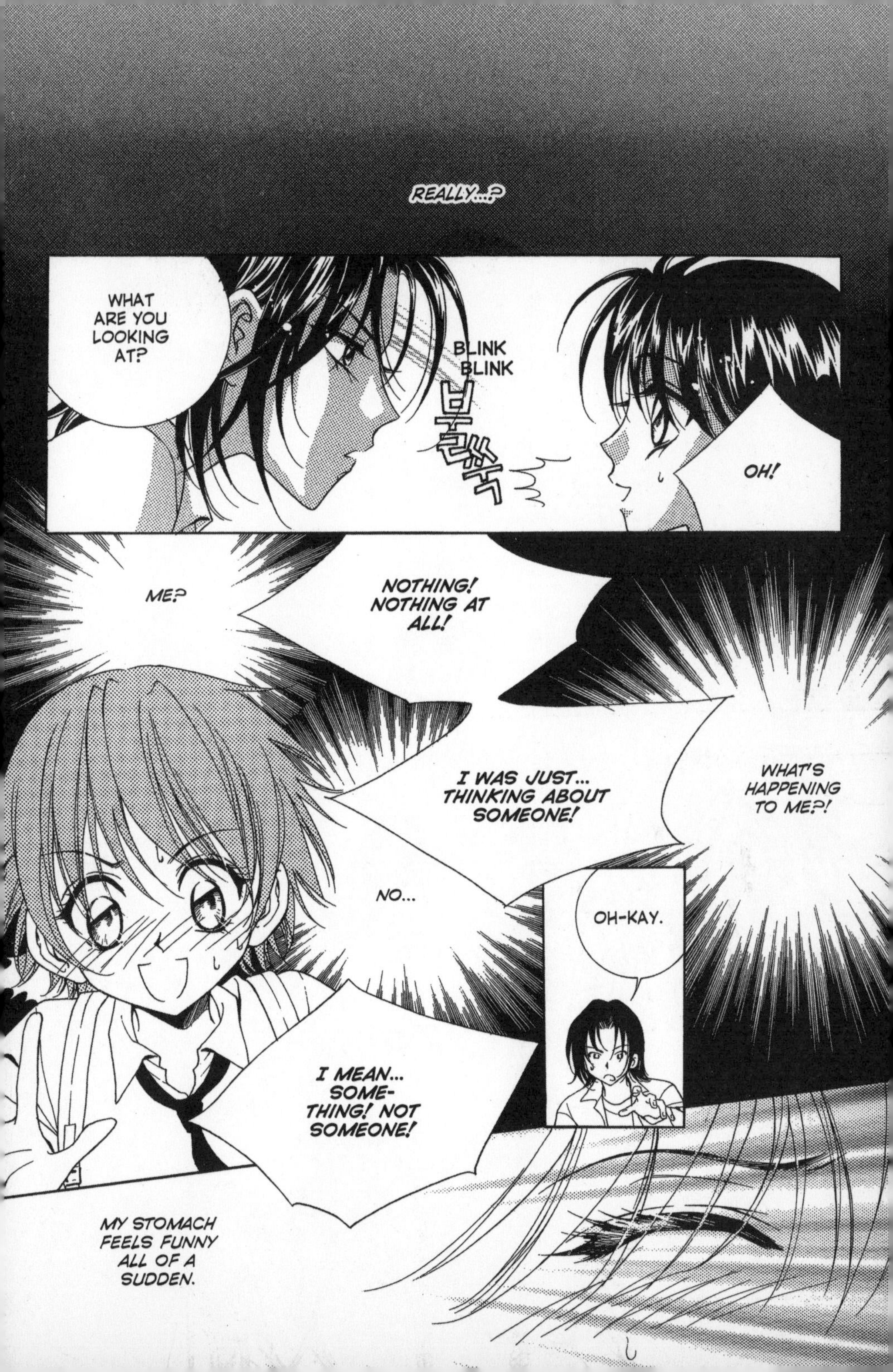
REALLY...?
WHAT ARE YOU LOOKING AT?
BLINK BLINK
OH!
ME?
NOTHING! NOTHING AT ALL!
I WAS JUST... THINKING ABOUT SOMEONE!
WHAT'S HAPPENING TO ME?!
NO...
OH-KAY.
I MEAN... SOME-THING! NOT SOMEONE!
MY STOMACH FEELS FUNNY ALL OF A SUDDEN.

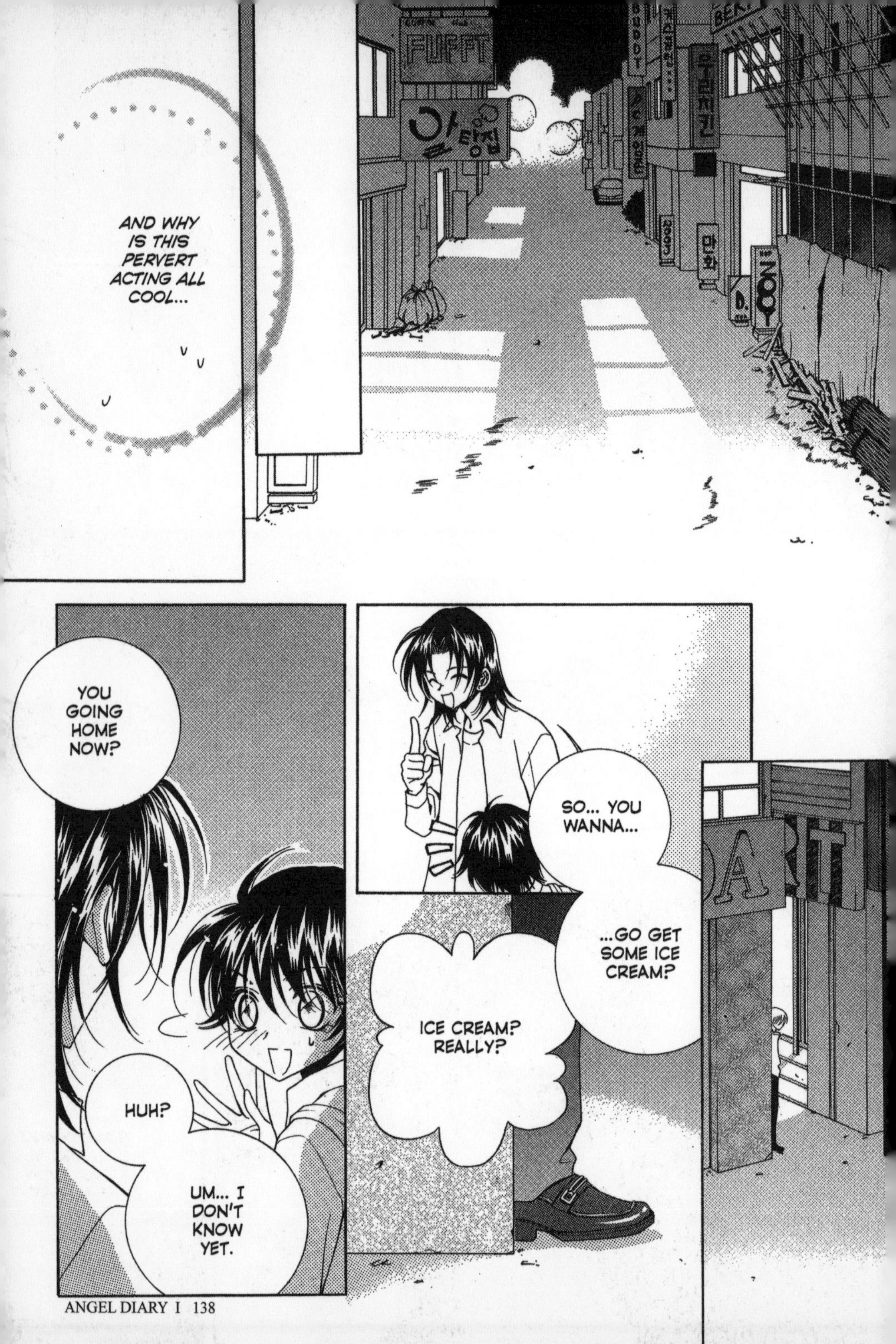
AND WHY IS THIS PERVERT ACTING ALL COOL...
YOU GOING HOME NOW?
HUH?
UM... I DON'T KNOW YET.
SO... YOU WANNA...
...GO GET SOME ICE CREAM?
ICE CREAM? REALLY?

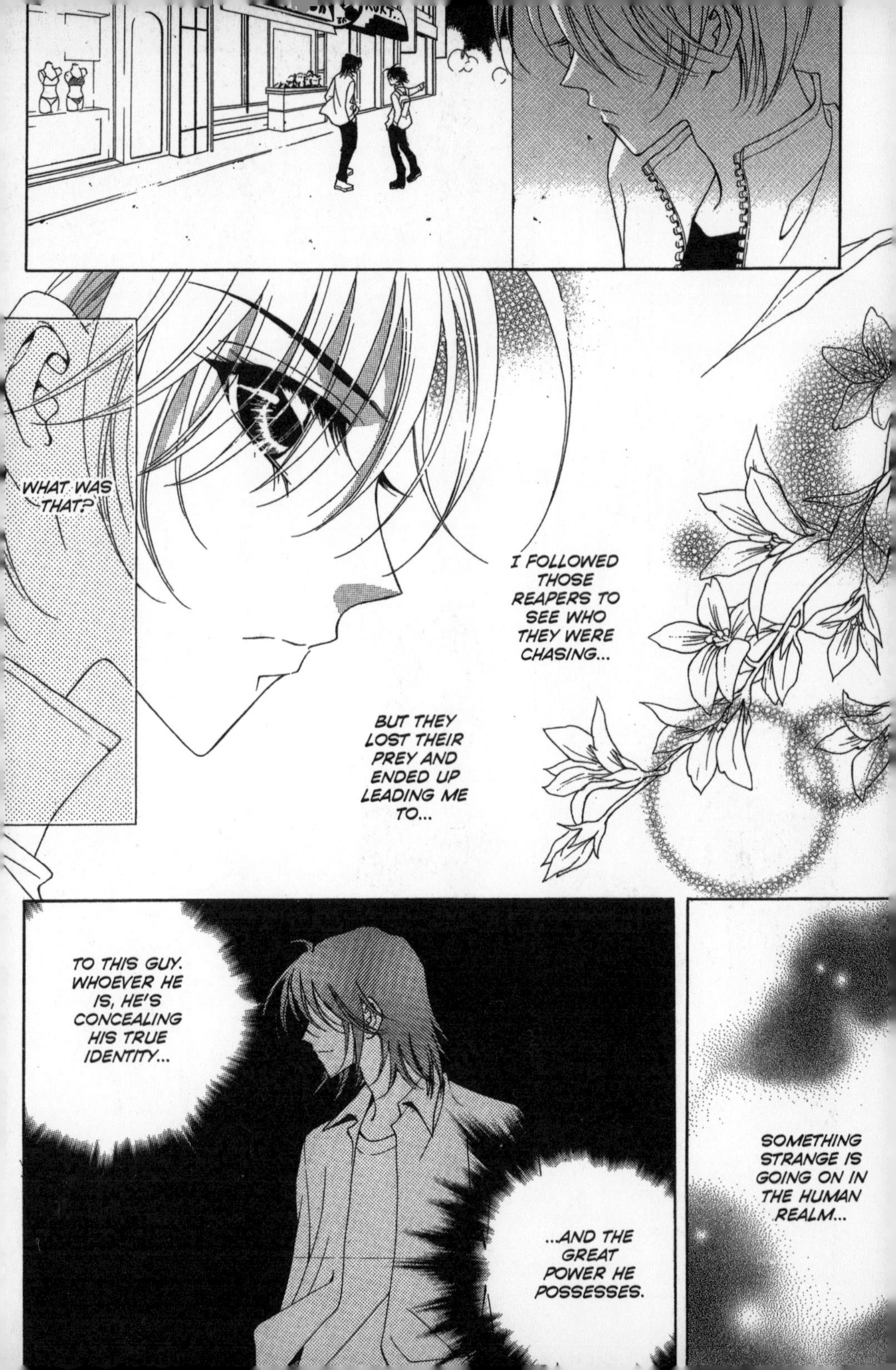
WHAT WAS THAT?
I FOLLOWED THOSE REAPERS TO SEE WHO THEY WERE CHASING...
BUT THEY LOST THEIR PREY AND ENDED UP LEADING ME TO...
TO THIS GUY. WHOEVER HE IS, HE'S CONCEALING HIS TRUE IDENTITY...
...AND THE GREAT POWER HE POSSESSES.
SOMETHING STRANGE IS GOING ON IN THE HUMAN REALM...

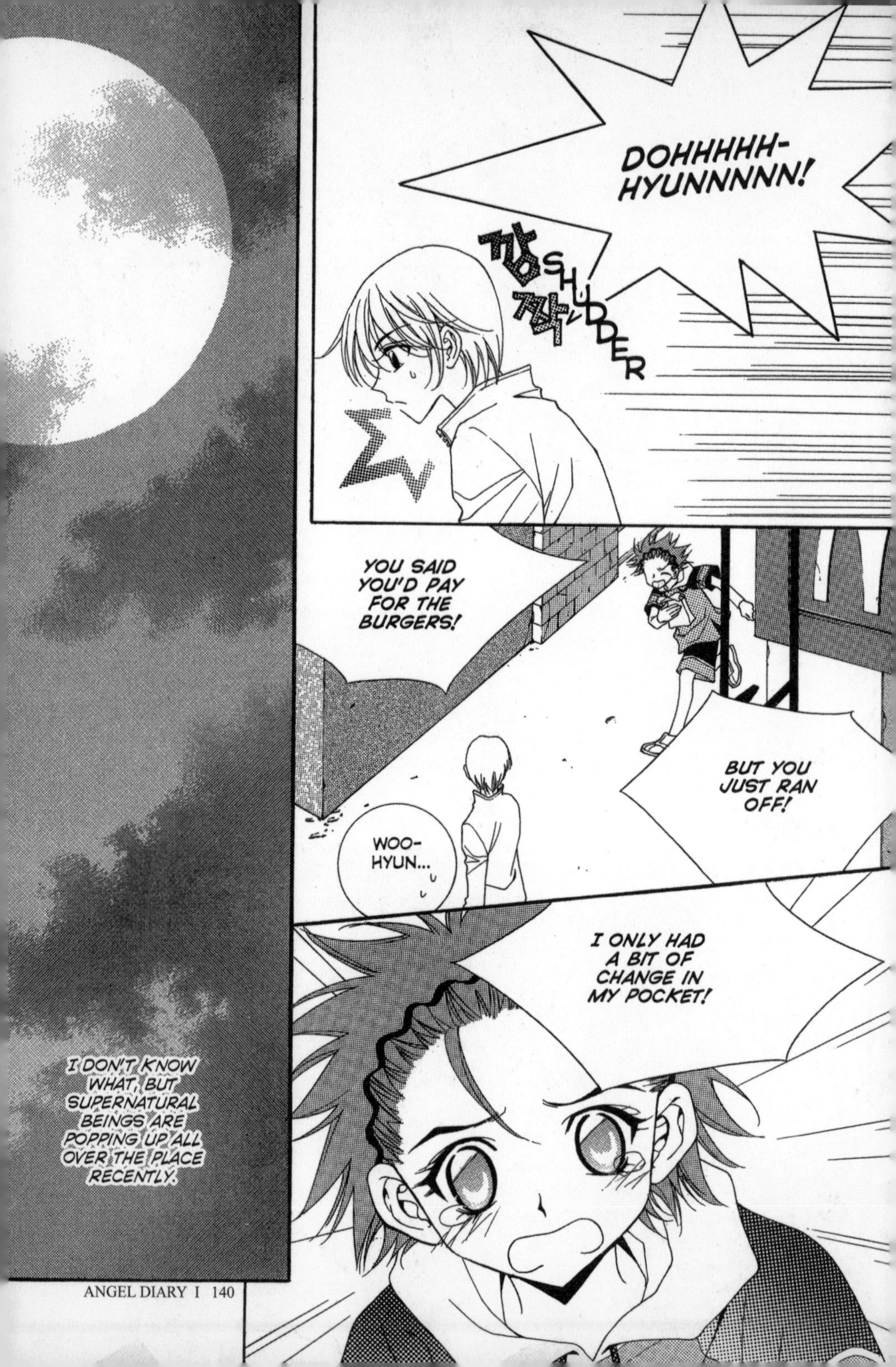
I DON'T KNOW WHAT, BUT SUPERNATURAL BEINGS ARE POPPING UP ALL OVER THE PLACE RECENTLY.
DOHHHHH-HYUNNNNN!
SHUDDER
YOU SAID YOU'D PAY FOR THE BURGERS!
BUT YOU JUST RAN OFF!
WOO-HYUN...
I ONLY HAD A BIT OF CHANGE IN MY POCKET!

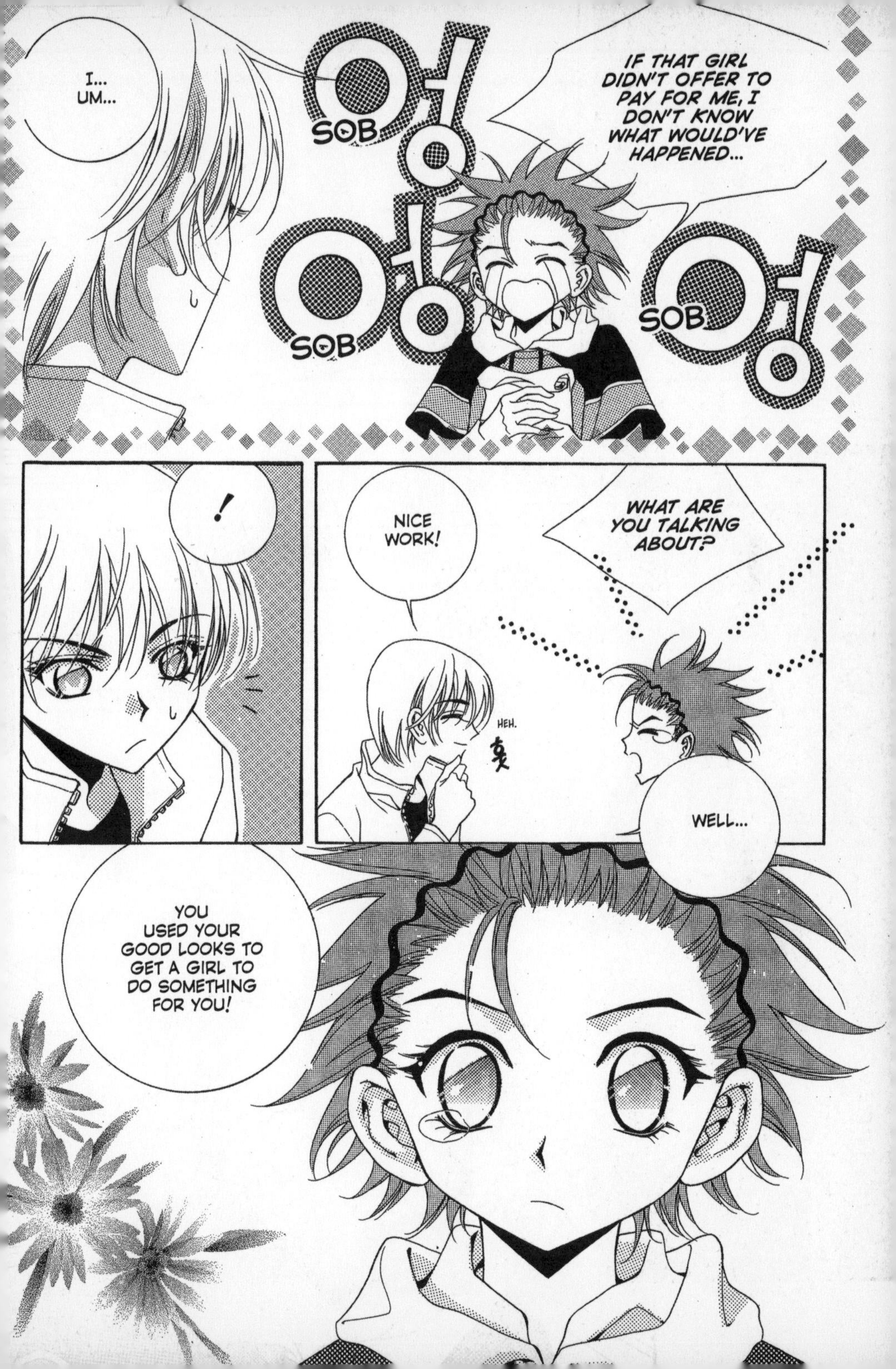
I... UM...
엉 SOB
IF THAT GIRL DIDN'T OFFER TO PAY FOR ME, I DON'T KNOW WHAT WOULD'VE HAPPENED...
엉 SOB
엉 SOB
!
NICE WORK!
WHAT ARE YOU TALKING ABOUT?
HEH.
WELL...
YOU USED YOUR GOOD LOOKS TO GET A GIRL TO DO SOMETHING FOR YOU!

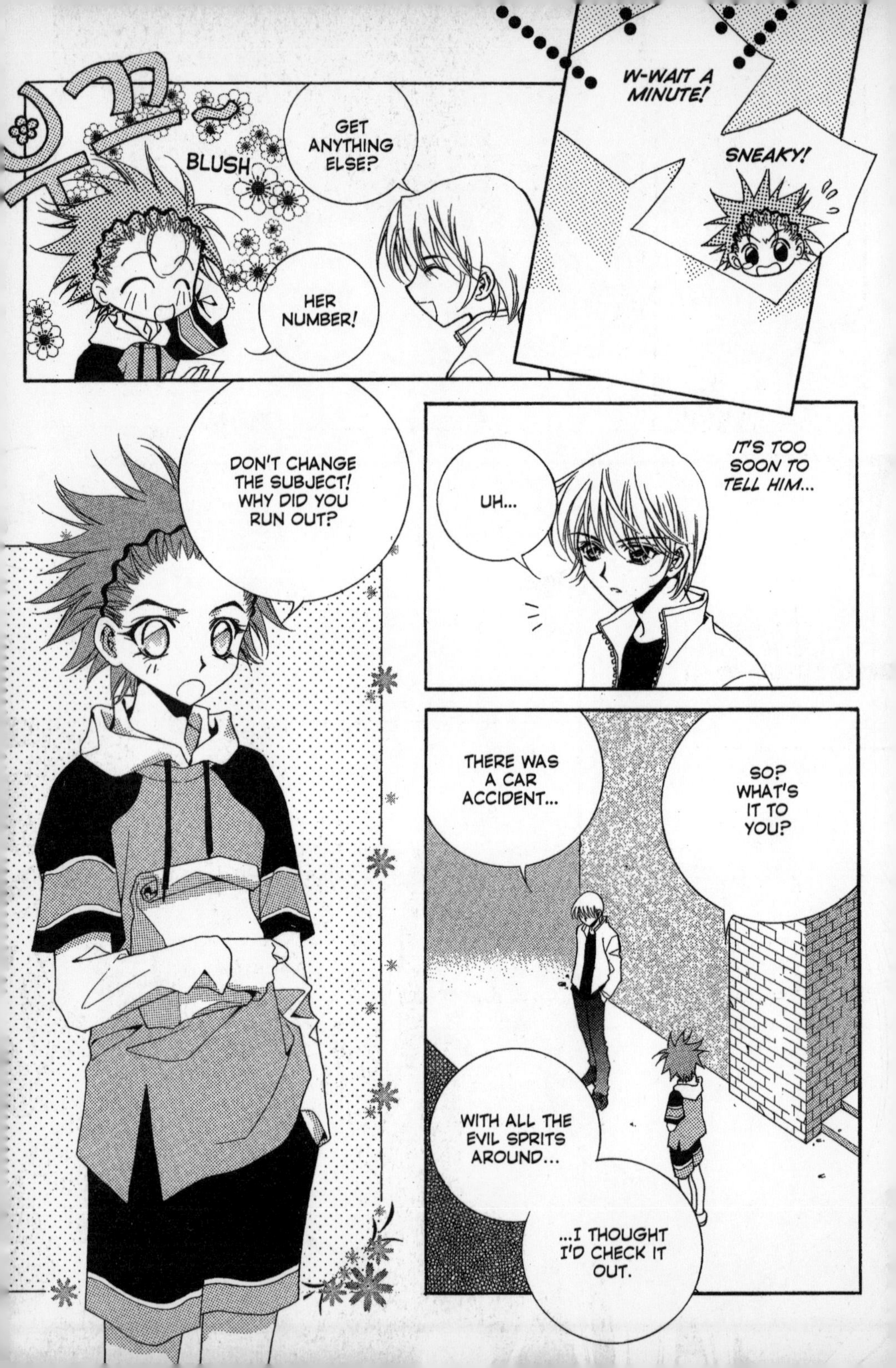

BLUSH
GET ANYTHING ELSE?
HER NUMBER!
W-WAIT A MINUTE!
SNEAKY!
DON'T CHANGE THE SUBJECT! WHY DID YOU RUN OUT?
UH...
IT'S TOO SOON TO TELL HIM...
THERE WAS A CAR ACCIDENT...
SO? WHAT'S IT TO YOU?
WITH ALL THE EVIL SPRITS AROUND...
...I THOUGHT I'D CHECK IT OUT.

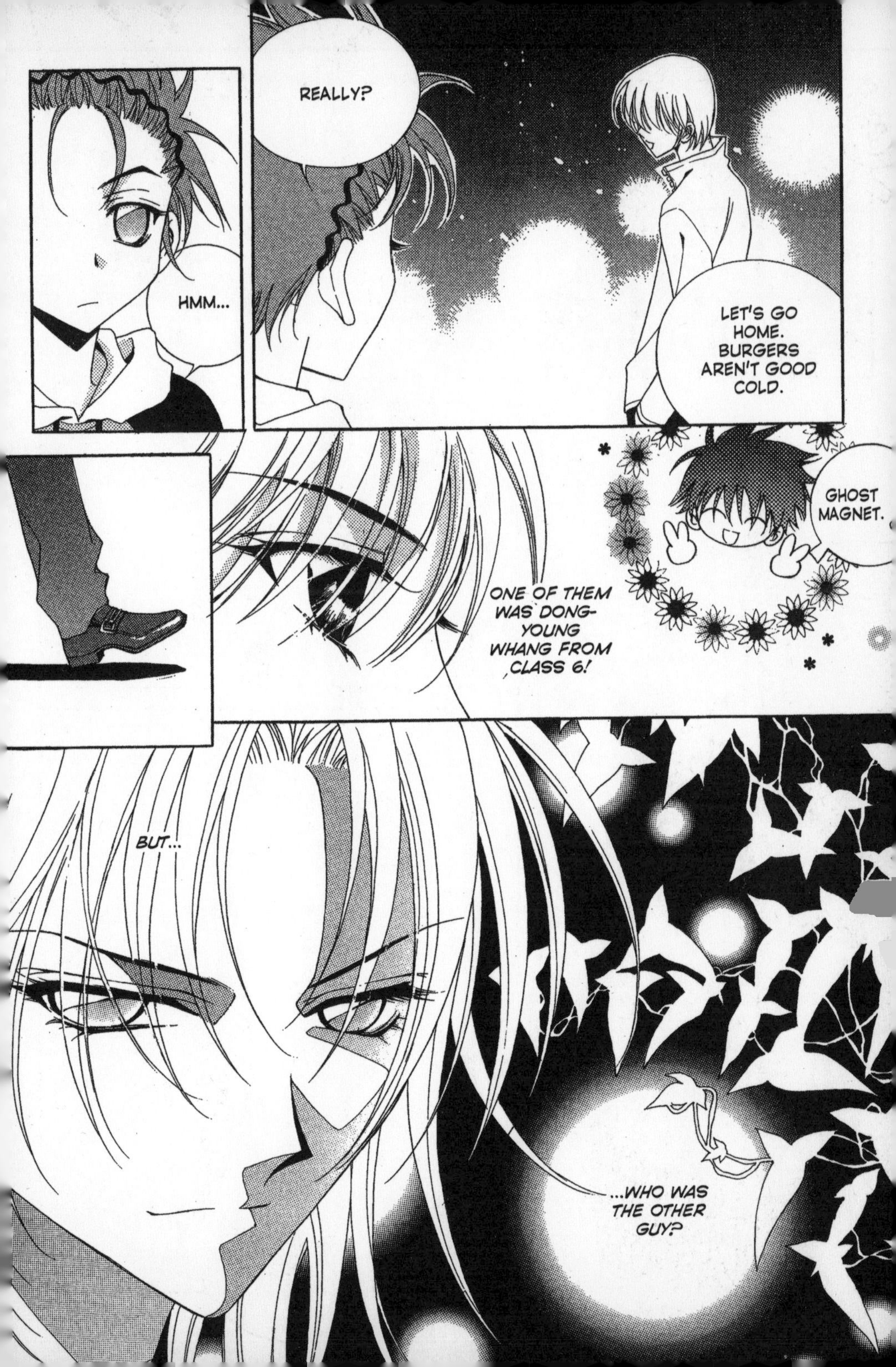
HMM...
REALLY?
LET'S GO HOME. BURGERS AREN'T GOOD COLD.
ONE OF THEM WAS DONG-YOUNG WHANG FROM CLASS 6!
GHOST MAGNET.
BUT...
...WHO WAS THE OTHER GUY?

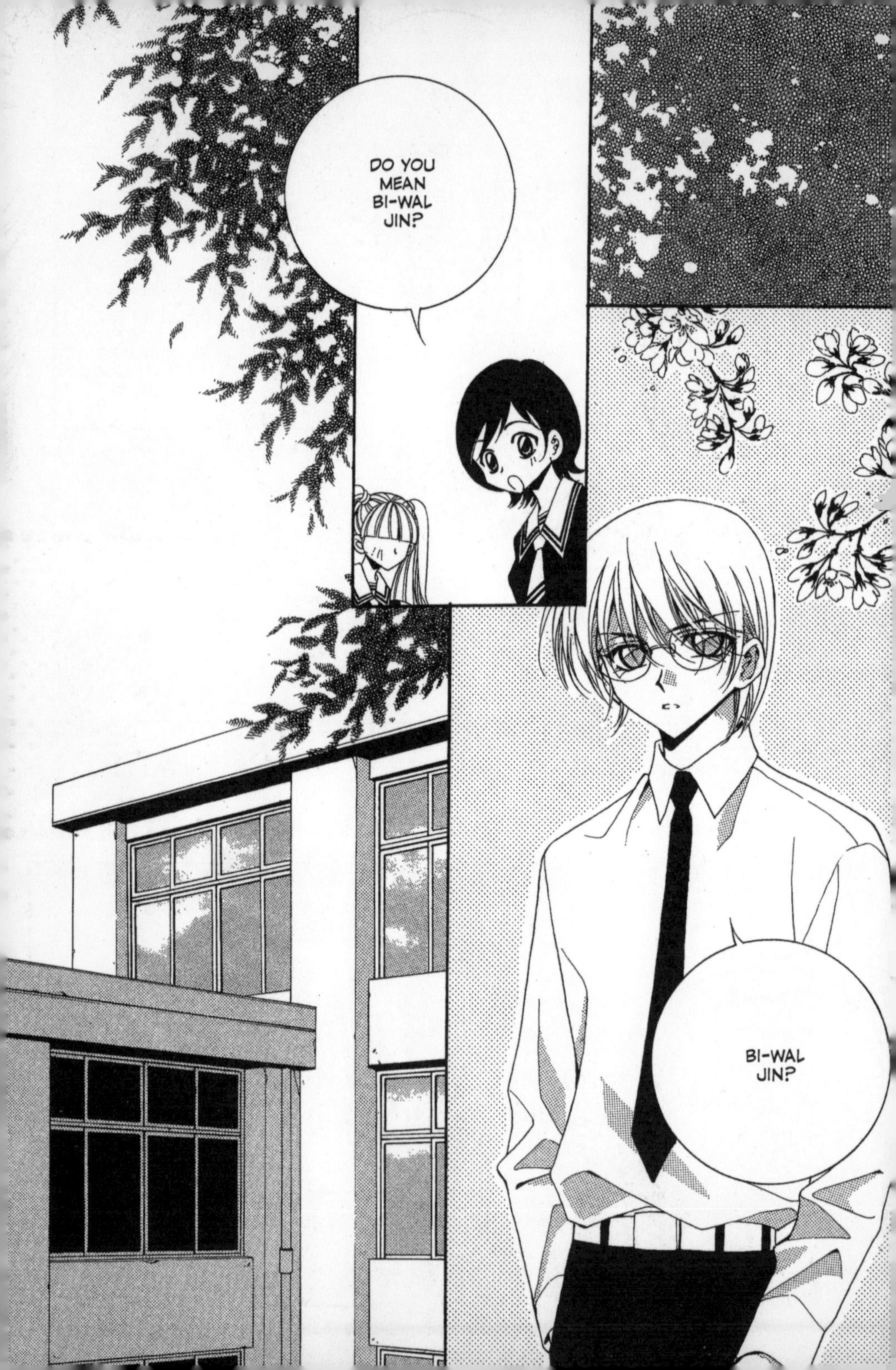
DO YOU MEAN BI-WAL JIN?
BI-WAL JIN?

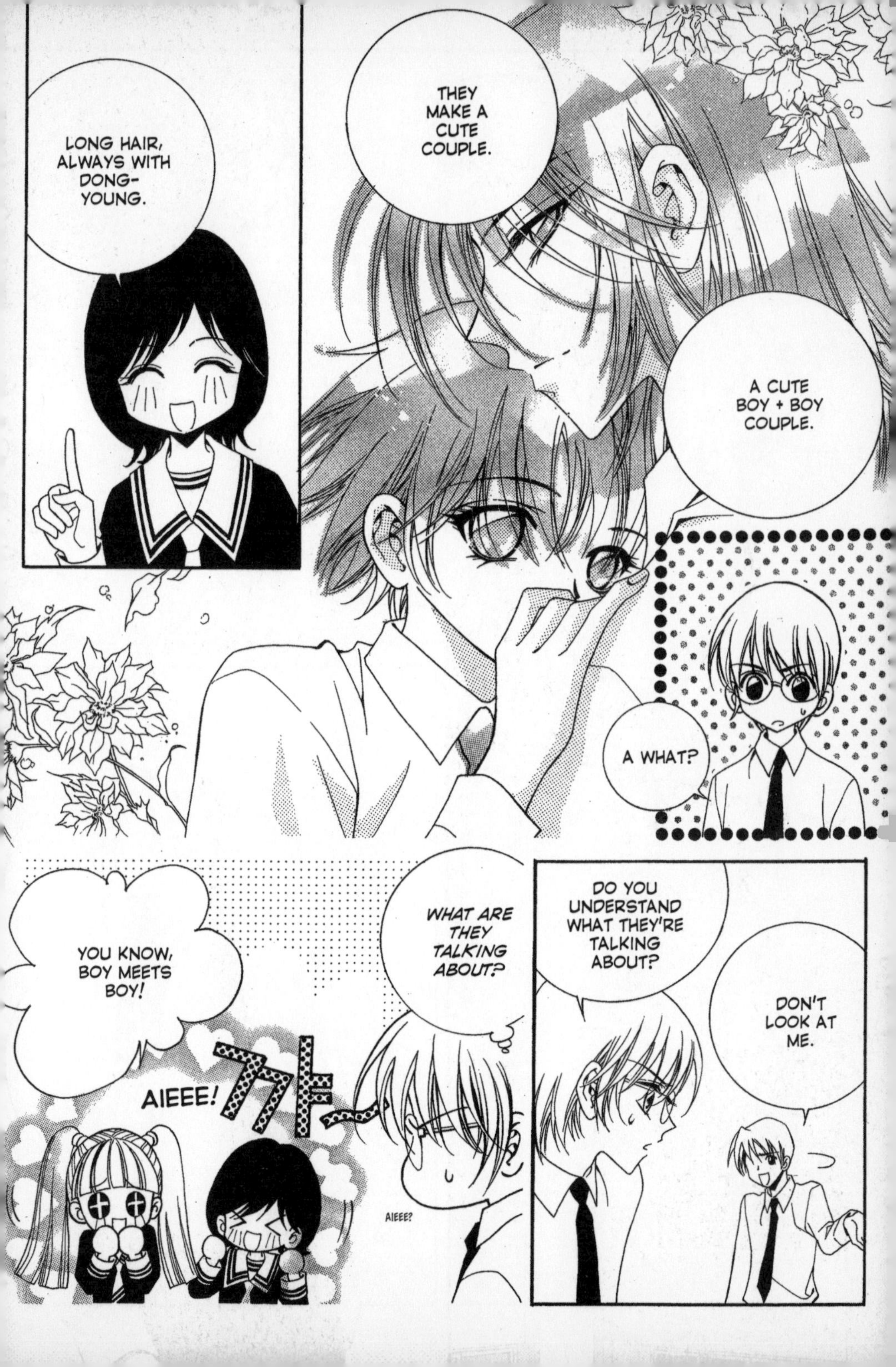
LONG HAIR, ALWAYS WITH DONG-YOUNG.
THEY MAKE A CUTE COUPLE.
A CUTE BOY + BOY COUPLE.
A WHAT?
YOU KNOW, BOY MEETS BOY!
AIEEE!
WHAT ARE THEY TALKING ABOUT?
AIEEE?
DO YOU UNDERSTAND WHAT THEY'RE TALKING ABOUT?
DON'T LOOK AT ME.

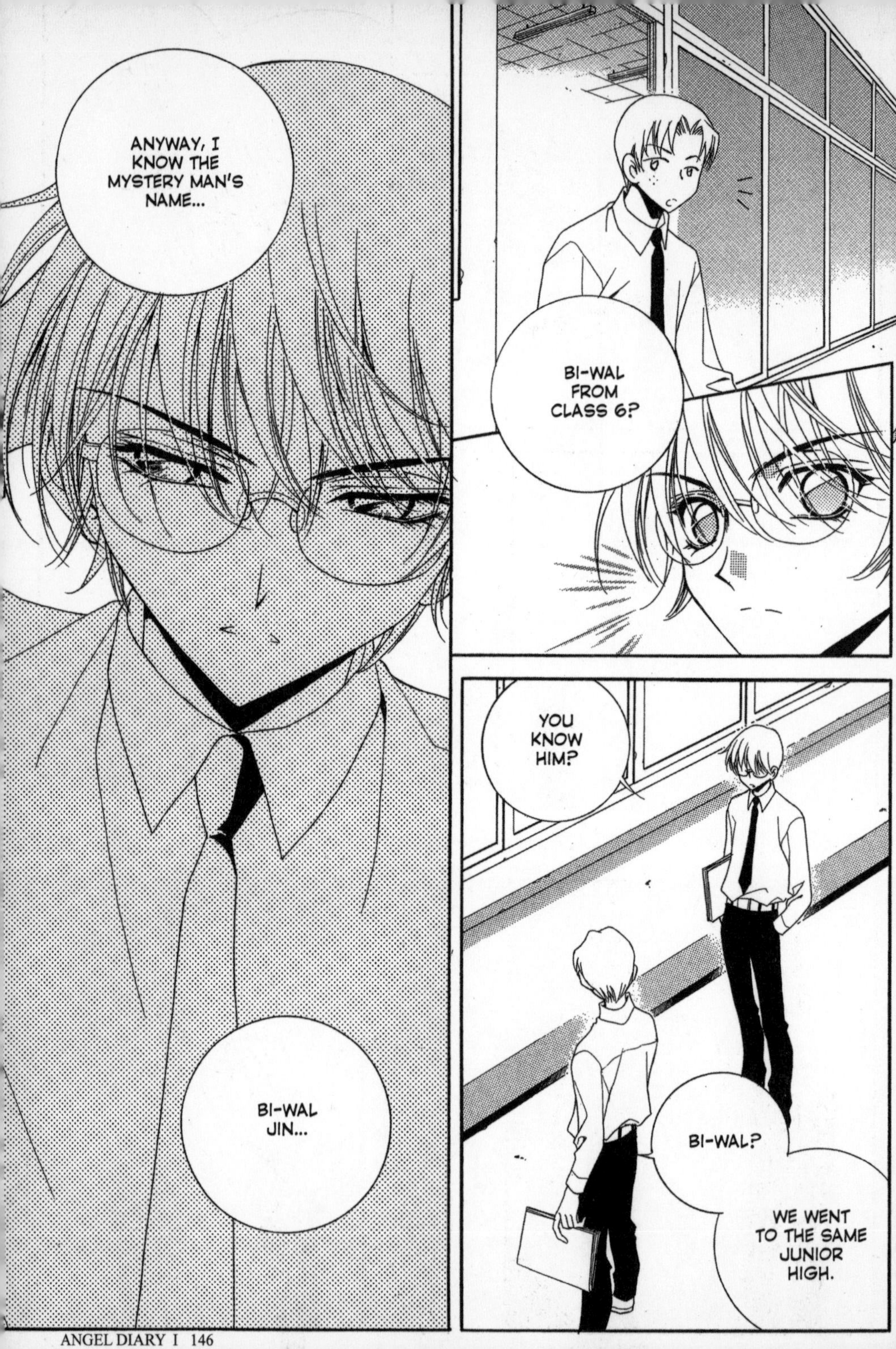
ANYWAY, I KNOW THE MYSTERY MAN'S NAME...
BI-WAL JIN...
BI-WAL FROM CLASS 6?
YOU KNOW HIM?
BI-WAL?
WE WENT TO THE SAME JUNIOR HIGH.

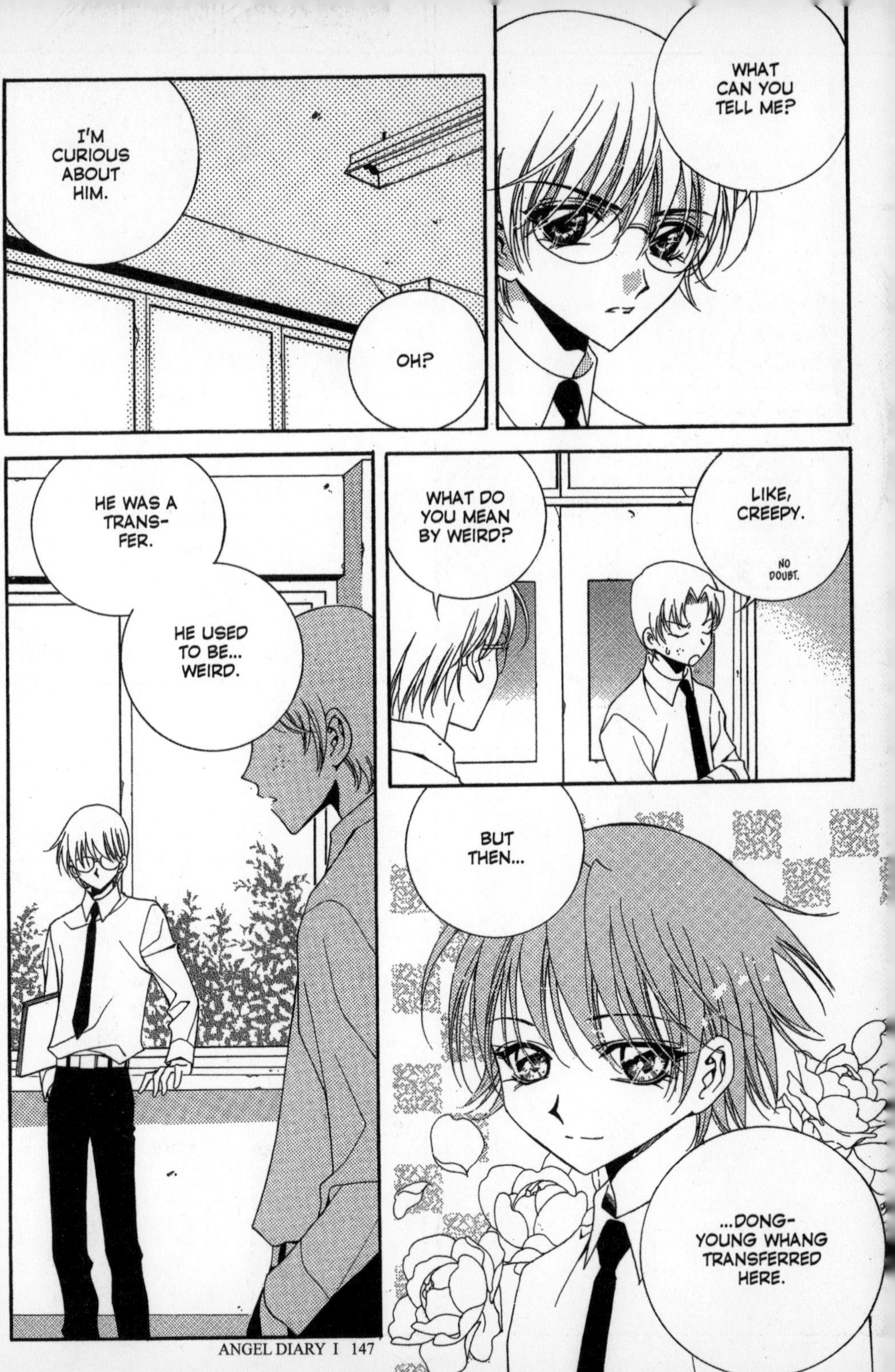
I'M CURIOUS ABOUT HIM.
OH?
WHAT CAN YOU TELL ME?
HE WAS A TRANS-FER.
HE USED TO BE... WEIRD.
WHAT DO YOU MEAN BY WEIRD?
LIKE, CREEPY.
NO DOUBT.
BUT THEN...
...DONG-YOUNG WHANG TRANSFERRED HERE.

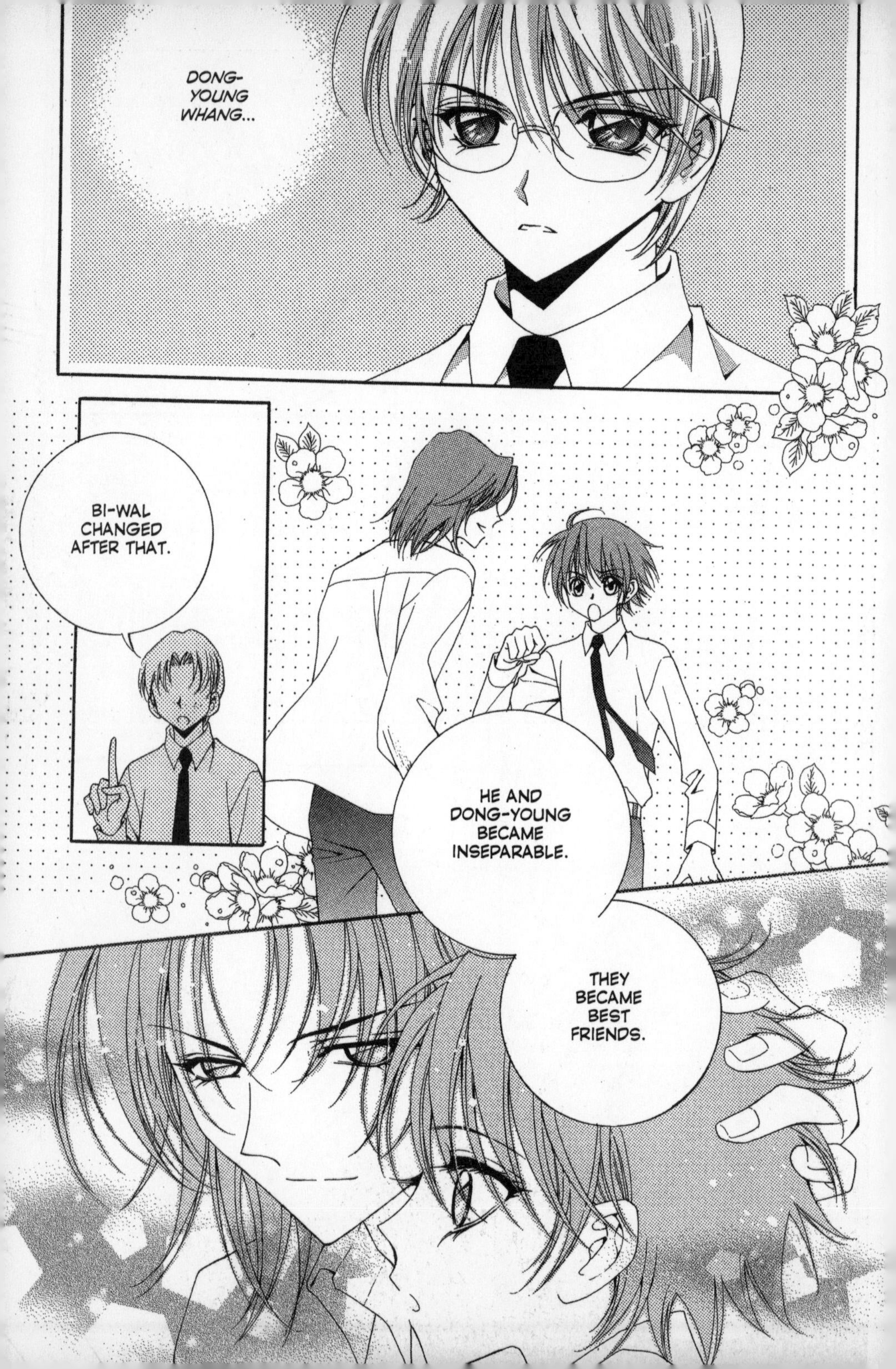
DONG-YOUNG WHANG...
BI-WAL CHANGED AFTER THAT.
HE AND DONG-YOUNG BECAME INSEPARABLE.
THEY BECAME BEST FRIENDS.

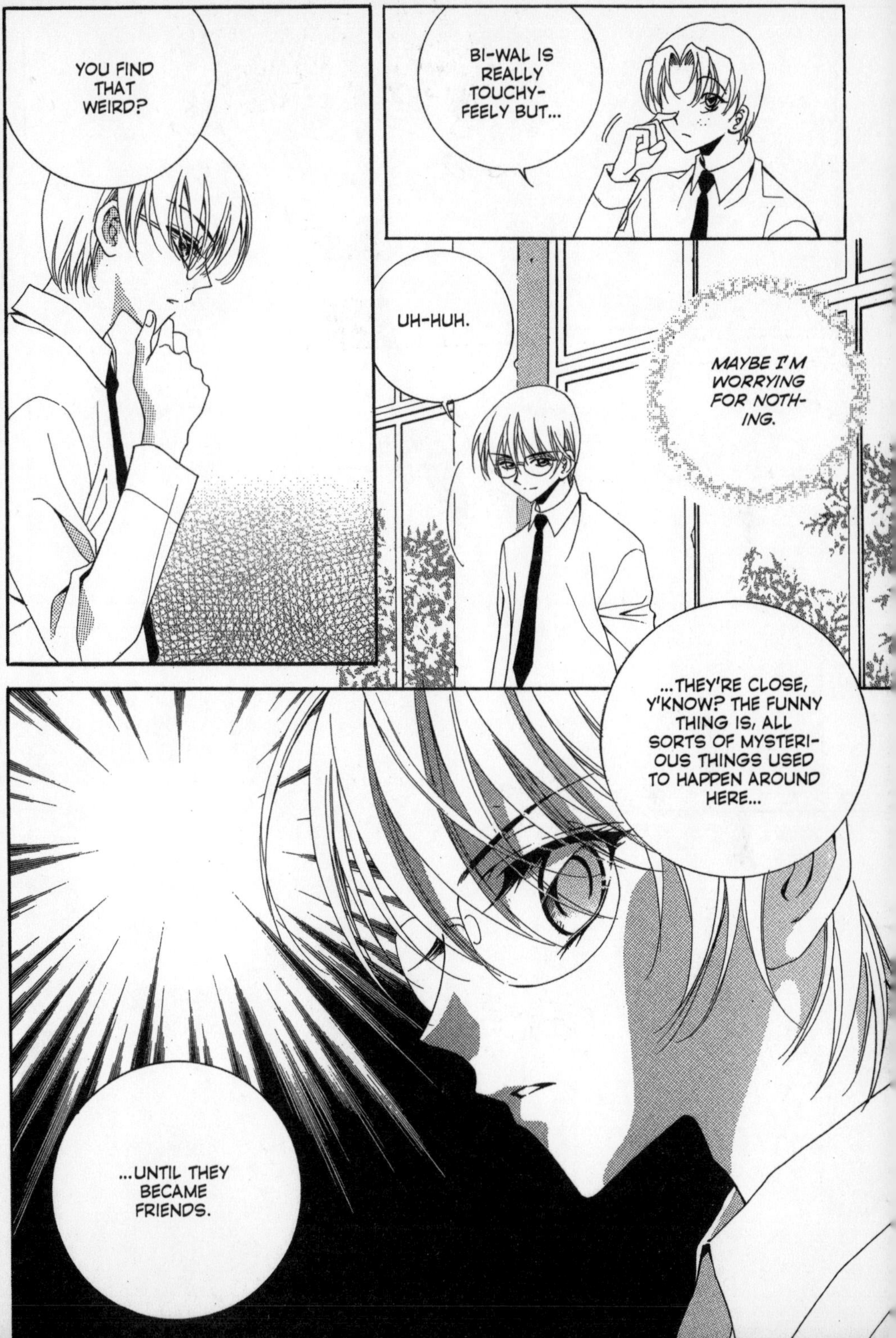
YOU FIND THAT WEIRD?
BI-WAL IS REALLY TOUCHY-FEELY BUT...
UH-HUH.
MAYBE I'M WORRYING FOR NOTH-ING.
...THEY'RE CLOSE, Y'KNOW? THE FUNNY THING IS, ALL SORTS OF MYSTERI-OUS THINGS USED TO HAPPEN AROUND HERE...
...UNTIL THEY BECAME FRIENDS.

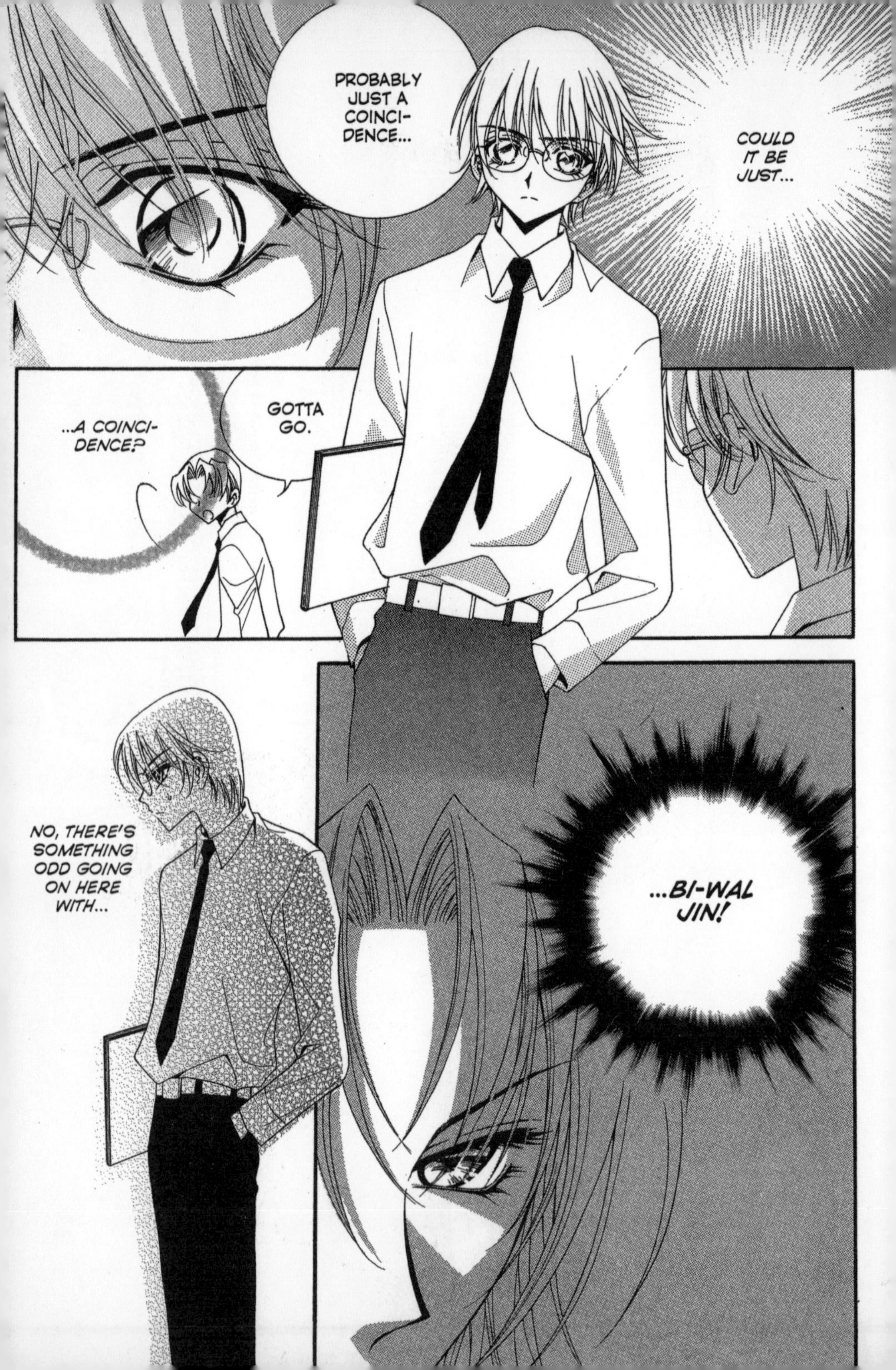
PROBABLY JUST A COINCI-DENCE...
COULD IT BE JUST...
...A COINCI-DENCE?
GOTTA GO.
NO, THERE'S SOMETHING ODD GOING ON HERE WITH...
...BI-WAL JIN!

II FIELD TRIP

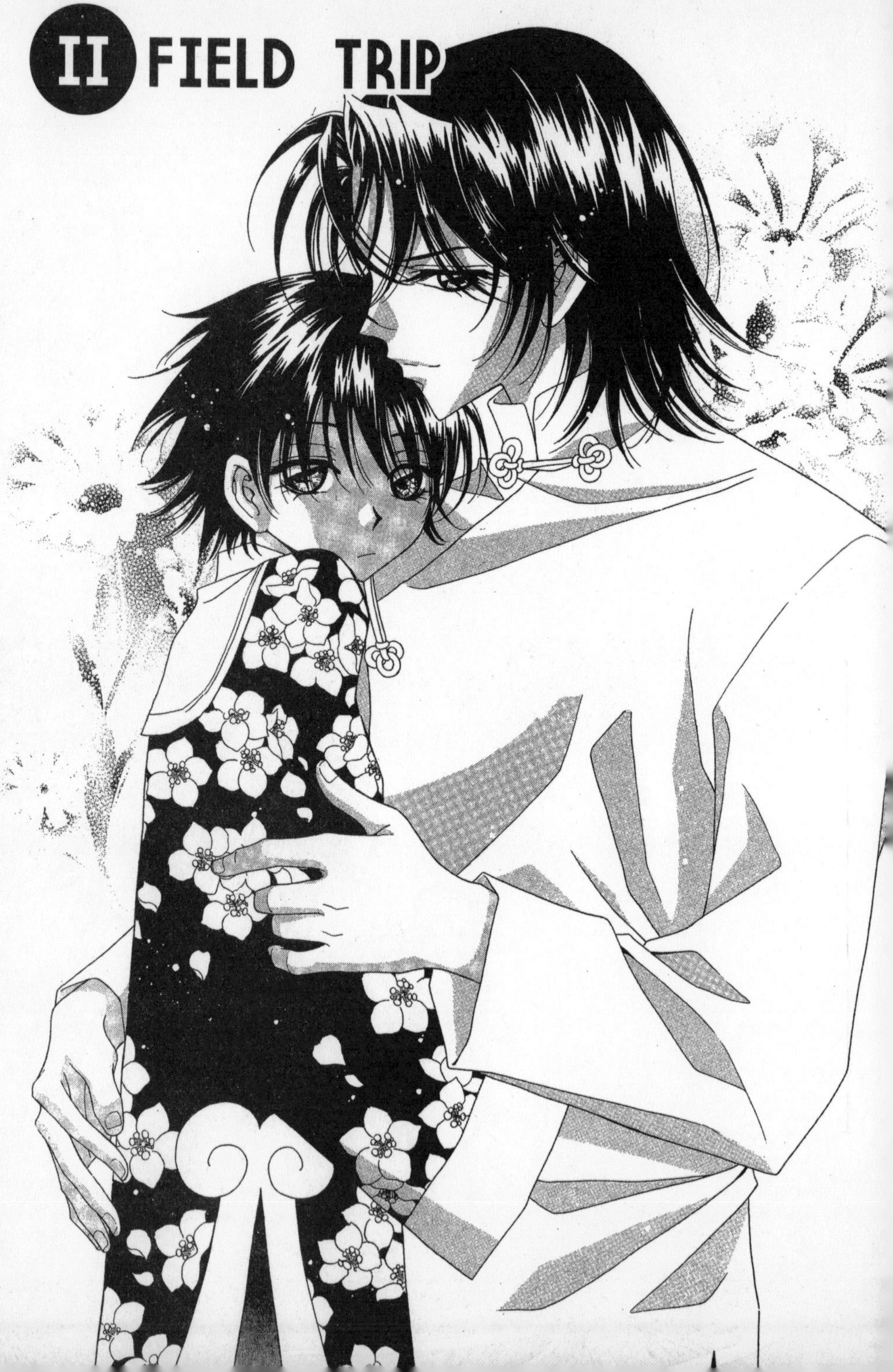

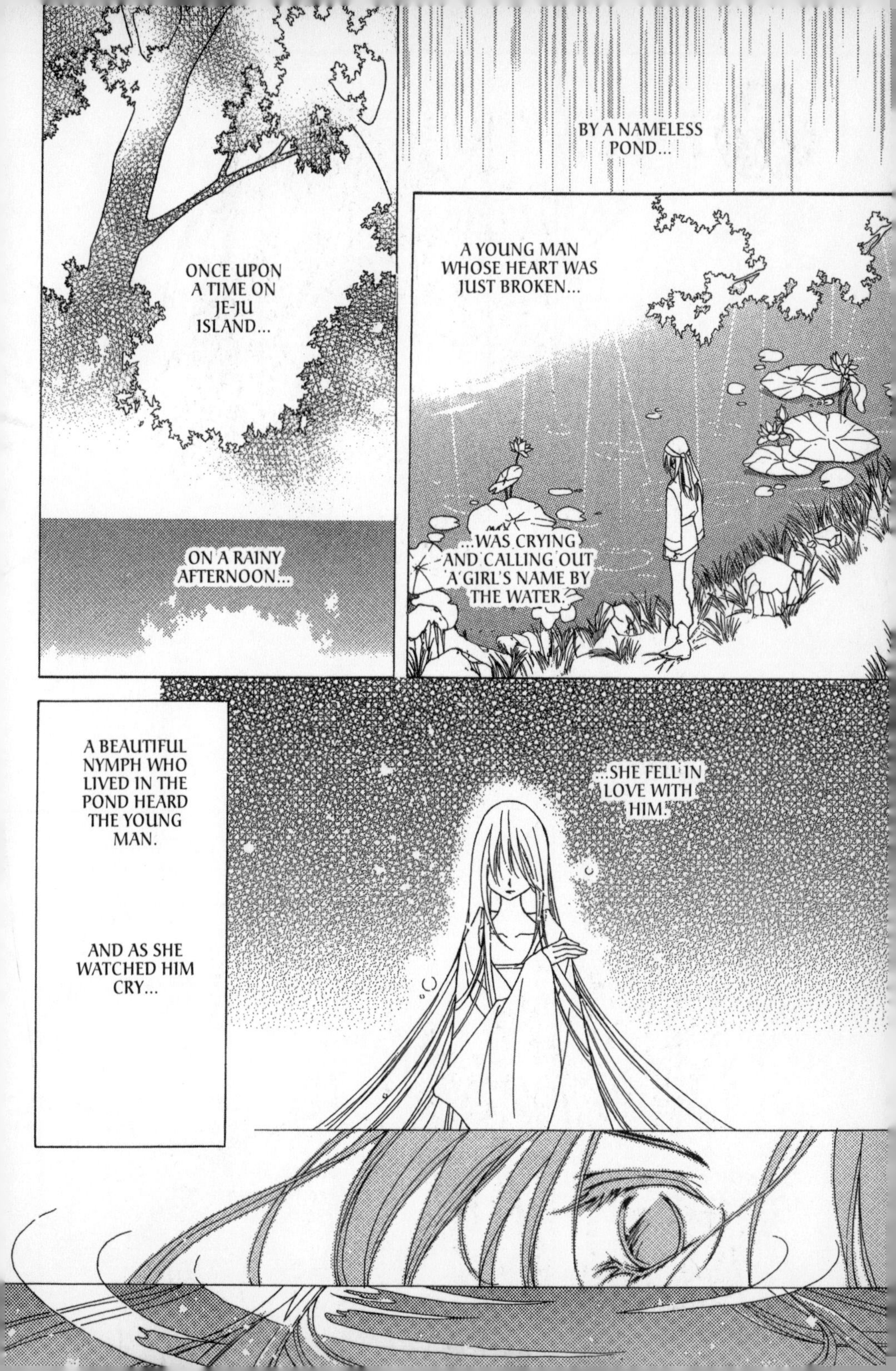
ONCE UPON A TIME ON JE-JU ISLAND...
ON A RAINY AFTERNOON...
BY A NAMELESS POND...
A YOUNG MAN WHOSE HEART WAS JUST BROKEN...
...WAS CRYING AND CALLING OUT A GIRL'S NAME BY THE WATER.
A BEAUTIFUL NYMPH WHO LIVED IN THE POND HEARD THE YOUNG MAN.
AND AS SHE WATCHED HIM CRY...
...SHE FELL IN LOVE WITH HIM.

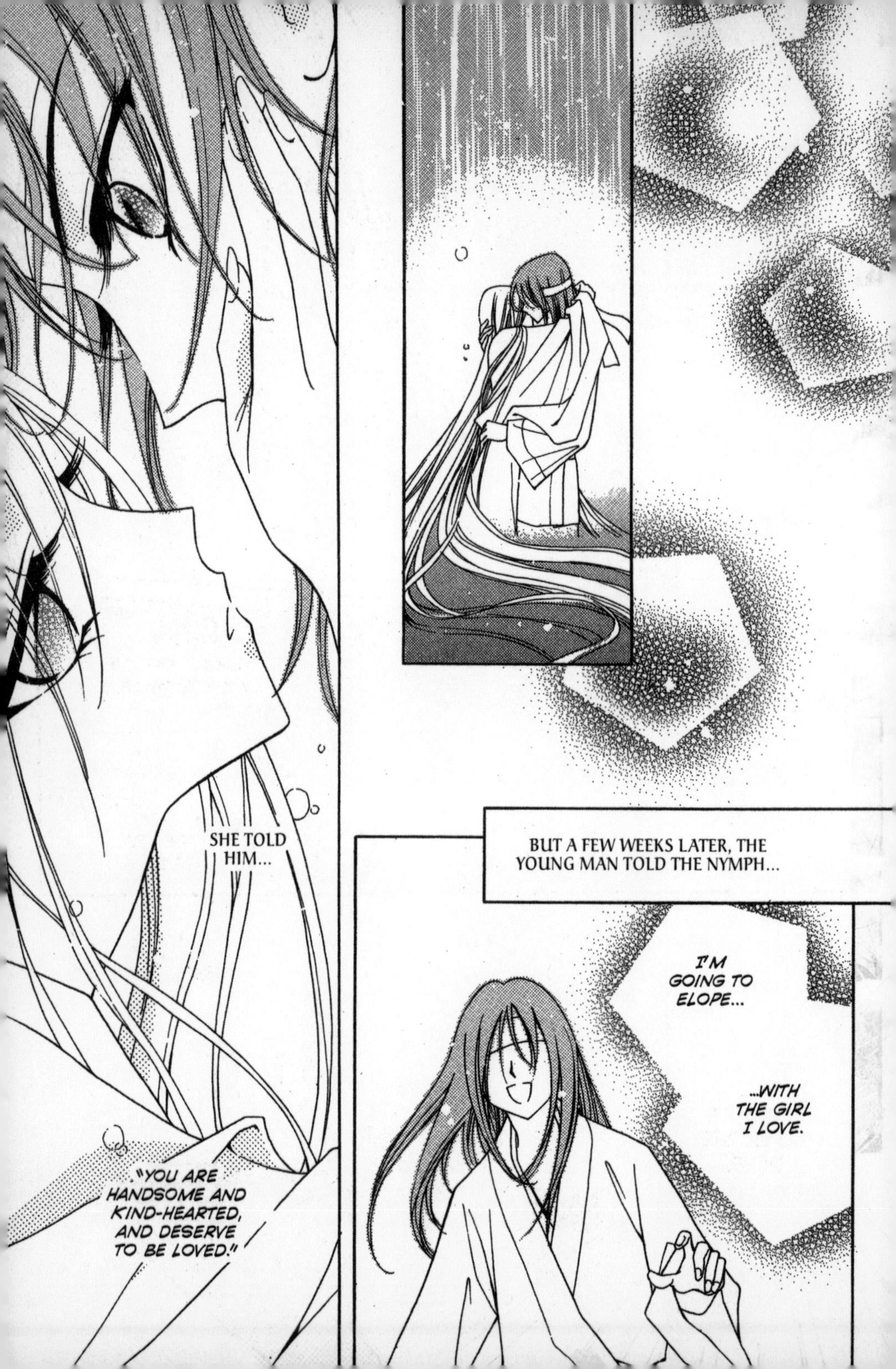
SHE TOLD HIM...
..."YOU ARE HANDSOME AND KIND-HEARTED, AND DESERVE TO BE LOVED."
BUT A FEW WEEKS LATER, THE YOUNG MAN TOLD THE NYMPH...
I'M GOING TO ELOPE...
...WITH THE GIRL I LOVE.

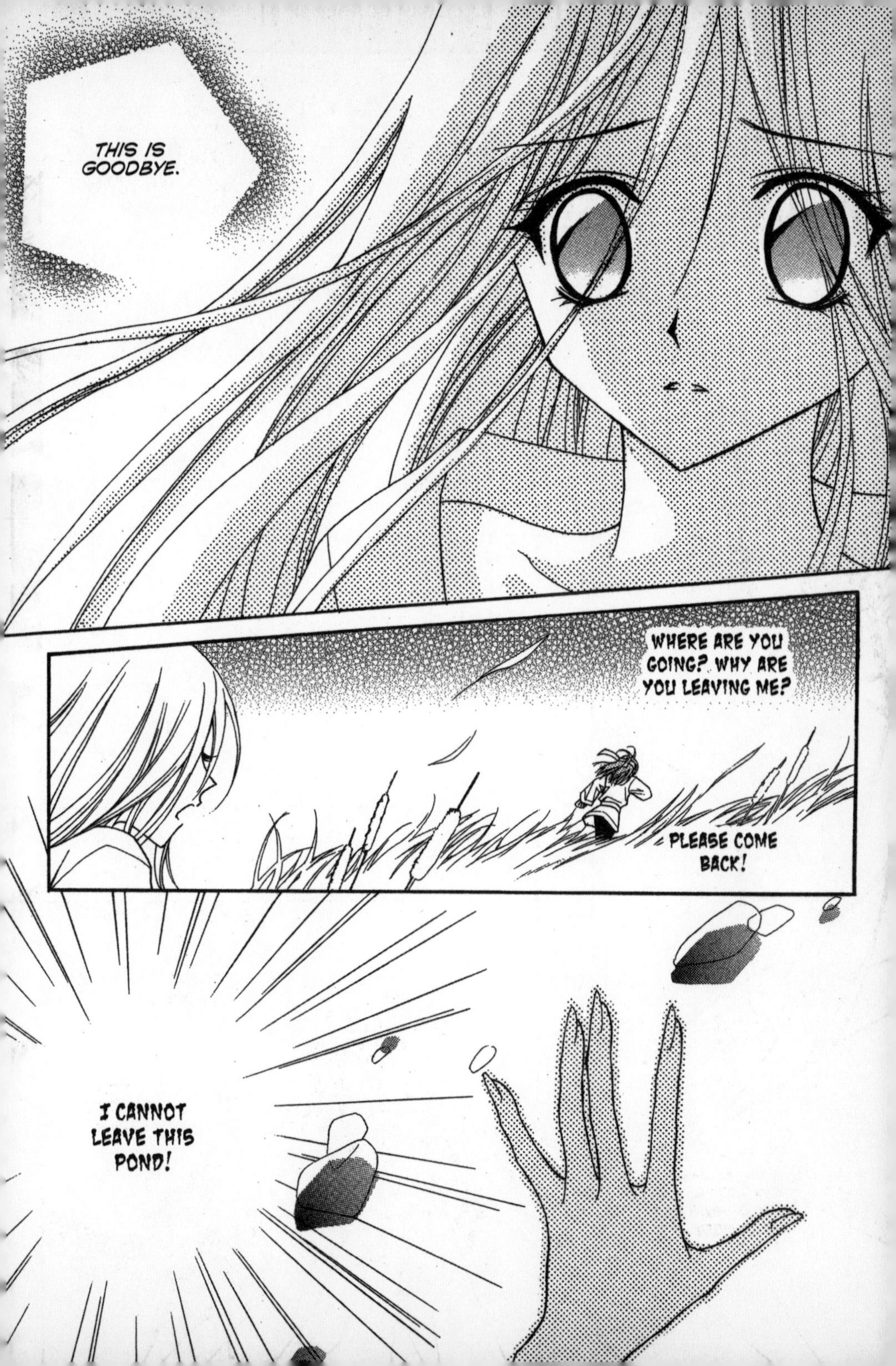
THIS IS GOODBYE.
WHERE ARE YOU GOING? WHY ARE YOU LEAVING ME?
PLEASE COME BACK!
I CANNOT LEAVE THIS POND!

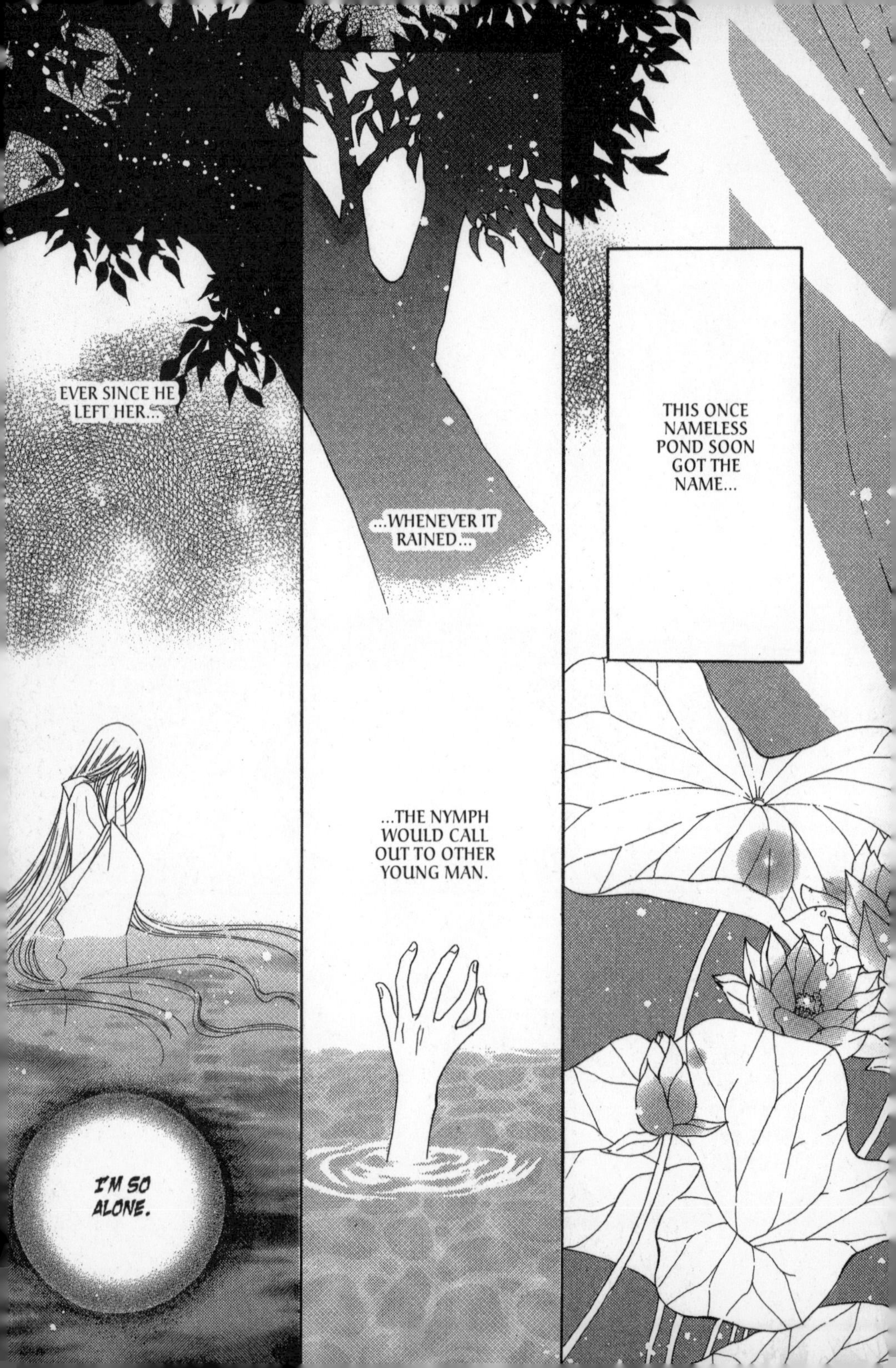
EVER SINCE HE LEFT HER...
I'M SO ALONE.
...WHENEVER IT RAINED...
...THE NYMPH WOULD CALL OUT TO OTHER YOUNG MAN.
THIS ONCE NAMELESS POND SOON GOT THE NAME...

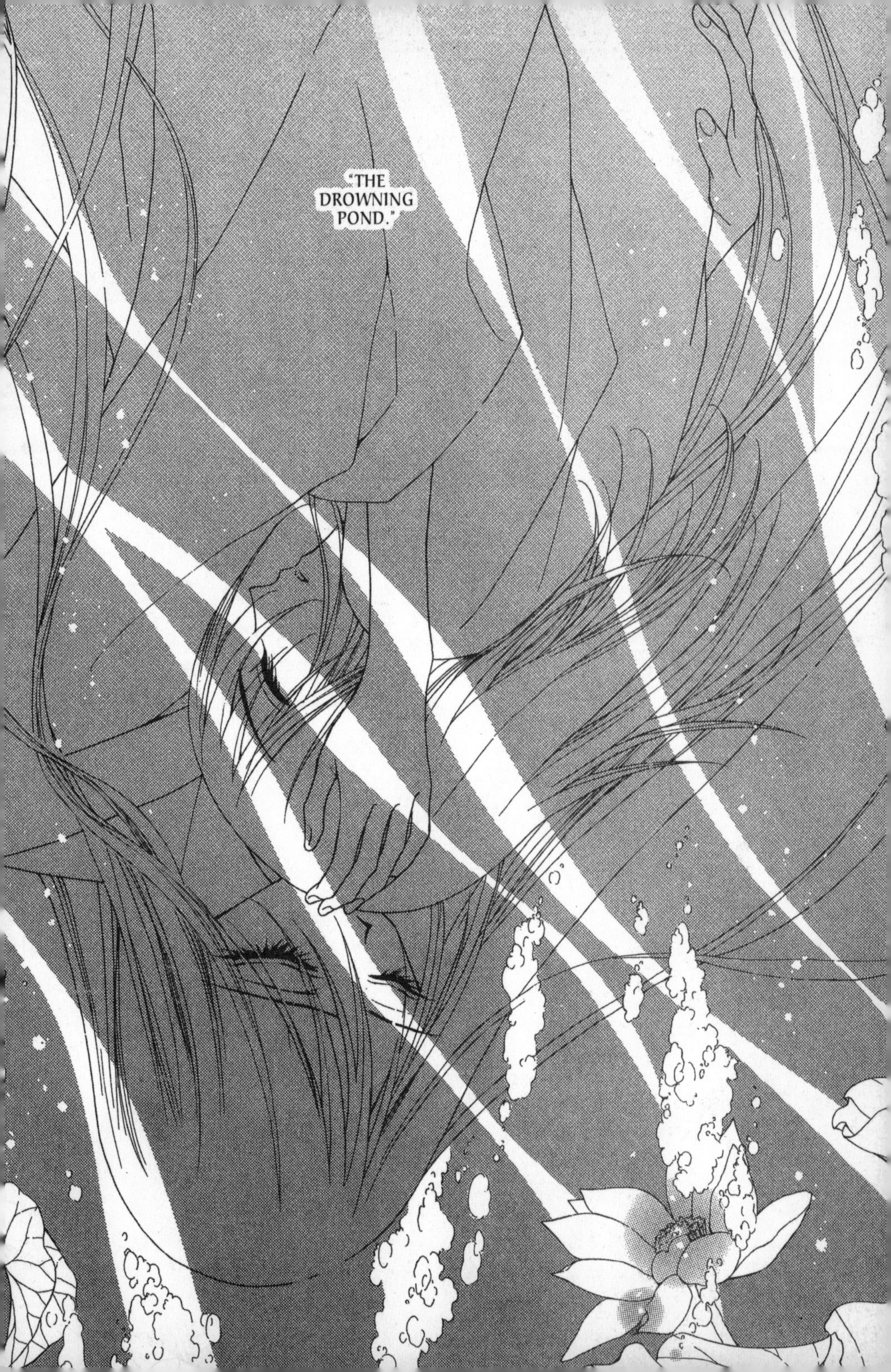
"THE DROWNING POND."

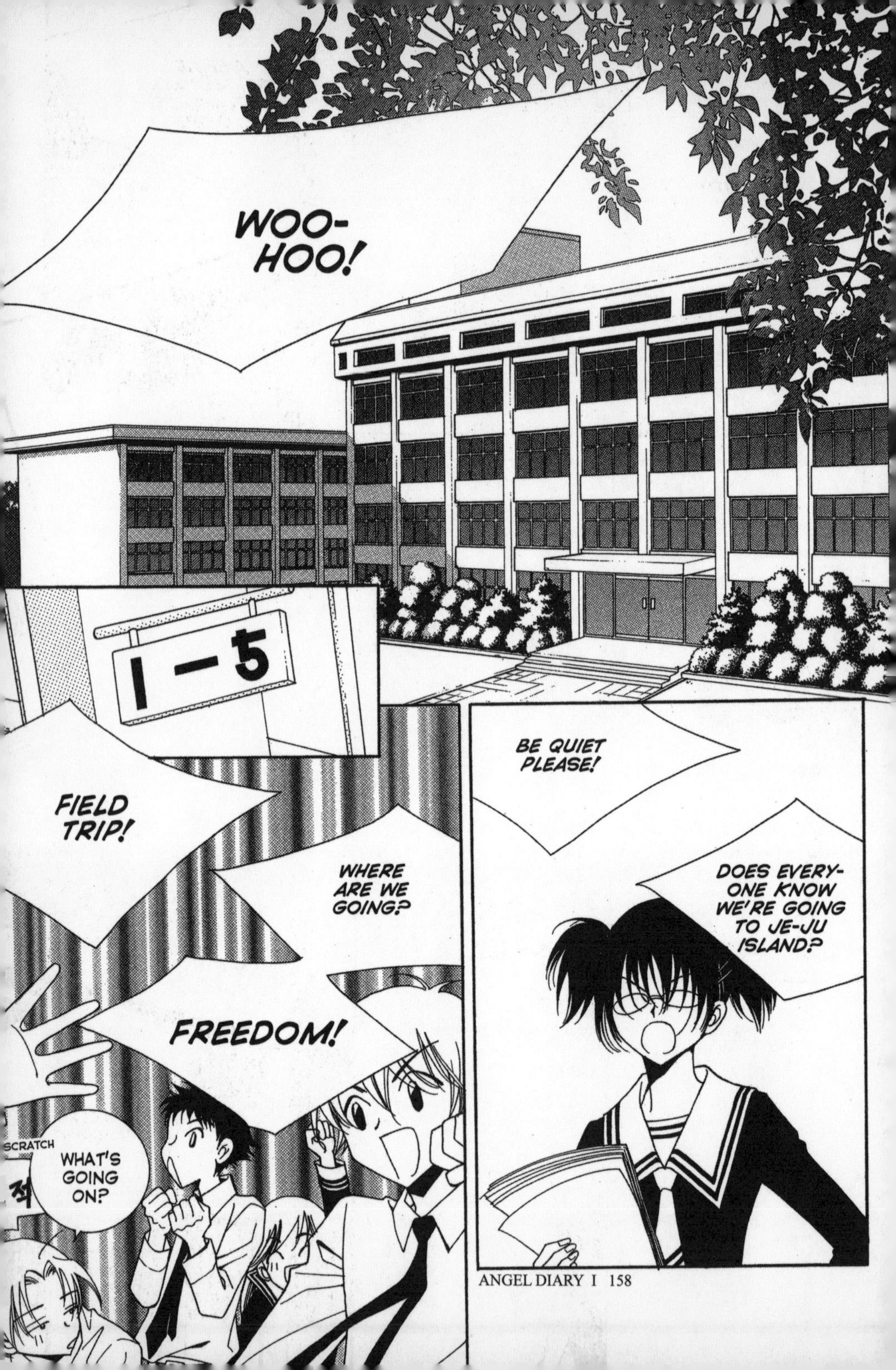
WOO-HOO!
1-5
FIELD TRIP!
WHERE ARE WE GOING?
FREEDOM!
SCRATCH
WHAT'S GOING ON?
BE QUIET PLEASE!
DOES EVERY-ONE KNOW WE'RE GOING TO JE-JU ISLAND?

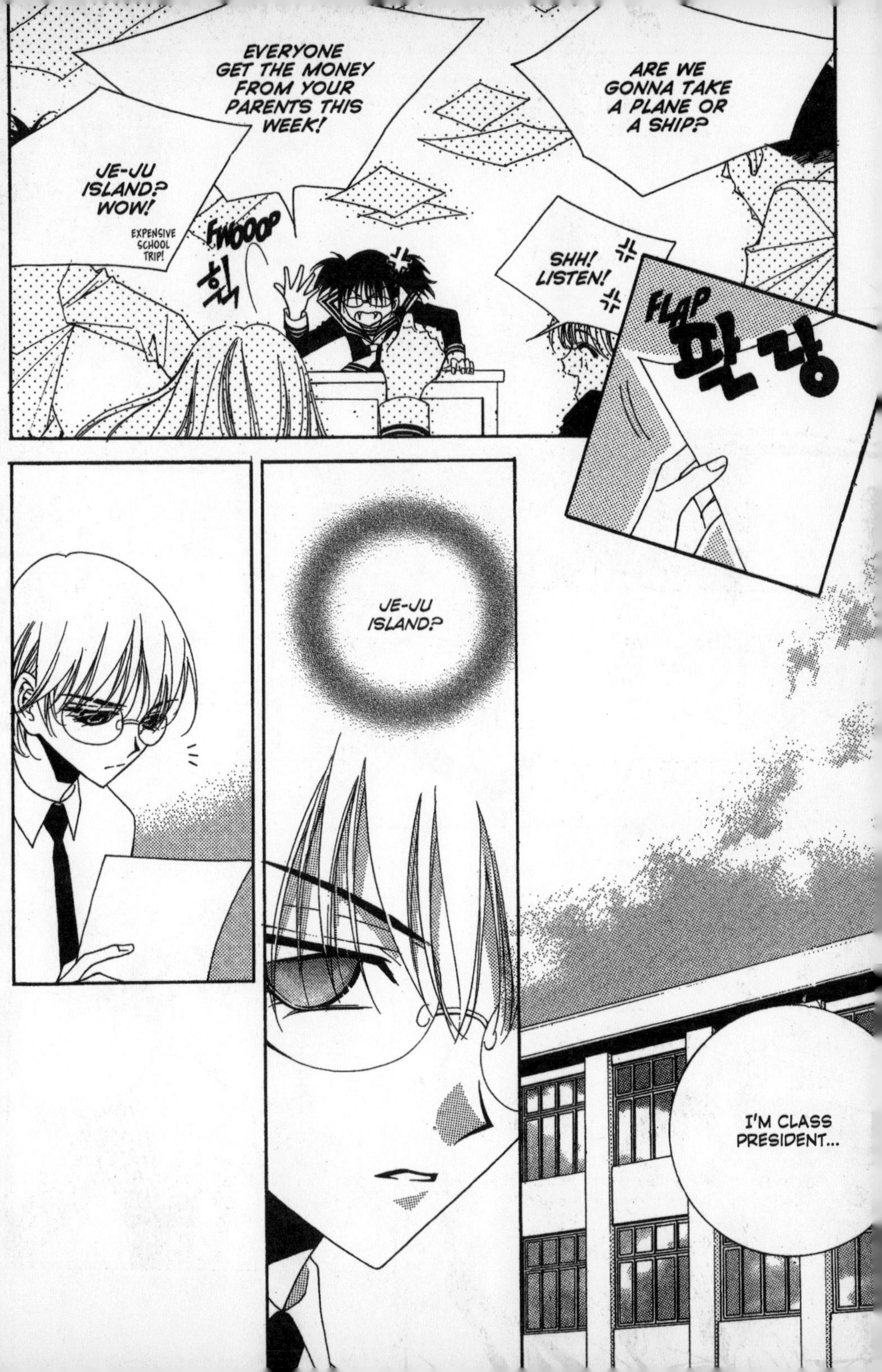
EVERYONE GET THE MONEY FROM YOUR PARENTS THIS WEEK!
ARE WE GONNA TAKE A PLANE OR A SHIP?
JE-JU ISLAND? WOW!
EXPENSIVE SCHOOL TRIP!
FWOOOP
휙
SHH! LISTEN!
FLAP
팔랑
JE-JU ISLAND?
I'M CLASS PRESIDENT...

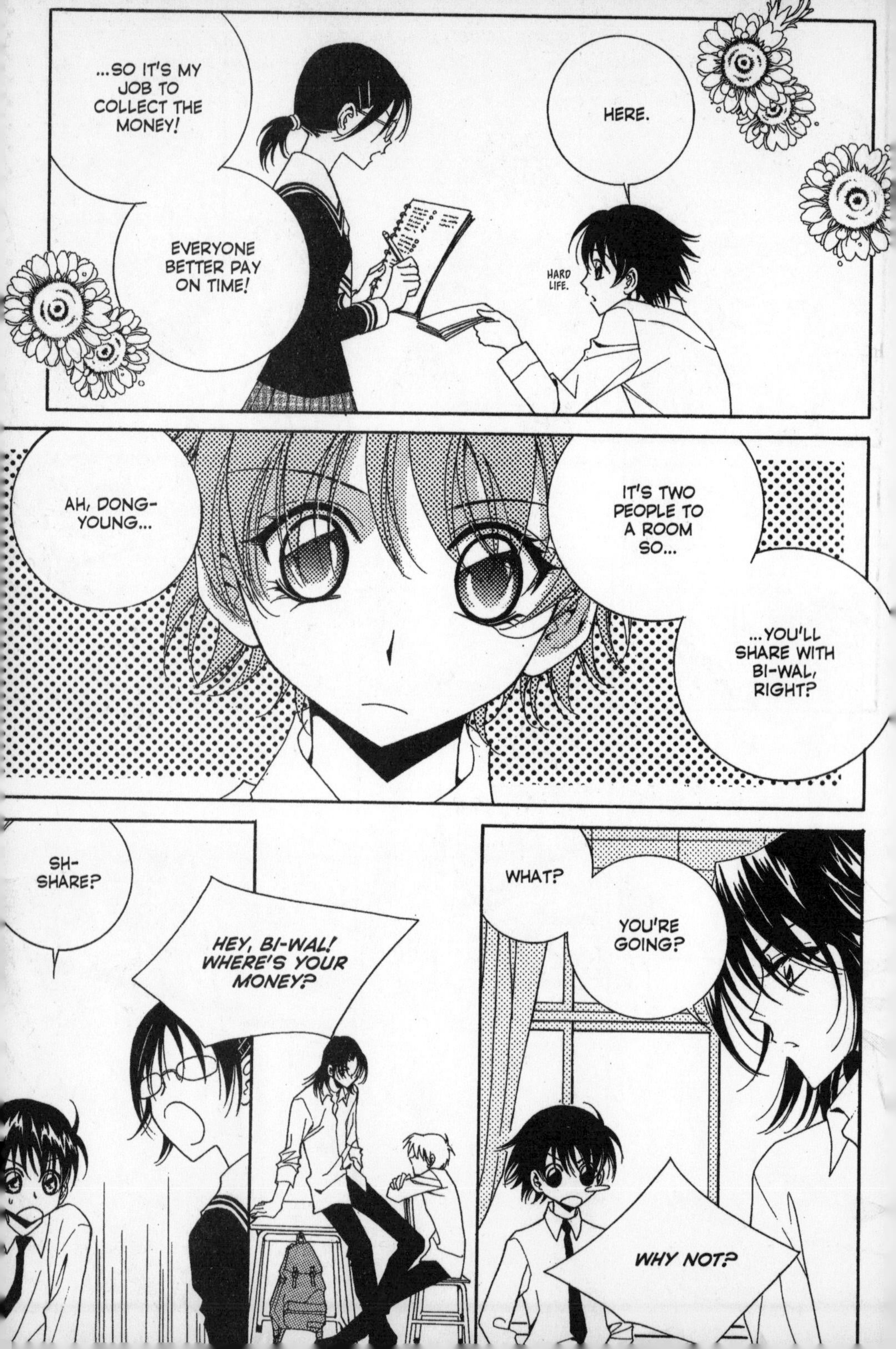
...SO IT'S MY JOB TO COLLECT THE MONEY!
EVERYONE BETTER PAY ON TIME!
HERE.
HARD LIFE.
AH, DONG-YOUNG...
IT'S TWO PEOPLE TO A ROOM SO...
...YOU'LL SHARE WITH BI-WAL, RIGHT?
SH-SHARE?
HEY, BI-WAL! WHERE'S YOUR MONEY?
WHAT?
YOU'RE GOING?
WHY NOT?

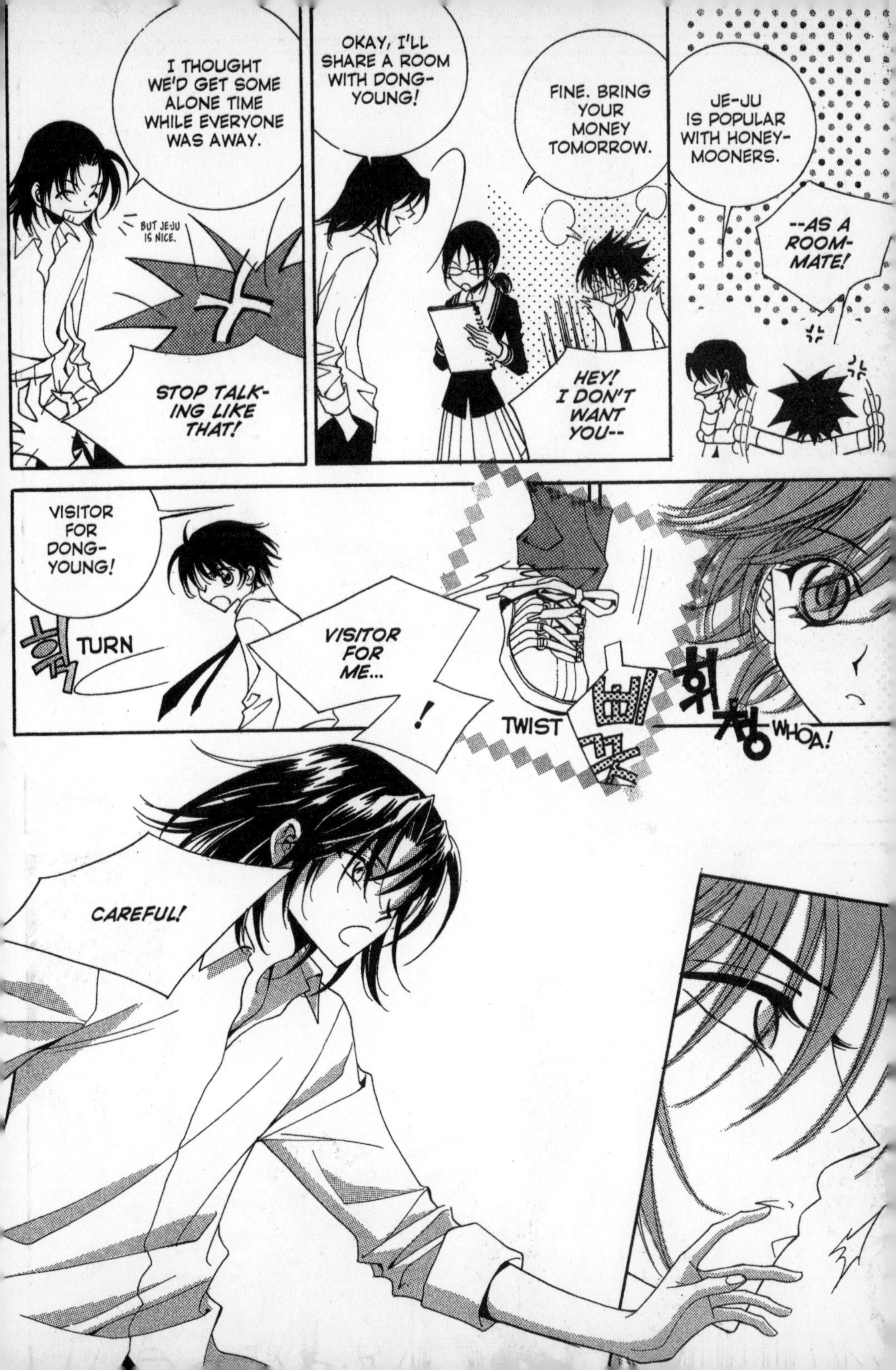
I THOUGHT WE'D GET SOME ALONE TIME WHILE EVERYONE WAS AWAY.
BUT JE-JU IS NICE.
STOP TALKING LIKE THAT!
OKAY, I'LL SHARE A ROOM WITH DONG-YOUNG!
FINE. BRING YOUR MONEY TOMORROW.
HEY! I DON'T WANT YOU--
JE-JU IS POPULAR WITH HONEY-MOONERS.
--AS A ROOM-MATE!
VISITOR FOR DONG-YOUNG!
TURN
VISITOR FOR ME...
!
TWIST
WHOA!
CAREFUL!

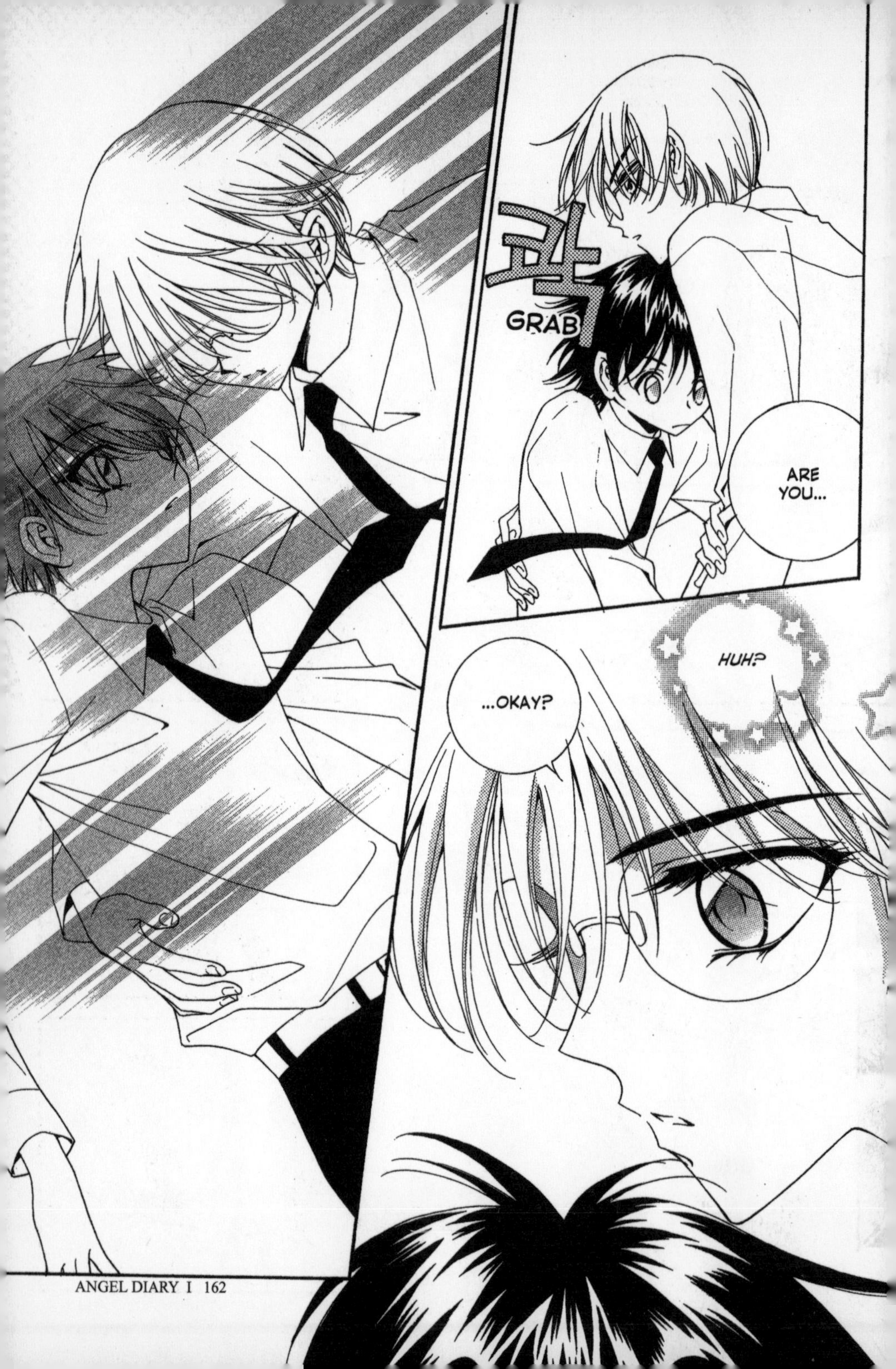
콱
GRAB
ARE YOU...
...OKAY?
HUH?

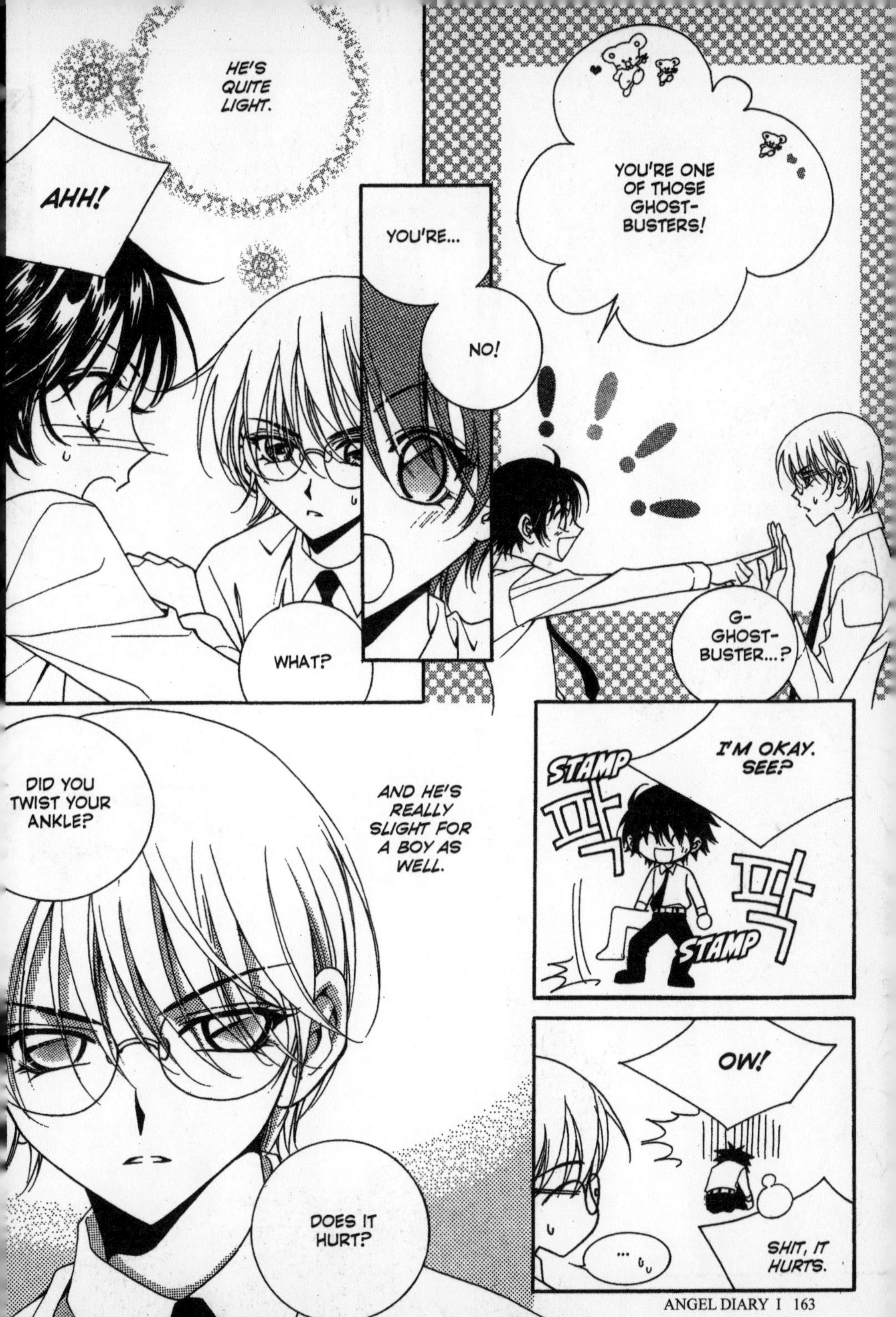
HE'S QUITE LIGHT.
AHH!
WHAT?
YOU'RE...
NO!
YOU'RE ONE OF THOSE GHOST-BUSTERS!
G-GHOST-BUSTER...?
DID YOU TWIST YOUR ANKLE?
AND HE'S REALLY SLIGHT FOR A BOY AS WELL.
DOES IT HURT?
I'M OKAY. SEE?
STAMP
팍
팍
STAMP
OW!
...
SHIT, IT HURTS.

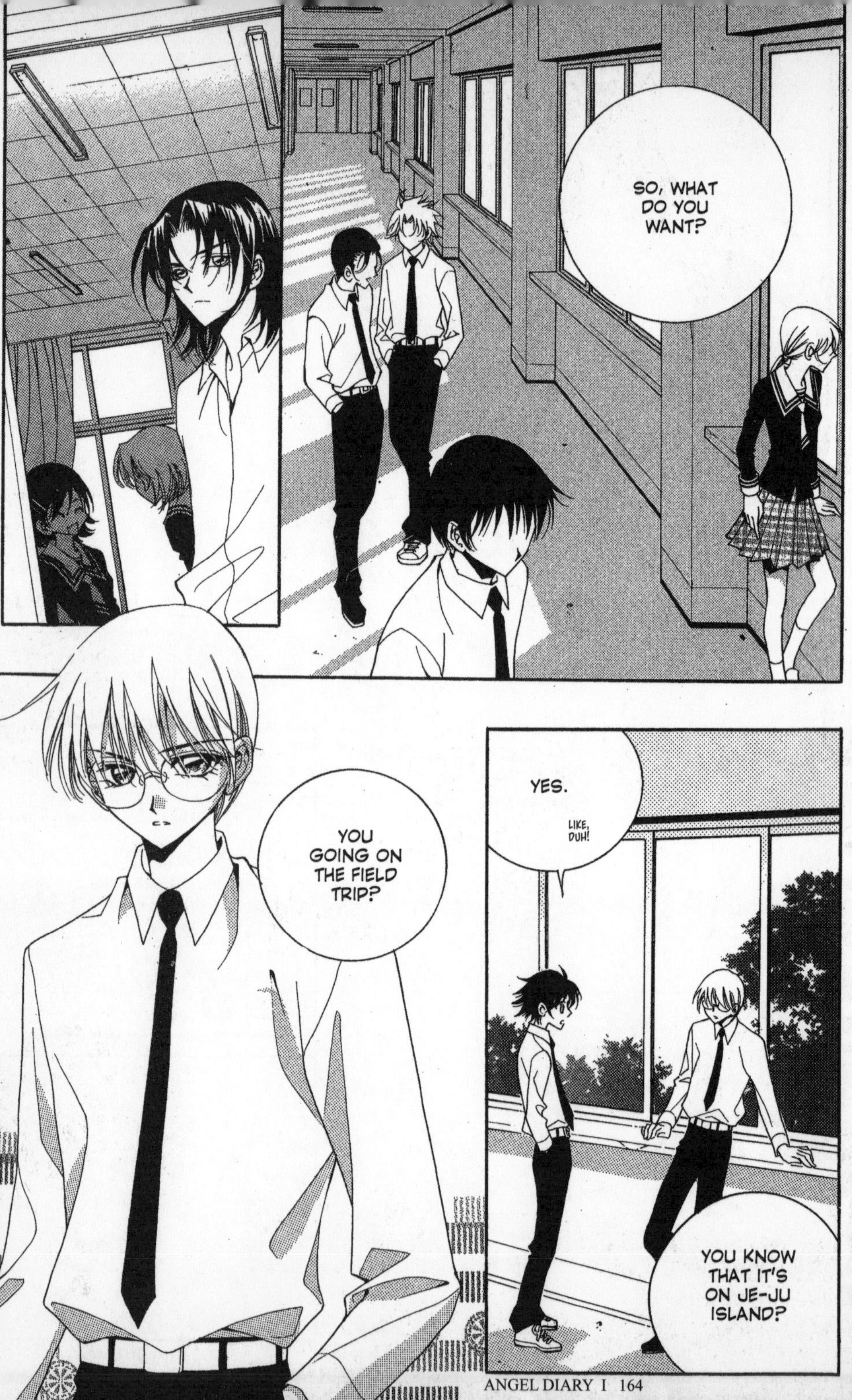
SO, WHAT DO YOU WANT?
YOU GOING ON THE FIELD TRIP?
YES.
LIKE, DUH!
YOU KNOW THAT IT'S ON JE-JU ISLAND?

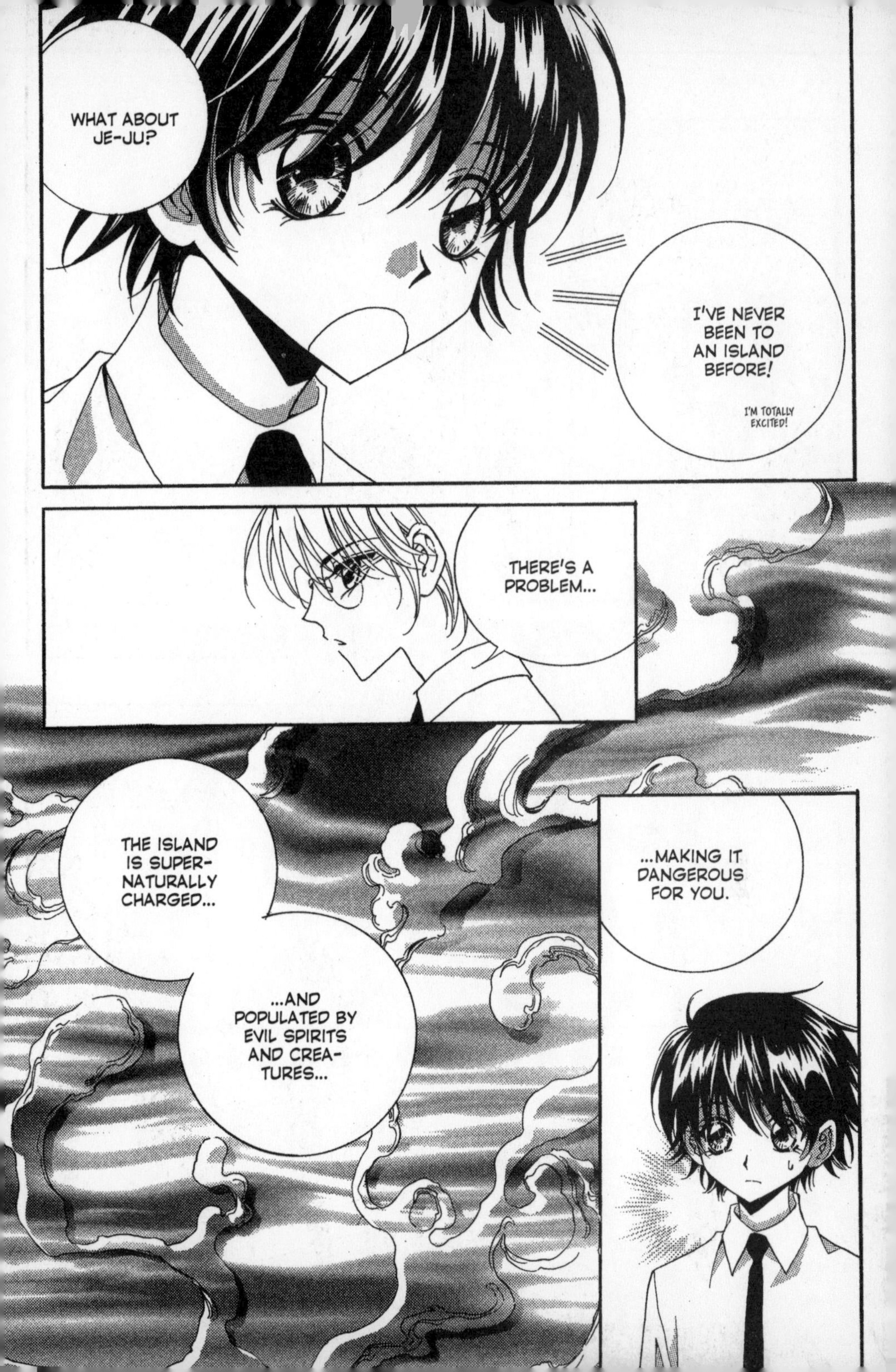
WHAT ABOUT JE-JU?
I'VE NEVER BEEN TO AN ISLAND BEFORE!
I'M TOTALLY EXCITED!
THERE'S A PROBLEM...
THE ISLAND IS SUPER-NATURALLY CHARGED...
...AND POPULATED BY EVIL SPIRITS AND CREA-TURES...
...MAKING IT DANGEROUS FOR YOU.

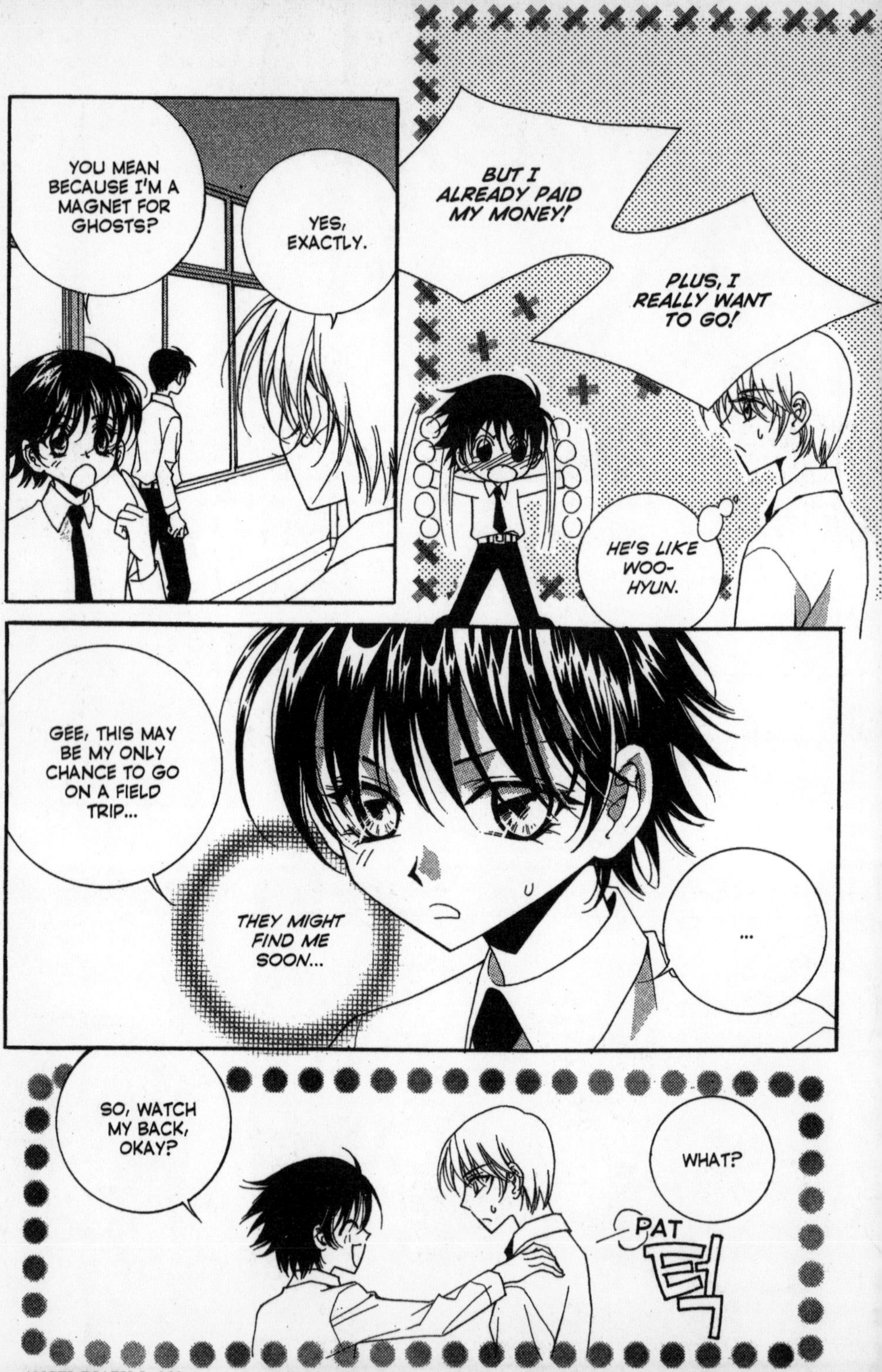
YOU MEAN BECAUSE I'M A MAGNET FOR GHOSTS?
YES, EXACTLY.
BUT I ALREADY PAID MY MONEY!
PLUS, I REALLY WANT TO GO!
HE'S LIKE WOO-HYUN.
GEE, THIS MAY BE MY ONLY CHANCE TO GO ON A FIELD TRIP...
THEY MIGHT FIND ME SOON...
...
SO, WATCH MY BACK, OKAY?
WHAT?
PAT
턱

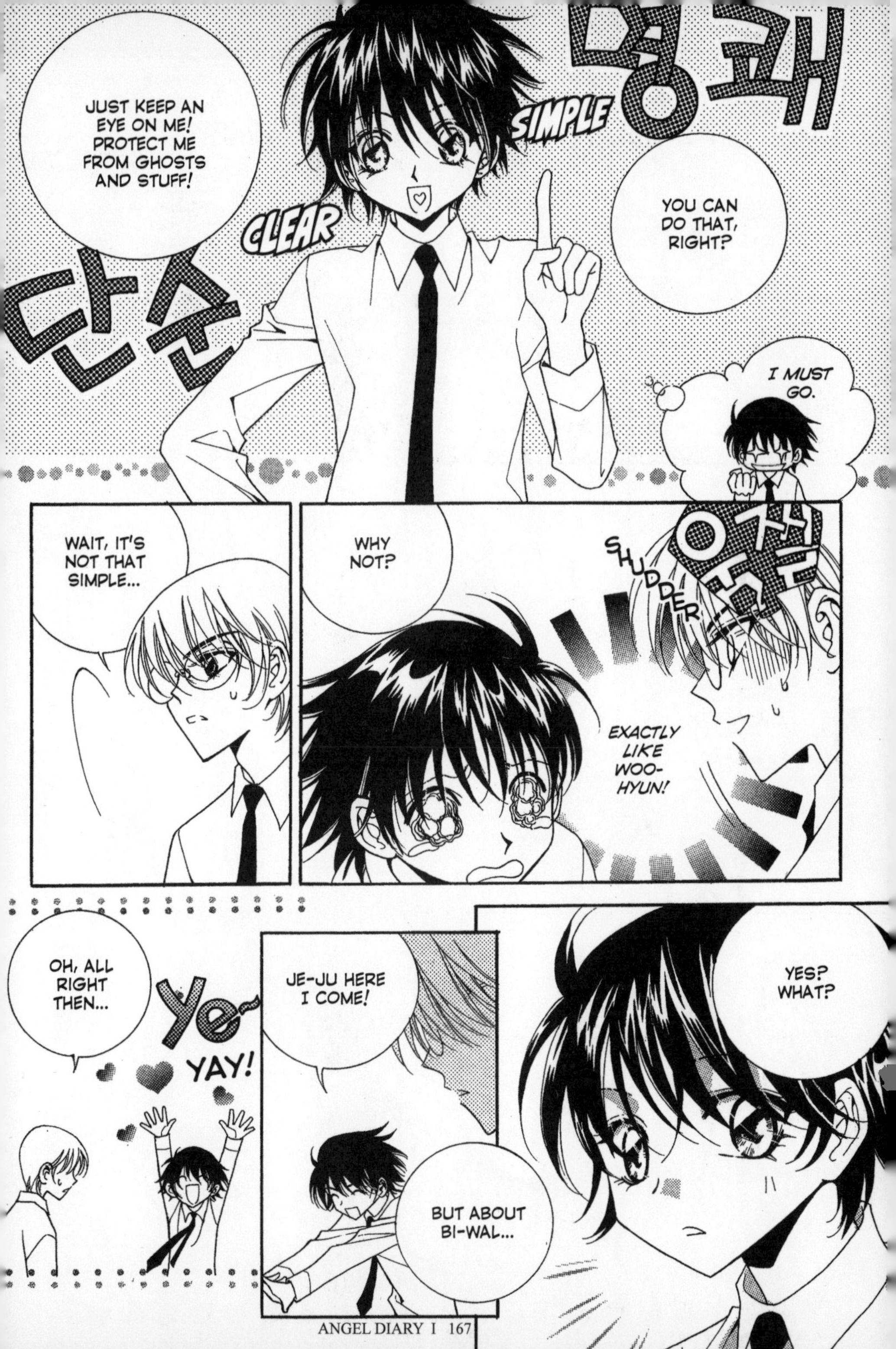
JUST KEEP AN EYE ON ME! PROTECT ME FROM GHOSTS AND STUFF!
단순
CLEAR
명쾌
SIMPLE
YOU CAN DO THAT, RIGHT?
I MUST GO.
WAIT, IT'S NOT THAT SIMPLE...
WHY NOT?
SHUDDER
EXACTLY LIKE WOO-HYUN!
OH, ALL RIGHT THEN...
Ye~
YAY!
JE-JU HERE I COME!
BUT ABOUT BI-WAL...
YES? WHAT?

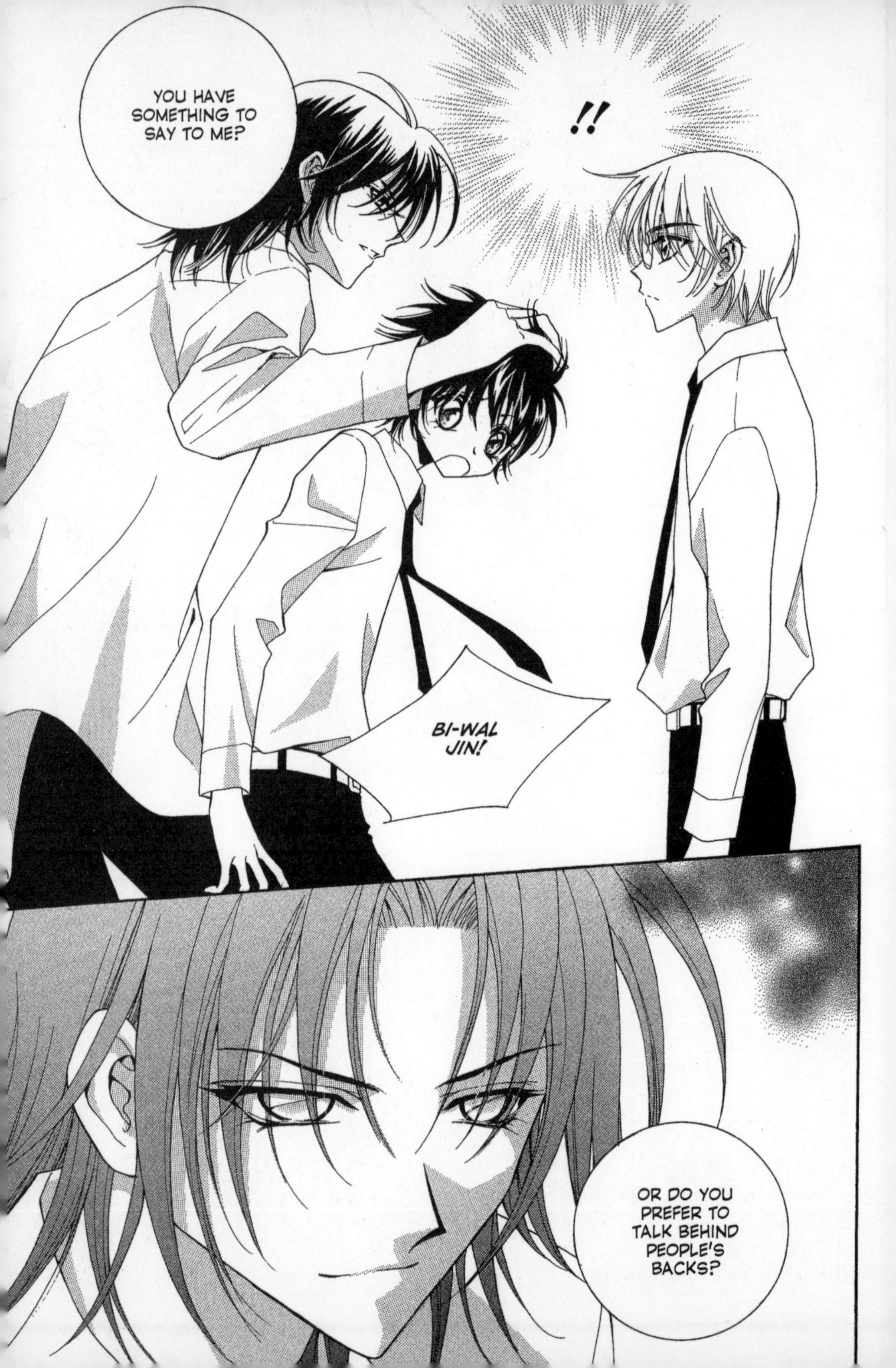
YOU HAVE SOMETHING TO SAY TO ME?
!!
BI-WAL JIN!
OR DO YOU PREFER TO TALK BEHIND PEOPLE'S BACKS?

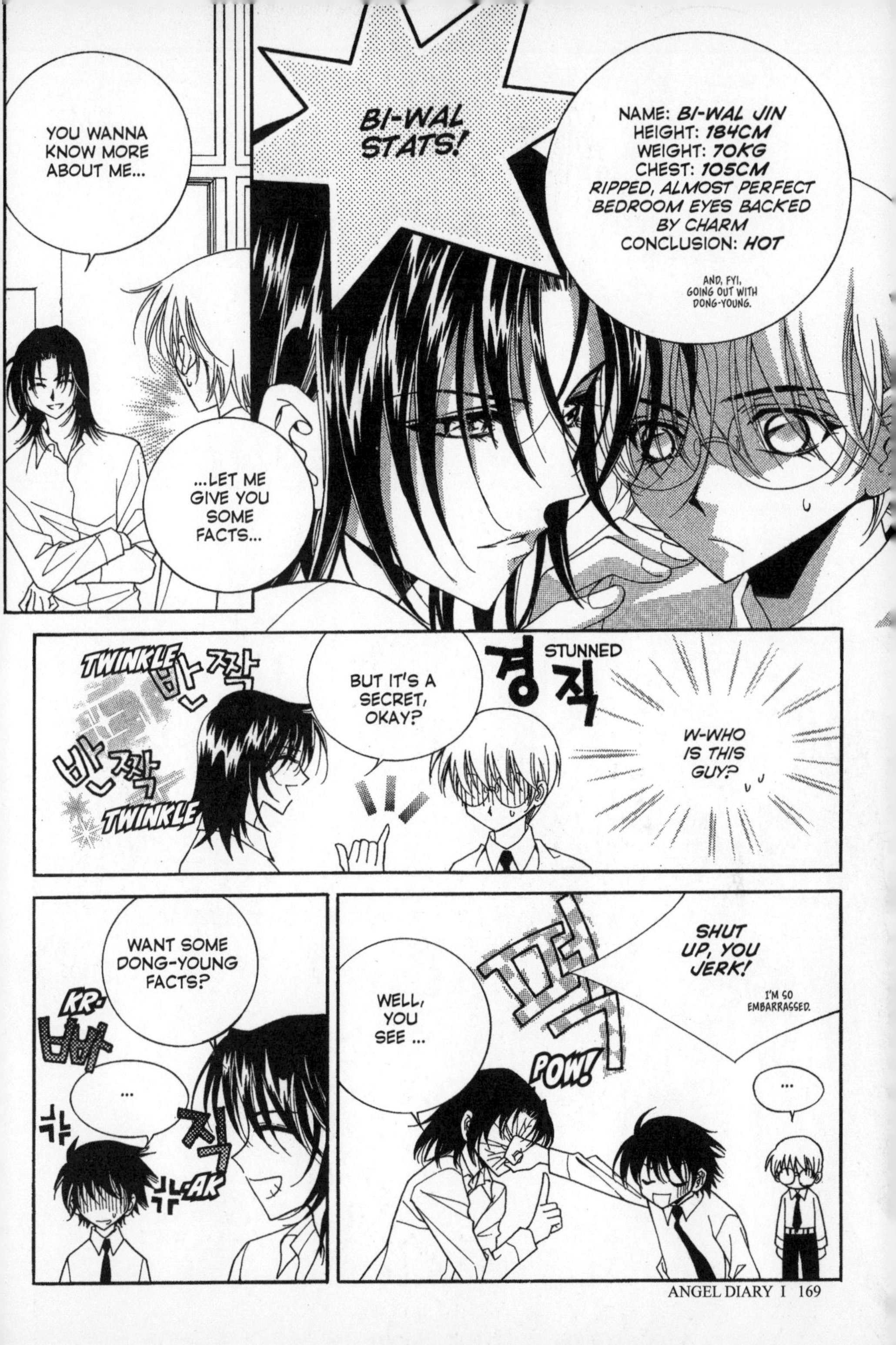

YOU WANNA KNOW MORE ABOUT ME...
...LET ME GIVE YOU SOME FACTS...
BI-WAL STATS!
NAME: BI-WAL JIN
HEIGHT: 184CM
WEIGHT: 70KG
CHEST: 105CM
RIPPED, ALMOST PERFECT
BEDROOM EYES BACKED BY CHARM
CONCLUSION: HOT
AND, FYI, GOING OUT WITH DONG-YOUNG.
TWINKLE 반짝
반짝 TWINKLE
BUT IT'S A SECRET, OKAY?
경직 STUNNED
W-WHO IS THIS GUY?
WANT SOME DONG-YOUNG FACTS?
KR- 바직 -AK
...
WELL, YOU SEE ...
퍽 POW!
SHUT UP, YOU JERK!
I'M SO EMBARRASSED.
...

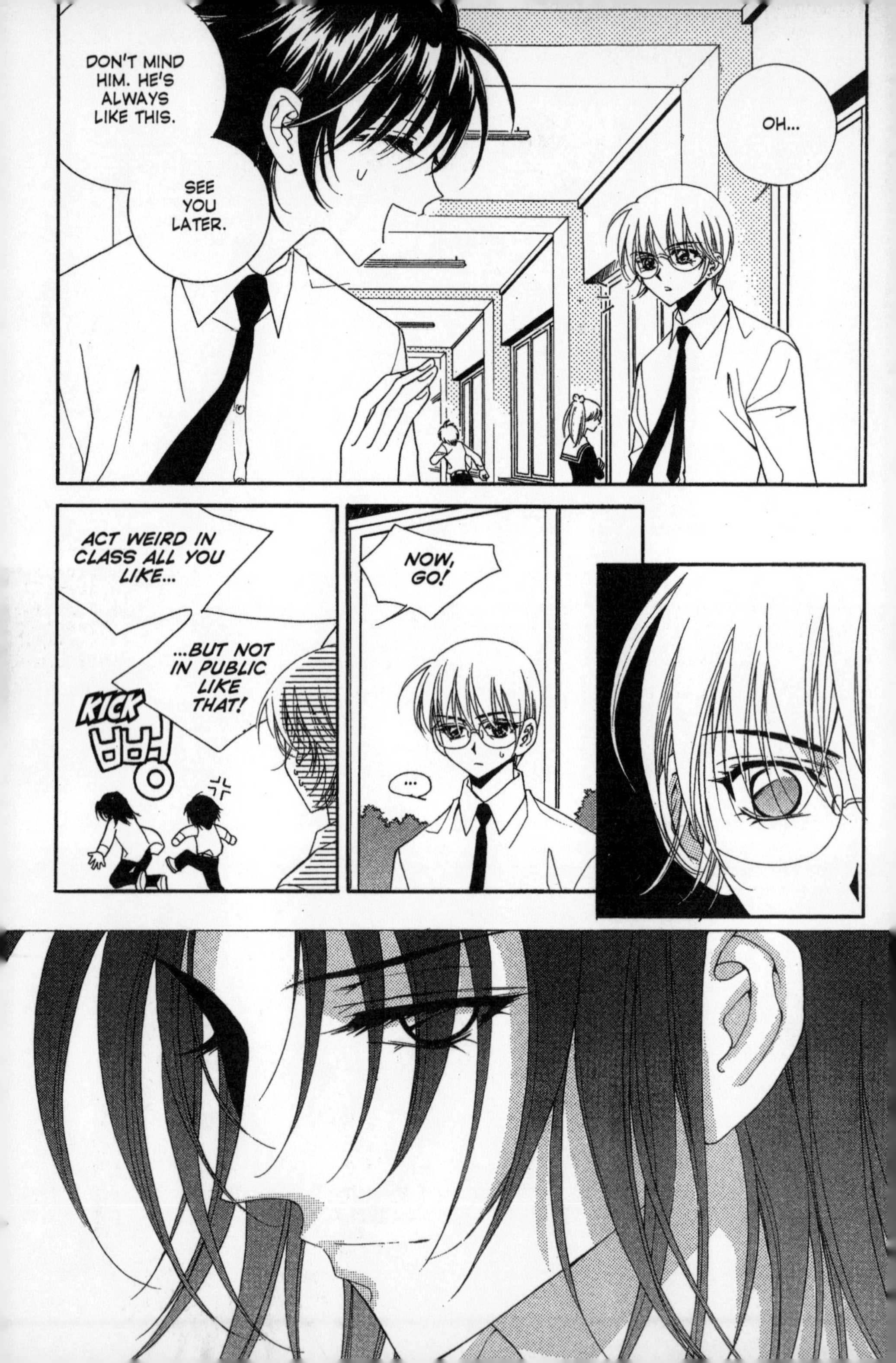
DON'T MIND HIM. HE'S ALWAYS LIKE THIS.
SEE YOU LATER.
OH...
ACT WEIRD IN CLASS ALL YOU LIKE...
...BUT NOT IN PUBLIC LIKE THAT!
KICK
NOW, GO!
...

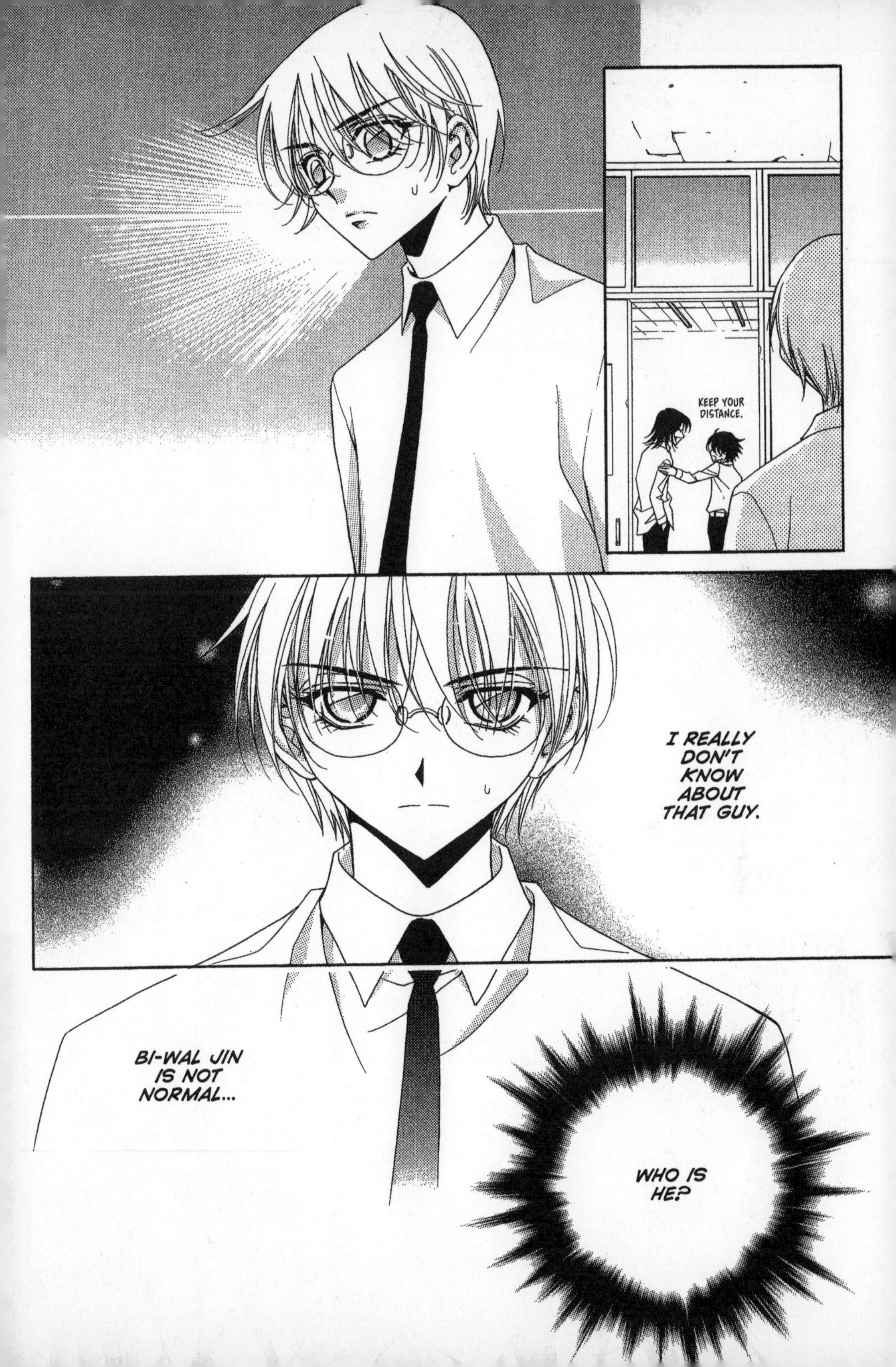
KEEP YOUR DISTANCE.
I REALLY DON'T KNOW ABOUT THAT GUY.
BI-WAL JIN IS NOT NORMAL...
WHO IS HE?

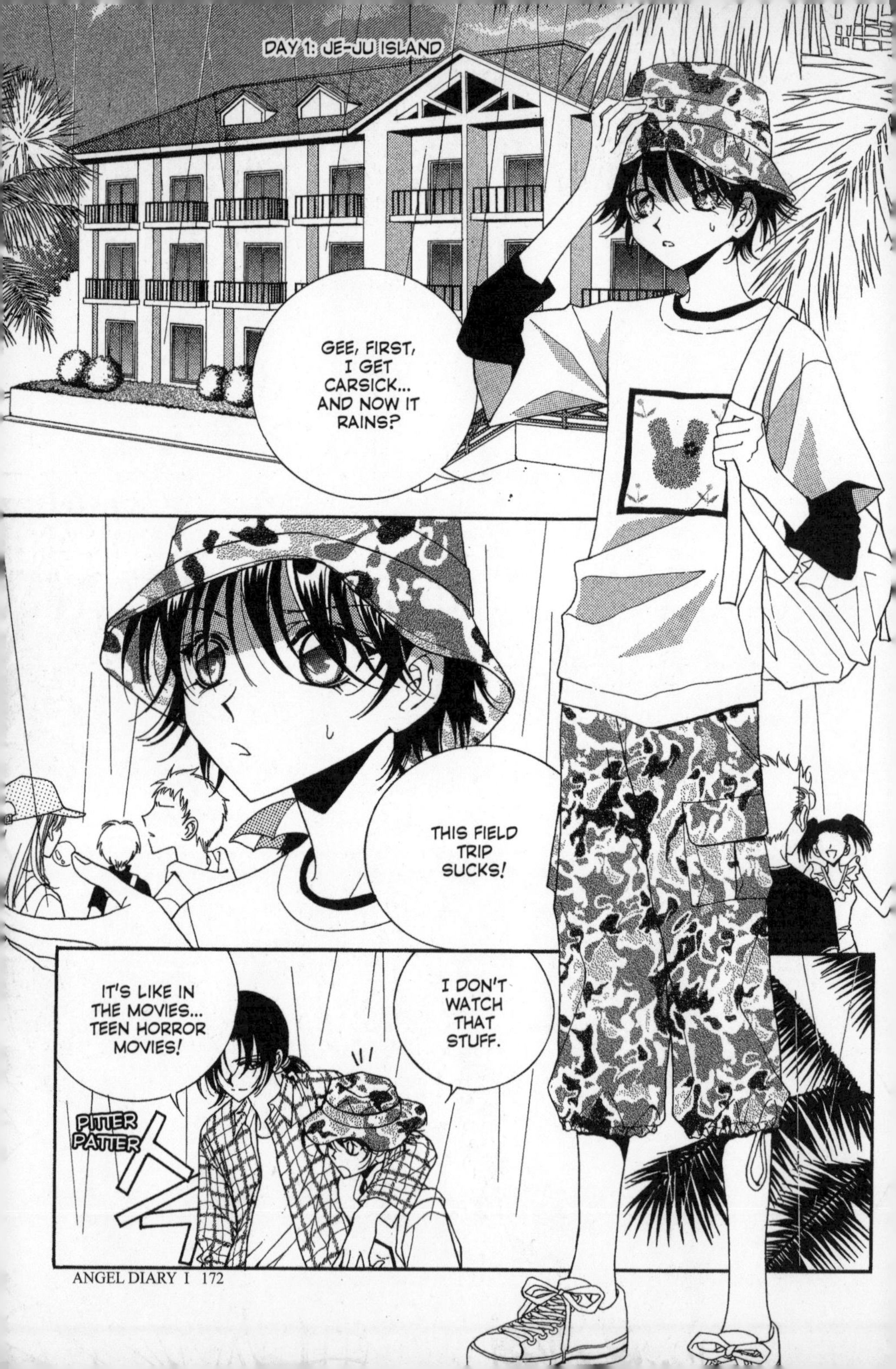
DAY 1: JE-JU ISLAND
GEE, FIRST, I GET CARSICK... AND NOW IT RAINS?
THIS FIELD TRIP SUCKS!
IT'S LIKE IN THE MOVIES... TEEN HORROR MOVIES!
PITTER PATTER
I DON'T WATCH THAT STUFF.

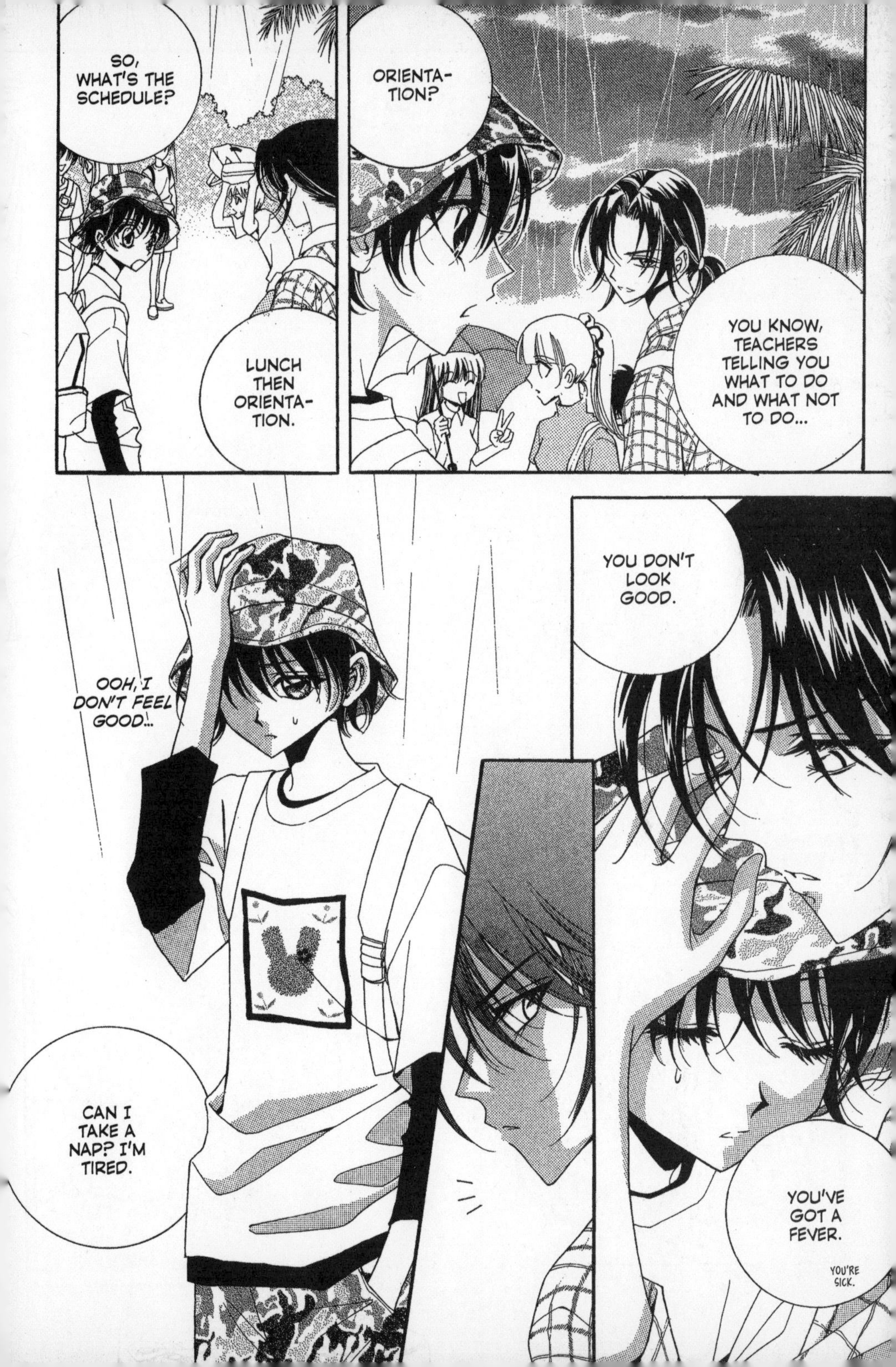
SO, WHAT'S THE SCHEDULE?
LUNCH THEN ORIENTA-TION.
ORIENTA-TION?
YOU KNOW, TEACHERS TELLING YOU WHAT TO DO AND WHAT NOT TO DO...
OOH, I DON'T FEEL GOOD...
CAN I TAKE A NAP? I'M TIRED.
YOU DON'T LOOK GOOD.
YOU'VE GOT A FEVER.
YOU'RE SICK.

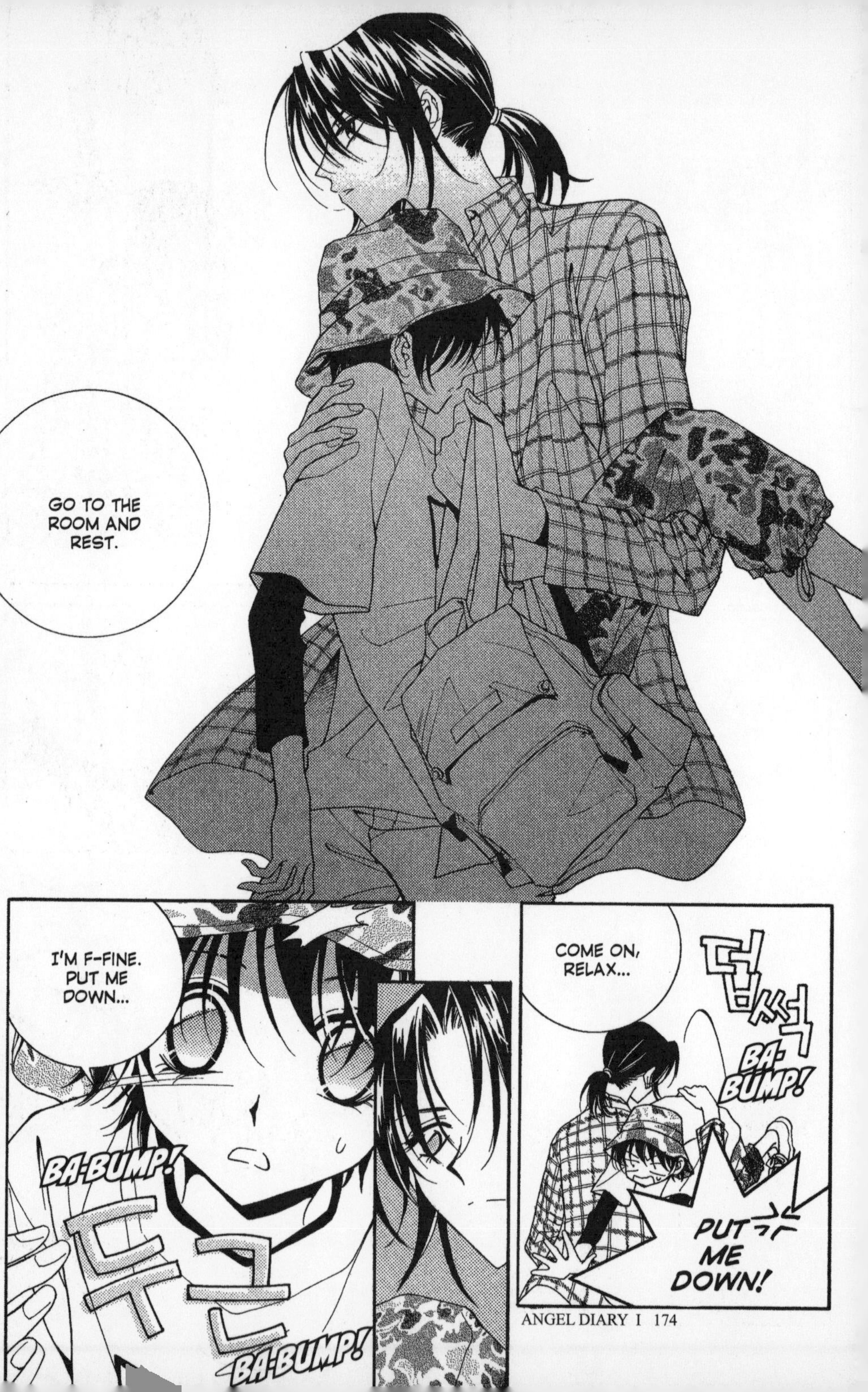
GO TO THE ROOM AND REST.
I'M F-FINE. PUT ME DOWN...
BA-BUMP!
BA-BUMP!
COME ON, RELAX...
BA-BUMP!
PUT ME DOWN!

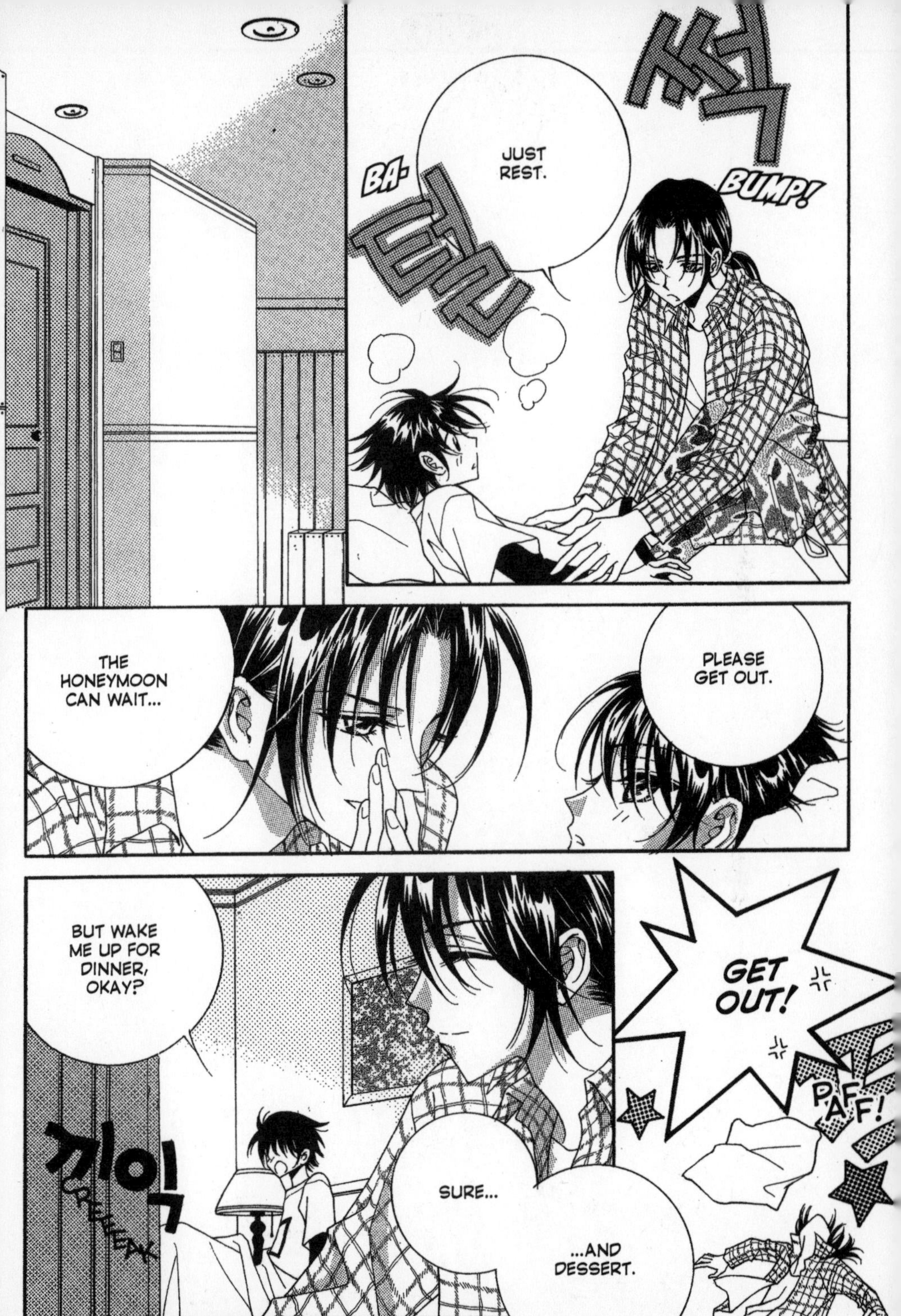
JUST REST.
BA-
BUMP!
THE HONEYMOON CAN WAIT...
PLEASE GET OUT.
BUT WAKE ME UP FOR DINNER, OKAY?
끼이익
CREEEAK
SURE...
...AND DESSERT.
GET OUT!
PAF!

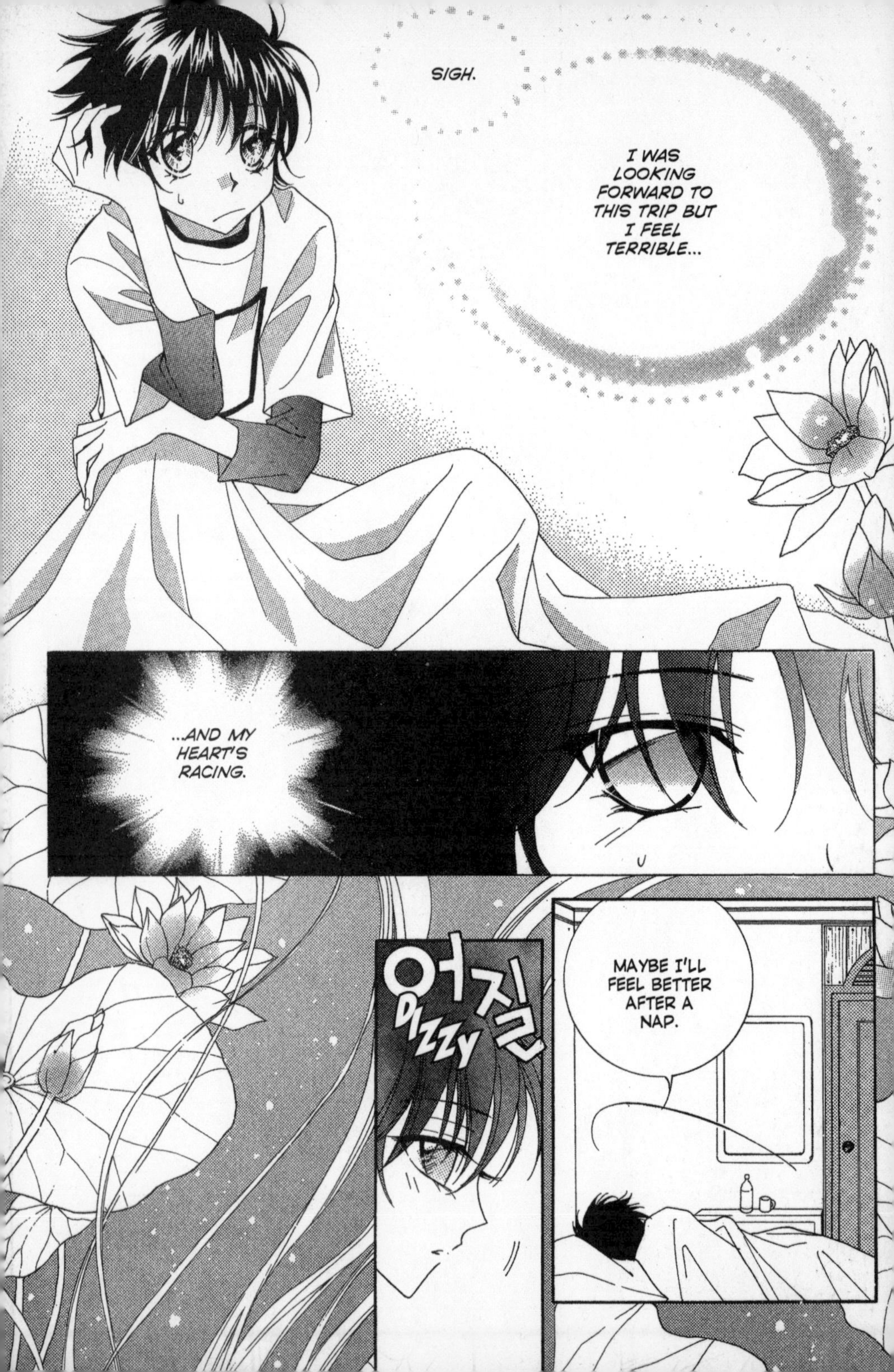
SIGH.
I WAS LOOKING FORWARD TO THIS TRIP BUT I FEEL TERRIBLE...
...AND MY HEART'S RACING.
어질
DIZZY
MAYBE I'LL FEEL BETTER AFTER A NAP.

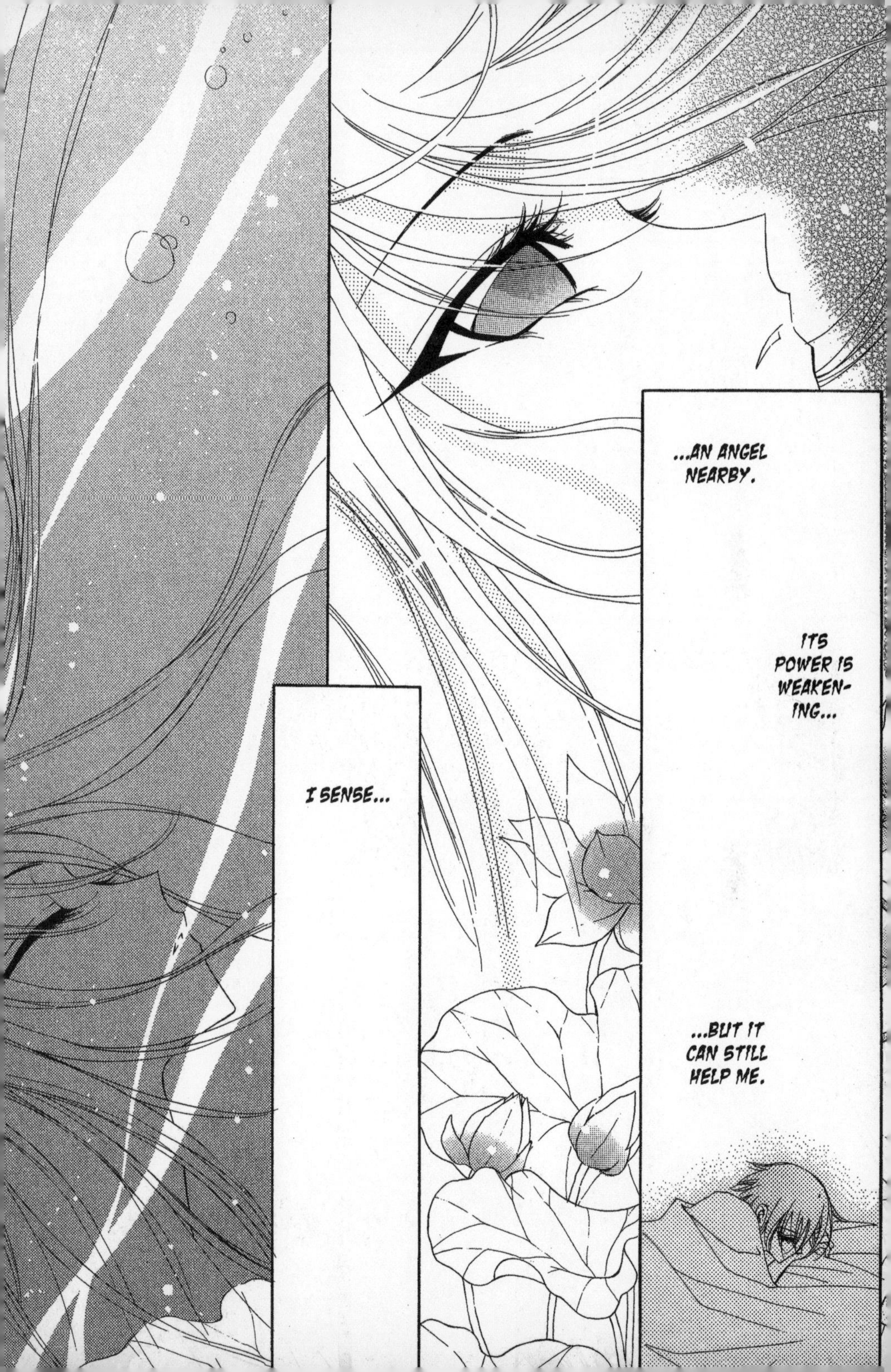
I SENSE...
...AN ANGEL NEARBY.
ITS POWER IS WEAKEN-ING...
...BUT IT CAN STILL HELP ME.

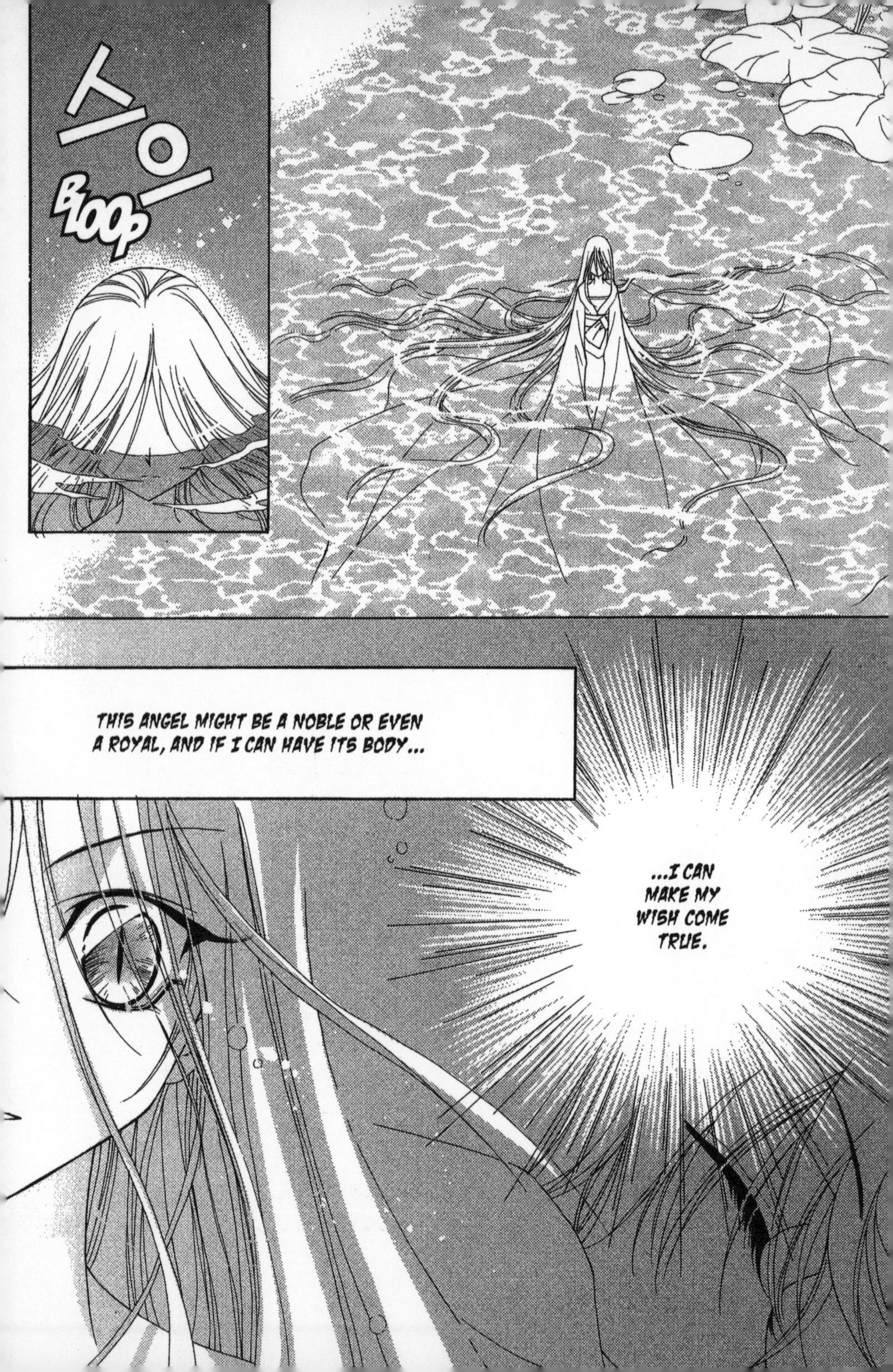
BLOOP
THIS ANGEL MIGHT BE A NOBLE OR EVEN A ROYAL, AND IF I CAN HAVE ITS BODY...
...I CAN MAKE MY WISH COME TRUE.

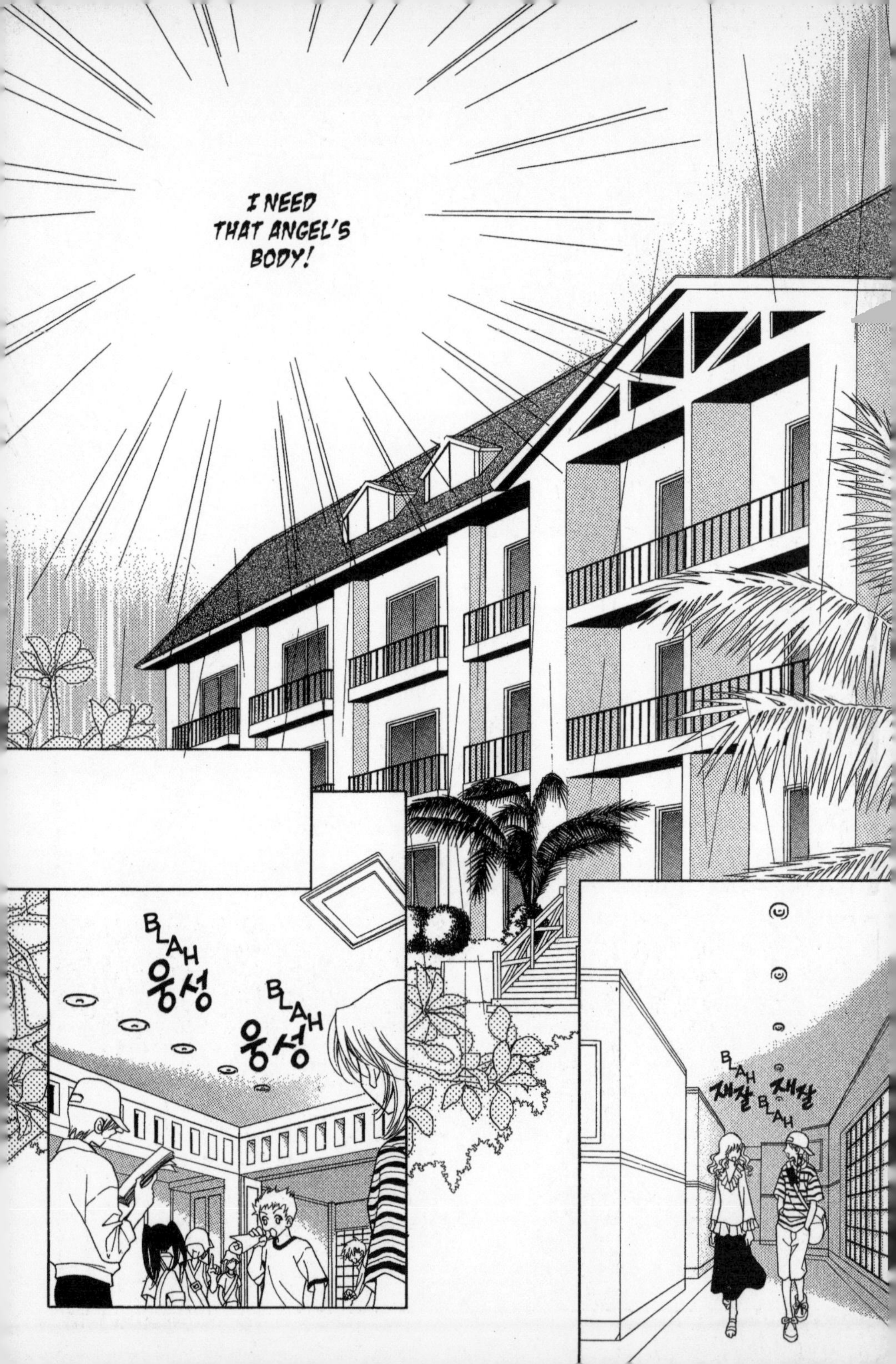
I NEED THAT ANGEL'S BODY!
BLAH 웅성
BLAH 웅성
BLAH 재잘
재잘 BLAH

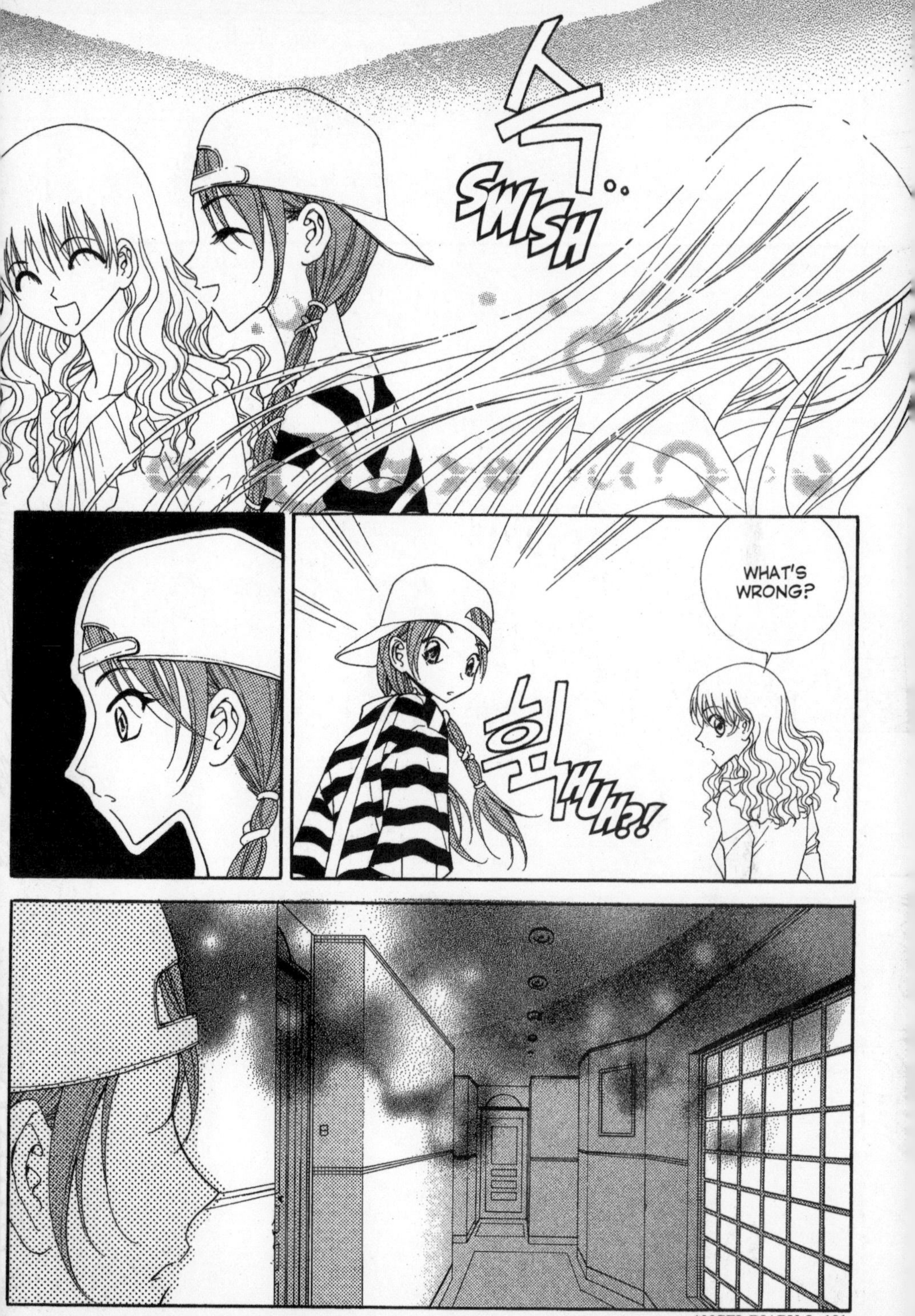

스윽..
SWISH
WHAT'S WRONG?
휙
HUH?!

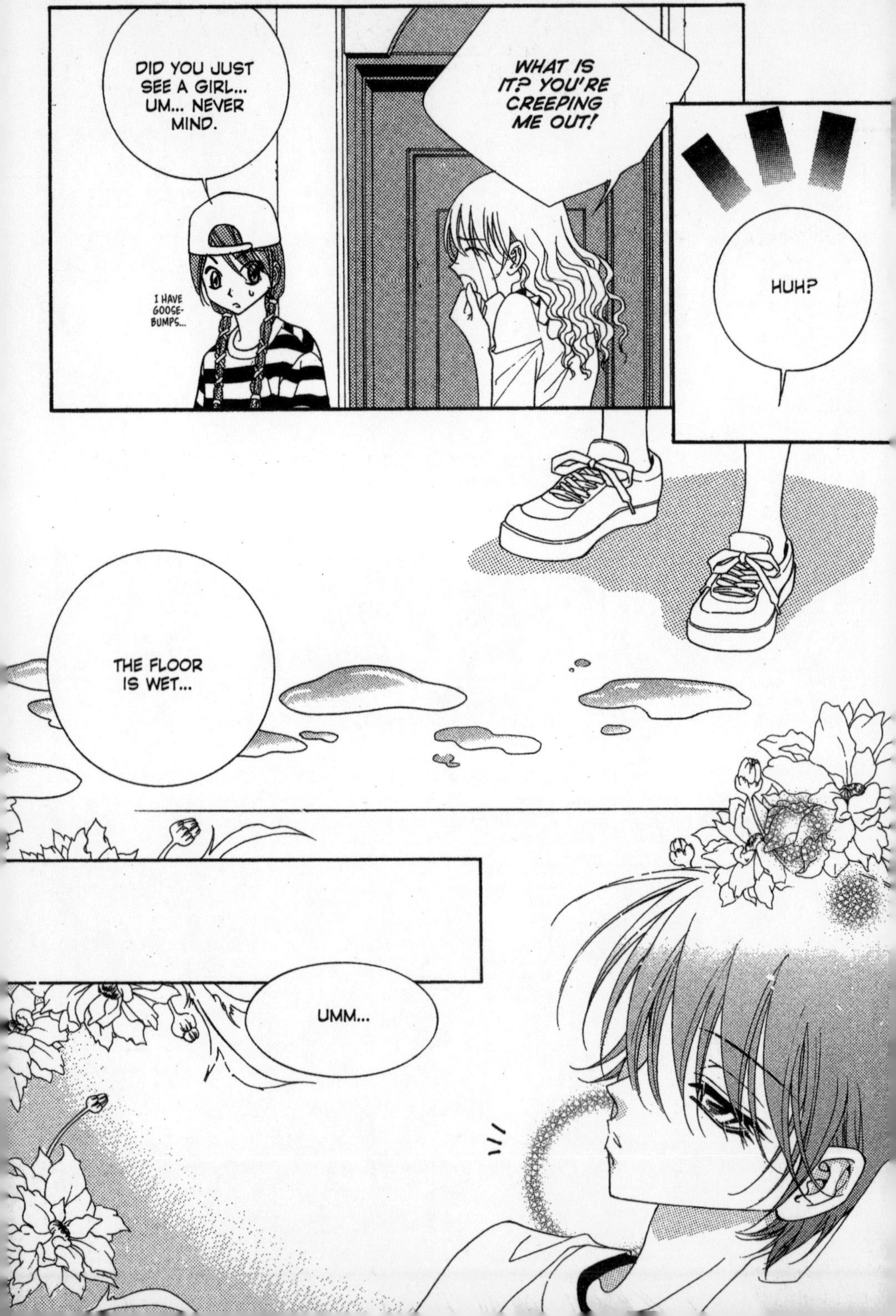
DID YOU JUST SEE A GIRL... UM... NEVER MIND.
I HAVE GOOSE-BUMPS...
WHAT IS IT? YOU'RE CREEPING ME OUT!
HUH?
THE FLOOR IS WET...
UMM...

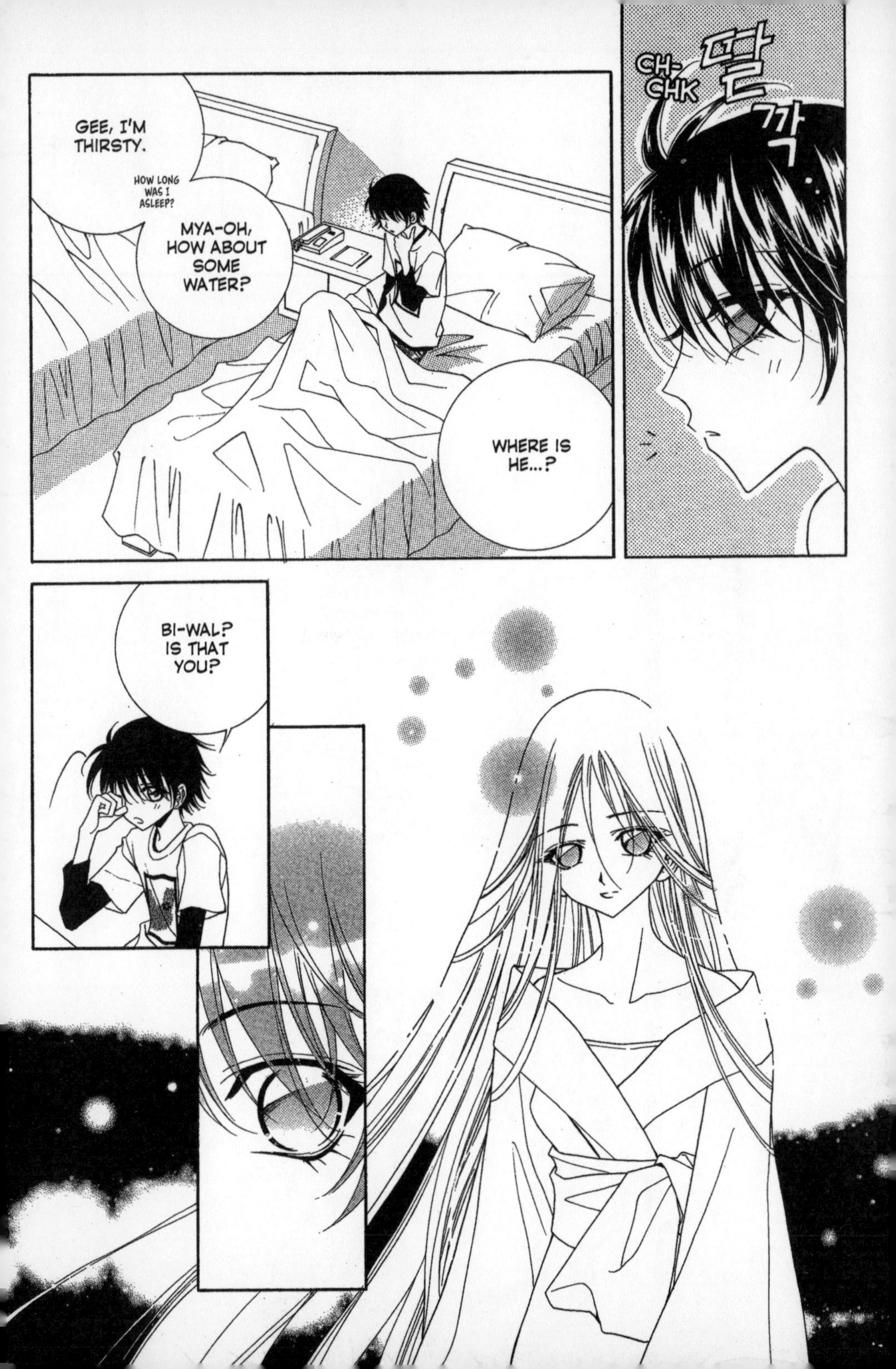
GEE, I'M THIRSTY.
HOW LONG WAS I ASLEEP?
MYA-OH, HOW ABOUT SOME WATER?
WHERE IS HE...?
CH-CHK
딸깍
BI-WAL? IS THAT YOU?

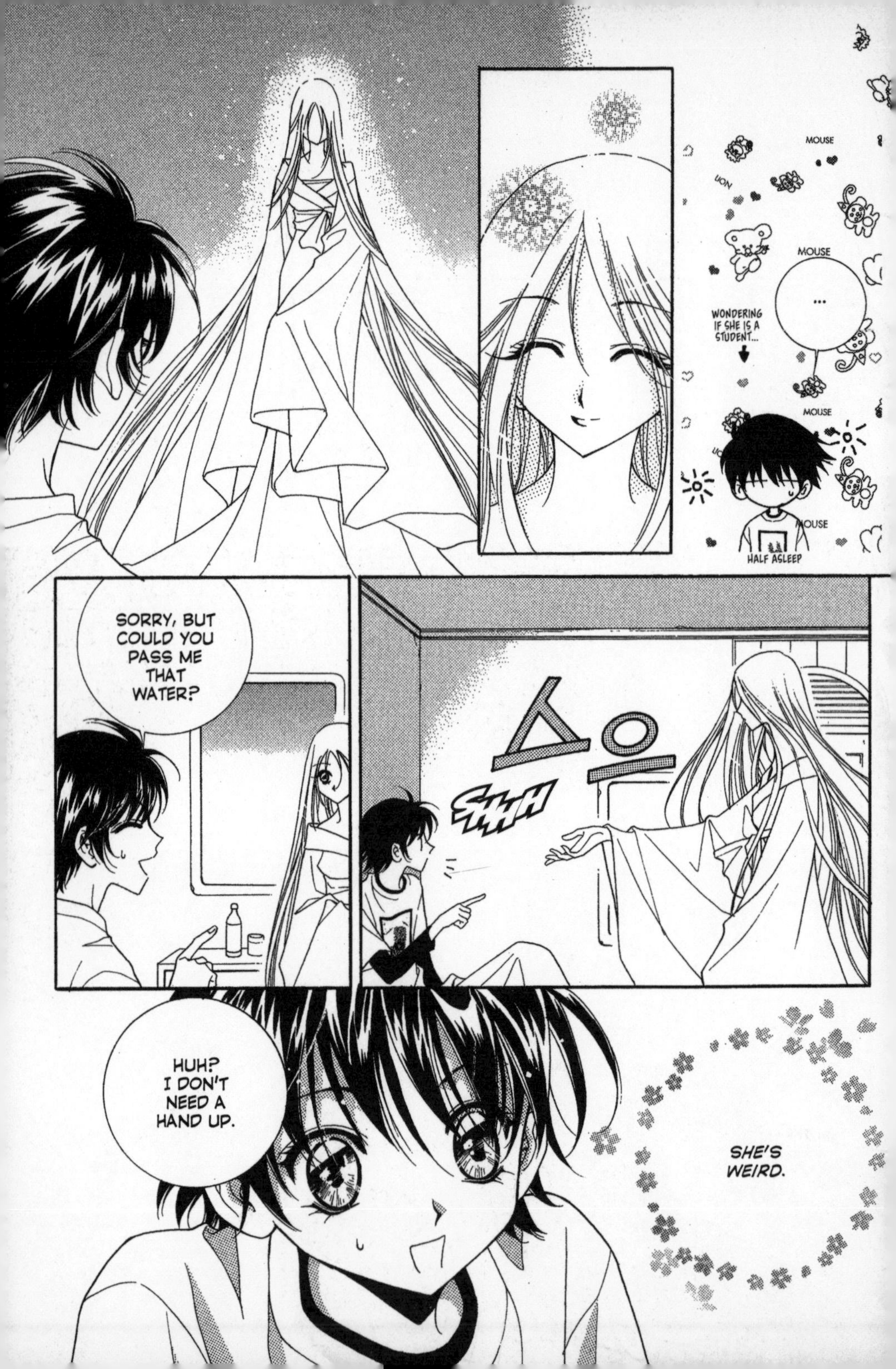
MOUSE
UON
MOUSE
...
WONDERING IF SHE IS A STUDENT...
MOUSE
MOUSE
HALF ASLEEP
SORRY, BUT COULD YOU PASS ME THAT WATER?
SHHH
HUH? I DON'T NEED A HAND UP.
SHE'S WEIRD.

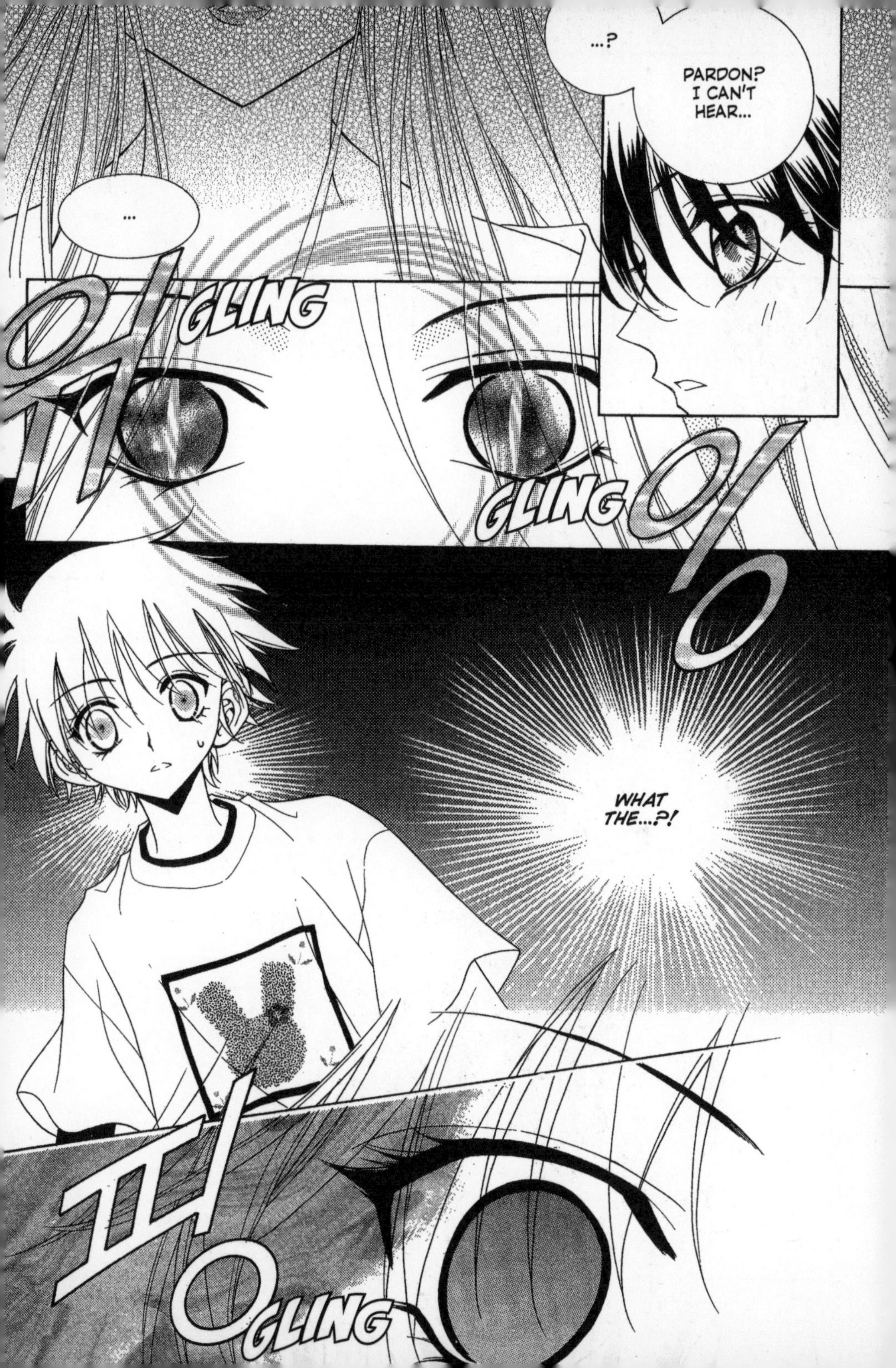
...
...?
PARDON? I CAN'T HEAR...
GLING
GLING
WHAT THE...?!
GLING

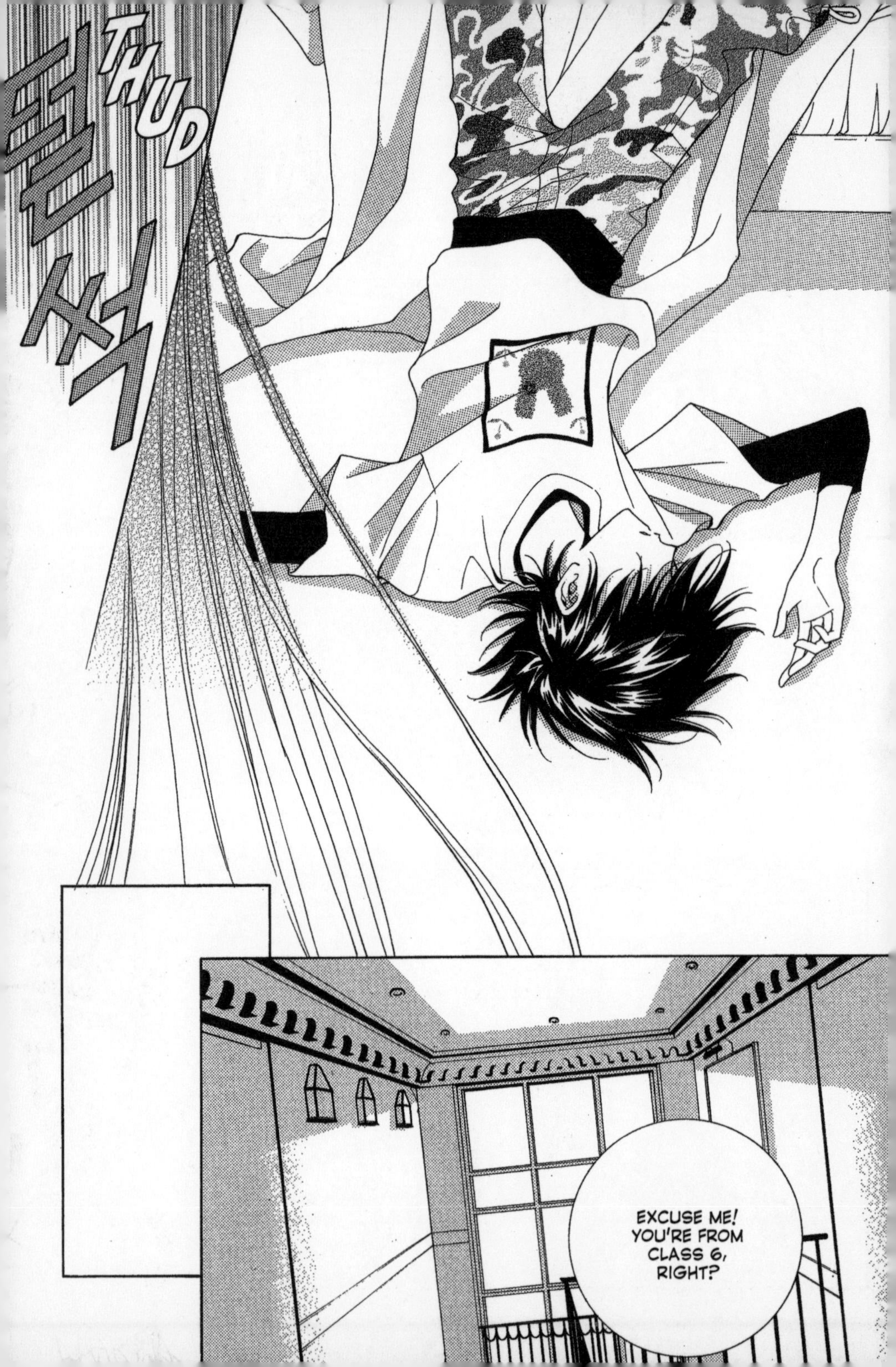
털썩
THUD
EXCUSE ME! YOU'RE FROM CLASS 6, RIGHT?

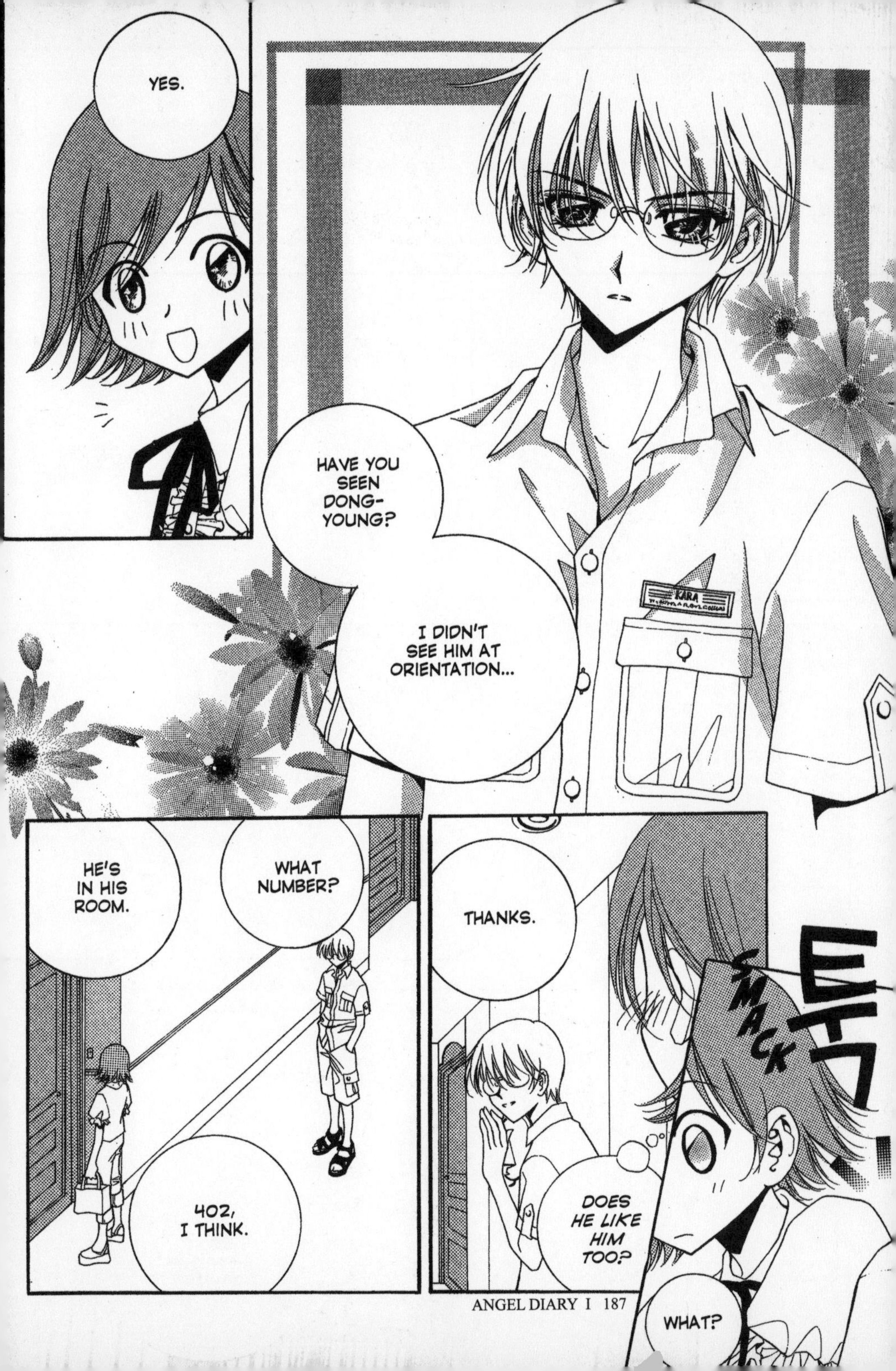
YES.
HAVE YOU SEEN DONG-YOUNG?
KARA
I DIDN'T SEE HIM AT ORIENTATION...
HE'S IN HIS ROOM.
WHAT NUMBER?
402, I THINK.
THANKS.
SMACK
DOES HE LIKE HIM TOO?
WHAT?

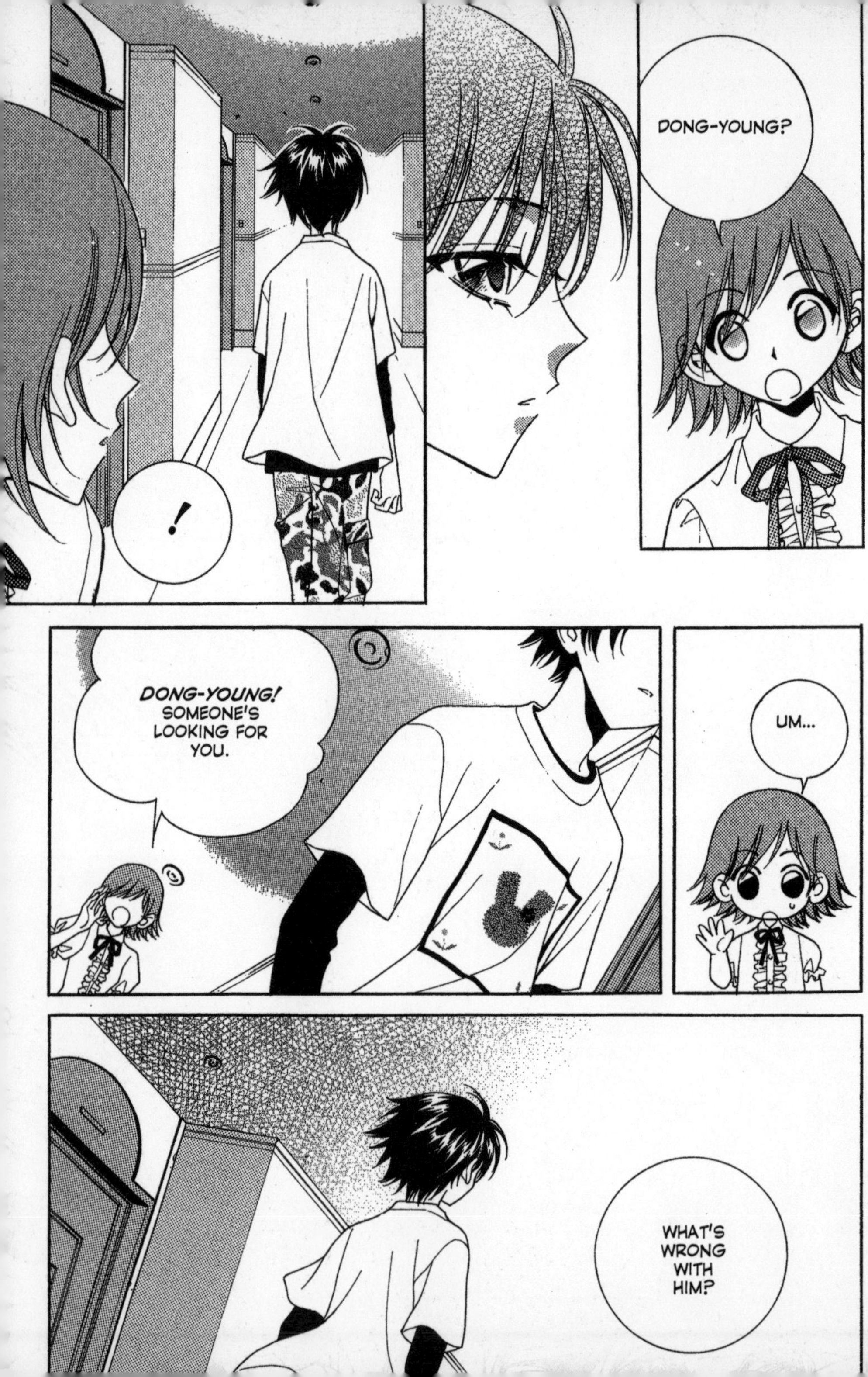
!
DONG-YOUNG?
DONG-YOUNG! SOMEONE'S LOOKING FOR YOU.
UM...
WHAT'S WRONG WITH HIM?

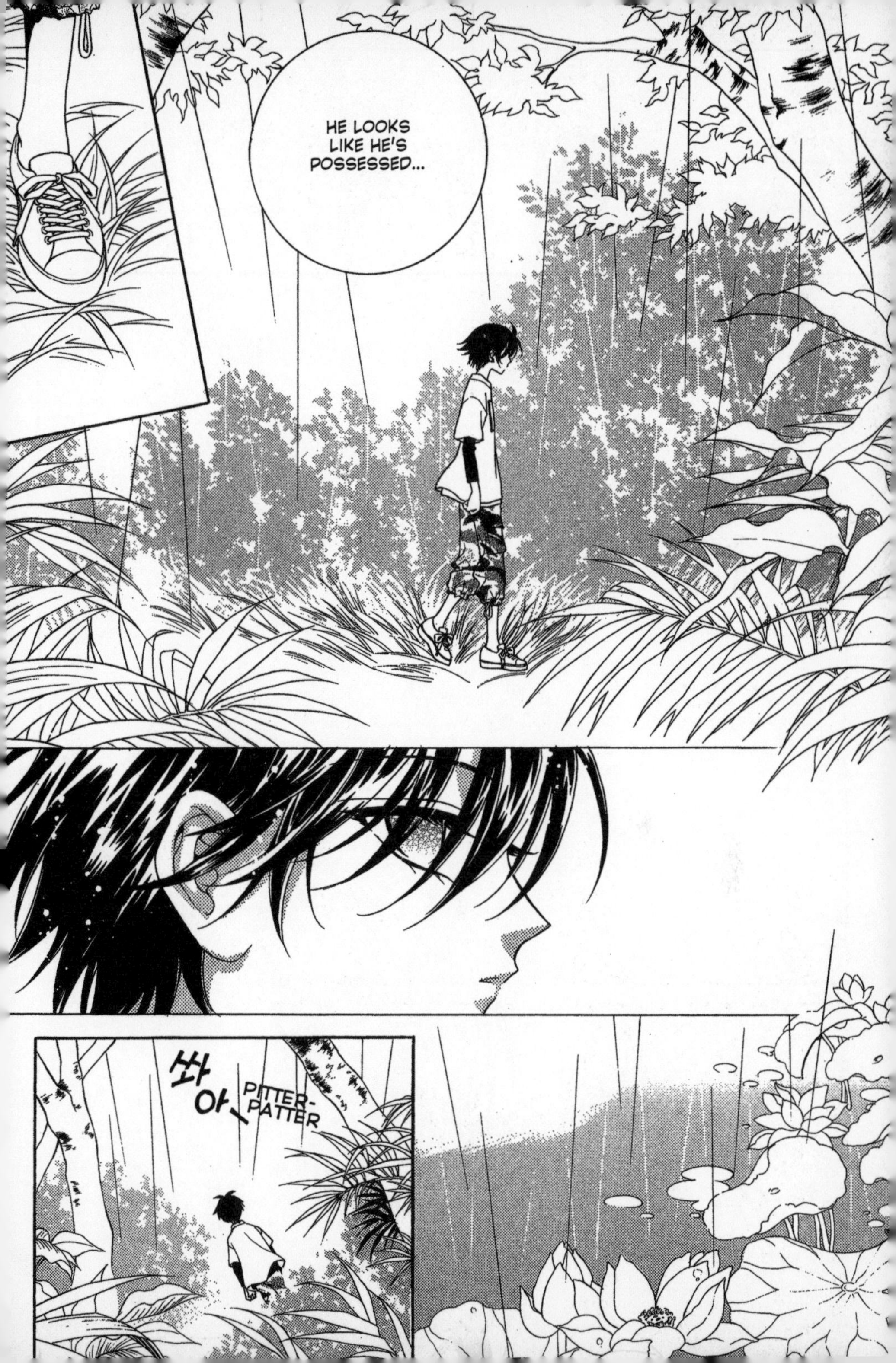
HE LOOKS LIKE HE'S POSSESSED...
쏴아-
PITTER-PATTER

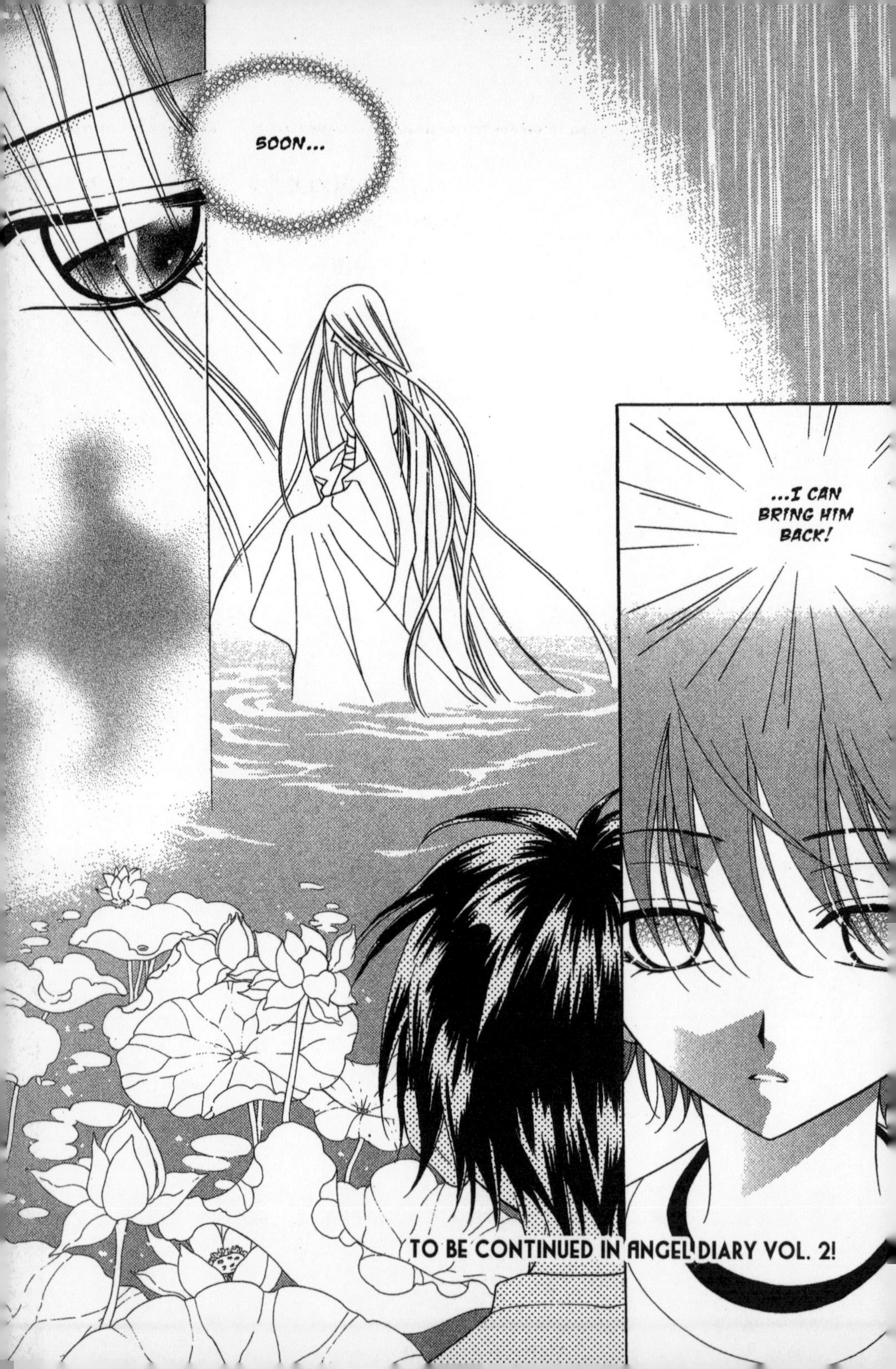
SOON...
...I CAN BRING HIM BACK!
TO BE CONTINUED IN ANGEL DIARY VOL. 2!

APPENDIX

Angel Diary

About the creator

Angel Diary
Kara/Yun-Hee Lee

Artist : Kara
Yoon-Kyung Kim (born on January 6th) and Eun-Sook Jung (born on October 25th) form the art team known as Kara. Yoon-Kyung pencils the story while Eun-Sook inks it. Their first book, <Terra>, won the first annual "Cake Comic Book Award" in Korea. <Angel Diary> debuted in a bi-weekly Korean comic magazine called "Bijou."

Writer : Yun-Hee Lee
Yun-Hee Lee was born on December 15th. She was recruited to help write <Devil Diary> after Kara read her work online. She officially joined the creative team with book two. Her favorite character from <Angel Diary> is Bi-Wal and one other character we have yet to meet...

Other Major Works
<Terra>, <Crystal Heart>, <Demon Diary>, <Legend>

Quick Chat with the Creator

Top fantasy creator troop
Kara/Yun-Hee Lee

The best manhwa team ever,
Kara & Yun-Hee Lee.
They spent countless days and nights
talking about their loves for cats and
fantasy stories.
Always on time and always the best !

How did three of you get together?
Both members of Kara used to study
manhwa together under the same master.
Yun-Hee's case... well, it was because our
(Kara's) story wasn't interesting enough
before. So we decided that we need a good
writer. We searched all over the internet,
and found Yun-Hee.

You guys ever get into a fight?
Kara and Yun-Hee never got into a fight.
But both members of Kara always fight
each others. -.-;

**What's some of the difficulties or
advantages about working as a team?**
Difficulties... hmm... The story could go
three different direction sometimes since we
have 3 different minds. An advantage would
be less stress. Three different people
working together on a single title means less
work for each of us which leads to much
less stress and more enjoyable working
environment. So, it's quite fun working
together.

**What if one of Kara gets married one
day?**
Then that one has to find a cutie for the
other one to get married too. :)

**Yun-Hee, You are well known for being a
huge online game fan. What do you like
about them?**
Lately, I've been playing Ragnarok Online
the most. I love their 2D characters in 3D
environments. I think the main attraction of
online games is to meet new people
through the game. It's so much fun to chat
and hunt together with people you meet
online.

**And what is the <Angel Diary> all about?
And what's some of the most interesting
elements about it?**
<Angel Diary> is a record of angels and
demons in a modern human world.
1. Curse. =_= I like the curse doll that
comes out often. It's a character too.
2. Many Bishounens. So you can choose
the one for your taste. Hehehe.

Kara & Yun-Hee Lee

Super-Cute Fantasy♥

Since their previous project, <Demon Diary>, Kara's unique and colorful characters with Yun-Hee Lee's exciting story has captured the hearts of many fans. Now, once more, this highly talented creative combo takes you to another exciting world.

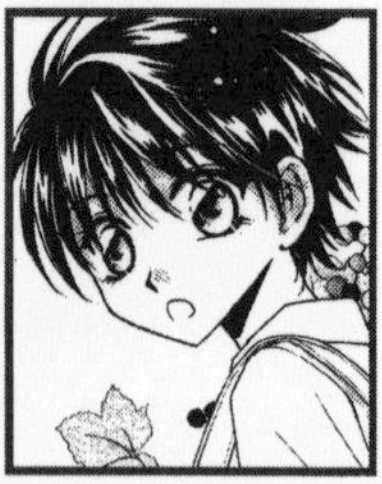

Dong-Young

Her real name is Chun-Yoo. She is the one and only princess of heaven. She ran away to the human world because she was betrothed to the king of the underworld. She's currently disguised as a high school boy in the human world.

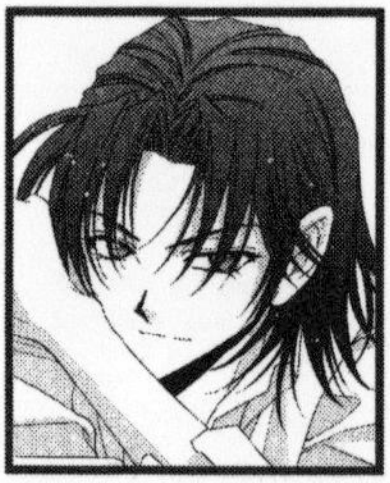

Bi-Wal

A classmate of Dong-Young. His ambiguous expression of love toward Dong-Young makes people think they are a couple. However, he's a mysterious character who even knows about Dong-Young being the lost princess.

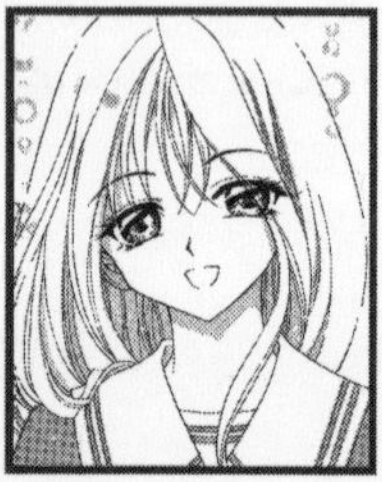

Ah-Hin

White Tiger (guardian of West) of the Four Guardians of heaven. She looks cute and naive, but her real personality is quite the contrary. She has been Dong-Young's closest friend since their childhood.

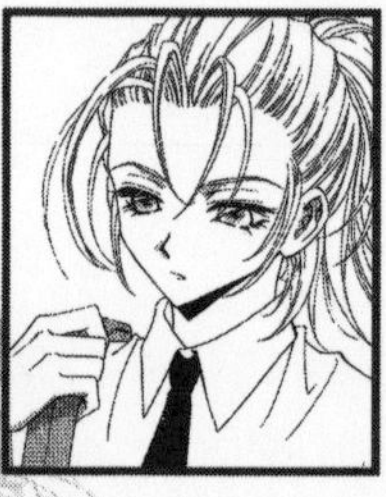

Ee-Jung

Red Phoenix (guardian of South) of the Four Guardians of heaven. He always follows his big sister Ah-Hin everywhere she goes. Mostly cool about everything, but is very protective of Ah-Hin.

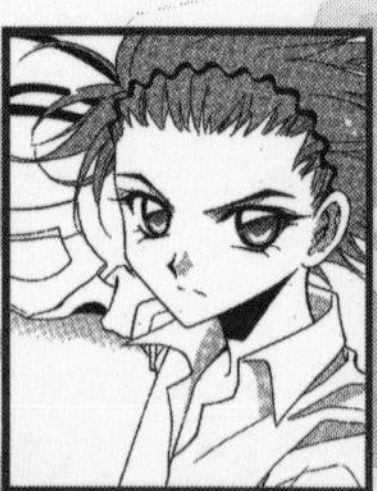

Woo-Hyun

Blue Dragon (guardian of East) of the Four Guardians of heaven. His simple mind and straight forward character gets him into a lot of trouble, but that is part of his charm. Always works with Doh-Hyun.

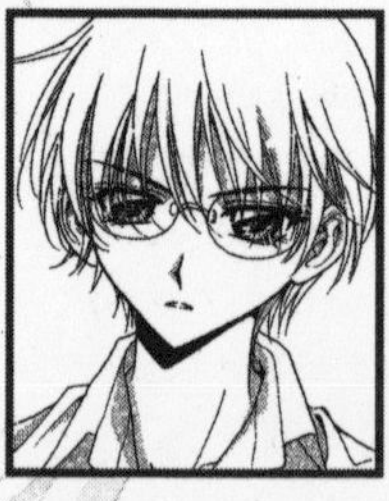

Doh-Hyun

Black Turtle (guardian of North) of the Four Guardians of heaven. He's smart, athletic, and even has a good heart. Because of his cautious and careful personality, he works great as a teammate of Woo-Hyun.

Behind the Story

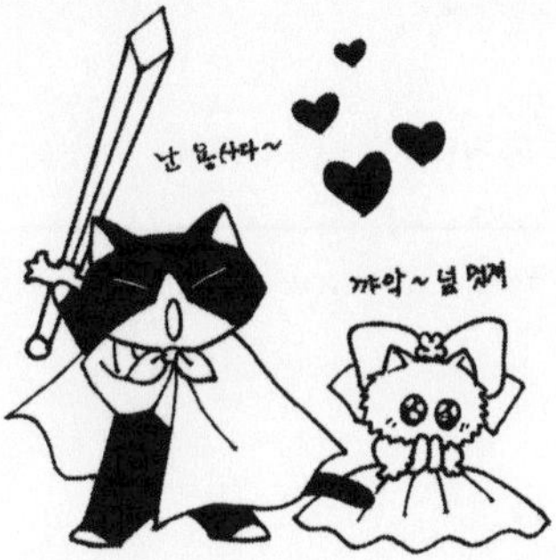
난 용사다~
꺄악~ 넘 멋져

Kara, the creators of successful fantasy titles such as <Demon Diary> and <Angel Diary>, talks about "Fantasy" and what it means to them.
Also, well-known game maniac Yun-Hee Lee will unveils the secret behind the names in <Angel Diary>.

Incite into Fantasy -Kara-

■ Invitation to the world of imagination!

To us, "Fantasy" is a collection of imaginations that are not bound by time or space. We live in a very structured world where everything follows natural laws and rules. Nothing outside of those is accepted, and we live very repetitive and boring lives in it day after day. That's the reason why people fall so deeply into the new and exciting worlds that are so different from our own when they read fantasy literature. The readers want to escape from their lives, and fantasy can fulfill that desire. That's the main attraction of "Fantasy" to us. If we take <Angel Diary> for example, it makes us feel as if we live in the same world with the angels, guardians, and demons that we never actually encounter in real life. We believe the readers feel the same way while they enjoy the books. As creators, it gives us tremendous satisfaction and joy creating new worlds and characters out of our imaginations. But in the end, creators of fantasy manhwa like us are simply fantasy maniacs also.

Love for video games behind the <Angel Diary> -Yun-Hee Lee-

■ Character names?

Everyone knows that I'm a big video game maniac. Out of all the games, I especially love playing Ragnarok Online and have been playing it for several years already. The truth is, many of the names in <Angel Diary> came from people I met online in the game. At the planning stage of the <Angel Diary>, I couldn't think of any good names for one of the main characters. But then I met someone named "Bi-Wal" in the game, and I used that name immediately because I thought that was such an interesting name. After that, of course, many more names migrated from the game into our <Angel Diary>. This game is quite dangerous since you constantly meet new and interesting people online all the time; which makes you get addicted to the game.

Preview

11th CAT

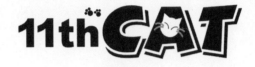

vol.1

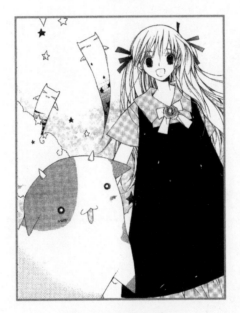

Kim MiKyung

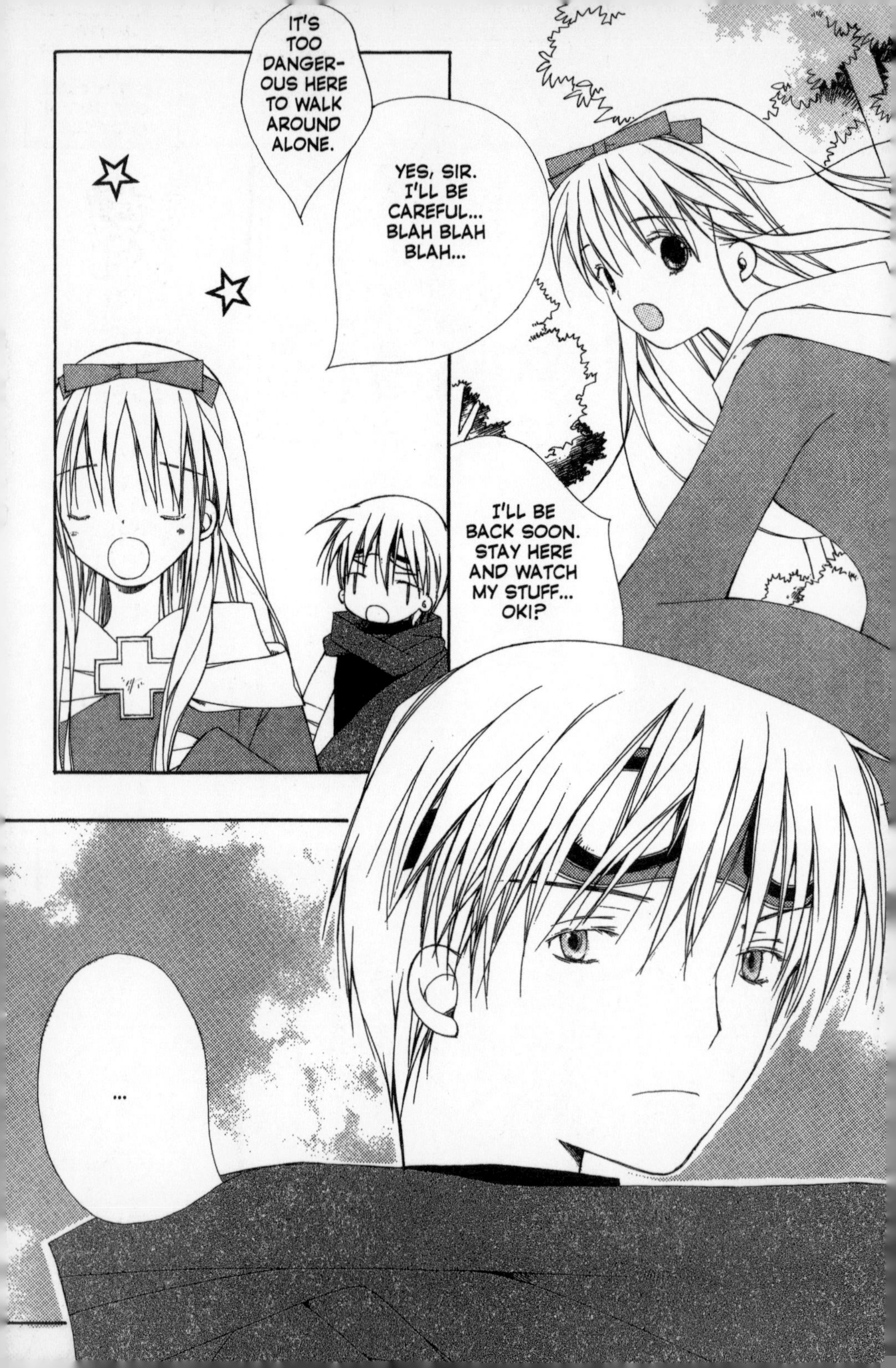
IT'S TOO DANGER-OUS HERE TO WALK AROUND ALONE.
YES, SIR. I'LL BE CAREFUL... BLAH BLAH BLAH...
I'LL BE BACK SOON. STAY HERE AND WATCH MY STUFF... OKI?
...

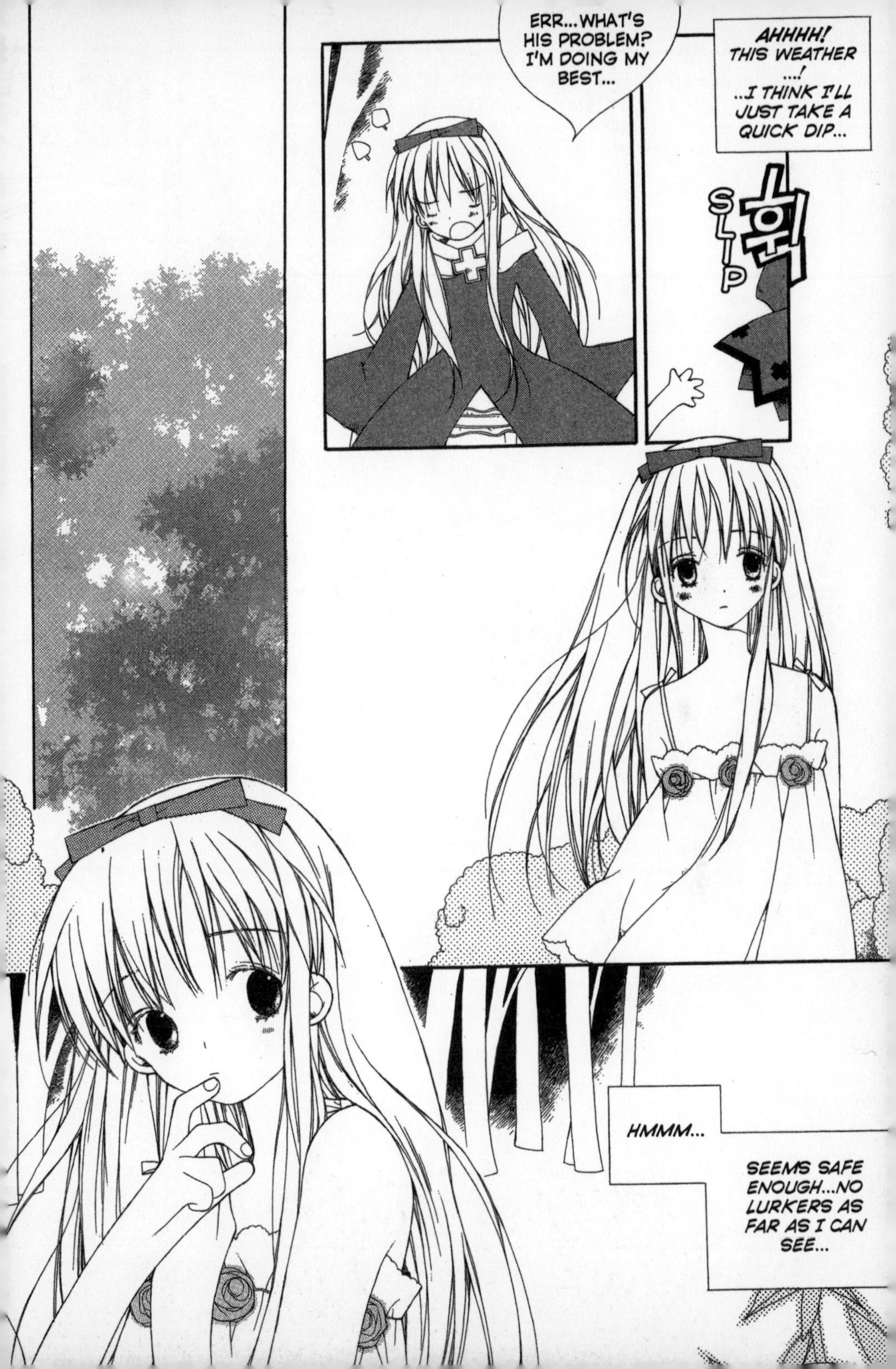

ERR...WHAT'S HIS PROBLEM? I'M DOING MY BEST...
AHHHH! THIS WEATHER ...! ...I THINK I'LL JUST TAKE A QUICK DIP...
SLIP
HMMM...
SEEMS SAFE ENOUGH...NO LURKERS AS FAR AS I CAN SEE...

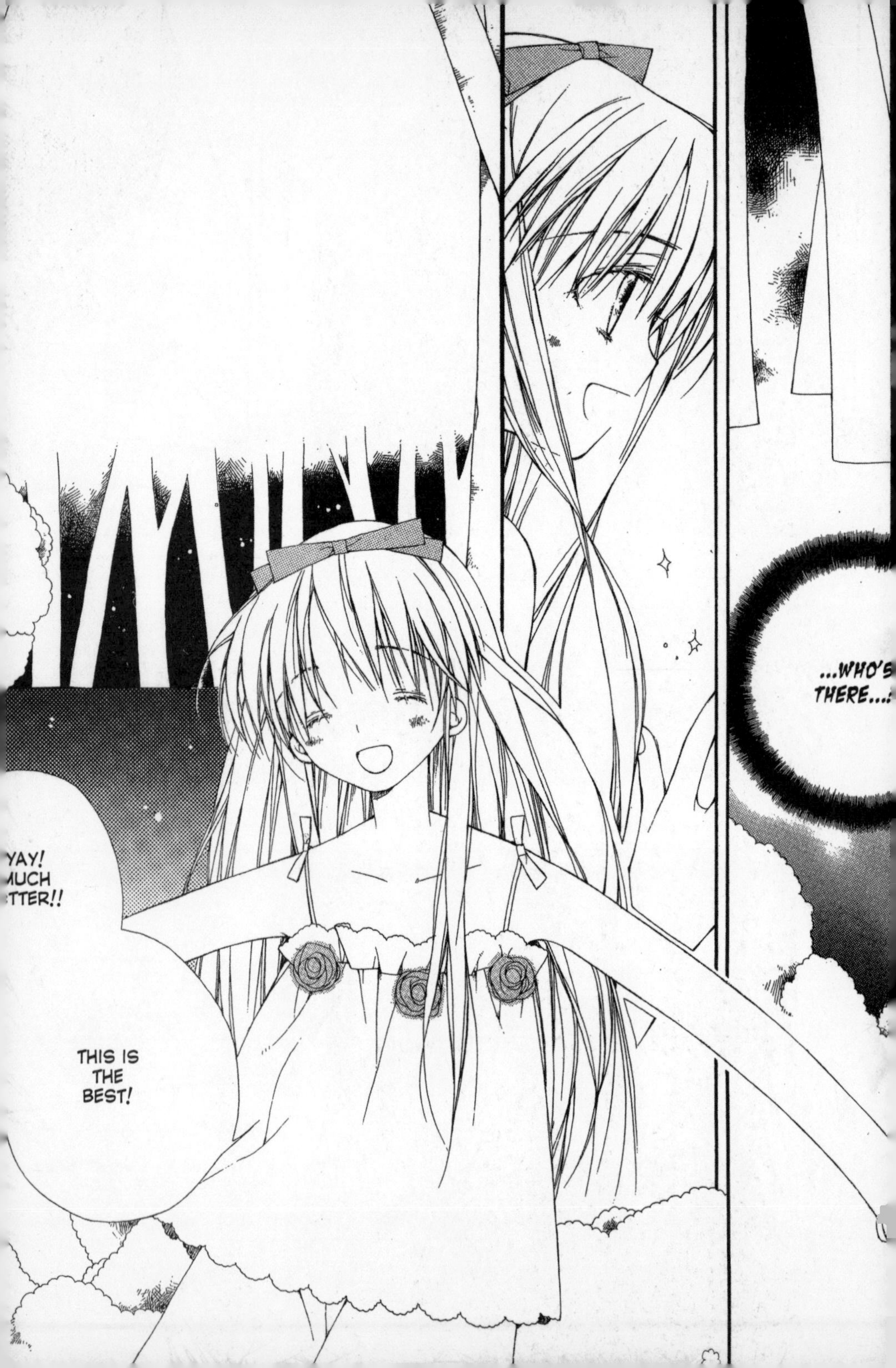
YAY! MUCH ETTER!!
THIS IS THE BEST!
...WHO'S THERE...

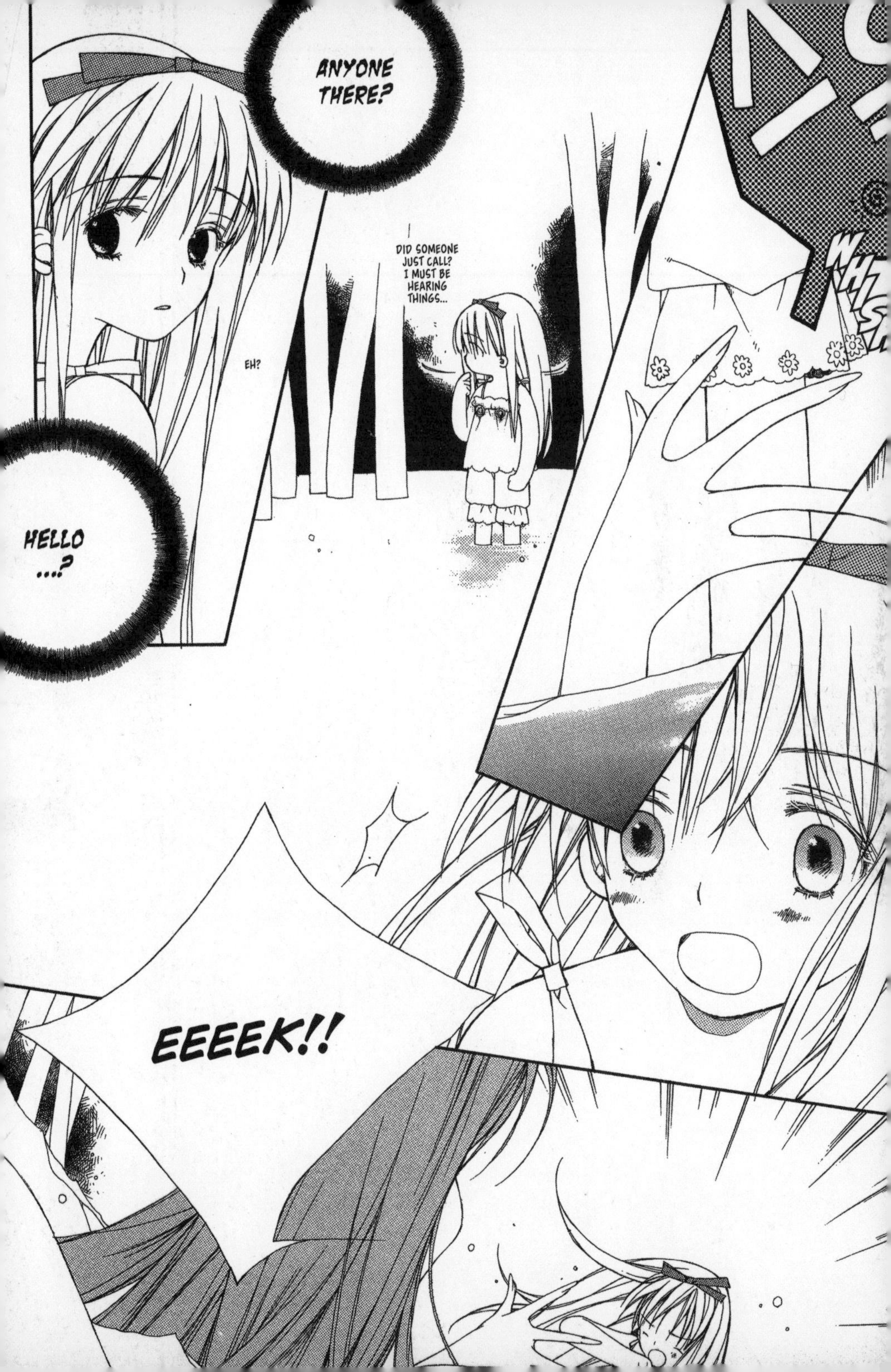
ANYONE THERE?
HELLO ...?
EH?
DID SOMEONE JUST CALL? I MUST BE HEARING THINGS...
EEEEK!!

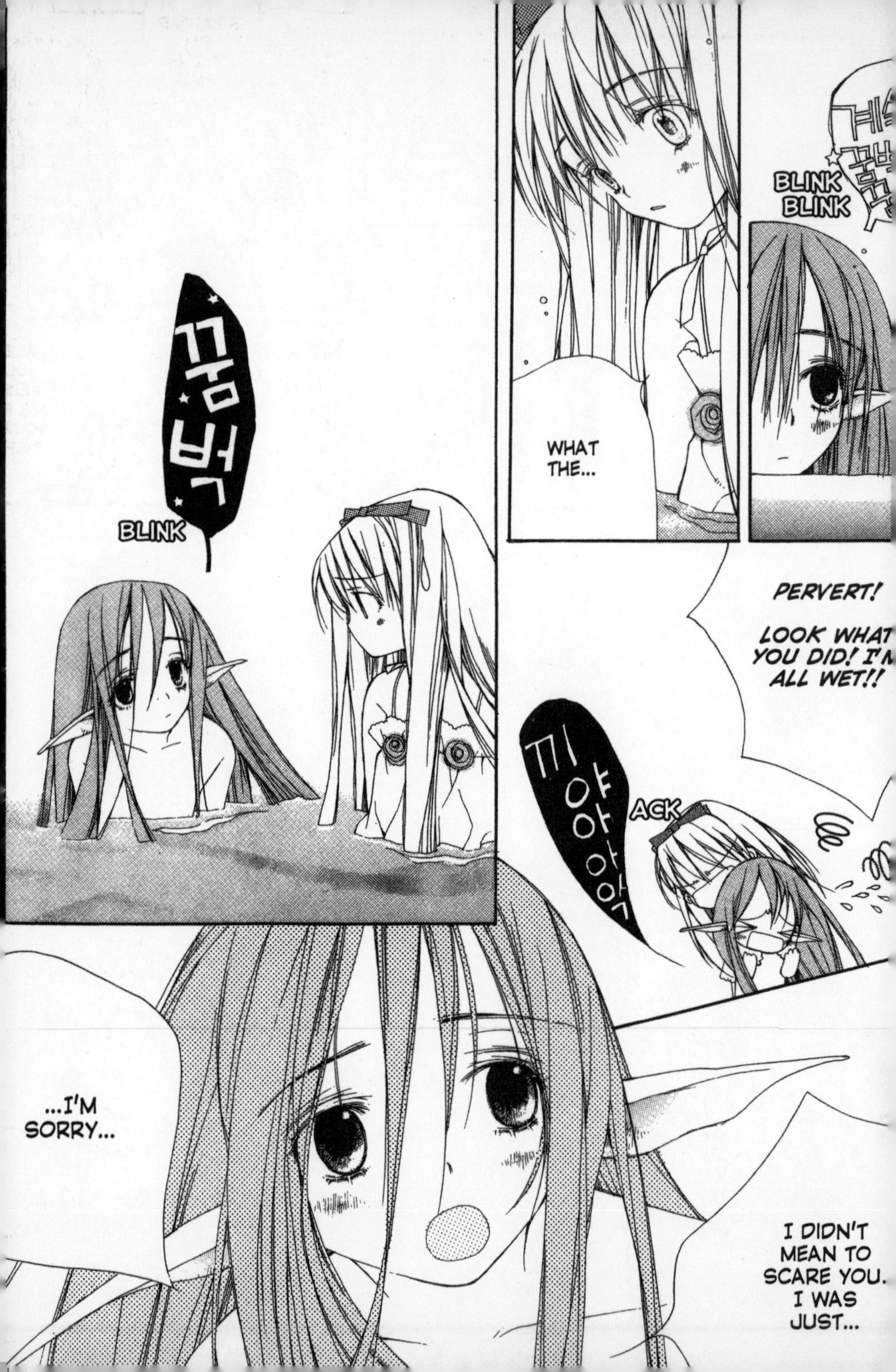
BLINK
WHAT THE...
BLINK BLINK
PERVERT!
LOOK WHAT YOU DID! I'M ALL WET!!
ACK
...I'M SORRY...
I DIDN'T MEAN TO SCARE YOU. I WAS JUST...

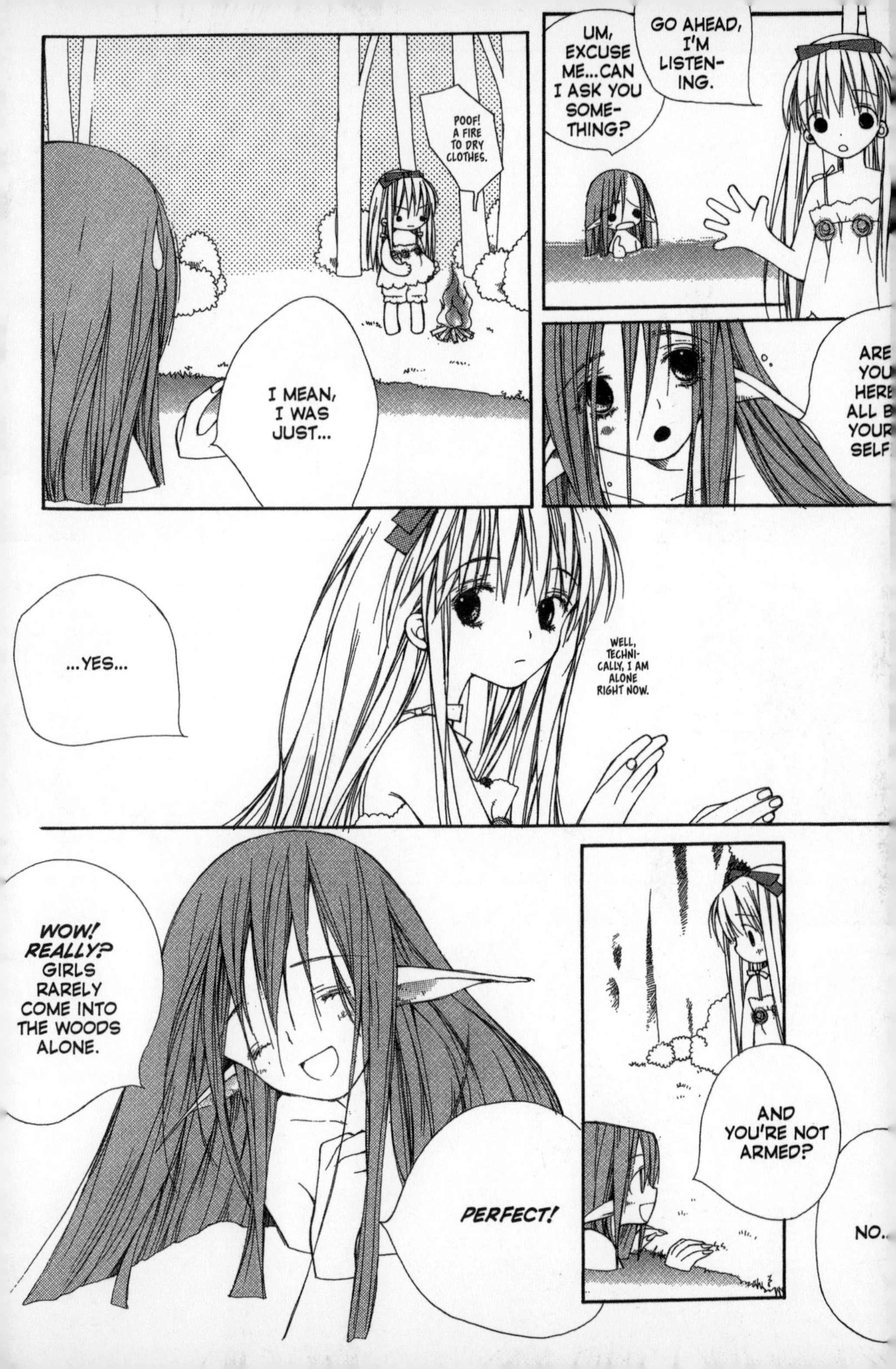
POOF! A FIRE TO DRY CLOTHES.
I MEAN, I WAS JUST...
UM, EXCUSE ME...CAN I ASK YOU SOME-THING?
GO AHEAD, I'M LISTEN-ING.
ARE YOU HERE ALL B YOUR SELF
...YES...
WELL, TECHNI-CALLY, I AM ALONE RIGHT NOW.
WOW! REALLY? GIRLS RARELY COME INTO THE WOODS ALONE.
PERFECT!
AND YOU'RE NOT ARMED?
NO..

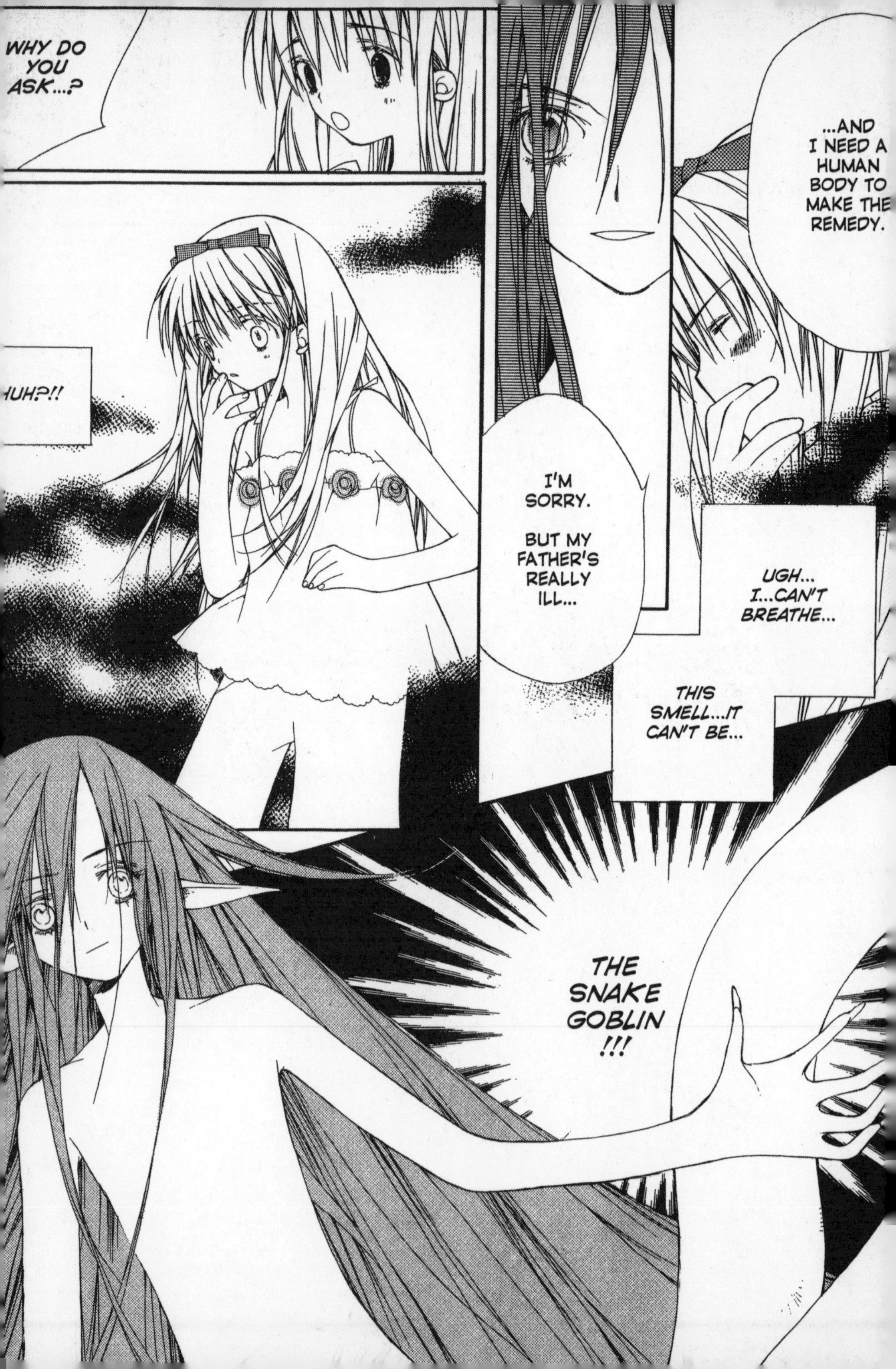
WHY DO YOU ASK...?
HUH?!!
I'M SORRY.
BUT MY FATHER'S REALLY ILL...
...AND I NEED A HUMAN BODY TO MAKE THE REMEDY.
UGH... I...CAN'T BREATHE...
THIS SMELL...IT CAN'T BE...
THE SNAKE GOBLIN!!!

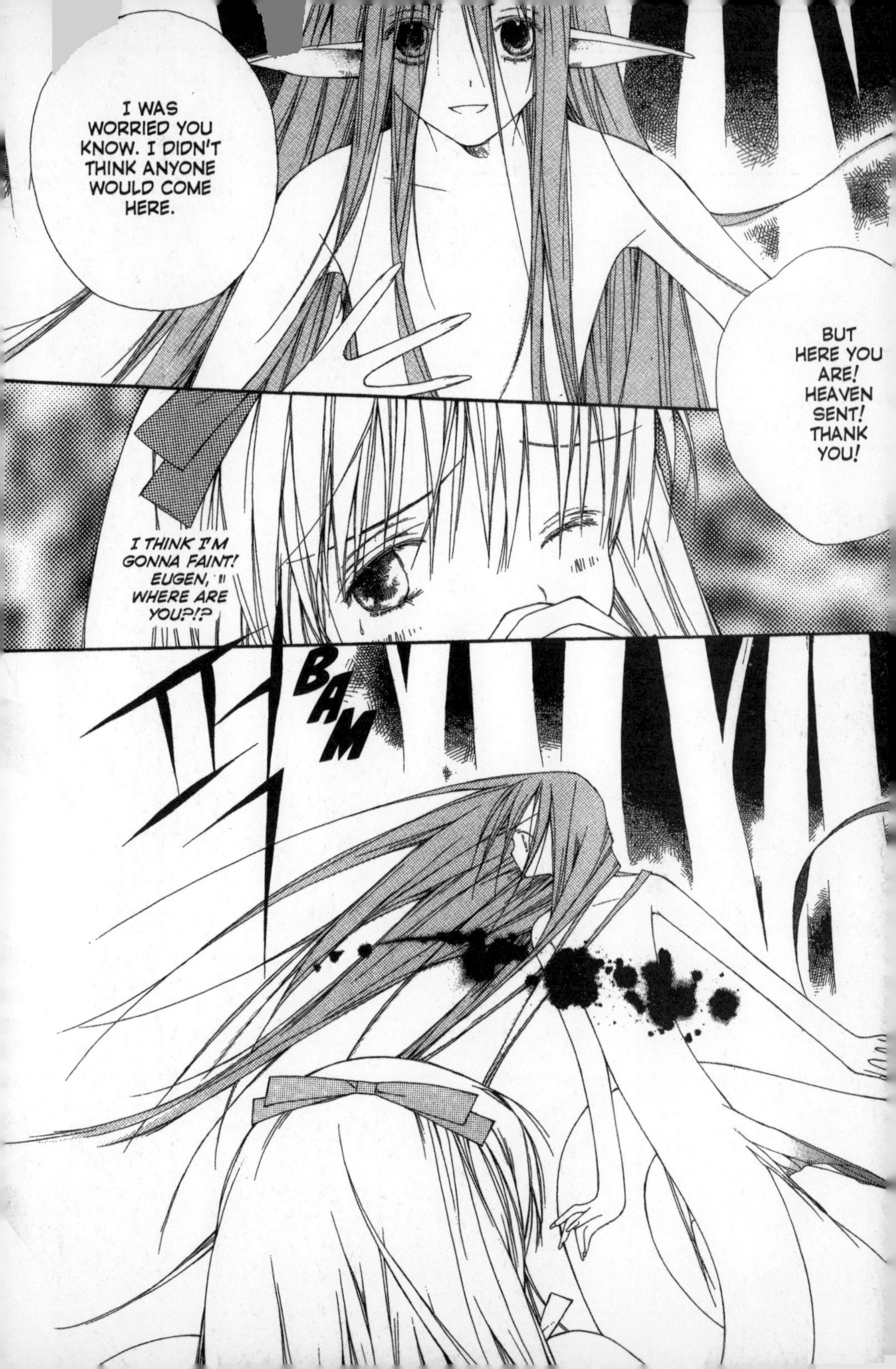
I WAS WORRIED YOU KNOW. I DIDN'T THINK ANYONE WOULD COME HERE.
BUT HERE YOU ARE! HEAVEN SENT! THANK YOU!
I THINK I'M GONNA FAINT! EUGEN, WHERE ARE YOU?!?
BAM

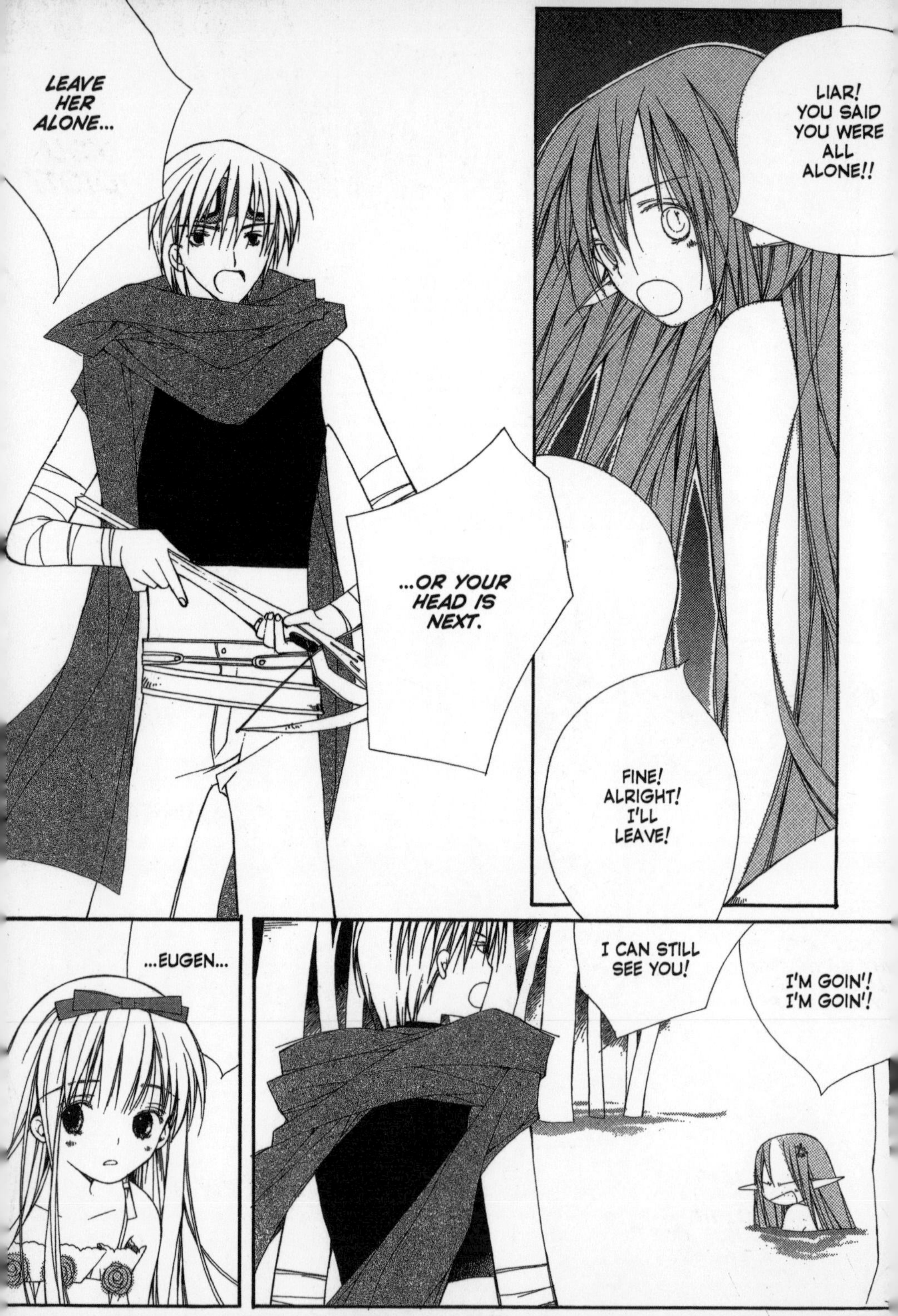
LEAVE HER ALONE...
...OR YOUR HEAD IS NEXT.
LIAR! YOU SAID YOU WERE ALL ALONE!!
FINE! ALRIGHT! I'LL LEAVE!
...EUGEN...
I CAN STILL SEE YOU!
I'M GOIN'! I'M GOIN'!

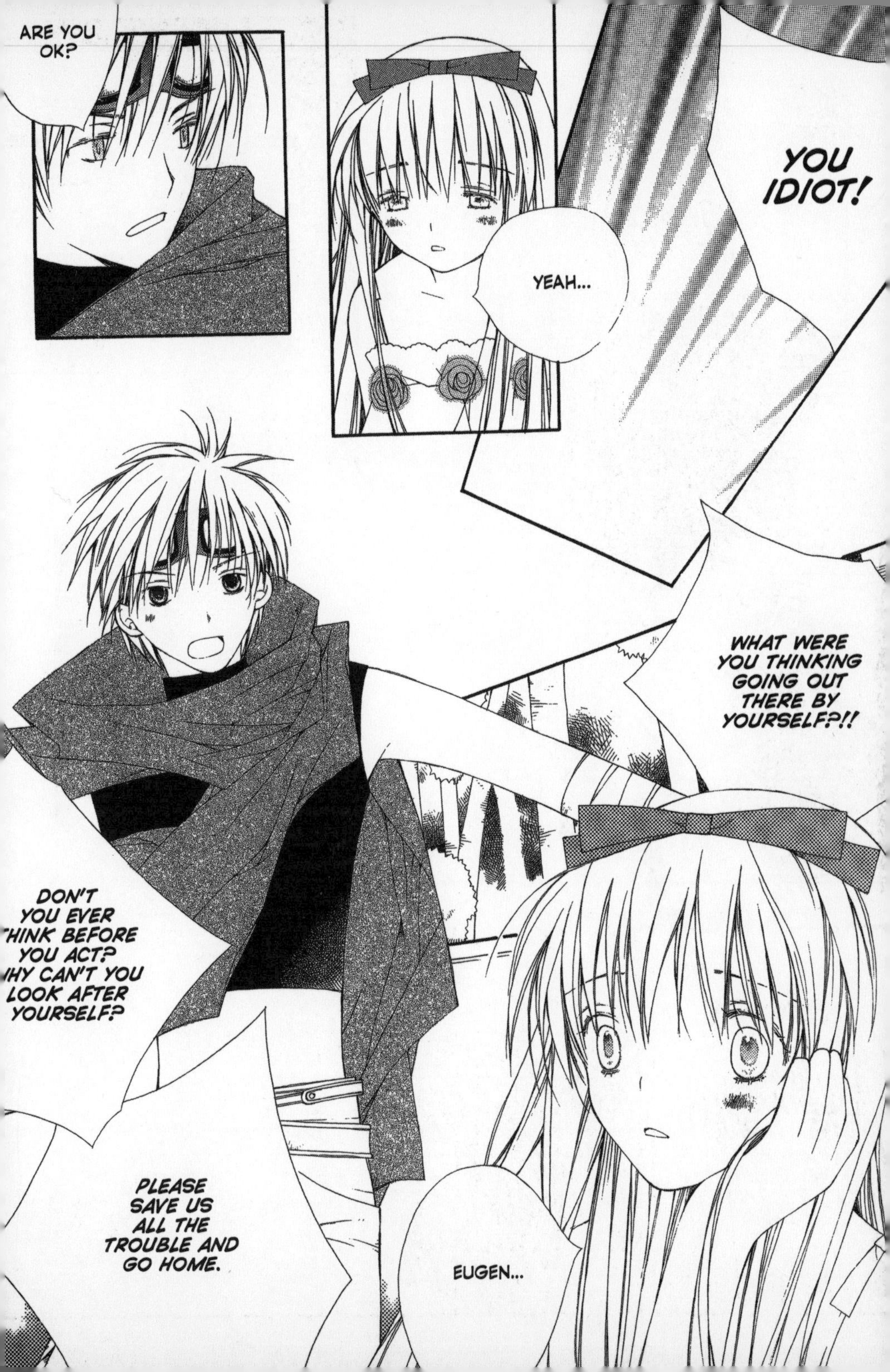
ARE YOU OK?
YEAH...
YOU IDIOT!
WHAT WERE YOU THINKING GOING OUT THERE BY YOURSELF?!!
DON'T YOU EVER THINK BEFORE YOU ACT? WHY CAN'T YOU LOOK AFTER YOURSELF?
PLEASE SAVE US ALL THE TROUBLE AND GO HOME.
EUGEN...

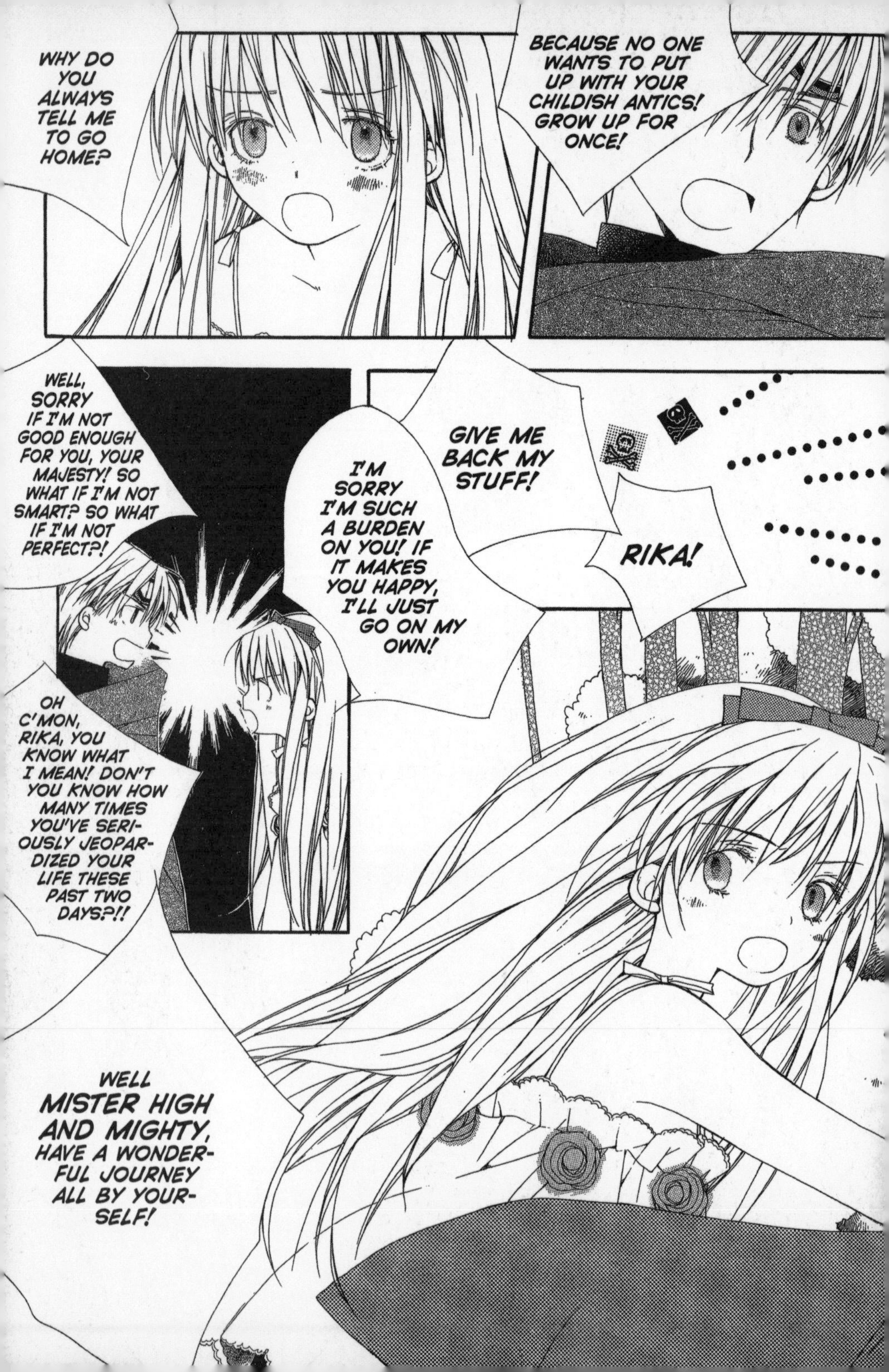

WHY DO YOU ALWAYS TELL ME TO GO HOME?
BECAUSE NO ONE WANTS TO PUT UP WITH YOUR CHILDISH ANTICS! GROW UP FOR ONCE!
WELL, SORRY IF I'M NOT GOOD ENOUGH FOR YOU, YOUR MAJESTY! SO WHAT IF I'M NOT SMART? SO WHAT IF I'M NOT PERFECT?!
OH C'MON, RIKA, YOU KNOW WHAT I MEAN! DON'T YOU KNOW HOW MANY TIMES YOU'VE SERIOUSLY JEOPARDIZED YOUR LIFE THESE PAST TWO DAYS?!!
I'M SORRY I'M SUCH A BURDEN ON YOU! IF IT MAKES YOU HAPPY, I'LL JUST GO ON MY OWN!
GIVE ME BACK MY STUFF!
RIKA!
WELL MISTER HIGH AND MIGHTY, HAVE A WONDERFUL JOURNEY ALL BY YOURSELF!

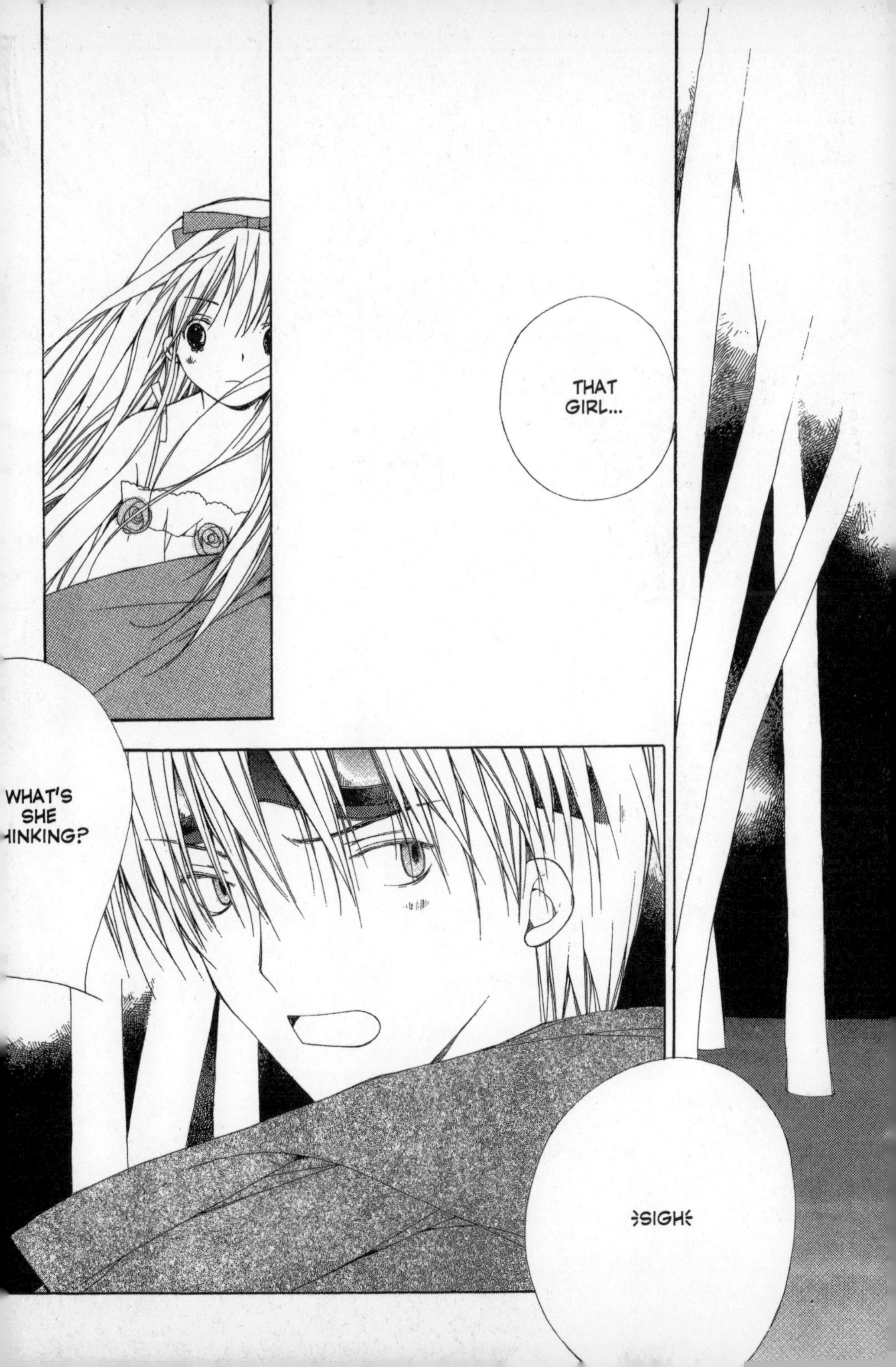
THAT GIRL...
WHAT'S SHE HINKING?
SIGH

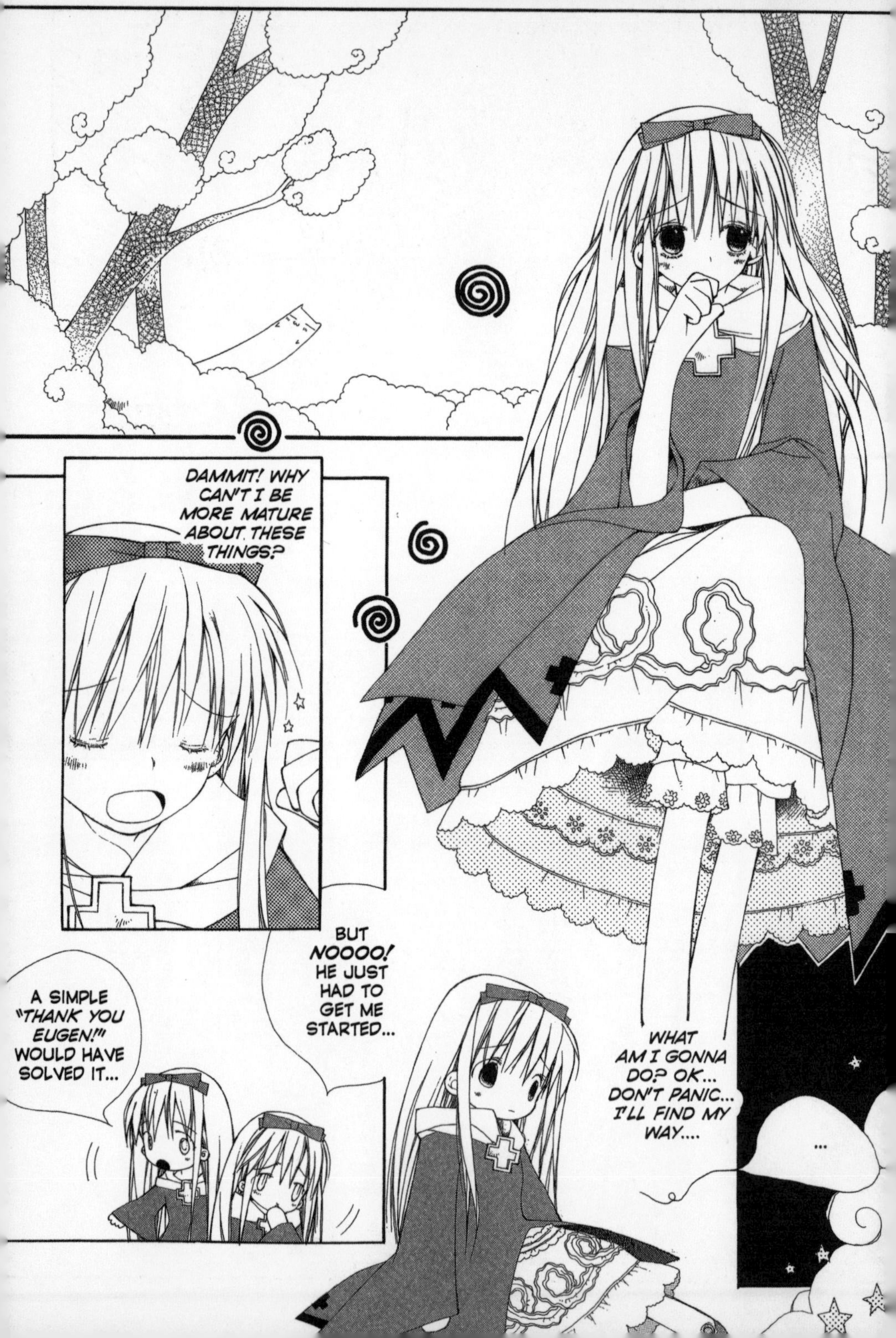
DAMMIT! WHY CAN'T I BE MORE MATURE ABOUT THESE THINGS?
A SIMPLE "THANK YOU EUGEN!" WOULD HAVE SOLVED IT...
BUT NOOOO! HE JUST HAD TO GET ME STARTED...
WHAT AM I GONNA DO? OK... DON'T PANIC... I'LL FIND MY WAY....
...

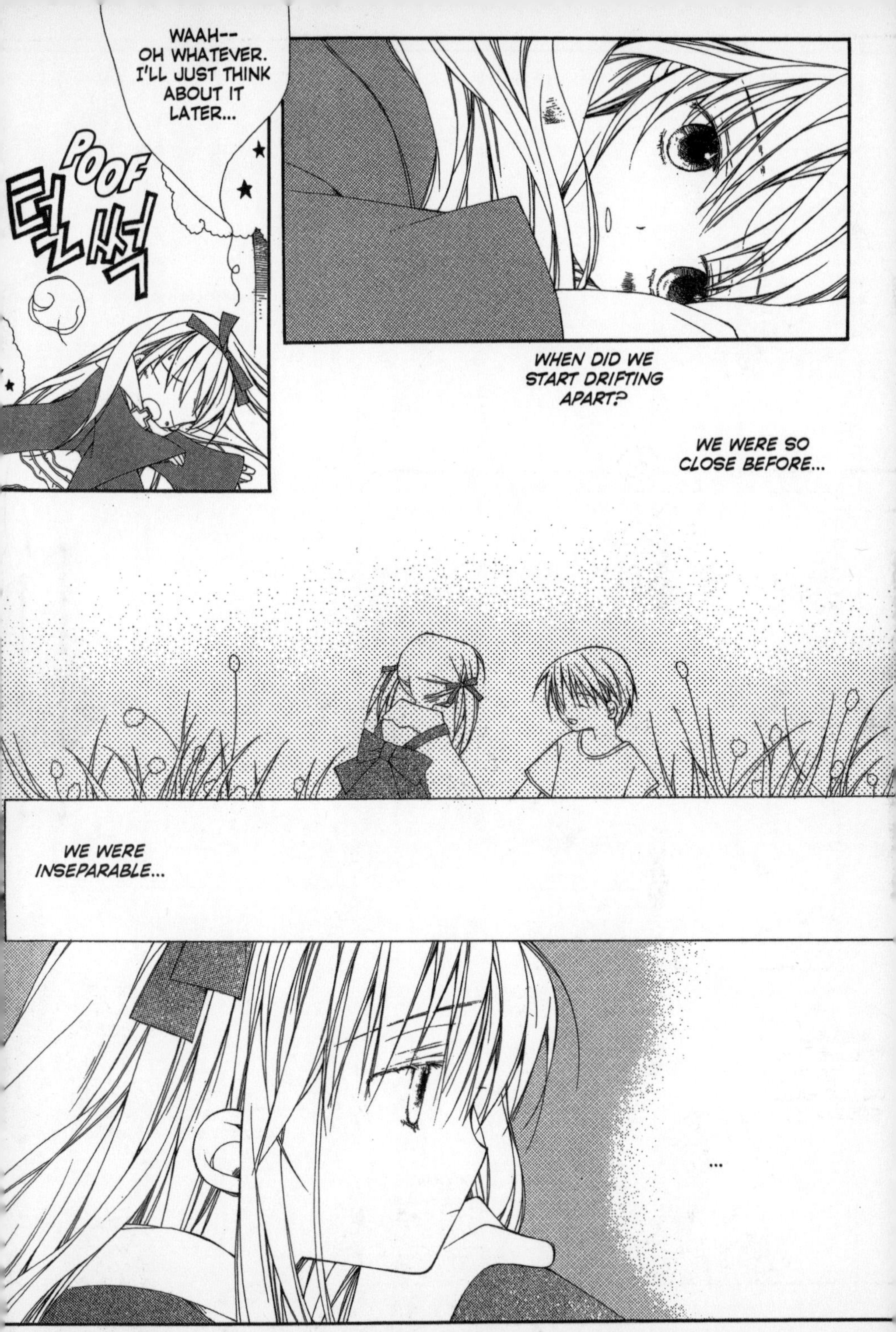
WAAH-- OH WHATEVER. I'LL JUST THINK ABOUT IT LATER...
POOF
털썩
WHEN DID WE START DRIFTING APART?
WE WERE SO CLOSE BEFORE...
WE WERE INSEPARABLE...
...

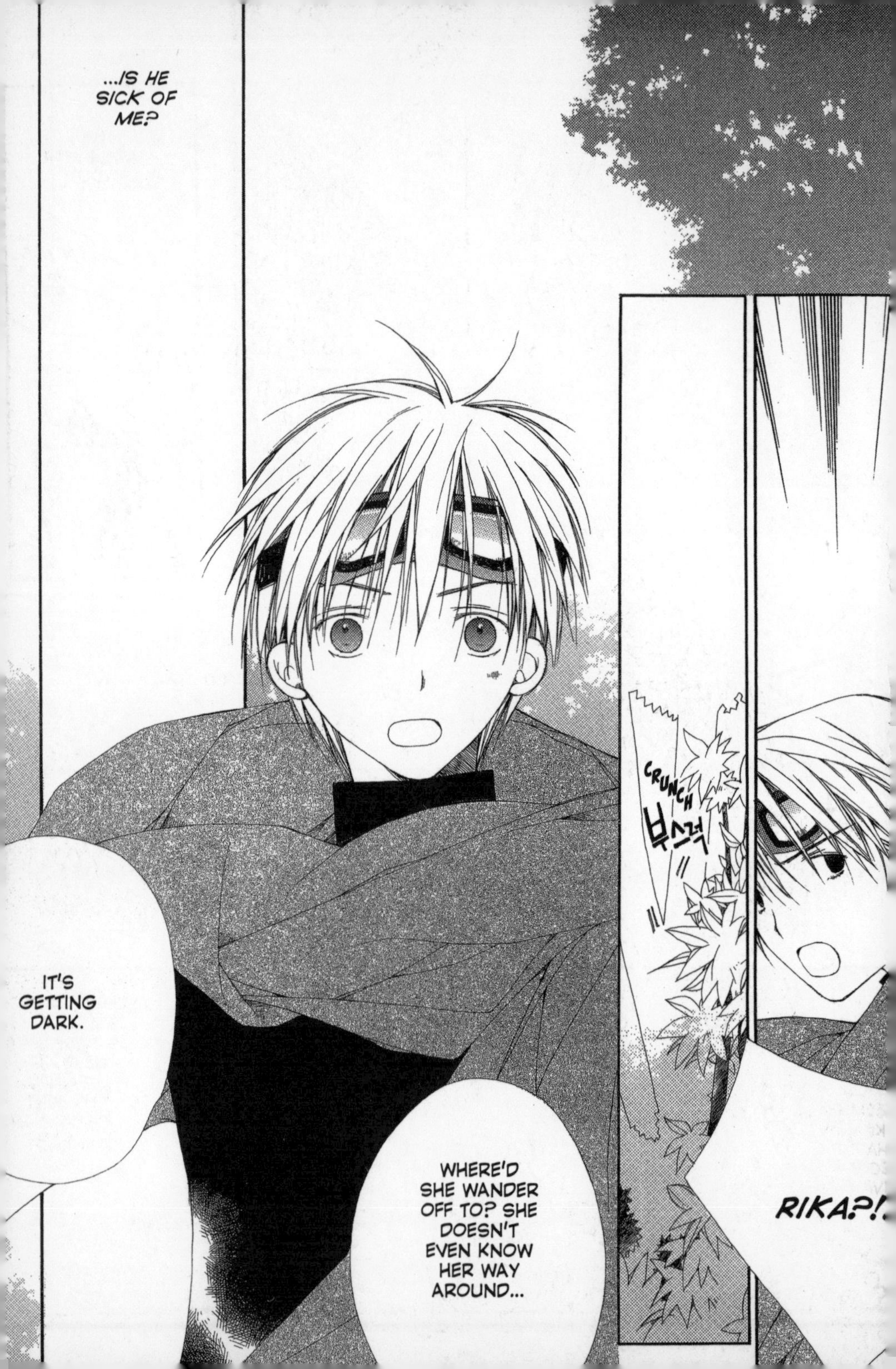
...IS HE SICK OF ME?
IT'S GETTING DARK.
WHERE'D SHE WANDER OFF TO? SHE DOESN'T EVEN KNOW HER WAY AROUND...
CRUNCH
부스럭
RIKA?!

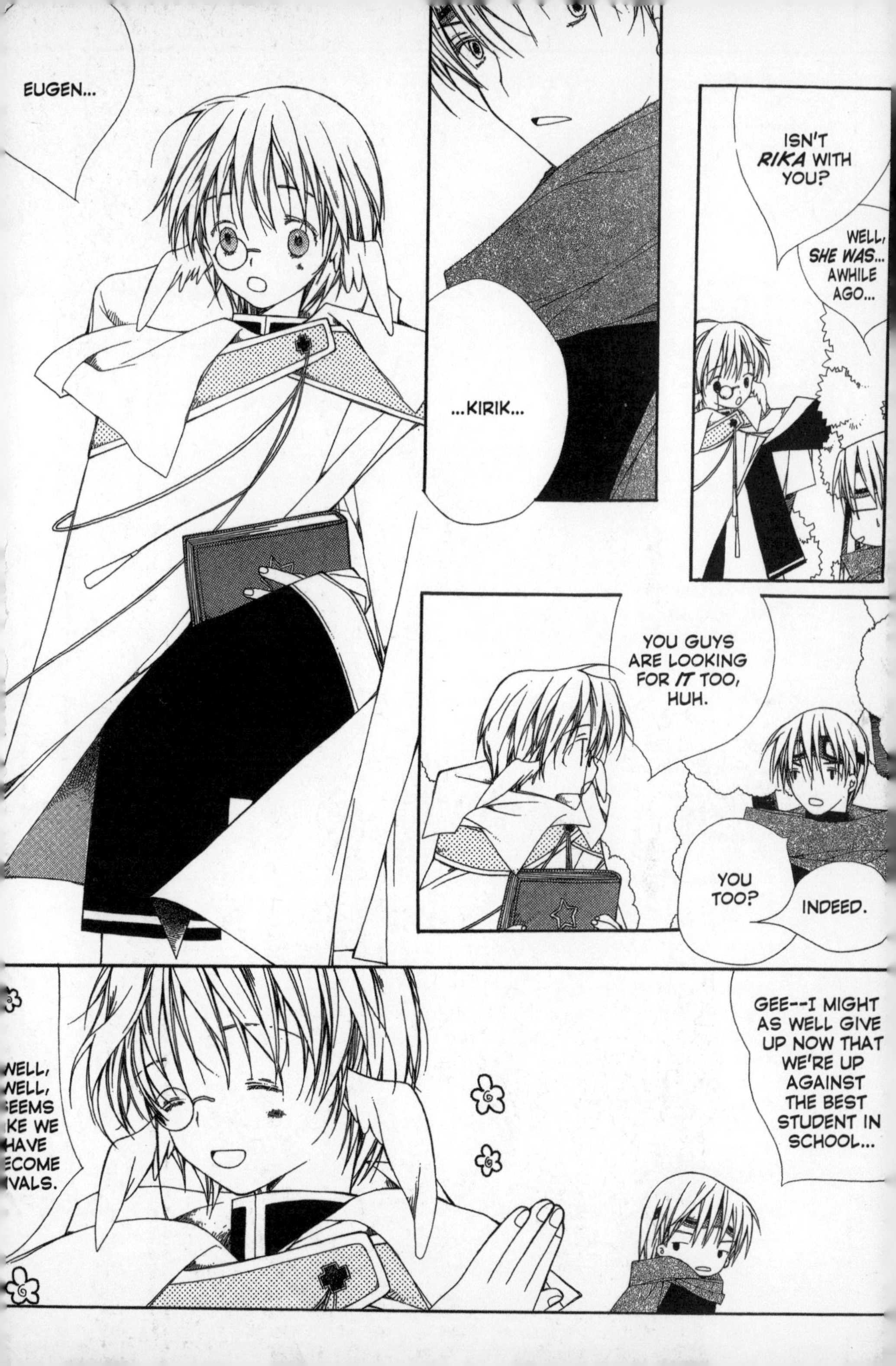
EUGEN...
...KIRIK...
ISN'T *RIKA* WITH YOU?
WELL, *SHE WAS*... AWHILE AGO...
YOU GUYS ARE LOOKING FOR *IT* TOO, HUH.
YOU TOO?
INDEED.
WELL, WELL, SEEMS IKE WE HAVE ECOME IVALS.
GEE--I MIGHT AS WELL GIVE UP NOW THAT WE'RE UP AGAINST THE BEST STUDENT IN SCHOOL...

Danbi Original

Angel Diary vol.1

Story by YunHee Lee
Art by KARA

Translation HyeYoung Im · J. Torres
English Adaptation J. Torres
Touch-up and Lettering Marshall Dillon
Graphic Design EunKyung Kim · YoungAh Cho
Editor JuYoun Lee

ICE Kunion

Project Manager Chan Park
Marketing Manager Erik Ko
Editor in Chief Eddie Yu
Publishing Director JeongHyun Chin
Publisher and C.E.O. JaeKook Chun

Angel Diary © 2005 Kara · YunHee Lee
First published in Korea in 2002 by SIGONGSA Co., Ltd.
English text translation rights arranged by SIGONGSA Co., Ltd.
English text © 2005 ICE KUNION

Published by ICE Kunion
SIGONGSA 2F Yeil Bldg. 1619-4, Seocho-dong, Seocho-gu, Seoul, 137-878, Korea

ISBN : 89-527-4467-5

First printing, October 2005
10 9 8 7 6 5 4 3 2 1
Printed in Canada

www.ICEkunion.com/www.koreanmanhwa.com